A·N·N·U·A·L E·D·I·T·I·O·N·S

World Religions 03/04

First Edition

EDITOR

Ramdas Lamb

University of Hawaii at Manoa

Ramdas Lamb received his doctorate in Religious Studies at the University of California at Santa Barbara. He has been a faculty member of the Religion Department at the University of Hawaii at Manoa since 1989 and is currently Graduate Chair and Associate Professor. The areas of his research, teaching, and writing include comparative religion, South Asian religious traditions, devotionalism, and monasticism.

McGraw-Hill/Dushkin

530 Old Whitfield Street, Guilford, Connecticut 06437

Visit us on the Internet
http://www.dushkin.com

Credits

1. **Understanding Religion**
   Unit photo—EPA-Documerica.
2. **Oral and Indigenous Religions**
   Unit photo—Australian Information Service photo.
3. **India: Jainism, Hinduism, and Sikhism**
   Unit photo—United Nations/WT/ARA photo.
4. **Buddhism**
   Unit photo—Photo by Christine Asenjo.
5. **Religions of China and Japan (Non-Buddhist)**
   Unit photo—Courtesy of Dean Collinwood.
6. **Judaism**
   Unit photo—United Nations photo by John Isaac.
7. **Christianity**
   Unit photo—Courtesy of Louis Raucci Jr.
8. **Islam**
   Unit photo—United Nations photo by John Isaac.
9. **Religions in Dialogue and Confrontation**
   Unit photo—Courtesy of Israeli Tourist Office.
10. **Religion Facing the Modern World**
    Unit photo—NYT Pictures by Melissa Springer.

Copyright

Cataloging in Publication Data
Main entry under title: Annual Editions: World Religions. 2003/2004.
1. World Religions—Periodicals. I. Lamb, Ramdas, *comp.* II. Title: World Religions.
ISBN 0–07–254868–1   658'.05

First Edition

Cover image © 2003 PhotoDisc, Inc.
Printed in the United States of America   1234567890BAHBAH543   Printed on Recycled Paper

Editors/Advisory Board

Members of the Advisory Board are instrumental in the final selection of articles for each edition of ANNUAL EDITIONS. Their review of articles for content, level, currentness, and appropriateness provides critical direction to the editor and staff. We think that you will find their careful consideration well reflected in this volume.

To the Reader

In publishing ANNUAL EDITIONS we recognize the enormous role played by the magazines, newspapers, and journals of the public press in providing current, first-rate educational information in a broad spectrum of interest areas. Many of these articles are appropriate for students, researchers, and professionals seeking accurate, current material to help bridge the gap between principles and theories and the real world. These articles, however, become more useful for study when those of lasting value are carefully collected, organized, indexed, and reproduced in a low-cost format, which provides easy and permanent access when the material is needed. That is the role played by ANNUAL EDITIONS.

It is estimated that more than 10,000 separate religions are being practiced in the world today. Within Christianity alone, there are said to be more than 30,000 different denominations. Thus, the plethora of religious beliefs and practices in the contemporary world extends far beyond the grasp of any textbook or university course. A study of world religions can, therefore, only scratch the surface of this vast, complex, and fascinating realm. At the same time, it is a necessary and valuable step in an increasingly interconnected world.

The purpose of this anthology, *Annual Editions: World Religions 03/04,* is twofold. First, it is meant to serve as a set of supplementary readings, in conjunction with a primary textbook, for use in a survey course on the major religions of the world. As such, it does not cover most of the basic background information on the formation and development of the various religions, except as might not be covered in a general text. It should be read as offering alternate and supplementary views. Second, because it is to be updated on a regular basis, it is meant to provide a glimpse of current events and changes that take place in contemporary religion and the broader world. The assorted articles in the collection have been drawn from a wide variety of sources, most of them having been written since the mid-1990s. Those that have been culled from older writings are included because of the information or perspective that they contribute. The material has been divided into 10 units, based both on my years of experience in teaching the material in a classroom setting and on how it is often segregated in world religion textbooks. While no two texts are alike, they nevertheless tend to follow similar patterns of organization.

The units have been organized in order that they may be easily utilized in a world religions course. The first two units look at religion in general and at various indigenous understandings of things considered religious. The next three units focus on the religious traditions of Asia. India has played an important role in the development of religion, having given birth to a variety of the world's major religious traditions. Thus, unit 3 has articles on several of these traditions, including Jainism, Hinduism, and Sikhism. Although Buddhism also has its origins in India, its development and its influence during the last 1,500 years have been primarily in Asian lands outside of India. Unit 4 gives a sampling of some of the different views in Buddhism.

Like India, China and Japan have had a great deal of religious and cultural influence on the rest of the world. While the two have historically shared much in terms of culture and religion over the last two millennia, they have also developed unique and lasting traditions. Unit 5 offers a look at a few of these manifestations.

Judaism, Christianity, and Islam comprise a family of related religious traditions, all of whose origins and early development occurred in and around the lands of Israel and the Mediterranean Sea. Units 6, 7, and 8 each focus on one of these traditions, respectively. Unit 9 presents some thoughts on both the interactions and the tensions that exist between traditions today. Lastly, unit 10 considers some of the issues that arise when religious traditions confront the contemporary world.

This volume contains a number of features that are designed to be useful to students and professionals. These include the *table of contents* with summaries of each article and key concepts in italics, a *topic guide* for locating articles on specific subjects related to world religions, and a comprehensive *index.* Also included are selected *World Wide Web* sites that can be used to further explore article topics.

Your comments, opinions, and recommendations about *Annual Editions: World Religions 03/04* will be greatly appreciated and will help shape future editions. Please take a moment to complete the postage-paid *article rating form* on the last page of this book. Any book can be improved, and with your help this one will continue to be.

Ramdas Lamb
Editor

Contents

UNIT 1
Understanding Religion

Four articles in this section examine the need to understand the cross-cultural dynamics of differing religions.

Unit Overview   xvi

UNIT 2
Oral and Indigenous Religions

Six articles in this section discuss some religions that are unique to smaller groups of people: Australian Aborigines, Native Americans, and Haitian Vodoun, among others.

Unit Overview   14

The concepts in bold italics are developed in the article. For further expansion, please refer to the Topic Guide and the Index.

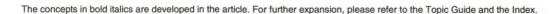

UNIT 3
India: Jainism, Hinduism, and Sikhism

Five selections in this section discuss various Indian religions and their historical traditions.

Unit Overview   **32**

The concepts in bold italics are developed in the article. For further expansion, please refer to the Topic Guide and the Index.

UNIT 4
Buddhism

Five selections in this section trace the history and development of Buddhism in the religious world.

UNIT 5
Religions of China and Japan (Non-Buddhist)

Seven articles in this section examine the various non-Buddhist religious traditions of China and Japan.

The concepts in bold italics are developed in the article. For further expansion, please refer to the Topic Guide and the Index.

UNIT 6
Judaism

Six selections in this section examine the development of Judaism, and the important role that this religion has played in world affairs.

The concepts in bold italics are developed in the article. For further expansion, please refer to the Topic Guide and the Index.

UNIT 7
Christianity

Six articles in this section discuss some of the traditions of Christianity, and the impact that some recent movements are having on Christian culture.

The concepts in bold italics are developed in the article. For further expansion, please refer to the Topic Guide and the Index.

UNIT 8
Islam

Five articles in this section discuss the development of Islam: the Koran, the shared theological heritage with the Jews, and the current state of the religion.

UNIT 9
Religions in Dialogue and Confrontation

Four selections in this section discuss some of the current challenges facing the interrelations between various world religions.

The concepts in bold italics are developed in the article. For further expansion, please refer to the Topic Guide and the Index.

UNIT 10
Religion Facing the Modern World

Four selections in this section examine how religion is evolving in today's society.

The concepts in bold italics are developed in the article. For further expansion, please refer to the Topic Guide and the Index.

Topic Guide

This topic guide suggests how the selections in this book relate to the subjects covered in your course. You may want to use the topics listed on these pages to search the Web more easily.

On the following pages a number of Web sites have been gathered specifically for this book. They are arranged to reflect the units of this *Annual Edition*. You can link to these sites by going to the DUSHKIN ONLINE support site at *http://www.dushkin.com/online/*.

ALL THE ARTICLES THAT RELATE TO EACH TOPIC ARE LISTED BELOW THE BOLD-FACED TERM.

Afterlife
20. Buddhism and Abortion: "The Way to Memorialize One's Mizuko"
22. Stories from an Illustrated Explanation of the *Tract of the Most Exalted on Action and Response*
41. In the Beginning, There Were the Holy Books

Art
8. Becoming Part of It
9. Veve: The Sacred Symbol of Vodoun
10. The Hula in Hawaiian Life and Thought
13. Seeing the Sacred
27. Matsuri

Buddhism
11. Ancient Jewel
16. The Beginnings of Buddhism
17. The Marrow of Zen
18. An Essential Commitment
19. "Shinran and Jodoshinshu"
20. Buddhism and Abortion: "The Way to Memorialize One's Mizuko"

Christianity
34. The Changing Face of the Church
35. Pluralism and the Catholic University
36. Raising Christian Children in a Pagan Culture
37. Child's Death Raises Questions About Faith
38. Resuscitating Passion
39. Handmaid or Feminist?
47. Cross Meets Crescent: An Interview With Kenneth Cragg
48. Islam & Christianity Face to Face: An Old Conflict: Prospects for a New Ending

Creation
5. Sun Mother Wakes the World: Australian Aborigine
6. First Tale
7. Kalevala: An Epic Poem That Gave Birth to a Nation
24. Izanagi-No-Mikoto and Izanami-No-Mikoto

Culture
2. Body Ritual Among the Nacirema
7. Kalevala: An Epic Poem That Gave Birth to a Nation
8. Becoming Part of It
10. The Hula in Hawaiian Life and Thought
21. Confucius
23. Asceticism in Early Taoist Religion: Introduction
25. Japanese Religions in the New Millennium
28. The Sacred Space of Judaism
29. Dreaming of Altneuland
30. The Politics of Holiness in Jerusalem
34. The Changing Face of the Church
36. Raising Christian Children in a Pagan Culture
41. In the Beginning, There Were the Holy Books
46. The Case for 'Yellow Theology'
52. Fundamentalism

Evil and sin
20. Buddhism and Abortion: "The Way to Memorialize One's Mizuko"
33. Holocaust Remembrance Day Brings Memories of Evil, Courage
36. Raising Christian Children in a Pagan Culture
37. Child's Death Raises Questions About Faith
41. In the Beginning, There Were the Holy Books
43. The Sacred Is Allah, the One True God

Founders
16. The Beginnings of Buddhism
18. An Essential Commitment
19. "Shinran and Jodoshinshu"
21. Confucius
26. The Goddess Emerges From her Cave: Fujita Himiko and her Dragon Palace Family
39. Handmaid or Feminist?
40. What Is the Koran?
42. The Dome of the Rock: Jerusalem's Epicenter

Freedom of religion
33. Holocaust Remembrance Day Brings Memories of Evil, Courage
36. Raising Christian Children in a Pagan Culture
37. Child's Death Raises Questions About Faith
46. The Case for 'Yellow Theology'
47. Cross Meets Crescent: An Interview With Kenneth Cragg
51. Doper or Devotee?
52. Fundamentalism

Fundamentalism
34. The Changing Face of the Church
36. Raising Christian Children in a Pagan Culture
41. In the Beginning, There Were the Holy Books
45. Religion; It Sounds Like Hate, but Is It?
48. Islam & Christianity Face to Face: An Old Conflict: Prospects for a New Ending
52. Fundamentalism

Gods and goddesses
5. Sun Mother Wakes the World: Australian Aborigine
6. First Tale
7. Kalevala: An Epic Poem That Gave Birth to a Nation
9. Veve: The Sacred Symbol of Vodoun
12. The Jain Deities
13. Seeing the Sacred
19. "Shinran and Jodoshinshu"
24. Izanagi-No-Mikoto and Izanami-No-Mikoto
26. The Goddess Emerges From her Cave: Fujita Himiko and her Dragon Palace Family
39. Handmaid or Feminist?
50. Oh, Gods!

Hinduism
11. Ancient Jewel
13. Seeing the Sacred
14. The Hindu Ethic of Nonviolence
15. The Sacred Is the One True Reality of Brahman

World Wide Web Sites

The following World Wide Web sites have been carefully researched and selected to support the articles found in this reader. The easiest way to access these selected sites is to go to our DUSHKIN ONLINE support site at *http://www.dushkin.com/online/*.

AE: World Religions

The following sites were available at the time of publication. Visit our Web site—we update DUSHKIN ONLINE regularly to reflect any changes.

General Sources

Comparative Religion
http://religion.rutgers.edu/vri/comp_rel.html

Rutgers University offers this virtual religion index that contains directories that cover all the world religions as well as textbooks and anthologies of sacred texts, guides to myths and mysticism, and much more.

Martin's Favorite Links
http://www.sacredsites.com/links.html

Among Martin's favorites in this 16-page index are the Stone Circle Webring, the Earth Mysteries and Sacred Sites Ring, Pilgrim's Route to Santiago de Compostela, Hindu Pilgrimage Sites of India, and many others.

Sacred Traditions
http://www.concentric.net/~Cosmas/sacred_traditions.htm

This site brings together a number of resources dealing with various sacred traditions. The site covers every religion, old or new.

UNIT 1: Understanding Religion

World Religion Gateway
http://www.academicinfo.net/religindex.html

Look up Sikhism, Gnosticism, Goddess, Rastafarianism, Jewish Studies, Alternative Spirituality, and many more words at Mike Madin's site of Academic Info at the University of Washington.

World Scripture: A Comparative Anthology of Sacred Texts
http://www.ettl.co.at/uc/ws/

This site is a collection of over 4,000 scriptural passages from 268 sacred texts and 55 oral traditions, and is organized into 164 different themes.

UNIT 2: Oral and Indigenous Religions

Aboriginal Beliefs
http://www.fcps.k12.va.us/DeerParkES/Dreamweaver/Australia/aborigines/beliefs.html

Told through their art, music, dance, and storytellings, the history and beliefs of the Aboriginal people are available at this site.

Creation Myths
http://www.magictails.com/creationlinks.html

Here are a large group of links to creation myths from a variety of cultures from around the world, everything from Babylonian to Mayan to Tahitian and Inuit, and many others.

Hopi Creation Story
http://www.dreamscape.com/morgana/umbriel.htm

Here is the Hopi creation story from *The World of Myth* by David Adams Leeming.

Ku Anthropologist
http://www.ku.edu/~kuanth/feb01.htm

The article "The Role of Exchange in the Formation of an Ewe Gorovodu Shrine in Southern Ghana" appears in the February 2001 issue of the University of Kansas's newsletter.

Vodun (and related religions)
http://www.religioustolerance.org/voodoo.htm

In this section of About Alternative Religions, Vodun, commonly called Voodoo, as well as related religions, such as Candombie, Lucumi, Macumba, and Yoruba, are explored.

Witchcraft, Magic and Religion Sources
http://www.people.virginia.edu/~ccf4f/magic/relig.html

Internet resources, assembled by Chris Fennell of the Department of Anthropology at the University of Virginia, that approach the subjects of witchcraft, magic, and religion are available at this site.

Zulu Religion and Superstitions
http://www.kzn-deat.gov.za/tourism/culture/religion/menu.htm

Zulu culture and traditions, including ancestor worship, superstition, the Sangoma, burials, and the Inyanga, are explained at this site.

Vodou, Vodun, Voodoo
http://dmoz.org/Society/Religion_and_Spirituality/African/Diasporic/Vodou,_Vodun,_Voodoo/

This site leads to many essays and discussions of the origins, history, and practice of voodoo.

UNIT 3: India: Jainism, Hinduism, and Sikhism

Hinduism Online
http://www.himalayanacademy.com

Everything from art and aums, from Hawaii Ashram to Gurudeva, and Hinduism today is covered at this site.

Introduction to Hinduism
http://www.uni-giessen.de/~gk1415/hinduism.htm

This is a guide to various aspects of Indian religious thought and interreligious understanding and tolerance. The main index is arranged so that subjects can easily be found in its 27 pages.

Introduction to Sikhism
http://photon.bu.edu/~rajwi/sikhism/mansukh1.html

Written by the late S. Gobind Singh Mansukhani, this online text covers everything important to the principles, history, sacred literature, and worship of Sikhs.

Jainism
http://www.cs.colostate.edu/~malaiya/jainhlinks.html

Anything you might want to know about Jainism is available at this extended listing of links.

UNIT 4: Buddhism

Buddhist Studies WWW Virtual Library
http://www.ciolek.com/WWWVL-Buddhism.html

This major Internet guide to Buddhist studies is edited by Dr. T. Matthew Ciolek and others, and the site keeps track of leading information facilities in the field of Buddhism.

www.dushkin.com/online/

Koan Studies Pages
http://www.ciolek.com/WWWVLPages/ZenPages/KoanStudy.html

The purpose of this site is to provide comprehensive and factual information about koans as used in Zen training.

Pure Land Buddhism WWW Virtual Library: Jodo-Shinshu
http://www.pitaka.ch/shinshu.htm

Here is a good starting place to enter the Jodo Ring on the Web.

Rissho Kosei Kai
http://philtar.ucsm.ac.uk/encyclopedia/easia/rissho.html

This encyclopedia entry briefly explains the history, symbols, and adherents of Rissho Kosei Kai.

Zen Buddhism WWW Virtual Library
http://www.ciolek.com/WWWVL-Zen.html

Complete information about the practice of Zen Buddhism is available at this site.

UNIT 5: Religions of China and Japan (Non-Buddhist)

Internet Resources on China: Philosophy and Religion
http://newton.uor.edu/Departments& Programs/AsianStudiesDept/china-phil.html

This annotated directory covers religious life in mainland China in the last century, religion and rebellion in China, Shamanism, the study of the Yao religion, and much more.

New Religions
http://www.kokugakuin.ac.jp/ijcc/wp/cpjr/newreligions/index.html

New Japanese religions are listed on these pages, with links to materials translated and published by Norman Havens.

Tenrikyo Official Home Page
http://www.tenrikyo.or.jp

These pages contain a quick summary of the teaching, key words in Tenrikyo, salvation stories, and a Tenrikyo-Christian dialogue.

UNIT 6: Judaism

Judaism and Jewish Resources
http://shamash.org/trb/judaism.html

Here is a gateway on the Internet to Jewish resources. It covers everything that needs to be known about Judaism.

Judaism
http://www.religioustolerance.org/judaism.htm

This site covers the beliefs and practices of Judaism, a description of Judaism, Jewish humanism, Christian-Jewish relationships, the Nazi Holocaust and religious strife and intolerance in Israel, as well as currently updated news.

UNIT 7: Christianity

ATLA World Christianity Website
http://www.yale.edu/adhoc/research_resources/wcig.htm

This Web site has been established to facilitate the acquisition and description of documentation of World Christianity, to share the information, and to promote its use. The site consists of Existing Collections and World Christianity Internet links.

History, Beliefs, Practices, Deeds, etc., of the Roman Catholic Church
http://www.religioustolerance.org/rcc.htm

Everything there is to know about the Roman Catholic Church is available at this Religious Tolerance.com site.

Mark A. Foster's Religious Studies Resource Links: Christianity
http://old.jccc.net/~mfoster/christian.html

Here are five pages of clickable resources on Christianity that range from Roman Catholic and Evangelical Episcopal to the Religious Society of Friends and Elbert Hubbard's Roycrofters.

Special Report: American Catholics Survey
http://www.natcath.com/NCR_Online/archives/102999/web/index.htm

The *National Catholic Reporter* prepared this statistical report about Catholics in the United States in 1999.

Wikipedia: Christianity
http://www.wikipedia.com/wiki/Christianity/

This encyclopedic report on Christianity contains recent changes, and is filled with links such as Christology, Jehovah's Witness, and Unification Church, which appear in the text in click-on form.

World Religions: Comparative Analysis
http://www.comparativereligion.com

This five-page site contains an article, "A Comparative Analysis of the Major World Religions from a Christian Perspective," whose goal is to investigate whether or not there is sufficient evidence to prove that world religions are complementary and equally true.

UNIT 8: Islam

Muslim Scientists and Islamic Civilization
http://cyberistan.org/islamic/

Here is the Web page for Muslim contributions to humanity and Islamic civilization. It includes biographies of scientists and humanists, links to glimpses of Islamic civilization, the Qur'an, the Prophet Muhammad and his companions, and much more.

UNIT 9: Religions in Dialogue and Confrontation

Center for Strategic and International Studies (CSIS)
http://www.csis.org/prevdip/cp_index.htm

This site describes current projects in preventive diplomacy being carried out by CSIS, such as a project on improving religious-ethnic relations in the former Yugoslavia, reviving the memory of Muslim Spain, and resolving the religious-secular divide in Israel.

UNIT 10: Religion Facing the Modern World

American Religion Resources
http://www.academicinfo.net/amrelig.html

This site covers church and state, Buddhism, Christianity, Islam, Judaism, Native American religions and spirituality, new religious movements, and religion in the American West, as well as a Clergy Abuse Tracker: A Coverage Weblog.

New Religious Movements Resources
http://www.gtu.edu/library/LibraryNRMLinks.html

These new religious movement links include megalinks like Academic Info: New Religious Movements; Ontario Consultants for Religious Tolerance; and Religious Movements Homepage at the University of Virginia, and links to communal, metaphysical, spiritualist, psychic, and new age families.

We highly recommend that you review our Web site for expanded information and our other product lines. We are continually updating and adding links to our Web site in order to offer you the most usable and useful information that will support and expand the value of your Annual Editions. You can reach us at: *http://www.dushkin.com/annualeditions/*.

UNIT 1
Understanding Religion

Unit Selections

1. **The "Comparative" Study of Religion**, Ninian Smart
2. **Body Ritual Among the Nacirema**, Horace Miner
3. **Baseball Magic**, George Gmelch
4. **Each Religion Expresses an Important Part of the Truth**, Raimundo Panikkar

Key Points to Consider

- What are the purposes and goals of the comparative study of religion?
- What role do rituals play in our lives? Wha is the difference between religious and nonreligious rituals?
- Is it possible to understand another person's religious beliefs from his or her own point of view? Explain.
- What are some of the commonalties that can be found in the various different religious traditions?
- Can people of one faith find things of value in other belief systems?

 **Links: www.dushkin.com/online/**
These sites are annotated in the World Wide Web pages.

World Religion Gateway
http://www.academicinfo.net/religindex.html

World Scripture: A Comparative Anthology of Sacred Texts
http://www.ettl.co.at/uc/ws/

The study of world religions can be both an exciting and an eye-opening adventure for those who have learned little or nothing about belief systems other than their own. Such study moves students in the direction of learning to understand better people from other cultures and religious traditions with respect to why they think and act the way that they do. Increasingly, our world is becoming smaller, more integrated, and interdependent. Since September 11, 2001, many Americans have come to realize that the United States is no longer isolated or immune from the views and actions of people around the world, which are frequently influenced by their religious and cultural values. The old saying, "ignorance is bliss," clearly does not apply to our world today. At best, ignorance can leave us ill-prepared to relate to, learn from, and exist in peace with the rest of the world. At worst, it can lead us into fear and hatred, suffering, and, ultimately, demise. On the other hand, the study of the religious cultures and history of the world can open up a vast awareness of the values, beauty, difficulties, and wisdom that can be found in every country and in every religious culture.

The goal of a comparative study of religion is not to convert students to a particular belief system. Instead, it is to help students become more aware and to gain a greater understanding of the world around them, including their neighbors. There was once a time in America when large portions of the population lived in relatively isolated communities and almost exclusively associated with others who looked, believed, and acted in a similar manner. Many Americans in past generations seldom knew, or even met, people whose ways of thinking and being were vastly different from their own. To most, "a different religion" simply meant a different denomination of Christianity. Moreover, many Christians believed that there were no religions other than Christianity, at least no "real" religions.

Much has changed in the last several decades, during which time large numbers of immigrants to the United States have come from South America, Asia, Africa, and the Pacific, bringing with them a great variety of new religious and cultural traditions. Starting in the 1950s, universities gradually began to teach courses on world religions, although the non-Christian traditions were rarely discussed with any depth or accuracy. Nearly all the professors were Protestant Christian, and many had degrees from theological seminaries as opposed to secular universities. However, as American students became more interested in and familiar with non-European religious traditions, there was an increasing demand for courses covering these topics. By the mid-1970s, there were world religion courses at most large universities. With an increasing percentage of multiethnic, multiracial, multicultural, and multireligious student populations and faculty, the awareness of other traditions has become both more possible and more necessary. Consequently, students now have a greater opportunity than ever before to learn from those around them and to develop a broader religious and cultural awareness of the world in a more personal way. The study of world religions can help to augment this process, and it can also give us the tools we need to live at peace with our neighbors.

Among the first academics to promote the comparative study of religion at the university level were Professors Huston Smith in the United States and Ninian Smart in England. Smith was the child of Christian missionaries in China. Having spent most of his formative years in Asia, he was exposed to a large variety of the region's religious traditions. His book, *The Religions of Man* (Perennial, 1989), was one of the first academic books to look at religions from a perspective of appreciation and understanding, and it became one of the primary texts for the study of comparative religion in America for several decades. In many ways, it pointed the way to an empathetic study of other religions.

Within a few years, Smart's *World Religions: A Dialogue* (Diane Publishing, 2001)was published and became an important source for the study of comparative religion in the United Kingdom, and then in the United States as well. Born in Scotland and raised in the Episcopal Church, Smart's studies and travels inspired in him a great interest in the religions of Asia. By the time of his death in 2001, he had written several dozen more volumes related to religion and its study. The first article in unit 1 is an extract from Smart's *Worldviews: Crosscultural Explorations of Human Beliefs.* In it, he discusses the approach that he thinks students should take in the comparative study of religion. The next two articles are presented to help students understand both the value and some conceptual tools for approaching this study.

The last article in this unit was written with the same mind set as the first. It comes from a Catholic priest, Fr. Raimundo Panikkar, whose career involved the teaching of religion within a secular, academic institution, the University of California at Santa Barbara. Like Smart and Smith, Panikkar has long taught the importance of a broad-based understanding of religion. This article is meant to inspire students to think beyond the narrow confines of what is traditionally understood as religion.

Together, the articles in this unit set the stage for a broader understanding of what religion is and why it is both important and useful to study.

The "Comparative" Study of Religion

For a long time, and especially in Europe, a strange division arose between religious scholars who belonged largely to Christian faculties of theology or divinity schools, and scholars engaged in the comparative study of religion. It was as though all religions other than Christianity (and, by implication, Judaism because it belonged to the same tradition of "revealed" religion) were to be treated as a separate group. It was sometimes argued that Christianity is unique and cannot seriously be compared to other religions. Only in the 1960s did the English-speaking world, and to some degree northern Europe, arrive at a broader and more integrated conception of the study of religion in which various religions and worldviews, Christianity included, are dealt with together. Thus, the modern study of religion emerged partly out of the comparative study of religion and looks at Christianity, too, as a "world religion"—not as the exclusive concern of Christian scholars.

However, many of the best historians of religion have been Christians. Although there have been problems among those Christian theologians who think that comparative religion makes people comparatively religious (to echo a famous and disdainful quip by the Roman Catholic writer Ronald Knox), many Christians have had a more encouraging view of the modern study of religion. (Actually, as far as my experience goes, Knox is quite wrong.)

So far, in sketching some of the threads woven into the fabric of religious studies, I have used, interchangeably, the phrases "history of religions" and "comparative study of religion." Both phrases have somewhat confusingly been in vogue.

People have used "the comparative study of religion" because, as a famous slogan has it, "If you know one, you know none." This means that knowledge of one religion can throw light upon another, and knowledge of another upon one's own, or that of one's own culture. For instance, in a number of traditions water is a symbol of chaos, and so even of death. Knowing this helps illuminate the ritual of total immersion practiced by many Christians at baptism. The devotee dies to the world and then rises again out of the waters of chaos and death with the risen Christ. Another example is this: Some Christian mystics say that it is impossible to refer to God with words, for in the higher stages of the path of meditation all words and images disappear. It turns out that similar things are said in Buddhism and in the Hindu tradition. So this similarity of expression suggests that there may be here some kind of universal human experience, and that the comparative study of religion helps bring this universality to light.

Moreover, if I cross the frontiers of my own culture and travel into the minds and hearts of another tradition, I am bound to make some kinds of comparisons, even if only in realizing that I must not read the assumptions of my own background into the lives of other people. If I as a Christian explore the meaning of the Sabbath for a Jew, I must become aware of deep differences in attitude, despite the use of a common word, namely "Sabbath." In order to understand the Buddhism of Sri Lanka or Thailand I must put behind me the thought that the supreme focus of faith is God, for the Buddhism of Sri Lanka does not focus on a Creator and has quite a different picture of the universe from that found in Genesis. I must not start from the assumptions of baseball in trying to understand cricket. Exploring another tradition should bring contrasts, not just similarities, to the surface; this is what making comparisons means. So, in an important sense, every time I cross the mental frontiers of my tradition and society I am engaged in a comparative study. And indeed, comparative study is possible within traditions and societies, as well as outside them. I am an Episcopalian, and the adjustments I need to make in order to understand what it is like to be a Southern Baptist or a Mormon or a New England Catholic are already considerable. I must not assume that I know my neighbor. And even if for some purposes it is useful to talk about Christianity or Buddhism, it is in fact more realistic to speak of Christianities and Buddhisms. Each has more than fifty-seven varieties. In brief, then, the whole enterprise of crosscultural understanding is comparative.

It also happens that modern scholars of religion have done much work on themes and types, looking at similar phenomena across the board. I have mentioned mysticism—here trying to see if there is a single shining core of inner experience to be found among those in different religions who engage in meditation. Another example is this: Different stories of creation and myths of catastrophe have recurring patterns, such as the story of the Flood. Or, we can see how there are types of religious leadership in both East and West—there are monks and nuns, priests, prophets, and other ecstatic visionaries. Or again, the notion of religious sacrifice seems to be a widespread religious phenomenon. All these observations are to do with *types* of religious phenomena.

Somewhat confusingly, a number of well-known writers (such as Gerardus van der Leeuw, the Dutch scholar; Geo Widengren, the Swede; and Mariasusai Dhavamony, the Indian) have used the term "phenomenology of religion" when referring to their comparative studies of religious themes and types. We thus have another meaning for that lengthy word "phenomenology." I think it is clearer if we refer to this particular kind of study as "typology" or thematic comparison," or perhaps even "morphology," the cataloging of forms.

But although it is true that there is a comparative element in the study of religion, the phrase "comparative study of religion" is rather awkward and is in any case dated. It sometimes had negative connotations; as we have seen, in the old days it could be a conscious or unconscious means of expressing Western superiority when other faiths were compared to their detriment. Partly because of the influence of the modern Chicago school of religion, led by Mircea Eliade, and partly because the International Association for the History of Religions uses the term, it is more common now to talk of "the history of religions." This covers both the writing of the history of individual faiths as well as thematic reflections about contrasts and comparisons.

Some like also to use the word "crosscultural" to express the fact that we have to see the world religions together. The term has great merit in that it suggests that the traffic is not all from one culture to others, but can cross in differing cultural directions, East and West and North and South. The message here is that we should not be busy merely imposing Western themes and categories on non-Western faiths, but that we should also be using Eastern and other categories to throw light on Western religion. Thus, for example, a major element in the Hindu tradition is the fervent worship of a personal God, thought of as Vishnu, or Krishna, or Shiva, or the divine female Kali. (About the last, an anecdote is told: A Hindu swami, or religious teacher, was once pressed to tell on television what God is really like; he surprised his American white male interviewer by saying, "She is black.") Anyway, such devotion—or faith—called *bhakti* is an important strand both in Hinduism and in later Buddhism. It is reasonable, vis-a-vis Christianity, to say that many Protestant hymns and Paul's theology also express a variety of *bhakti*. There are many other non-Western categories that could be used across the board with profit. We could begin to ask questions like "What is distinctive about Christian *bhakti?*" so the modern study of religion can also be looked on as crosscultural.

This makes sense; we do, after all, live on the same globe. We are now moving into a period of global civilization in which we begin to share one another's ancestors and achievements. Beethoven is played in Tokyo and Indian music in New York, and the citizen of the world can draw on the ancestral wisdom of both Socrates and Confucius and the art of Paris and Nigeria. So too can the modern study of religion become genuinely crosscultural and therefore global.

These comparative themes become especially important when we begin to test wide-ranging theories about religion. For instance, the great sociologist Max Weber (1864–1920) hypothesized that Protestantism was a main factor in the rise of capitalism in the West. To test his theory, he looked at how things fared outside Europe, in the Islamic, Indian, and Chinese worlds. For if we say that certain religious factors A and B give rise to result C in one culture, then we need to discover whether A and B are present in other cultures that do *not* manifest C. Either they are not present, or at least, not jointly; or, if they are present, then we should look for some further factor D to tell us why A and B

gave rise to C in one culture but not in the others. We cannot put human societies and human histories into a laboratory, but we can use global history as a kind of laboratory. This is where the social sciences can make crosscultural comparisons. Weber was a major crosscultural pioneer in the fields of religion and economics. He described religious attitudes that, in his view, greatly influenced the rise of capitalism. The Protestant faith, according to Weber, placed great emphasis on inner-worldly asceticism, in which the faithful lived actively, but austerely, in the world (rather than living the more contemplative life of the monastery, which other faiths emphasize). In particular, Weber identified the influence of Protestant reformer John Calvin, whose teachings, coupled with his establishment of a religiously controlled state in Geneva, were important. These factors motivated the middle classes to work hard and spend moderately, and were thus central to the rise of capitalism. What, by the way, do we say about the Buddhist and Confucian values lying deep in the social structures of Japan? How far have they been the source of Japan's great technological and economic miracle?

The fact that the modern study of religion is crosscultural helps strengthen the belief that we should include secular worldviews within its scope. For although it may seem to us in the West that the division between secular and sacred is "natural," and that political ideologies such as Marxism belong to a different category from religions, other, non-Western perspectives may not necessarily divide human realities the same way. Thus, if we look to China, we find that Maoism comes as a direct alternative to the old tradition of Confucius, which likewise contained a philosophy of how to run society.

We can sum up what has been said or implied about the modern study of religion as follows:

First, it is plural, dealing with the many religions and secular worldviews of the globe.

Second, it is open-ended in the sense that considers belief-systems and symbols lying beyond the frontiers of traditional religions.

Third, it treats worldviews both historically and systematically, and attempts to enter, through structured empathy, into the viewpoint of the believers.

Fourth, it makes thematic comparisons that help illuminate the separate traditions.

Fifth, it is polymethodic: It uses many methods drawn from various disciplines—history, art history, philology, archaeology, sociology, anthropology, philosophy, and so on.

Sixth, it aims to show the power of religious ideas and practices and their interactions with other aspects of human existence.

Seventh, it can set the scene not only for an educated understanding of the world and its various belief-systems, but also for a personal quest for spiritual truth.

Structured empathy plays a central part in all this. It is the way we cross our own horizons into the worlds of other people.

From *Worldviews: Crosscultural Explorations of Human Beliefs,* 3/E by Ninian Smart. © 1999. Reprinted by permission of Pearson Education, Inc., Upper Saddle River, NJ.

Body Ritual Among the Nacirema

Horace Miner
University of Michigan

The anthropologist has become so familiar with the diversity of ways in which different peoples behave in similar situations that he is not apt to be surprised by even the most exotic customs. In fact, if all of the logically possible combinations of behavior have not been found somewhere in the world, he is apt to suspect that they must be present in some yet undescribed tribe. This point has, in fact, been expressed with respect to clan organization by Murdock (1949: 71). In this light, the magical beliefs and practices of the Nacirema present such unusual aspects that it seems desirable to describe them as an example of the extremes to which human behavior can go.

Professor Linton first brought the ritual of the Nacirema to the attention of anthropologists twenty years ago (1936: 326), but the culture of this people is still very poorly understood. They are a North American group living in the territory between the Canadian Cree, the Yaqui and Tarahumare of Mexico, and the Carib and Arawak of the Antilles. Little is known of their origin, though tradition states that they came from the east. According to Nacirema mythology, their nation was originated by a culture hero, Notgnishaw, who is otherwise known for two great feats of strength—the throwing of a piece of wampum across the river Pa-To-Mac and the chopping down of a cherry tree in which the Spirit of Truth resided.

Nacirema culture is characterized by a highly developed market economy which has evolved in a rich natural habitat. While much of the people's time is devoted to economic pursuits, a large part of the fruits of these labors and a considerable portion of the day are spent in ritual activity. The focus of this activity is the human body, the appearance and health of which loom as a dominant concern in the ethos of the people. While such a concern is certainly not unusual, its ceremonial aspects and associated philosophy are unique.

The fundamental belief underlying the whole system appears to be that the human body is ugly and that its natural tendency is to debility and disease. Incarcerated in such a body, man's only hope is to avert these characteristics through the use of the powerful influences of ritual and ceremony. Every household has one or more shrines devoted to this purpose. The more powerful individuals in the society have several shrines in their houses and, in fact, the opulence of a house is often referred to in terms of the number of such ritual centers it possesses. Most houses are of wattle and daub construction, but the shrine rooms of the more wealthy are walled with stone. Poorer families imitate the rich by applying pottery plaques to their shrine walls.

While each family has at least one such shrine, the rituals associated with it are not family ceremonies but are private and secret. The rites are normally only discussed with children, and then only during the period when they are being initiated into these mysteries. I was able, however, to establish sufficient rapport with the natives to examine these shrines and to have the rituals described to me.

The focal point of the shrine is a box or chest which is built into the wall. In this chest are kept the many charms and magical potions without which no native believes he could live. These preparations are secured from a variety of specialized practitioners. The most powerful of these are the medicine men, whose assistance must be rewarded with substantial gifts. However, the medicine men do not provide the curative potions for their clients, but decide what the ingredients should be and then write them down in an ancient and secret language. This writing is understood only by the medicine men and by the herbalists who, for another gift, provide the required charm.

The charm is not disposed of after it has served its purpose, but is placed in the charm-box of the household shrine. As these magical materials are specific for certain ills, and the real or imagined maladies of the people are many, the charm-box is usually full to overflowing. The magical packets are so numerous that people forget what their purposes were and fear to use them again. While the natives are very vague on this point, we can only assume that the idea in retaining all the old magical materials is that their presence in the charm-box, before which the body rituals are conducted, will in some way protect the worshipper.

Beneath the charm-box is a small font. Each day every member of the family, in succession, enters the shrine room, bows his head before the charm-box, mingles different sorts of holy water in the font, and proceeds with a brief rite of ablution.

The holy waters are secured from the Water Temple of the community, where the priests conduct elaborate ceremonies to make the liquid ritually pure.

In the hierarchy of magical practitioners, and below the medicine men in prestige, are specialists whose designation is best translated "holy-mouth-men." The Nacirema have an almost pathological horror and fascination with the mouth, the condition of which is believed to have a supernatural influence on all social relationships. Were it not for the rituals of the mouth, they believe that their teeth would fall out, their gums bleed, their jaws shrink, their friends desert them, and their lovers reject them. (They also believe that a strong relationship exists between oral and moral characteristics. For example, there is a ritual ablution of the mouth for children which is supposed to improve their moral fiber.)

The daily body ritual performed by everyone includes a mouth-rite. Despite the fact that these people are so punctilious about care of the mouth, this rite involves a practice which strikes the uninitiated stranger as revolting. It was reported to me that the ritual consists of inserting a small bundle of hog hairs into the mouth, along with certain magical powders, and then moving the bundle in a highly formalized series of gestures.

In addition to the private mouth-rite, the people seek out a holy-mouth-man once or twice a year. These practitioners have an impressive set of paraphernalia, consisting of a variety of augers, awls, probes, and prods. The use of these objects in the exorcism of the evils of the mouth involves almost unbelievable ritual torture of the client. The holy-mouth-man opens the client's mouth and, using the above mentioned tools, enlarges any holes which decay may have created in the teeth. Magical materials are put into these holes. If there are no naturally occurring holes in the teeth, large sections of one or more teeth are gouged out so that the supernatural substance can be applied. In the client's view, the purpose of these ministrations is to arrest decay and to draw friends. The extremely sacred and traditional character of the rite is evident in the fact that the natives return to the holy-mouth-men year after year, despite the fact that their teeth continue to decay.

It is to be hoped that, when a thorough study of the Nacirema is made, there will be a careful inquiry into the personality structure of these people. One has but to watch the gleam in the eye of a holy-mouth-man, as he jabs an awl into an exposed nerve, to suspect that a certain amount of sadism is involved. If this can be established, a very interesting pattern emerges, for most of the population shows definite masochistic tendencies. It was to these that Professor Linton referred in discussing a distinctive part of the daily body ritual which is performed only by men. This part of the rite involves scraping and lacerating the surface of the face with a sharp instrument. Special women's rites are performed only four times during each lunar month, but what they lack in frequency is made up in barbarity. As part of this ceremony, women bake their heads in small ovens for about an hour. The theoretically interesting point is that what seems to be a preponderantly masochistic people have developed sadistic specialists.

The medicine men have an imposing temple, or *latipso*, in every community of any size. The more elaborate ceremonies required to treat very sick patients can only be performed at this temple. These ceremonies involve not only the thaumaturge but a permanent group of vestal maidens who move sedately about the temple chambers in distinctive costume and headdress.

The *latipso* ceremonies are so harsh that it is phenomenal that a fair proportion of the really sick natives who enter the temple ever recover. Small children whose indoctrination is still incomplete have been known to resist attempts to take them to the temple because "that is where you go to die." Despite this fact, sick adults are not only willing but eager to undergo the protracted ritual purification, if they can afford to do so. No matter how ill the supplicant or how grave the emergency, the guardians of many temples will not admit a client if he cannot give a rich gift to the custodian. Even after one has gained admission and survived the ceremonies, the guardians will not permit the neophyte to leave until he makes still another gift.

The supplicant entering the temple is first stripped of all his or her clothes. In every-day life the Nacirema avoids exposure of his body and its natural functions. Bathing and excretory acts are performed only in the secrecy of the household shrine, where they are ritualized as part of the body-rites. Psychological shock results from the fact that body secrecy is suddenly lost upon entry into the *latipso*. A man, whose own wife has never seen him in an excretory act, suddenly finds himself naked and assisted by a vestal maiden while he performs his natural functions into a sacred vessel. This sort of ceremonial treatment is necessitated by the fact that the excreta are used by a diviner to ascertain the course and nature of the client's sickness. Female clients, on the other hand, find their naked bodies are subjected to the scrutiny, manipulation, and prodding of the medicine men.

Few supplicants in the temple are well enough to do anything but lie on their hard beds. The daily ceremonies, like the rites of the holy-mouth-men, involve discomfort and torture. With ritual precision, the vestals awaken their miserable charges each dawn and roll them about on their beds of pain while performing ablutions, in the formal movements of which the maidens are highly trained. At other times they insert magic wands in the supplicant's mouth or force him to eat substances which are supposed to be healing. From time to time the medicine men come to their clients and jab magically treated needles into their flesh. The fact that these temple ceremonies may not cure, and may even kill the neophyte, in no way decreases the people's faith in the medicine men.

There remains one other kind of practitioner, known as a "listener." This witch-doctor has the power to exorcise the devils that lodge in the heads of people who have been bewitched. The Nacirema believe that parents bewitch their own children. Mothers are particularly suspected of putting a curse on children while teaching them the secret body rituals. The counter-magic of the witch-doctor is unusual in its lack of ritual. The patient simply tells the "listener" all his troubles and fears, beginning with the earliest difficulties he can remember. The memory displayed by the Nacirema in these exorcism sessions is truly remarkable. It is not uncommon for the patient to bemoan the rejection he felt upon being weaned as a babe, and a few individuals even see their troubles going back to the traumatic effects of their own birth.

In conclusion, mention must be made of certain practices which have their base in native esthetics but which depend upon the pervasive aversion to the natural body and its functions. There are ritual fasts to make fat people thin and ceremonial feasts to make thin people fat. Still other rites are used to make women's breasts large if they are small, and smaller if they are large. General dissatisfaction with breast shape is symbolized in the fact that the ideal form is virtually outside the range of human variation. A few women afflicted with almost inhuman hyper-mammary development are so idolized that they make a handsome living by simply going from village to village and permitting the natives to stare at them for a fee.

Reference has already been made to the fact that excretory functions are ritualized, routinized, and relegated to secrecy. Natural reproductive functions are similarly distorted. Intercourse is taboo as a topic and scheduled as an act. Efforts are made to avoid pregnancy by the use of magical materials or by limiting intercourse to certain phases of the moon. Conception is actually very infrequent. When pregnant, women dress so as to hide their condition. Parturition takes place in secret, without friends or relatives to assist, and the majority of women do not nurse their infants.

Our review of the ritual life of the Nacirema has certainly shown them to be a magic-ridden people. It is hard to understand how they have managed to exist so long under the burdens which they have imposed upon themselves. But even such exotic customs as these take on real meaning when they are viewed with the insight provided by Malinowski when he wrote (1948:70):

Looking from far and above, from our high places of safety in the developed civilization, it is easy to see all the crudity and irrelevance of magic. But without its power and guidance early man could not have mastered his practical difficulties as he has done, nor could man have advanced to the higher stages of civilization.

REFERENCES

Linton, Ralph. 1936. *The Study of Man.* New York, D. Appleton-Century Co.

Malinowski, Bronislaw. 1948. *Magic, Science, and Religion.* Glencoe, The Free Press.

Murdock, George P. 1949. *Social Structure.* New York, The Macmillan Co.

Baseball Magic

George Gmelch

On each pitching day for the first three months of a winning season, Dennis Grossini, a pitcher on a Detroit Tiger farm team, arose from bed at exactly 10:00 a.m. At 1:00 p.m. he went to the nearest restaurant for two glasses of iced tea and a tuna sandwich. Although the afternoon was free, he changed into the sweatshirt and supporter he wore during his last winning game, and, one hour before the game, he chewed a wad of Beech-Nut chewing tobacco. After each pitch during the game he touched the letters on his uniform and straightened his cap after each ball. Before the start of each inning he replaced the pitcher's resin bag next to the spot where it was the inning before. And after every inning in which he gave up a run, he washed his hands.

When asked which part of the ritual was most important, he said, "You can't really tell what's most important so it all becomes important. I'd be afraid to change anything. As long as I'm winning, I do everything the same."

Trobriand Islanders, according to anthropologist Bronislaw Malinowski, felt the same way about their fishing magic. Among the Trobrianders, fishing took two forms: in the *inner lagoon* where fish were plentiful and there was little danger, and on the *open sea* where fishing was dangerous and yields varied widely. Malinowski found that magic was not used in lagoon fishing, where men could rely solely on their knowledge and skill. But when fishing on the open sea, Trobrianders used a great deal of magical ritual to ensure safety and increase their catch.

Baseball, America's national pastime, is an arena in which players behave remarkably like Malinowski's Trobriand fishermen. To professional ballplayers,

baseball is more than just a game. It is an occupation. Since their livelihoods depend on how well they perform, many use magic to try to control the chance that is built into baseball. There are three essential activities of the game—pitching, hitting, and fielding. In the first two, chance can play a surprisingly important role. The pitcher is the player least able to control the outcome of his own efforts. He may feel great and have good stuff warming up in the bullpen and then get into the game and not have it. He may make a bad pitch and see the batter miss it for a strike out or see it hit hard but right into the hands of a fielder for an out. His best pitch may be blooped for a base hit. He may limit the opposing team to just a few hits yet lose the game, or he may give up a dozen hits but still win. And the good and bad luck don't always average out over the course of a season. Some pitchers end the season with poor won-loss records but good earned run averages, and vice versa. For instance, this past season Andy Benes gave up over one run per game more than his teammate Omar Daal but had a better won-loss record. Benes went 14–13, while Daal was only 8–12. Both pitched for the same team—the Arizona Diamondbacks—which meant they had the same fielders behind them. Regardless of how well a pitcher performs, on every outing he depends not only on his own skill, but also upon the proficiency of his teammates, the ineptitude of the opposition, and luck.

Hitting, which many observers call the single most difficult task in the world of sports, is also full of risk and uncertainty. Unless it's a home run, no matter how well the batter hits the ball, fate determines whether it will go into a waiting

glove, whistle past a fielder's diving stab, or find a gap in the outfield. The uncertainty is compounded by the low success rate of hitting: the average hitter gets only one hit in every four trips to the plate, while the very best hitters average only one hit every three trips. Fielding, as we will return to later, is the one part of baseball where chance does not play much of a role.

How does the risk and uncertainty in pitching and hitting affect players? How do they try to exercise control over the outcomes of their performance? These are questions that I first became interested in many years ago as both a ballplayer and an anthropology student. I'd devoted much of my youth to baseball, and played professionally as first baseman in the Detroit Tigers organization in the 1960s. It was shortly after the end of one baseball season that I took an anthropology course called "Magic, Religion, and Witchcraft." As I listened to my professor describe the magical rituals of the Trobriand Islanders, it occurred to me that what these so-called "primitive" people did wasn't all that different from what my teammates and I did for luck and confidence at the ball park.

ROUTINES AND RITUALS

The most common way players attempt to reduce chance and their feelings of uncertainty is to develop and follow a daily routine, a course of action which is regularly followed. Talking about the routines ballplayers follow, Pirates coach Rich Donnelly said:

They're like trained animals. They come out here [ballpark] and everything has to be the same, they don't like anything that knocks them off their routine. Just look at the dugout and you'll see every guy sitting in the same spot every night. It's amazing, everybody in the same spot. And don't you dare take someone's seat. If a guy comes up from the minors and sits here, they'll say, 'Hey, Jim sits here, find another seat.' You watch the pitcher warm up and he'll do the same thing every time. And when you go on the road it's the same way. You've got a routine and you adhere to it and you don't want anybody knocking you off it.

Routines are comforting, they bring order into a world in which players have little control. And sometimes practical elements in routines produce tangible benefits, such as helping the player concentrate. But what players often do goes beyond mere routine. Their actions become what anthropologists define as *ritual*—prescribed behaviors in which there is no empirical connection between the means (e.g., tapping home plate three times) and the desired end (e.g., getting a base hit). Because there is no real connection between the two, rituals are not rational, and sometimes they are actually irrational. Similar to rituals are the nonrational beliefs that form the basis of taboos and fetishes, which players also use to reduce chance and bring luck to their side. But first let's look more closely at rituals.

Most rituals are personal, that is, they're performed by individuals rather than by a team or group. Most are done in an unemotional manner, in much the same way players apply pine tar to their bats to improve the grip or dab eye black on their upper cheeks to reduce the sun's glare. Baseball rituals are infinitely varied. A ballplayer may ritualize any activity—eating, dressing, driving to the ballpark—that he considers important or somehow linked to good performance. For example, Yankee pitcher Denny Neagle goes to a movie on days he is scheduled to start. Pitcher Jason Bere listens to the same song on his Walkman on the days he is to pitch. Jim Ohms puts another penny in the pouch of his supporter after

each win. Clanging against the hard plastic genital cup, the pennies made a noise as he ran the bases toward the end of a winning season. Glenn Davis would chew the same gum every day during hitting streaks, saving it under his cap. Infielder Julio Gotay always played with a cheese sandwich in his back pocket (he had a big appetite, so there might also have been a measure of practicality here). Wade Boggs ate chicken before every game during his career, and that was just one of dozens of elements in his pre and post game routine, which also included leaving his house for the ballpark at precisely the same time each day (1:47 for a 7:05 game). Former Oriole pitcher Dennis Martinez would drink a small cup of water after each inning and then place it under the bench upside down, in a line. His teammates could always tell what inning it was by counting the cups.

Many hitters go through a series of preparatory rituals before stepping into the batter's box. These include tugging on their caps, touching their uniform letters or medallions, crossing themselves, tapping or bouncing the bat on the plate, or swinging the weighted warm-up bat a prescribed number of times. Consider Red Sox Nomar Garciaparra. After each pitch he steps out of the batters box, kicks the dirt with each toe, adjusts his right batting glove, adjusts his left batting glove, and touches his helmet before getting back into the box. Mike Hargrove, former Cleveland Indian first baseman, had so many time consuming elements in his batting ritual that he was known as "the human rain delay." Both players believe their batting rituals helped them regain their concentration after each pitch. But others wonder if they have become prisoners of their own superstitions. Also, players who have too many or particularly bizarre rituals risk being labeled as "flakes," and not just by teammates but by fans and media as well. For example, pitcher Turk Wendell's eccentric rituals, which included wearing a necklace of teeth from animals he had killed, made him a cover story in the *New York Times Sunday Magazine*.

Some players, especially Latin Americans, draw upon rituals from their Roman Catholic religion. Some make the sign of the cross or bless themselves be-

fore every at bat, and a few like the Rangers' Pudge Rodriguez do so before every pitch. Others, like the Detroit Tiger Juan Gonzalez, also visibly wear religious medallions around their necks, while some tuck them discretely inside their undershirts.

One ritual associated with hitting is tagging a base when leaving and returning to the dugout between innings. Some players don't "feel right" unless they tag a specific base on each trip between the dugout and the field. One of my teammates added some complexity to his ritual by tagging third base on his way to the dugout only after the third, sixth, and ninth innings. Asked if he ever purposely failed to step on the bag, he replied, "Never! I wouldn't dare. It would destroy my confidence to hit." Baseball fans observe a lot of this ritual behavior, such as fielders tagging bases, pitchers tugging on their caps or touching the resin bag after each bad pitch, or smoothing the dirt on the mound before each new batter or inning, never realizing the importance of these actions to the player. The one ritual many fans do recognize, largely because it's a favorite of TV cameramen, is the "rally cap"—players in the dugout folding their caps and wearing them bill up in hopes of sparking a rally.

Most rituals grow out of exceptionally good performances. When a player does well, he seldom attributes his success to skill alone. He knows that his skills were essentially the same the night before. He asks himself, "What was different about today which explains my three hits?" He decides to repeat what he did today in an attempt to bring more good luck. And so he attributes his success, in part, to an object, a food he ate, not having shaved, a new shirt he bought that day, or just about any behavior out of the ordinary. By repeating that behavior, he seeks to gain control over his performance. Outfielder John White explained how one of his rituals started:

I was jogging out to centerfield after the national anthem when I picked up a scrap of paper. I got some good hits that night and I guess I decided that the paper had something to do with it. The next night I picked up a gum wrapper and had another good night at the plate… I've been picking up paper every night since.

Outfielder Ron Wright of the Calgary Cannons shaves his arms once a week and plans to continue doing so until he has a bad year. It all began two years before when after an injury he shaved his arm so it could be taped, and proceeded to hit three homers over the next few games. Now he not only has one of the smoothest swings in the minor leagues, but two of the smoothest forearms. Wade Boggs' routine of eating chicken before every game began when he was a rookie in 1982. He noticed a correlation between multiple hit games and poultry plates (his wife has over 40 chicken recipes). One of Montreal Expos farmhand Mike Saccocio's rituals also concerned food, "I got three hits one night after eating at Long John Silver's. After that when we'd pull into town, my first question would be, "Do you have a Long John Silver's?" Unlike Boggs, Saccocio abandoned his ritual and looked for a new one when he stopped hitting well.

When in a slump, most players make a deliberate effort to change their rituals and routines in an attempt to shake off their bad luck. One player tried taking different routes to the ballpark; several players reported trying different combinations of tagging and not tagging particular bases in an attempt to find a successful combination. I had one manager who would rattle the bat bin when the team was not hitting well, as if the bats were in a stupor and could be aroused by a good shaking. Similarly, I have seen hitters rub their hands along the handles of the bats protruding from the bin in hopes of picking up some power or luck from bats that are getting hits for their owners. Some players switch from wearing their contact lenses to glasses. Brett Mandel described his Pioneer League team, the Ogden Raptors, trying to break a losing streak by using a new formation for their pre-game stretching.[1]

TABOO

Taboos are the opposite of rituals. The word taboo comes from a Polynesian term meaning prohibition. Breaking a taboo, players believe, leads to undesirable consequences or bad luck. Most players observe at least a few taboos, such as never stepping on the white foul lines. A few, like the Mets Turk Wendell and Red Sox Nomar Garciaparra, leap over the entire basepath. One teammate of mine would never watch a movie on a game day, despite the fact that we played nearly every day from April to September. Another teammate refused to read anything before a game because he believed it weakened his batting eye.

Many taboos take place off the field, out of public view. On the day a pitcher is scheduled to start, he is likely to avoid activities he believes will sap his strength and detract from his effectiveness. Some pitchers avoid eating certain foods, others will not shave on the day of a game, refusing to shave again as long as they are winning. Early in the 1989 season Oakland's Dave Stewart had six consecutive victories and a beard by the time he lost.

Taboos usually grow out of exceptionally poor performances, which players, in search of a reason, attribute to a particular behavior. During my first season of pro ball I ate pancakes before a game in which I struck out three times. A few weeks later I had another terrible game, again after eating pancakes. The result was a pancake taboo: I never again ate pancakes during the season. Pitcher Jason Bere has a taboo that makes more sense in dietary terms: after eating a meatball sandwich and not pitching well, he swore off them for the rest of the season.

While most taboos are idiosyncratic, there are a few that all ball players hold and that do not develop out of individual experience or misfortune. These form part of the culture of baseball, and are sometimes learned as early as Little League. Mentioning a no-hitter while one is in progress is a well-known example. It is believed that if a pitcher hears the words "no-hitter," the spell accounting for this hard to achieve feat will be broken and the no-hitter lost. This taboo is also observed by many sports broadcasters, who use various linguistic subterfuges to inform their listeners that the pitcher has not given up a hit, never saying "no-hitter."

FETISHES

Fetishes or charms are material objects believed to embody "supernatural" power that can aid or protect the owner. Good luck charms are standard equipment for some ballplayers. These include a wide assortment of objects from coins, chains, and crucifixes to a favorite baseball hat. The fetishized object may be a new possession or something a player found that happens to coincide with the start of a streak and which he holds responsible for his good fortune. While playing in the Pacific Coast League, Alan Foster forgot his baseball shoes on a road trip and borrowed a pair from a teammate. That night he pitched a no-hitter, which he attributed to the shoes. Afterwards he bought them from his teammate and they became a fetish. Expo farmhand Mark LaRosa's rock has a different origin and use:

> I found it on the field in Elmira after I had gotten bombed. It's unusual, perfectly round, and it caught my attention. I keep it to remind me of how important it is to concentrate. When I am going well I look at the rock and remember to keep my focus, the rock reminds me of what can happen when I lose my concentration.

For one season Marge Schott, former owner of the Cincinnati Reds, insisted that her field manager rub her St. Bernard "Schotzie" for good luck before each game. When the Reds were on the road, Schott would sometimes send a bag of the dog's hair to the field manager's hotel room.

During World War II, American soldiers used fetishes in much the same way. Social psychologist Samuel Stouffer and his colleagues found that in the face of great danger and uncertainty, soldiers developed magical practices, particularly the use of protective amulets and good luck charms (crosses, Bibles, rabbits' feet, medals), and jealously guarded articles of clothing they associated with past experiences of escape from danger.[2] Stouffer also found that prebattle preparations were carried out in fixed ritual-like order, similar to ballplayers preparing for a game.

Uniform numbers have special significance for some players who request their lucky number. Since the choice is usually limited, they try to at least get a uniform that contains their lucky number, such as 14, 24, 34, or 44 for the player whose lucky number is four. When Ricky Henderson came to the Blue Jays in 1993 he paid outfielder Turner Ward $25,000 for the right to wear number 24. Oddly enough, there is no consensus about the effect of wearing number 13. Some players will not wear it, others will, and a few request it. Number preferences emerge in different ways. A young player may request the number of a former star, hoping that—through what anthropologists call *imitative* magic—it will bring him the same success. Or he may request a number he associates with good luck. While with the Oakland A's Vida Blue changed his uniform number from 35 to 14, the number he wore as a high-school quarterback. When 14 did not produce better pitching performance, he switched back to 35. Former San Diego Padre first baseman Jack Clark changed his number from 25 to 00, hoping to break out of a slump. That day he got four hits in a double header, but also hurt his back. Then, three days later, he was hit in the cheekbone by a ball thrown in batting practice.

Colorado Rockies Larry Walker's fixation with the number three has become well known to baseball fans. Besides wearing 33, he takes three practice swings before stepping into the box, he showers from the third nozzle, sets his alarm for three minutes past the hour and he was wed on November 3 at 3:33 p.m. Fans in ballparks all across America rise from their seats for the seventh inning stretch before the home club comes to bat because the number seven is lucky, although the origin of this tradition has been lost.

Clothing, both the choice and the order in which they are put on, combine elements of both ritual and fetish. Some players put on their uniform in a ritualized order. Expos farmhand Jim Austin always puts on his left sleeve, left pants leg, and left shoe before the right. Most players, however, single out one or two lucky articles or quirks of dress for ritual elaboration. After hitting two home runs in a

game, for example, ex-Giant infielder Jim Davenport discovered that he had missed a buttonhole while dressing for the game. For the remainder of his career he left the same button undone. For outfielder Brian Hunter the focus is shoes, "I have a pair of high tops and a pair of low tops. Whichever shoes don't get a hit that game, I switch to the other pair." At the time of our interview, he was struggling at the plate and switching shoes almost every day. For Birmingham Baron pitcher Bo Kennedy the arrangement of the different pairs of baseball shoes in his locker is critical:

I tell the clubies [clubhouse boys] when you hang stuff in my locker don't touch my shoes. If you bump them move them back. I want the Pony's in front, the turfs to the right, and I want them nice and neat with each pair touching each other…. Everyone on the team knows not to mess with my shoes when I pitch.

During streaks—hitting or winning—players may wear the same clothes day after day. Once I changed sweatshirts midway through the game for seven consecutive nights to keep a hitting streak going. Clothing rituals, however, can become impractical. Catcher Matt Allen was wearing a long sleeve turtle neck shirt on a cool evening in the New York-Penn League when he had a three-hit game. "I kept wearing the shirt and had a good week," he explained. "Then the weather got hot as hell, 85 degrees and muggy, but I would not take that shirt off. I wore it for another ten days—catching—and people thought I was crazy." Also taking a ritual to the extreme, Leo Durocher, managing the Brooklyn Dodgers to a pennant in 1941, is said to have spent three and a half weeks in the same gray slacks, blue coat, and knitted blue tie. During a 16-game winning streak, the 1954 New York Giants wore the same clothes in each game and refused to let them be cleaned for fear that their good fortune might be washed away with the dirt. Losing often produces the opposite effect. Several Oakland A's players, for example, went out and bought new street clothes in an attempt to break a fourteen-game losing streak.

Baseball's superstitions, like most everything else, change over time. Many of the rituals and beliefs of early baseball are no longer observed. In the 1920s and 1930s sportswriters reported that a player who tripped en route to the field would often retrace his steps and carefully walk over the stumbling block for "insurance." A century ago players spent time on and off the field intently looking for items that would bring them luck. To find a hairpin on the street, for example, assured a batter of hitting safely in that day's game. Today few women wear hairpins—a good reason the belief has died out. To catch sight of a white horse or a wagon-load of barrels were also good omens. In 1904 the manager of the New York Giants, John McGraw, hired a driver with a team of white horses to drive past the Polo Grounds around the time his players were arriving at the ballpark. He knew that if his players saw white horses, they'd have more confidence and that could only help them during the game. Belief in the power of white horses survived in a few backwaters until the 1960s. A gray haired manager of a team I played for in Drummondville, Quebec, would drive around the countryside before important games and during the playoffs looking for a white horse. When he was successful, he would announce it to everyone in the clubhouse.

One belief that appears to have died out recently is a taboo about crossed bats. Some of my Latino teammates in the 1960s took it seriously. I can still recall one Dominican player becoming agitated when another player tossed a bat from the batting cage and it landed on top of his bat. He believed that the top bat might steal hits from the lower one. In his view, bats contained a finite number of hits, a sort of baseball "image of limited good." It was once commonly believed that when the hits in a bat were used up no amount of good hitting would produce any more. Hall of Famer Honus Wagner believed each bat contained only 100 hits. Regardless of the quality of the bat, he would discard it after its 100th hit. This belief would have little relevance today, in the era of light bats with thin handles—so thin that the typical modern bat is lucky to survive a dozen hits without being broken. Other superstitions about bats do survive, however. Position players on the Class A Asheville Tourists, for example, would not let pitchers touch or swing their bats, not even to warm up. Poor-hitting players, as most pitchers are, were said to pollute or weaken the bats.

UNCERTAINTY AND MAGIC

The best evidence that players turn to rituals, taboos, and fetishes to control chance and uncertainty is found in their uneven application. They are associated mainly with pitching and hitting—the activities with the highest degree of chance—and not fielding. I met only one player who had any ritual in connection with fielding, and he was an error prone shortstop. Unlike hitting and pitching, a fielder has almost complete control over the outcome of his performance. Once a ball has been hit in his direction, no one can intervene and ruin his chances of catching it for an out (except in the unlikely event of two fielders colliding). Compared with the pitcher or the hitter, the fielder has little to worry about. He knows that, in better than 9.7 times out of 10, he will execute his task flawlessly. With odds like that there is little need for ritual.

Clearly, the rituals of American ballplayers are not unlike that of the Trobriand Islanders studied by Malinowski many years ago.[3] In professional baseball, fielding is the equivalent of the inner lagoon while hitting and pitching are like the open sea.

While Malinowski helps us understand how ballplayers respond to chance and uncertainty, behavioral psychologist B. F. Skinner sheds light on why personal rituals get established in the first place.[4] With a few grains of seed Skinner could get pigeons to do anything he wanted. He merely waited for the desired behavior (e.g. pecking) and then rewarded it with some food. Skinner then decided to see what would happen if pigeons were rewarded with food pellets regularly, every fifteen seconds, regardless of what they did. He found that the birds associate the arrival of the food with a particular action, such as tucking their head under a wing or walking in clockwise circles. About ten seconds after the arrival of the last pellet, a bird would begin doing whatever it associated with getting the food and keep doing it until the next pellet arrived. In short, the pigeons behaved as if their actions made the food appear. They learned to associate particular behaviors with the reward of being given seed.

Ballplayers also associate a reward—successful performance—with prior behavior. If a player touches his crucifix and then gets a hit, he may decide the gesture was responsible for his good fortune and touch his crucifix the next time he comes to the plate. If he gets another hit, the chances are good that he will touch his crucifix each time he bats. Unlike pigeons, however, most ballplayers are quicker to change their rituals once they no longer seem to work. Skinner found that once a pigeon associated one of its actions with the arrival of food or water, only sporadic rewards were necessary to keep the ritual going. One pigeon, believing that hopping from side to side brought pellets into its feeding cup, hopped ten thousand times without a pellet before finally giving up. But, then, didn't Wade Boggs eat chicken before every game, through slumps and good times, for seventeen years?

Obviously the rituals and superstitions of baseball do not make a pitch travel faster or a batted ball find the gaps between the fielders, nor do the Trobriand rituals calm the seas or bring fish. What both do, however, is give their practitioners a sense of control, with that added confidence, at no cost. And we all know how important that is. If you really believe eating chicken or hopping over the foul lines will make you a better hitter, it probably will.

BIBLIOGRAPHY

Malinowski, B. *Magic, Science and Religion and Other Essays* (Glencoe, Ill., 1948).

Mandel, Brett. *Minor Players, Major Dreams.* Lincoln, Nebraska: University of Nebraska Press, 1997.

Skinner, B.F. *Behavior of Organisms: An Experimental Analysis* (D. Appleton-Century Co., 1938).

Skinner, B.F. *Science and Human Behavior* (New York: Macmillan, 1953).

Stouffer, Samuel. *The American Soldier.* New York: J. Wiley, 1965.

Torrez, Danielle Gagnon. *High Inside: Memoirs of a Baseball Wife.* New York: G.P. Putnam's Sons, 1983.

NOTES

1. Mandel, *Minor Players, Major Dreams*, 156.
2. Stouffer, *The American Soldier*
3. Malinowski, B. *Magic, Science and Religion and Other Essays*
4. Skinner, B.F. *Behavior of Organisms: An Experimental Analysis*

Department of Anthropology, Union College; e-mail gmelchg@union.edu

Revised version of "Superstition and Ritual in American Baseball" from *Elysian Fields Quarterly,* Vol. 11, No. 3, 1992, pp. 25-36. © September 2000, McGraw-Hill/Dushkin, with permission of the author, George Gmelch.

Each Religion Expresses an Important Part of the Truth

RAIMUNDO PANIKKAR

Like Cobb, Raimundo Panikkar rejects any form of religious "pluralism" that would conclude that religions share a common "essence." His own religious and intellectual history is remarkably complex. He was born of a Hindu father and a Roman Catholic mother, and became a Catholic priest who holds doctorates in the sciences, philosophy, and theology. He has written that in his encounter with other religions, "I 'left' as a christian, 'found' myself a hindu and 'return' a buddhist, without having ceased to be a christian." His approach to other religions reflects this complexity, as he argues that we must strive to understand each religion in its own "language" of concepts. We cannot gloss over the differences to conclude that "all shall be one," nor can we ignore what others have to say. Each religion "reflects, corrects, complements, and challenges the other" in the intricate web of interconnections he calls "intrareligious" dialogue.

QUESTIONS

1. How does Panikkar compare religions to languages, complete with the difficulties of translation? How does this shape the task of dialogue with others?
2. Why is there no "absolute center" to the universe of religions, in Panikkar's view?
3. Why is truth "neither one nor many," according to Panikkar?

Whatever theory we may defend regarding the origin and nature of religion, whether it be a divine gift or a human invention or both, the fact remains that it is at least a human reality and as such coextensive with another also at least human reality called language....

Any religion is complete as any language is also capable of expressing everything that it feels the need to express. Any religion is open to growth and evolution as any language is. Both are capable of expressing or adopting new shades of meaning, of shifting idioms or emphases, refining ways of expression and changing them. When a new need is felt in any religious or linguistic world, there are always means of dealing with that need. Furthermore, although any language is a world in itself, it is not without relations with neighboring languages, borrowing from them and open to mutual influences. And yet each language only takes as much as it can assimilate from a foreign language. Similarly with religions: they influence each other and borrow from one another without losing their identity. As an extreme case a religion, like a language, may disappear entirely. And the reasons also seem very similar—conquest, decadence, emigration, etc.

From the internal point of view of each language and religion, it makes little sense to say that one language is more perfect than another, for you can in your language (as well as in your religion) say all that you feel you need to say. If you would feel the need to say something else or something different, you would say it. If you use only one word for camel and hundreds for the different metals, and another language does just the opposite, it is because you have different patterns of differentiation for camels and metals. It is the same with religions. You may have only one word for wisdom, God, compassion or virtue and another religion scores of them.

The great problem appears when we come to the encounter of languages—and religions. The question here is translation. Religions are equivalent to the same extent that languages are translatable, and they are unique as much as languages are untranslatable. There is the common world of objectifiable objects. They are the objects of empirical or logical verification. This is the realm of terms. Each term is an epistemic sign standing for an empirically or logically verifiable object. The terms 'tree,' 'wine,' 'atom,' 'four,' can be translated into any given language if we have a method of empirically pointing out a visible thing (tree), a physically recognizable substance (wine), a physicomathematically definable entity (atom) and a logical cipher (four). Each of these cases demands some specific conditions, but we may assume that these conditions can all be empirically or logically verifiable once a certain axiom is accepted. In short, all terms are translatable insofar as a name could easily be invented or adopted even by a language which might lack a particular term ('atom' for instance). Similarly, all religions have a translatable sphere: all refer to the human being, to his well-being, to overcoming the possible obstacles to it and the like. Religious terms—qua terms—are translatable.

The most important part of a language as well as of a religion, however, is not terms but words, i.e., not epistemic signs to orient us in the world of objects, but living symbols to allow us to live in the world of Men and Gods. Now, words are not objectifiable. A word is not totally separable from the meaning we give to it and each of us in fact gives different shades of meaning to the same word. A word reflects a total human experience and cannot be severed from it. A word is not empirically or logically detectable. When we say 'justice,' 'dharma,' 'karuna,' we cannot point to an object, but have to refer to crystallizations of human experiences that vary with people, places, ages, etc. We cannot properly speaking translate words. We can only transplant them along with a certain surrounding context which gives them meaning and offers the horizon over against which they can be understood, i.e., assimilated within another horizon. And even then the transplanted word, if it survives, will soon extend its roots in the soil and acquire new aspects, connotations, etc. Similarly with religions: they are not translatable like terms; only certain transplants are possible under appropriate conditions. There is not an object 'God,' 'justice,' or 'Brahman,' a thing in itself independent of those living words, over against which we may check the correction of the translation. In order to translate them we have to transplant the corresponding world view that makes those words say what they intend to say....

The translator has to speak the 'foreign' language as his own. As long as we speak a language translating from another, we shall never speak fluently or even correctly. Only when we speak that language, only when you 'speak' that religion as your own will you really be able to be a spokesman for it, a genuine translator. And this obviously implies at the same time that you have not forgotten your native tongue, that you are equally capable of expressing yourself in the other linguistic world....

The mention of pluralism by way of conclusion may not be out of place. The aim of the intrareligious dialogue is understanding. It is not to win over the other or to come to a total agreement or a universal religion. The ideal is communication in order to bridge the gulfs of mutual ignorance and misunderstandings between the different cultures of the world, letting them speak and speak out their own insights in their own languages. Some may wish even to reach communion, but this does not imply at all that the aim is a uniform unity or a reduction of all the pluralistic variety of Man into one single religion, system, ideology or tradition. Pluralism stands between unre-lated plurality and a monolithic unity. It implies that the human condition in its present reality should not be neglected, let alone despised in favor of an ideal (?) situation of human uniformity. On the contrary, it takes our factual situation as real and affirms that in the actual polarities of our human existence we find our real being....

Either Christians "stick" to their "Christ" and become exclusivistic, or they give up their claims, dilute their beliefs, and become, at best, inclusivistic. These two horns of the dilemma are equally unacceptable. The parallel Copernican revolution consists in shifting the center from linear history to a theanthropocosmic vision, a kind of trinitarian notion, not of the godhead alone, but of reality. The center is neither the earth (our particular religion), nor the sun (God, transcendence, the Absolute...). Rather, each solar system has its own center, and every galaxy turns reciprocally around the other. There is no absolute center. Reality itself is concentric inasmuch as each being (each tradition) is the center of the universe—of its own universe to begin with. The theanthropocosmic insight (which sees the unity between the divine-human-cosmic) suggests a sort of trinitarian dynamism in which all is implied in all (each person represents the community and each tradition reflects, corrects, complements, and challenges the other)....

This attitude may be summed up in the following statements:

1. Pluralism does not mean plurality or a reduction of plurality to unity. It is a fact that there is a plurality of religions. It is also a fact that these religions have not been reduced to any sort of unity. Pluralism means something more than sheer acknowledgment of plurality and the mere wishful thinking of unity.

2. Pluralism does not consider unity an indispensable ideal, even if allowance is made for variations within that unity. Pluralism accepts the irreconcilable aspects of religions without being blind to their common aspects. Pluralism is not the eschatological expectation that in the end all shall be one.

3. Pluralism affirms neither that the truth is one nor that it is many. If truth were one, we could not accept the positive tolerance of a pluralistic attitude and would have to consider pluralism a connivance with error. If truth were many, we would fall into a plain contradiction. We said already that pluralism does not stand for plurality—a plurality of truths in this case. Pluralism adopts a nondualistic, advaitic, attitude that defends the pluralism of truth because reality itself is pluralistic—that is, incommensurable with either unity or plurality.

Excerpted from *The Intrareligious Dialogue*, by Raimundo Panikkar, 1978, pp 86–90. © 1978 by Paulist Press, www.paulistpress.com.

UNIT 2
Oral and Indigenous Religions

Unit Selections

5. **Sun Mother Wakes the World: Australian Aborigine**, Diane Wolkstein
6. **First Tale**, George M. Mullett
7. **Kalevala: An Epic Poem That Gave Birth to a Nation**, Ann Bahr
8. **Becoming Part of It**, Joseph Epes Brown
9. **Veve: The Sacred Symbol of Vodoun**, Lilith Dorsey
10. **The Hula in Hawaiian Life and Thought**, John Charlot

Key Points to Consider

- What are cosmogonic myths? From where do they come?
- What role do creation myths play in a culture?
- What does a culture's creation myths reveal about it?
- What are some of the unique aspects of indigenous religious traditions?
- What role do the arts play in traditional religions?
- Describe the different concepts of the divine as found in various indigenous traditions.

 **Links: www.dushkin.com/online/**
These sites are annotated in the World Wide Web pages.

Aboriginal Beliefs
http://www.fcps.k12.va.us/DeerParkES/Dreamweaver/Australia/aborigines/beliefs.html

Creation Myths
http://www.magictails.com/creationlinks.html

Hopi Creation Story
http://www.dreamscape.com/morgana/umbriel.htm

Ku Anthropologist
http://www.ku.edu/~kuanth/feb01.htm

Vodun (and related religions)
http://www.religioustolerance.org/voodoo.htm

Witchcraft, Magic and Religion Sources
http://www.people.virginia.edu/~ccf4f/magic/relig.html

Zulu Religion and Superstitions
http://www.kzn-deat.gov.za/tourism/culture/religion/menu.htm

Vodou, Vodun, Voodoo
http://dmoz.org/Society/Religion_and_Spirituality/African/Diasporic/Vodou,_Vodun,_Voodoo/

Religion has been said to have origins in people seeking to know their own origins, and also their destinies. Questions as to where we came from and where we will go after death were surely among those posed by some of the earliest humans who reflected on their world and on their existence. In some of the most ancient of myths about which we have any knowledge, we can see ideas and beliefs being formed as to the source of the world and of humans. As to our destiny, we can find evidence in the earliest human graves discovered by archaeologists suggesting that many of our ancient ancestors had a belief in an afterlife of some sort. At such sites, food stuffs, tools, and weapons have all been discovered among the items buried with the dead, probably placed there for use in the next life, or to whatever form of existence the particular culture believed the departed beings would go. It is here that religious beliefs and practices reveal their beginnings.

Hand-in-hand with the development of a culture has typically been its beliefs and attitudes toward, and people's relationship to, the realm of the unseen, the spirit world, the divine. In understanding the various religious traditions, a variety of methods are used. One of these separates ethnic and prophetic traditions. The former are those that have their genesis in, and are predominantly followed by, members of a specific ethnic and cultural group. Such traditions tend to be rooted and find validation within a specific cultural and geographic domain as well. It is for this reason that they often, although not always, stay within geographic and/or ethnocultural boundaries. Examples of such religions in the United States include those traditionally practiced by Native American tribes, native Hawaiians, and Eskimos. When such a tradition is closely connected with a particular land and people, it is often referred to as an indigenous religion, which is the label that will generally be employed. While Judaism, Hinduism, and Shinto are, in many ways, ethnic/indigenous religious traditions as well, their domain of influence is vast enough to be discussed in separate units in this anthology.

Within indigenous religious traditions, beliefs and practices are typically passed on orally and visually through rituals and myths, or sacred stories, rather than through texts and scriptures. For them, storytelling and ritual enactment are important vehicles for the dissemination and preservation of tradition. Stories and rituals tend to connect members of the group to a place or places, as well as to the spirit world, and to each other. These myths usually contain sacred knowledge. Thus, indigenous tra-

ditions typically have a much closer connection to the natural world than do prophet-based traditions. The land, the animals, the humans, and the world of the spirits all are seen to be connected in a sacred relationship. The stories and myths explain these relationships and what one must do to keep them in order. Here, deeds and actions are generally given more emphasis than belief, and ritual action plays a very important part.

Among the most foundational stories of indigenous peoples are their creation myths. (This can be seen in the case of Jews and the stories of Genesis, which are later adopted by Christians.) Creation stories tell people of the origins of the world, how order comes out of chaos, and who is responsible for this order. The first three articles in this unit provide examples of such myths. The next three articles look at the role of ritual, various art forms, and the role these play in identity, communication, and connectedness.

Sun Mother Wakes the World

Australian Aborigine

The Australian Aborigines believe that their first ancestors created the world and its laws. They also believe that the world is still being created, and they call this continual process of creation the Dreamtime. In order to enter into creation—past, present, and future—the Aborigines perform ceremonies during which they describe the Dreamtime in paintings, dances, songs, and stories. Just as each of their ancestors appeared on earth in a certain place, which is called their Dreaming, so, too, the place where each Aborigine is born is called his or her Dreaming. The birthplaces of the ancestors and the people living on earth are considered sacred. Aborigines go on journeys to tend to the birthplaces of their ancestors and the different people in the tribe. On such an occasion, they perform ceremonies to renew themselves and to keep the earth alive.

THE EARTH WAS ASLEEP. The spirits of all living beings were sleeping. No fish swam. No animal stirred. The wind did not whisper. In the sky, Sun Mother was also asleep. In her sleep, a voice whispered to her, "Wake, wake, my child."

Sun Mother opened her eyes. Light appeared.

"My daughter," the voice spoke again. "It is time for you to wake the sleeping earth." Sun Mother stretched and the light became brighter. Swift as a shooting star, Sun Mother sped to the earth. The earth was gray and empty. There was no color. No sound. No movement.

Sun Mother began to travel. With each step she took, grass, plants, and trees sprouted in her footprints. Sun Mother traveled north, south, east, and west, waking all the earth. Then she rested, surrounded by green plants and trees. Again a voice called to her. "My daughter, it is time for you to go to the dark caves to wake the sleeping animal spirits."

Sun Mother entered a large cave. Light flooded the cave. The witchety grubs, beetles, and caterpillars cried: "*Kkkt! Kkkt!* Why do you wake us?" But when the crawling creatures opened their eyes and saw the beauty of Sun Mother, they followed her out of the dark cave onto the earth. Insects of every color and shape appeared, and the earth became more beautiful.

As Sun Mother entered the next cave, ice melted under her feet, forming a stream. Her warmth woke the lizards, frogs, and snakes. "*Sssssst!* Go away!" they hissed. But when they saw beautiful Sun Mother, they followed her, and a stream filled with fish flowed after her.

Accompanied by the crawling and moving creatures, Sun Mother walked to the coldest, darkest cave. Along the ledges of the dark cave were sleeping birds and animals of every kind. "*HOOOOO!*" the cave owl hooted, and the caterpillars and beetles quaked in terror. The large animals laughed and followed Sun Mother out of the cave.

Sun Mother lay down under a large rivergum tree and rested. All the animals gathered near her. The wind stirred the leaves. All the creatures were content with the gift of life they had received.

AFTER RESTING, SUN MOTHER SPOKE to the crawling, moving, feathery, furry creatures and said, "My children, I woke you as a seed is woken in the spring. Now my work is done and I can return to my home in the sky. Treat the earth with care, for it is the earth who has guarded and will guard your sleeping spirits."

Swift as a shooting star, Sun Mother soared up into the western sky. The animals watched in fear. Where was she going? "Come back!" they called. "Sun Mother—" The earth became darker and darker. After a time, it was completely dark. The wind did not whisper. No animal stirred. No fish swam. Everything was still.

Then a little frog croaked loudly. From the corner of her big eye, the frog saw light. Sun Mother was returning in the eastern sky. "Welcome, welcome, Sun Mother!" the animals cried joyously. But Sun Mother did not return to earth. She glided westward across the sky and disappeared.

Again, there was darkness. But the animals were not as frightened as they were before. They understood that Sun Mother had returned to her home in the sky, but each day she would visit them on earth.

But as time passed, the animals forgot the moment when they first received the gift of life. They looked at each other, and they wanted what they did not have. Emu wanted longer legs. Owl wanted larger eyes. Wombat wanted stronger claws. They insulted each other. They mimicked each other. They quarrelled so loudly that their cries reached the home of Sun Mother.

Swift as a shooting star, Sun Mother sped to the earth. She gathered everyone together and said, "My children, I love each of you. I wish you to be happy. If you are unhappy with the form you have been given, you will have a chance to choose another one. Consider very carefully now, for the form you choose will be yours for a long time."

Emu grew longer legs so she could run faster than any other bird. Kangaroo grew a pouch so she could keep her babies close to her. Wombat grew stronger claws so he could dig tunnels under the earth. Platypus could not decide what she wanted or where she wanted to live. So she chose everything: a beak, fur, webbed feet, and a tail! Then she moved to a land of flowing waters.

Sun Mother was so amazed watching the animals change shape. She too wanted something new. That night she gave birth to Moon and Morning Star.

A third time Sun Mother spoke to all the creatures and said, "Now when I leave you in the evening, my daughter Moon and my son Morning Star will be with you to give you light."

Moon and Morning Star grew brighter. Moon became big, beautiful, and ready. Some time after Morning Star crossed her path, Moon gave birth to the first woman and the first man.

"Welcome, welcome, little ones," Sun Mother said to the first woman and the first man. "All around you are your relations—the crawling, moving, feathery, and furry creatures—the water, the grass, the hills, and the wind. This is their place. Now it is your place, too. The place you were born will be called your Dreaming. The place your children will be born will be called their Dreaming.

"Begin your travels. Care for the place of your Dreaming and for all the land for your grandmothers and grandfathers, as well as for your grandchildren. I traveled every step of the earth and it is alive. As I visit the earth each morning, so you too must travel the earth to keep it alive."

With these words, Sun Mother soared up into the sky.

Each morning Sun Mother travels the earth. She brings light to her children, continuing to keep the promise she made at creation.

—Retold by Diane Wolkstein

Author's Note: In his book, Myths and Legends of the Australian Aboriginals, *Ramsay Smith attributed the story of Sun Mother to Kardin-Nilla (Laughing Waters) of the Karraru tribe. In order to find out more about the story and tribe, I made three journeys to Australia, but was finally informed by anthropologist Bill Edwards at the University of Adelaide that the Karraru tribe no longer exists. Nevertheless, I consulted with, told, and read the story to tribal people throughout Australia to try to capture the voice and tone of this ancient Dreaming. The story will be published by Morror Junior in 2000.*

First Tale

IN THE BEGINNING there were only two: Tawa, the Sun God, and Spider Woman, the Earth Goddess. All the mysteries and power in the Above belonged to Tawa, while Spider Woman controlled the magic of the Below. In the Underworld, abode of the gods, they dwelt and they were All. There was neither man or woman, bird nor beast, no living thing until these Two willed it to be.

In time it came to them that there should be other gods to share their labors. So Tawa divided himself and there came Muiyinwuh, god of All Life Germs; Spider Woman also divided herself so that there was Huzruiwuhti, Woman of the Hard Substances, the goddess of all hard ornaments of wealth such as coral, turquoise, silver and shell. Huzruiwuhti became the always-bride of Tawa. They were the First Lovers and of their union there came into being those marvelous ones the Magic Twins—Puukonhoya, the Youth, and Palunhoya, the Echo. As time unrolled there followed Hicanavaiya, Ancient of Six (the Four World Quarters, the Above and Below), Man-Eagle, the Great Plumed Serpent and many others. But Masauwuh, the Death God, did not come of these Two but was bad magic who appeared only after the making of creatures.

And then it came about that these Two had one Thought and it was a mighty Thought—that they would make the Earth to be between the Above and the Below where now lay shimmering only the Endless Waters. So they sat them side by side, swaying their beautiful bronze bodies to the pulsing music of their own great voices, making the First Magic Song, a song of rushing winds and flowing waters, a song of light and sound and life.

"I am Tawa," sang the Sun God, "I am Light. I am Life. I am Father of all that shall ever come."

"I am Kokyanwuhti," the Spider Woman crooned in softer note. "I receive Light and nourish Life. I am Mother of all that shall ever come."

"Many strange thoughts are forming in my mind—beautiful forms of birds to float in the above, of beasts to move upon the Earth and fish to swim in the Waters," intoned Tawa.

"Now let these things that move in the Thought of my lord appear," chanted Spider Woman, the while with her slender fingers she caught up clay from beside her and made the Thoughts of Tawa take form. One by one she shaped them and laid them aside—but they breathed not nor moved.

"We must do something about this," said Tawa. "It is not good that they lie thus still and quiet. Each thing that has a form must also have a spirit. So now, my beloved, we must make a mighty Magic."

They laid a white blanket over the many figures, a cunningly woven woolen blanket, fleecy as a cloud, and made a mighty incantation over it, and soon the figures stirred and breathed.

"Now, let us make ones like unto you and me, so that they may rule over and enjoy these lesser creatures," sang Tawa, and Spider Woman shaped the Thoughts of her lord into man figures and woman figures like unto their own. But after the blanket magic had been made the figures still stayed inert. So Spider Woman gathered them all in her arms and cradled them in her warm young bosom, while Tawa bent his glowing eyes upon them. The two now sang the magic Song of Life over them, and at last each man fig-

ure and woman figure breathed and lived.

"Now that was a good thing and a mighty thing," quoth Tawa. "So now all this is finished, and there shall be no new things made by us. Those things we have made shall multiply, each one after his own kind. I will make a journey across the Above each day to shed my light upon them and return each night to Huzruiwuhti. And now I shall go to turn my blazing shield upon the Endless Waters, so that the Dry Land may appear. And this day will be the first day upon the Earth."

"Now I shall lead all these created things to the land that you shall cause to appear above the waters," said Spider Woman.

Then Tawa took down his burnished shield from the turquoise wall of the kiva and swiftly mounted his glorious way to the Above. After Spider Woman had bent her wise, all-seeing eyes upon the thronging creatures about her, she wound her way among them, separating them into groups.

"Thus and thus shall you be and thus shall you remain, each one in his own tribe forever. You are Zunis, you are Kohoninos, you are Pah-Utes—." The Hopis, all, all people were named by Kokyanwuhti then.

Placing her Magic Twins beside her, Spider Woman called all the people to follow where she led. Through all the Four Great Caverns of the Underworld she led them, until they finally came to an opening, a sipapu, which led above. This came out at the lowest depth of the Pisisbaiya (the Colorado River) and was the place where the people were to come to gather salt. So lately had the Endless Waters gone down that the Turkey, Koyona, pushing eagerly ahead, dragged his tail feathers in the black mud where the dark bands were to remain forever.

Mourning Dove flew overhead, calling to some to follow, and those who followed where his sharp eyes had spied out springs and built beside them were called "Huwinyamu" after him. So Spider Woman chose a creature to lead each clan to a place to build their house. The Puma, the Snake, the Antelope, the Deer, and other Horn creatures, each led a clan to a place to build their house. Each clan henceforth bore the name of the creature who had led them.

Then Spider Woman spoke to them thus: "The woman of the clan shall build the house, and the family name shall descend through her. She shall be house builder and homemaker. She shall mold the jars for the storing of food and water. She shall grind the grain for food and tenderly rear the young. The man of the clan shall build kivas of stone under the ground where he shall pay homage to his gods. In these kivas the man shall make sand pictures which will be his altars. Of colored sand shall he make them and they shall be called 'ponya'. After council I shall whisper to him; he shall make

prayer sticks or paho to place upon the ponya to bear his prayers. There shall be the Wupo Paho, the Great Paho, which is mine. There shall be four paho of blue, the Cawka Paho—one for the great Tawa, one for Muiyinwuh, one for Woman of the Hard Substances and one for the Ancient of Six. Each of these paho must be cunningly and secretly wrought with prayer and song. The man, too, shall weave the clan blankets with their proper symbols. The Snake clan shall have its symbol and the Antelope clan its symbol; thus it shall be for each clan. Man shall fashion himself weapons and furnish his family with game."

Stooping down, she gathered some sand in her hand, letting it run out in a thin, continuous stream. "See the movement of the sand. That is the life that will cause all things therein to grow. The Great Plumed Serpent, Lightning, will rear and strike the earth to fertilize it, Rain Cloud will pour down waters and Tawa will smile upon it so that green things will spring up to feed my children."

Her eyes now sought the Above where Tawa was descending toward his western kiva in all the glory of red and

gold. "I go now, but have no fear, for we Two will be watching over you. Look upon me now, my children, ere I leave. Obey the words I have given you and all will be well, and if you are in need of help call upon me and I will send my sons to your aid."

The people gazed wide-eyed upon her shining beauty. Her woven upper garment of soft white wool hung tunic-wise over a blue skirt. On its left side was woven a band bearing the woman's symbols, the Butterfly and the Squash Blossom, in designs of red and yellow and green with bands of black appearing between. Her beautiful neck was hung with heavy necklaces of turquoise, shell and coral, and pendants of the same hung from her ears. Her face was fair, with warm eyes and tender red lips, and her form most graceful. Upon her small feet were skin boots of gleaming white, and they now turned toward where the sand spun about in whirlpool fashion. She held up her right hand and smiled upon them, then stepped upon the whirling sand. Wonder of wonders, before their eyes the sands seemed to suck her swiftly down until she disappeared entirely from their sight.

Kalevala: An epic poem that gave birth to a nation

by Ann Marie Bahr

Feb. 28 is Kalevala Day. The Kalevala is the national epic of Finland. If an American is asked to name the most important document in the history of her nation, she is likely to say "the Declaration of Independence." If a Finn is asked the same question, he may well say "the Kalevala."

The Kalevala is an epic poem. (Other examples of epic poems are Gilgamesh of Mesopotamia, The Iliad and The Odyssey of Greece, and the Mahabharata of India.) An epic poem is a really good hero story that explains the origins and values of a national culture through a combination of history and myth.

The Kalevala has a creation story in which an egg breaks open. The lower half becomes the earth and the upper part the sky; the yolk becomes the sun and the white the moon. It has a singing duel in which the hero, an old man named Vainamoinen, magically enchants his opponent with his songs, and a maiden who is so reluctant to marry the old man that she rejects and taunts him.

It has healing spells and hunting charms, and the resurrection of a dead hero. There is a magical, mysterious object called a "Sampo," which brings good fortune. The sun and the moon are captured and released. It has romance and war, tragedy and magic—in short, all the elements of an epic tale.

The Kalevala was created when physician and folklorist Elias Lonnrot (1802–84) collected the songs of illiterate folk singers and wove them into a long narrative poem. In the first half of the 19th century, folk poetry was still a living tradition in eastern Finland. Old people would chant runes (poems) about the birth of fire and the world. Finns may have been singing those very verses even before the birth of Christ.

The Kalevala had the good fortune to appear just as a nationalistic spirit was sweeping through what was to become Finland. It was a nationalism that faced apparently insurmountable obstacles. There had never been an independent Finnish nation.

From the 12th century until 1809, the Finns had been a part of Sweden. In 1809 they became a grand duchy of the Russian Empire. Some went so far as to claim that since there had never been a nation named Finland, the Finns had no history or culture. How could a people who had literally never had a country aspire to nationhood?

Imagine, then, the excitement that greeted the appearance of the Kalevala, which appeared in final form in 1849. People felt that it contained both the history and mythology of the Finns, proving that they were a unique culture with a right to an independent nation.

There were other problems. The stories of the Kalevala were pre-Christian, many of them dating from the Iron Age (circa 500 B.C. to A.D. 400). Contemporary Finland is 90 percent Evangelical Lutheran; that percentage may have been even higher in the 19th century. How could a solidly Lutheran nation embrace a national epic filled with pagan religious beliefs?

The answer lies in the last rune, which chronicles the demise of the old ways as Christianity appears on the scene. It tells of Marjatta the virgin, who lives a pure and chaste life, but magically becomes pregnant. Shunned by her family, she goes off to a stable where she gives birth to a son.

Vainamoinen is called upon to question Marjatta, determine who the baby's father is, and decide whether the boy should live or die. Vainamoinen decides that the child should be left to die, but then the 1-month-old boy begins to speak, accusing Vainamoinen of false judgment.

Recognizing that his successor has come, Vainamoinen sails away, leaving behind his kantele (stringed musical instrument) and his songs for his people.

As he departs, he says that a time will come when his people will need him again. And it did.

The Kalevala remains alive in Finland. It inspires visual and literary artists, who use its mystical imagery to portray the universal and eternal facts of life: survival and death, love and heartbreak, tragedy and magical prosperity. It influences everyday life as well. Names of city quarters, streets, businesses and products are regularly drawn from the Kalevala. People, too, are named after Kalevala characters.

The Kalevala has been translated into 51 languages, more than any other work of Finnish literature. The first translation was in German and appeared in 1852, just three years after the appearance of the Finnish original.

This international recognition is surprising, given the fact that the language of the Kalevala is archaic, its poetic meter is ancient, and the Finnish cultural sphere is relatively small. My guess is that the recognition reflects the fact that the Kalevala is filled with magic, with high adventure, with romance, with the life and death of not only individuals, but also cultures. It is a striking portrayal of universal themes in a gripping adventure story.

ANN MARIE BAHR IS A PROFESSOR OF RELIGIOUS STUDIES AT SOUTH DAKOTA STATE UNIVERSITY.

Becoming Part of It

The following is a transcription (with some added material) of an address given at the American Museum of Natural History in January. It was part of a program entitled "I Become Part of It," which was presented by PARABOLA's *Society for the Study of Myth and Tradition.*

by Joseph Epes Brown

In talking about sacred dimensions in Native American life, I must proceed not just as a descriptive ethnographer but also as a historian of religion, and with what I hope is a basic humanistic concern; that is, I believe it important to ask about the relevance of these primal values to a dominant contemporary world with life-ways which are oriented towards very different directions and with contrasting priorities. One notices very clearly today our increasing malaise and sometimes even fear, which—at least in certain segments of our society—is leading to a growing mood for re-evaluation and reassessment, a wish even to take a backward look, so to say, at "progress," that concept which for so long has been an unquestioned quasi-religious dogma in our lives. Many of those early studies of Native American peoples and cultures suffered from the kinds of prejudices that came out of this prevailing concept of progress.

An expression of this new and growing mood is found in an increasing concern to seek out our ancient origins, with a view to rediscovering and perhaps even identifying with what is our own proper heritage. I put the question in this manner because very often when I speak about the relevance and the reality of American Indian values, I am misunderstood, especially by students who like to believe that what I am trying to say is that they should go out and live and be American Indians; this is not my point at all, because for those of us who are non-Indians it is an impossibility. One has to be brought up in these cultures and traditions, one has to live the languages, in order truly to identify with the ethos of an American Indian people. What I *am* trying to say is that these traditions could be taken as models which might provide us with answers to some of the dilemmas with which we are currently struggling in our own society.

In the '60s, in our restlessness with where we found ourselves, we began to turn to the religions and methods of the Orient, with all the attractions and mystique which distance provides. By the '70s, however, with our rapidly growing ecological concerns, there developed an increasing awareness that certain answers could be found in the spiritual traditions of the Native Americans; for here the sacred values which so many of us were seeking out were actually rooted in this land, where they have survived through some sixty to eighty thousand years. Out of this mood there has come a vast array of new literature, both genuine and spurious, relating to Native American life-ways and world view; and even if the approach has often been overly romantic, there is here a change from earlier attitudes and prejudices, which is a positive sign even if it is only a beginning.

Although greatly oversimplified and generalized, let me give at least a brief sampling of what I think are some of the core Native American values and perspectives, through which we can perhaps come to relearn a little bit about ourselves and about our own proper spiritual heritage, the hope being that what has been lost can still be rediscovered. Certainly the Native American people themselves, especially the younger ones today, are trying to regain and revitalize their own traditions which may have been lost, or taken from them through a variety of pressures and prejudices. We have, I suggest, in this struggle a model for our own proper quest. What are some of its contours?

Tribal cultures, it seems to me, present a model of what a religious tradition *is;* and this is a basic reality which we have lost sight of. That is, what really is a true religious tradition? What does it encompass, what are its dimensions? These cultures demonstrate how all components of a culture can be interconnected: how the presence of the sacred can permeate all life-ways to such a degree that what we call religion is here integrated into the totality of life and into all of life's activities. Religion here is so pervasive in life that there is probably no Native

American language in which there is a term which could be translated as "religion" in the way we understand it. As Peter Nabokov tells us in his book, *Indian Running,* when you track down a seemingly isolated or minimal feature of Indian life, such as running, the whole system opens before your eyes; and this is true because of the interrelatedness of all the components of a genuine tradition. Obviously in such a system life cannot be fragmented, due to that binding and interconnecting thread of the presence of the sacred.

In terms of interconnections, a dominant theme in all Native American cultures is that of relationship, or a series of relationships that are always reaching further and further out; relationships within the immediate family reaching out to the extended family, to the band, outward again to the clan, to the tribal group; and relationships do not stop there but extend out to embrace and relate to the environment: to the land, to the animals, to the plants, and to the clouds, the elements, the heavens, the stars; and ultimately those relationships that people express and live, extend to embrace the entire universe.

In the Plains area, to give an example, one of the most profound rites is that of the smoking of the pipe. In this ritual smoking of the pipe, all who participate are joined in a communal ritual act, and when it is finished, everybody who has shared in the smoking of the pipe recites the phrase, in Lakota in this case, *"mitakuye oyasin"*—"we are all relatives." We *are* all related, because in this rite we have all become one within a mystery that is greater than any of its parts. I shall talk more about the general importance of rituals and ceremonies later.

Associated with relationship there should be mentioned the theme of reciprocity which permeates so many aspects of North American cultures. Put very simply, reciprocity here refers again to that process wherein if you receive or take away you must also give back. This is a living statement of the importance of the cycle permeating all of life: the cycle of life and death, of life leading to old age and then coming back to life. Everything in their world of experience is conceived in terms of such cycles or of the circle; everything comes back upon itself. Black Elk so often said that all the forces of the world work in cycles or circles: the birds build their nests in circular form, the foxes have their dens in circles, the wind in its greatest power moves in a circle, and life is as a circle. I recall once how this reality was beautifully expressed in a living manner, when I noticed how this dignified old man would relate to little children. He would get down on his hands and knees and pretend he was a horse, and the children would squeal with joy on the old man's back. Here there obviously was no generation gap; he was one with the child. I once asked him how it was that he could so relate to the child, and he replied: "I who am an old man am about to return *to* the Great Mysterious" (*Wakan Tanka,* in Lakota) "and a young child is a being who has just come *from* the Great Mysterious; so it is that we are very close together." Because of

such cyclical understanding, both are very nearly at the same point.

Such attitudes could be spelled out in terms of any number of cultural expressions, but the point I want to draw from this is that we have here an example which contrasts with our own dominant concept of process which is in terms of linearity—the straight line which moves from here to there and onward indefinitely. Indeed, this theme of linearity permeates all aspects of our life. The way we read, for instance, is in lines; we have sayings in our vocabulary that tell us to "Line up!" "Let's get this straight!" Or if we refer to somebody who is a little bit crazy, we make a circular motion alongside our head, by which we indicate the reason is going in circles. There is something here from which we can learn, something about ourselves and our concept of progress, with all the loaded meanings which this term bears.

One must mention also the special nature of Native American languages, which contrasts with our understanding of language and our use of words. In Native languages the understanding is that the meaning *is* in the sound, it *is* in the word; the word is not a symbol for a meaning which has been abstracted out, word and meaning are together in one experience. Thus, to name a being, for example an animal, is actually to conjure up the powers latent in that animal. Added to this is the fact that when we create words we use our breath, and for these people and these traditions breath is associated with the principle of life; breath is life itself. And so if a word is born from this sacred principle of breath, this lends an added sacred dimension to the spoken word. It is because of this special feeling about words that people avoid using sacred personal names, because they contain the power of the beings named, and if you use them too much the power becomes dissipated. So usually one has to refer to a person in a very circuitous manner, or use a term which expresses relationship.

In this context one must also emphasize the positive values that could be attached to non-literacy. I use that term rather than illiteracy, which connotes the *inability* to read and write, which is negative and derogatory. Too often we have branded people as being backward and uncivilized if they are *illiterate,* whereas one can make a strong case for the advantages of growing up and living in a society which is *non-literate.* For in such a society all the lore which is central and sacred to the culture is borne *within* the individual in a living manner; you do not have to go outside of yourself, for all that is essential to life is carried with you, is ever-present. It seems that where you have people who are non-literate in this positive sense, you tend to have a special quality of person, a quality of being that cannot be described—a very different quality from that of the literate person. It has been my experience when among primal peoples in many parts of the world that there is something here that is very special.

Paralleling this primal concept of language, and of the word not as "symbol" but as an immediate event, is the quality of experiencing the visual arts and crafts. I should stress first of all that for primal peoples generally there is no dichotomy between the arts and crafts, in the manner that our art historians insist on, where art is one kind of thing that can be placed on a mantelpiece or hung on the wall, and the craft item is inferior because it is made for utilitarian ends. This seems to me a most artificial distinction and I think it is time that we outgrew it; indeed there is today evidence that we *are* reevaluating such prejudiced dichotomies. For why cannot a utilitarian object also be beautiful? All necessary implements, utensils, and tools in Native American life-ways are of technical excellence and are also beautiful. They must be made in special sacred ways, and the materials of the tools and objects made have to be gathered with prayer and offerings. Beauty and truth are here one! When a Pomo basketmaker, for example, goes out to collect the grasses for her basket, she prays to the grasses, she enters into a relationship with them as she gathers, and makes offerings in return for having taken their life. When a woman weaves a basket she will pass the grass between her lips to moisten it, but also to breathe upon it, to give her life breath into the grass and thus give to the basket a special sacred quality that is always present in its use and tangible presence.

Through these few selected examples which have been given, I am suggesting that, where such traditions are still alive and spiritually viable, there tend to be present, within all of life's necessary activities, dimensions and expressions of the sacred. Actions of such quality could therefore be considered to manifest a ritual element in the sense that they tend to *order* life around and toward a Center. In this context, however, one must also speak of those special great rites and ceremonies, many often related to the seasonal cycles, which serve not just to support continuing orientations toward the sacred in everyday activities, but work for the *intensification* of such Presence and experience; such rites may also be the source and origin of new rites, ceremonies, and other sacred expressions through the visual arts, songs, or special dance forms.

One example of a ritual complex which is central to the lives of Plains people is the well known "vision" or "guardian spirit quest." This ritualized retreat is for the benefit of the individual man and woman, and yet means are present for the eventual sharing of received vision powers or messages with the larger community. After rigorous preparations, which always include the rites of the purifying sweat lodge and instructions by a qualified elder, the candidate goes to a high and remote place with the resolve to fast and pray continually and to suffer through acts of sacrifice and exposure to the elements for a specified number of days. The ordeal is highly ritualized and may involve the establishing of an altar, or the setting out of poles at the center and to the four directions of space. The person may also be instructed to remain within this established space and not to move

about casually but to walk only out from the center to each of the poles in turn, always returning to the center. Prayers may be addressed to the powers of the four directions, and one may also use repetitive prayers such as the one the Lakota Black Elk has given us: "Grandfather, Great Mysterious, have pity on me." One may also remain silent, for it has been said that "silence *is* the voice of *Wakan-Tanka*, the *Great Mysterious*." If tired, one may sleep, for dreams of power may come to the candidate in this manner; yet it is understood that the true vision is of greater power than the dream. Often the sacred experience comes in the mysterious appearance of an animal or a winged being, or perhaps in one of the powers of nature. A special message is often communicated to the seeker, and this will serve as a guide and reminder throughout the person's life. After three or four days one returns to camp where a sweat lodge has again been prepared; within this lodge the candidate will explain the vision or dream which will be interpreted by the guiding elder, who will then give instructions as to what should now be accomplished in order to insure the continuity of the participation of the spiritual throughout the person's life. From such experiences have come the "medicine bundles" with rich and complex rites specific to each bundle and their ceremonial opening on special occasions. They have also been the origin of sacred types of art forms, such as the painted shields, or special songs of power, or even the great ritual dances, such as the horse dance, involving four groups of eight horses not representing, but *being* the powers of the four directions of space. It is in this manner that something of the sacred experience which had come to a particular individual is shared by all members of the larger community.

What is remarkable about the rites of the vision quest among the Plains peoples is that it is accomplished not just by special people as is the case in the Arctic, but that every man or woman after the age of puberty is expected to participate either once or even continually throughout his or her life.

What concerns us in this example is not just the detailed pattern of the ritual elements of the quest as such, which can encompass a multitude of very diverse possibilities, but that here we have one sample as a model of traditional ritual structures and acts which must involve initial purification, choice of appropriate site, the defining and delimiting of a special sacred place, and the fixing of a center. Further, ritualized *actions* are prescribed for the participant, which means that participation is not just with the mind, or a part of one's being, but with the totality of who one is. Also provided are means for continuity and development of the sacred experiences received, and the eventual responsibility for sharing something of them with the larger community.

As complement to the individually oriented "vision quest," one could mention the great communal "Sun Dance," referred to by different terms across the Plains groups. For this great complex of solemn rites, ceremonies, fasting, sacred song and dance fulfills not just the particular spiritual needs of the actively participating individuals, but also those of the entire tribal group gathered in circular camp for the occasion. The event is indeed for the welfare of the entire world. These are ceremonies, interspersed with special sacred rites, which celebrate world and life renewal at the time of spring. The ritualized dance forms again involve orientation around and towards a center which is either the sun itself or the cottonwood tree as axis of the world, standing at the center of a circular frame lodge carefully constructed in imitation of the cosmos. The ritual and ceremonial language of the total celebration speaks to and encompass a plurality of spiritual possibilities at the levels of microcosm, macrocosm, and metacosm. It is believed by many that should the sacrificial rites of this "thirst lodge" be neglected or forgotten, the energy of the world will run out and the cycle in which we are living will close. It is an example to the world that these rites and ceremonies are far from being neglected, for today in ever increasing numbers the people are participating and are finding renewed strength and spiritual resolve.

All spiritually effective rites must accomplish three cumulative possibilities which may be termed purification, expansion—wholeness or virtue—and identity. A ritual means which embodies these possibilities may be found in the sacred nature and use of the Plains Indian tobacco pipe, the smoking of which constitutes a communion. The shape of the pipe with its stem, bowl or "heart," and foot, is identified with the human person. In purifying the pipe before a ritual smoking there is an analogy to man's own purification; for in concentrating on the hollow of the straight stem leading to the bowl comes the understanding that one's mind should be this straight and pure. In filling the bowl of the pipe a prayer is said for each grain of tobacco in such a manner that everything in the world is mentioned. The filled bowl or the heart of man, in thus containing all possibilities, is then the universe. Finally the fire which is put to the tobacco is the Presence of the ultimate all-inclusive Principle, *Wakan Tanka*, the "Great Mysterious." In smoking the pipe through the aid of breath the totality of all creation is absorbed within this ultimate Principle. And since in the pipe there is a grain of tobacco identified with the one who smokes, there is here enacted a sacrificial communion of identity. With this understanding,

the phrase "we are all related," recited by the individual or group after the smoking, takes on the deepest possible meaning.

I will sum up by simply saying that in all that I have tried to speak of in such brief fashion, we have expressions through different means of a special quality among traditional peoples that could be called oneness of experience: a lack of dichotomizing or fragmenting, a unity in the word and in visual image. In the painted image, for example, the understanding is that in that being that is represented, or even in a depicted part of that being—the paw of a bear, let us say—all the power of the animal is present. One can draw from all Native American cultures examples to reinforce such interpretation. One final example I will use is that of the Navajo dry painting or "sand painting" as it is sometimes called. These are made in a rich ceremonial context for the curing of individuals who have gotten out of balance with their world. They are long ceremonies which can go on for four or five or up to ten days, during which time sacred chants are used with all the meaning of the *word* as I have tried to explain it. At a certain moment during the ceremony the ill person is placed at the center of one of the dry paintings; the understanding is that the person thus becomes identified with the power that is in the image painted on the earth with colored sand and pollen. And the singer takes some of the painted image and presses it to the body of the ill person, again to emphasize this element of identity: the painting is not a symbol of some meaning or power, the power *is* there present in it, and as the person identifies with it the appropriate cure is accomplished.

I conclude with this portion of a Navajo chant:

> The mountains, I become part of it…
> The herbs, the fir tree, I become part of it.
> The morning mists, the clouds, the
>   gathering waters,
> I become part of it.
> The wilderness, the dew drops, the
>   pollen…
> I become part of it.

And in the context of other chants, there is always the conclusion that indeed, I *am* the universe. We are not separate, but are one.

From *Parabola*, August 1982, pp. 6-12. © 1982 by Parabola, The Magazine of Myth and Tradition, www.parabola.org. Reprinted by permission.

Veve

The Sacred Symbol of Vodoun

Lilith Dorsey

IN THE UNITED STATES today there are upward of one million practitioners of Haitian Vodoun and its related traditions of Voodoo in New Orleans, Santeria in Cuba, and Umbanda and Candomble in Brazil. A central element in many spiritual houses of these religions is the *veve*.

The veve is simultaneously an offering, a petition, and praise for the ancient African gods and goddesses. Primarily it was the Yoruba deities who found themselves transported to the Americas in the hearts and minds of the enslaved Africans. Almost all of their traditional religious practices were forbidden, and the popularity of the veve grew out of a need for a temporary and simple way of honoring the *Lwa* or deities.

The word "veve" is derived from the ancient Fon term for the ritual palm oil used in drawing rectangular ground offerings. Similar drawings can be found among the Kongo people, the Ndembu people of Zambia, and the Pende people of Zaire. The veves of Vodoun, however, are more integrated and detailed than those of their African cousins.

Veves are most often created on the open ground in cornmeal, flour, rice powder, red brick dust, coffee, gunpowder, or other materials. Each Lwa has his or her own unique veve, which is danced on by the barefoot practitioners. This is done in order to draw down the divine energy into their bodies. The veve serves as a spiritual conduit for both the Vodoun practitioner and the Lwa. The presence of the veve insures the safe journey of all who dance these astral paths.

The artistry of the veve is both primal and divine. The lines are drawn simultaneously with both hands, and their thickness and thinness vary with each individual drawing, creating a unique manifestation of divine energy and divine art. The image can be drawn to honor a single Lwa, or many veves may be combined, incorporating different symbols for the various gods and goddesses.

Papa Legba is present in the veve form of an equal-armed cross, frequently embellished with stars. This beautifully illustrates Legba's title of central master of astral space. In Haitian Vodoun, Legba is the wise father who acts as an intermediary between the worlds of the visible and the invisible. He is always called first in any ceremony. It is Legba who opens the paths to our communication and contact with the other Lwa.

STUDENTS OF MANY of the world's religions will recognize the use of the sacred serpent in the Lwa Damballa (also referred to as Danballah) and his bride Aida Wedo. Their veves usually incorporate this divine pair facing each other with their tongues outstretched. Their spiritual domain is wealth, luck, and healing. Damballa and Aida Wedo represent a connection to Africa, as they are said to carry messages from Africa under the ocean to the New World and up to the Lwa in the sky via the rainbow. In New Orleans the use of snakes is vital to ritual. This reintroduction may be traced to the first great American Voodoo queen Marie Laveau.

Maitresse Erzulie (also known as Ezili) is the Vodoun mistress who rules over love, eloquence, help, beauty, and fortune, as well as vengeance, jealousy, and discord. Each one of these aspects is represented by a different veve, but all have a heart shape as a central theme.

The Lwa Ogou is a chief figure in many Haitian ceremonies. This is primarily due to his importance as the liberator of the Haitian people. Toussaint L'Ouverture, one of the central leaders of the Haitian revolution, is reputed to have been a child of the Lwa Ogou. This means that he embodied the same fiery spirit and virtues as this Lwa of war, technology, and the forge. Veves for this Lwa often contain swords or a diamond-shaped pattern that resembles a shield, and they are often constructed out of gunpowder. Using Ogou's ritual material for the veve brings extra power and blessings to the working or ceremony.

La Sirene is the mistress of the sea. She is depicted in veve form as a mermaid. She is the divinity in charge of the sacred songs of Vodoun, marrying the word and the music to bring about rapture.

The husband of La Sirene is Agwe, another deity of the ocean. This watery Lwa has as his domain all aspects of shipping, fishing, and navigation, and the veve most often used for him incorporates a sailboat. Agwe is called on in ritual to provide safe passage and to grant victory.

The most maligned deities in Haiti are Les Barons and Les Gedes: these represent both the essence of death and the unknown. Ancestor reverence is an integral part of many African Diasporan traditions. Veves in the shapes of coffins, crosses, top hats, and gravestones are often laid down before food offerings are left for Les Barons and Les Gedes. By honoring these people who cared for us most during our life and by continuing to interact with them after they have passed, the practitioner will receive guidance and blessings. The properly cared-for dead can give advice in dreams, gifts, and even lottery numbers. Part of the misunderstanding of these entities comes from their lewd and lascivious behavior. The raunchiest antics take place during the Gede festivals which occur on November 1 and 2 in most Vodoun temples. During this time members of the temple become possessed by the Gede, drink large quantities of rum, smoke cigars, and speak with foul language. They have been known to perform a kind of divine dirty dancing in which participants bump hips and groins with the possessed. After the practitioner has paid the Gede money, special blessings or favors can be granted. Many in western society revere death as the ultimate end, but Vodoun practitioners have found a way to embrace death as a new entry into the spiritual world. Baron and Gede veves are traditionally drawn with both flour and coffee, as black and white are two of the ritual colors of these energies.

VEVES ARE PRIMARILY used as a call to the Lwa during ceremony. They are traditionally drawn around a *poteau mitan* or centerpole. They may however, be constructed on food offering plates, as we see with Les Gedes, at the crossroads for Legba, on the railroad tracks for Ogou, on graves for Maman Brigitte, the mistress of the cemetery, or anywhere appropriate to the ritual working.

A popular Haitian artistic tradition has grown up around what are known as wall veves. These range from simple to complex hand-hammered metal cutouts and are created to bring the Lwa into a house or temple. Some of the more notable artists in this venue are Georges Littaud and Gabriel Ben-Aime.

Veves also manifest in the form of magical talismans, commonly drawn on parchment using dragon's blood ink, dove's blood ink, or blood or other bodily fluid. The symbols are simpler than the veves created on the floor and are used to bring about more specific blessings of the Lwa. Traditionally they are carried in a red flannel pouch worn about the person of the practitioner.

A recent trend toward Vodoun tattoos has given the Lwa a new forum for their veves. A veve tattoo brings one into direct and permanent contact with the Lwa. A blood offering is made by the practitioner during the process, and proper ritual must accompany any work of this type. Drums or other ritual music should be played. A veve is created on the floor with cornmeal—this should be done in complete silence. Appropriate offerings of food and drink are given both to the ancestors and to the entity which is being invoked, and a candle, preferably white, is lit to cleanse the area. The food and drink, as well as the cornmeal, should be left in place for at least a day if possible, after which it is to be gathered up and left under a large tree.

Veves come in many different forms and manifestations. Born of the spirituality of ancient Africa, they were transported to the Americas, where they have evolved into the divine symbols that they are today.

From *Parabola*, February 1999, pp. 44-47. © 1999 by Parabola, The Magazine of Myth and Tradition, www.parabola.org. Reprinted by permission.

The Hula in Hawaiian Life and Thought

What happens when you dance, Io?
"I don't know," she says. "I'm not there."

— *Iolani Luahine*, Advertiser, *Nov. 15, 1978*

"When I don't dance, I feel disconnected."

— *Iolani Luahine,* Advertiser, *Dec. 11, 1978*

By John Charlot

Cultures differ in their views of dance—the importance and purposes assigned to it—as much as in their dance styles. A study of the hula can lead to the very foundation of Hawaiian culture.

Hula is dance with chant, that is, the bodily gesture is always connected to language which makes it meaningful rather than abstract.

The basic Hawaiian experience of language is oral communication. The vehicle of the spoken word is the breath of life. The word emerges *mai nei loko,* from the insides, the seat of emotion and truthfulness. The breath in Hawaiian thinking is related to the winds, which also have characters and speak. Once voiced, the word lives on only in the remembering mind.

This experience of oral communication is the basis for a magical view of language in which a word has some real connection to the object it refers to. That connection is often revealed through onomatopoeia, the similarity of their sounds. Moreover, that connection makes a word powerful, capable of being used for good or ill. A call receives an

answer. A name reveals a person and a destiny. The power of an achieved prayer flies to its goal. This view of language is still a living element in the thinking of many Hawaiians.

The body that dances the word is also meaningful. Hawaiian thinkers connect parts of the human body to elements of the universe. Above the top of the head hover the ancestors. The navel attaches to mother and family; the genitals, to future generations. The sensitive palms receive emanations from the source toward which they are directed. Because the body is meaningful, the modern Hawaiian religious teacher Emma de Fries can read the character of an infant from it.

The body also has inherent powers. The bones of a great fisherman make particularly effective hooks. The potato farmer does his planting naked so that the fertility of his body will be communicated to his land. Because word and body are meaningful and powerful, their use is regulated. The child is taught not to speak and act thoughtlessly and haphazardly, but consciously and carefully.

This is genuine moral training, for word and deed come *mai nei loko,* from the insides, and are expressions of character. Indeed, word and gesture induce emotions, thoughts, and character traits. One can exercise one's way both to health and meditation.

Hawaiians are quick to note posture and read character from it:

*I 'ike 'ia no ke kanaka i ka noho
    mai o ke kanaka.*

The person is truly seen in the way
    he acts.

The head tilted back shows a sense of self-importance and superiority: tilted forward, humility. Folded arms hold others out, show an unwillingness to join and cooperate. Hands on hips remind Hawaiians of a chief or overseer ready to lord it over others.

Because the body is connected to elements of the universe, posture can be chosen to receive more powerfully communications from the desired regions. The palms can be held skyward toward the gods or turned down to receive emanations from the earth.

Gestures are powerful. They can effect changes, achieve results. Hands crossed behind the back are a curse, heap up troubles on the back of an enemy. The sorcerer writhes, miming the pain he sends to his victim. The planter staggers under the light banana sucker to ensure it will grow and bear a heavy load.

Often the regulations of word and gesture are coordinated. The fisherman on his way to work must avoid both certain statements and anything that would encumber his hands held at the ready. The warrior chants his taunt and gestures with his club before entering into single combat.

Dance is therefore not isolated in Hawaiian culture, but continuous with the rest of life. Dance concentrates and heightens a consciousness of the meaningfulness of one's words, body, and actions—a consciousness which can be found in every other activity.

A chant offering gathered wild plants to the hula goddess Laka expands her sphere of influence from her forest home to the voice of the chanter and finally to all things:

Oh Laka!
Clusters of greens, oh Laka!
Oh Laka in the voice
Oh Laka in the getting
Oh Laka in the riches
Oh Laka in all things!

This explains why Hawaiians can describe so much of life in terms of dance. The *Kumulipo*, a chant on the origin of the universe, describes the movement of reptiles:

O hulahula wale ka ne' ena a kolo
'O ka maewa huelo ka loloa.
Just like doing the hula, their
    squirming and crawling,
The tail swinging so long.

The giant shark slides past the diver and gives a flick of its tail—called the *ala hula,* the exit from the dance—just as a female dancer can give a final flip of her hips to say, "I could have had you if I'd wanted to."

The 19th century writer S. M. Kamakau describes the fisherman making his lure move "like an *'ala'apapa hula,* and many *he'e* [squid] came to embrace the dancer, unaware of the hook underneath. The octopus did not want the cowry or the stone to eat… but the fisherman enticed it with a sort of hula and the octopus was 'taken in.'"

Kamakau describes communal planting as a group dance with the planters dressed finely and decorated with leis: "A proud sight it was to see… as the *'o'o ku* [digging sticks] rose, fell, and were bent back all in perfect unison, the men's arms rising together as though beckoning."

A Pele chant describes an entire landscape doing the *ha'a* dance, the hula with bent knees:

Puna is dancing in the wind.
The *hala* grove at Kea'au dances,
Ha'ena dances with Hopoe.
The woman dances,
Rotating her hips in the sea of
    Nanahuki there,
A hula for beauty and excitement
In the sea of Nanakuki!

Land and human dance together in the same wind.

The style of hula emerges from this view of dance. The hula uses the "natural body" as opposed to the "extended body" of ballet. That is, the hula movements are not unusual, not splits, extraordinary leaps, stands on point, and so on. Hula movements are stylizations of everyday ones and require good conditioning, but not stretching the body into "unnatural" shapes.

In dancing, the trunk of the body usually forms a more or less stable center while the feet mark the time. The extended arms and hands create a space around the dancer.

Within that space, the hands gesture. The gesture is imitative; that is, it is meaningful because of the similarity of form between it and the object it imitates. Touching fingers and thumb pointed upward means the flower bud. Flickering fingers mark the rain. The palm held flat, vertical and high signifies the cliff.

In classical hula training, one learns the gesture through a kind of meditation. In the story of Keaomelemele, a young woman learns to hula by imitating the swaying of the branches and leaves she is observing. In a chant, the dancers' raised right hands, with their bracelets of mountain greenery, are compared to a famous grove of coconut trees.

The contemporary hula master John Kaimikaua… instructs his students to meditate before the object to be imitated until that within the dancer which is related to it wells up and emerges as the gesture. "Look at the wave until that which is wave inside you begins to act. Then the gesture will come from inside you and be real. So you can become the object you're trying to imitate."

When the great dancer Iolani Luahine posed for a portrait by my father, Jean Charlot, she sat on the floor and looked across the lanai to a hedge moving in a soft wind. As she looked, her hands slowly rose, holding the strands of her maile lei. They then began to sway and shiver slightly, tentatively. The gesture slowly became more regular and surer, and her torso began to participate in the movement. Finally, she was dancing the hedge.

This way of learning gesture is paralleled in chant training. The student goes to the beach and imitates the sound of the waves. He goes to a certain section of a valley to learn the peculiar sound of the wind there. Hawaiian chant and poetry make extensive use of the similarity of sound between the word and its referent.

The space the dancer creates with his arms and hands around his body can be understood as cosmic space. Above his eyes are the swaying trees, the cliffs, the arching rainbow and the sky. Below his shoulders sweep the broad expanse of beach and the billowing ocean. My daughter's teacher told the class not to open their fingers when their hands were above their heads: "Don't make spiders in the sky!"

In the teaching Kalahikiola Nali'ielua received from his mother, a dancer, the space from the shoulders up is the heavenly element, the torso is the area of earth, and below is the ocean and the underworld.

This sense of the cosmos is an essential element in the religious experience of the hula. Dance naturally comprehends the non-conscious. I once stood in the back row of a class doing its warm-up exercises. Each time the teacher struck the gourd, my body jumped—an unconscious reaction that seemed to start at the base of my spine. I jumped in disorder. The dancer's immediate, spontaneous reaction was a formed gesture. That is, the training, the culture, went very deep. Conversely, the dancer's gesture contained the unconscious body energy of the spinal reaction.

That meeting of culture and energy is living dance. The dancer seems transformed, electric. The term for dancer is *'olapa,* used also for the flash of lightning. The connection is made explicit in a chant to Laka which describes the entrance of the dancers:

The red mist rises on the ocean.
The spray arrives, covers the land.
Lightning flashes from the far sky,
Cracking, rumbling.
The crowd roars.
A hula of so many people!
Oh Laka!

A woman described to me her experience of the state of dancing hula. She felt enclosed. Beyond the reach of her arms and hands was only darkness. She felt she was being moved, impelled, by the words of the chant. She could not stop or act differently. She was totally dependent on the chanter.

In that state, the words of the chant took on a new meaning, a new feeling. The things the words named became presences, even if dim, if not totally defined or definable.

The dancer knew most of the things that became present: the rain, the wind, the clouds. But, at the word *lipolipo,* deep and dark—which she danced by an inviting gesture toward her left and low—she felt the presence of something she could not clearly see, but which seemed large and powerful. Disturbed, she later asked her grandmother what it was. She was told she would find out later.

Chanters can have similar experiences. In the family of the dancer was a young man who studied chant. All he can remember of his debut is mounting the stage and striking his gourd for the first time. He next remembers leaving the stage. His grandmother explained to him later that he came from a family of chanters so that, when he chanted, his ancestors took over.

When chanter and dancer reach this state, true hula occurs. The dancer realizes the cosmos chanted into presence.

Traditions speak of the origin of the hula in ecstatic prayer. The 19th century writer Moses Manu describes the hula beginning when people imitated the gestures made by a woman while she was in a trance. John Kaimikaua has received a similar tradition from oral sources: people became interested in the hula while watching a woman in prayer; when she became conscious again, they asked her to teach them.

Some dancers feel they become another person during the hula. Iolani Luahine said, while watching a videotape of herself dancing, "She's better than I am."

The intensity of the hula explains why it was placed under the protection of powerful gods and surrounded with ceremonies and tabus. Candidates for training were carefully screened and disciplined and were given a broad education.

Even today, moral as well as technical criteria are used in deciding whether to allow a student to advance to more serious dances. The dancer will need maturity and stability.

The advanced dancer, the great dancer, is one who can experience the dance ever more intensely and completely without being overwhelmed. The gesture moves from the hands and arms into the whole body. Iolani Luahine danced the *ua po'i,* the pouncing rain, not with a dipping movement of her hands, but with a crouching, cat-like leap. The whole dancer becomes the gesture. No part of the body need be reserved in order to maintain equilibrium.

Many dancers experience a change of mood as they emerge from the hula. Often female dancers will kiss the chanter, each other, or the person honored by their dance. Today this is a spontaneous act. But it is based on an earlier custom: the female dancer was obliged to kiss the first man who asked her after the dance. Martha Warren Beckwith calls this "doubtless a survival of more intimate advances once encouraged in the name of the lustful divinity supposed to be directly inspiring the successful dancer" (*The Kumulipo,* page 101).

Hawaiian chant most often has a sexual double meaning. This can be expressed in the dance by the movements of the hips—significantly more important than in ballet—while the shoulders and arms express the literal meaning of the chant. This is a reflection of Hawaiian body consciousness and the view that different parts of the body are related to different dimensions of reality. "Put your hands on your *'okole* [buttocks]" young girls are told. "If you don't know where it is, you can't use it." A teacher orders her pre-teen daughter to dance the *'ami* movement with a more circular rotation of her hips: "If you don't move it, I'll put you back with the boys."

Sexual abstinence was practiced during training in hula academies. Graduation marked, in some traditions, a readiness to accept the sexual relations stimulated by the dance. Beckwith states that the branch of *koa* placed on the hula altar plays on the word for courage: "Courage in a woman depends upon her meeting successfully the challenge of sex relations, and it was hence the power to excite erotic emotion that marked the triumph of a hula dancer."

Hula—like word and gesture on their own—has power, can effect change. Dance can bring the winds and rains, can make the clouds come down to the earth. Hula is not art for art's sake, not complete in itself, but fulfilled in its effect, made real by its relationship to its context. A dancer has described to me the circulation of energy she feels between the dancers, the viewers and the environment.

The ultimate context in Hawaiian thinking is the universe conceived as a continuing genealogy. Sky mates with earth, and, through succeeding generations, the universe is formed and completed: elements to plants to animals to the first gods and humans and down to the present generation which continues the genealogy into the next. Everything in the universe is truly related, on a branch of the same family tree. Everything is progeny and sexual; elements as well as plants and animals.

In a famous chant for the graduation of a dancer, Laka is pictured in the lush forest in the cool mists, trampling the wet, yielding forest floor—a traditional picture of sexual fertility. To her is offered the head of a pig, the snout of which is a phallic symbol. The pig is of the god Kane, Male, who is a man for Laka. They mate, and a plant takes root, sends up a trunk, leafs, buds, branches and fruits. The sexual act of the gods generates the energy of growth. The offspring is the plant and also the hula dancer it symbolizes. They are produced by the same life-force.

All Hawaiian culture—the arts, education, philosophy and religion—explores the ramifications of this view of humans and the universe. In the *Kumulipo,* each stage in the development of the universe can be understood as a stage in the conception, birth, and growth of a child to young adulthood. In lyric poetry, a description of a landscape is simultaneously one of human emotions. In hula, the dancer becomes a cosmos.

Humans are not conceived as somehow separate from nature, as essentially different from their environment—as in so much Western culture. Rather, Hawaiian culture invites us to realize the beauty and power of our identity as members of the universe.

John Charlot is HONOLULU's Visual Arts columnist.

From *Honolulu,* November/December 1979, pp. 18-24. © John Charlott 1979. Reprinted by permission.

UNIT 3
India: Jainism, Hinduism, and Sikhism

Unit Selections

11. **Ancient Jewel**, T. R. (Joe) Sundaram
12. **The Jain Deities**, Rev. E. Osborn Martin
13. **Seeing the Sacred**, Diana Eck
14. **The Hindu Ethic of Nonviolence**, *Hinduism Today*
15. **The Sacred Is the One True Reality of Brahman**, Swami Nikhilananda

Key Points to Consider

- Why do you think so many surviving religious traditions originated in the Indian subcontinent?

- What are some of the elements that Indian religions have in common?

- How are the concepts of karma and nonviolence connected?

- Can a religion exist without the belief in an eternal divinity? Explain.

- What are some of the differing ways in which Hindus conceive of the divine? How do these differ from Western concepts?

- What are some of the unique characteristics of Sikhism?

 **Links: www.dushkin.com/online/**
These sites are annotated in the World Wide Web pages.

Hinduism Online
http://www.himalayanacademy.com
Introduction to Hinduism
http://www.uni-giessen.de/~gk1415/hinduism.htm
Introduction to Sikhism
http://photon.bu.edu/~rajwi/sikhism/mansukh1.html
Jainism
http://www.cs.colostate.edu/~malaiya/jainhlinks.html

Two geographic areas, the Indian subcontinent and the Middle East, have historically given birth to the majority of the larger religions of the world. While the great Western religious traditions have come from the latter, the former has seen the genesis of the great Eastern religious traditions of Buddhism, Hinduism, Jainism, and Sikhism. Because of the development and early shift in the center of Buddhism beyond the borders of its homeland, it is the focus of the next unit.

India has long been a land of diverse peoples and traditions, possessing a religious and cultural history dating back more than 4,500 years. Archaeological discoveries in the region reveal an ancient culture in the northwestern part of the subcontinent that was indeed socially and technically sophisticated for its time. Since then, the evolution of the native peoples, along with the influences of invaders, travelers, and immigrants to the region, has inspired the growth of multiple forms of religious beliefs and expressions. Because of this diversity, it is virtually impossible to contain the prevailing range of religious concepts within any preconceived boundaries, especially those used to describe Western traditions.

Generally speaking, each of the religious movements in India has developed unique aspects while drawing upon and reformulating existing traditions. Rather than exclusiveness, inclusiveness has been the more typical approach. Consequently, each tradition has much in common with the others of the region. This can especially be seen in Jainism, Buddhism, and Hinduism. Although all three have their distinctions, they also share enough to make it sometimes difficult to ascertain where one tradition ends and another begins. Hindus will worship Jain and Buddhist deities. Buddhism has adopted various Hindu deities. All three adhere to and utilize, in one form or another, the concepts of *karma,* nonviolence, and rebirth. Sikhism is of quite late origin, in comparison to these other traditions, and rejects many of the concepts held by them. Nevertheless, it also shares certain central beliefs and is very obviously a product of their influences.

To help facilitate an introduction for the student to the religious landscape, this unit looks at some conceptions of divinity, or ultimacy, and of virtues perceived to help align one with that ultimate being, or state of being. Jainism, one of the earliest formalized religious traditions of India, had in its origin a lack of focus on a divinity as such. Instead, it looked at the interactions of the individual soul with the world or matter, time, and space, and the consequences, known as *karma,* of these interactions. As the tradition grew, it evolved an elaborate understanding of *karma,* a unique cosmology, and a belief in the power of *ahimsa,* or nonviolence. The first two articles in this unit look at these issues.

The next two articles address the issue of divinity in the Hindu tradition, and the many ways it is conceived and understood. The first of these focuses more on the phenomenal realm, which Hindus believe can be a powerful and useful medium of perception. The next article in the unit discusses the role of nonviolence in the various India-based religious traditions and theorizes on its practical relevance and importance for today. The last article looks more at Hinduism's transcendent nature.

Ancient Jewel

From early Greece to the modern civil rights movement, Indian thought and philosophy have had a wide-ranging influence on Western culture.

T. R. (Joe) Sundaram

The very word *India* conjures up exotic images in one's mind. Yet this name for the south Asian subcontinent is of Western making, mediated by the Persians and the Arabs. The name used in ancient Sanskrit texts is *Bharat* (for the land of Bharatha, a legendary king), which is also the official name of the modern republic. Other familiar Western words such as *Hindu, caste,* and *curry* are also totally foreign to India. The general knowledge that exists in the West about India, its early history, philosophy, and culture is, at best, superficial. Nevertheless, since it would be impossible in a brief article to do justice to even one of these topics, I shall provide a brief, accurate glimpse into each.

India covers about 1.2 million square miles and is home to a population of 895 million; in comparison, the United States covers 3.6 million square miles and has 258 million residents. Thus, the population density of India is nearly 10 times that of the United States. (The size of classical India—which includes modern-day India, Pakistan, Bangladesh, and parts of Afghanistan—is about two-thirds that of the continental United States.)

But statistics about India can be misleading. For example, while only about one-quarter of the population is "literate," able to read and write, this has to be viewed in light of the strong oral traditions present in India since antiquity. Therefore, while a "literate" American may often be unaware of the collective name of the first 10 amendments to the U.S. Constitution, an "illiterate" Indian peasant would be aware of the history of his ancestors from antiquity to the present day.

Not only is India one of the oldest civilizations in the world, being more than 6,000 years old, but also it may be the oldest continuing civilization in existence; that is, one without any major "gaps" in its history. As the renowned historian A. L. Basham has pointed out,

> Until the advent of archeologists, the peasant of Egypt or Iraq had no knowledge of the culture of his forefathers, and it is doubtful whether his Greek counterpart had any but the vaguest ideas about the glory of Periclean Athens. In each case there had been an almost complete break with the past. On the other hand, the earliest Europeans to visit India found a culture fully conscious of its own antiquity.

India is a land of many ancient "living" cities, such as, for example, Varanasi. Even at sites like Delhi, many successive cities have been built over thousands of years. Among old buried cities that have been unearthed in modern times by archaeologists are Mohenjo-Daro and Harappa.

Of these cities, the renowned archaeologist Sir John Marshall writes that they establish the existence

> in the fourth and third millennium B.C., of a highly developed city life; and the presence in many houses, of wells and bathrooms as well as an elaborate drainage system, betoken a social condition of the citizens at least equal to that found in Sumer, and superior to that prevailing in contemporary Babylonia and Egypt.

Thus, India was the "jewel of the world" long before the Greek and Roman civilizations.

Nor was classical India isolated from developing civilizations in other parts of the world. Clay seals from Mohenjo-Daro have been found in Babylonia and vice versa. Ancient Indian ar-

Embassy of India

Continuous civilization: Excavations at Mohenjo-Daro and Harappa reveal well-planned towns and a sophisticated urban culture dating back to 2500 B.C.

Crucible of Learning

- *India's may be the oldest continuing civilization in existence.*

- *To avoid misunderstanding India, it is essential to appreciate three central tenets of Indian thinking: assimilating ideas and experiences, a belief in cycles, and the coexistence of opposites.*

- *India has made numerous contributions to contemporary Western understanding of mathematics, science, and philosophy.*

---

tifacts such as beads and bangles have been found in many parts of the Middle East and Africa. India and Indian culture were known to the Greeks even before the time of Alexander the Great. The Greek historian Herodotus wrote extensively about India during the sixth century B.C. Also, during this period many Greeks, including Pythagoras, are known to have traveled to India.

Sixth century B.C. was a period of great religious and philosophical upheaval in India. Hinduism was already an established, "old" religion, and reform movements were beginning to appear, such as one by a prince known as Siddhartha Gautama, who later came to be known as the Buddha. The religion that was founded based on his teachings spread not only throughout Asia but also to many parts of the world, including Greece, and it helped spread Indian culture in the process.

In Alexander the Great's campaign to conquer the world, his ultimate goal was India; he died without achieving that objective. When Seleucus Nicator, Alexander's successor, tried to follow in Alexander's footsteps, he was soundly defeated by Indian emperor Chandragupta Maurya. A peace treaty was signed between the two, and Seleucus sent an ambassador, Megasthenes, to the court of Chandragupta. Megasthenes sent glowing reports back to Greece about India, and he pronounced Indian culture to be equal or superior to his own, a high compliment indeed, since Greece was then near its zenith.

For the next 1,500 years or so, India—rich in material wealth, scientific knowledge, and spiritual wisdom—enjoyed the reputation of being at the pinnacle of world civilizations. Arab writers of the Middle Ages routinely referred to mathematics as *hindsat,* the "Indian science."

And as is well known now, it was Columbus' desire to reach India that led to the discovery of America. Indeed, the explorer died thinking that he had discovered a new sea route to India, while he had merely landed on a Caribbean island. Columbus' mistake also led to the mislabeling of the natives of the land as "Indians," a label that survived even after the mistake had been discovered.

THE UPANISHADS

Indian philosophy is almost as old as Indian civilization, and its zenith was reached nearly 3,000 years ago with the compilation,

A terra-cotta toy cow: Ancient Indian civilizations featured highly talented artisans and craftsmen.

by unknown sages, of 108 ancient philosophical texts known as the Upanishads. These texts reflect even older wisdom, which was passed down from generation to generation through oral transmission. A Western commentator has remarked that in the Upanishads the Indian mind moved from cosmology to psychology, and that while most other contemporary civilizations were still asking the question "What am I?" the Indian mind was already asking, "Who am I?"

When translations of the Upanishads first became available in the West in the nineteenth century, the impact on European philosophers such as Goethe and Schopenhauer and on American writers such as Emerson and Whitman was profound. "In the whole world," wrote Schopenhauer emotionally, "there is no study as beneficial and as elevating as the Upanishads." Emerson wrote poems based on the texts.

One of the principal underlying themes in the Upanishads is the quest for a "personal reality." This quest began with the conviction that the limitations of our sensory perceptions give us an imperfect model to comprehend the real world around us; this is known as the concept of *maya*. Since individual perceptions can be different, different people can also have different "realities."

For example, a happy event for one individual may be an unhappy one for another. Recognition and perfection of our personal reality is the quintessential goal of Indian philosophy and is also the basic principle behind yoga. Indeed, the literal meaning of the Sanskrit word *yoga* is "union," and the union that is sought is not with any external entity but with one's self. This is, of course, also the principal tenet of modern psychoanalysis.

From a Western perspective, to avoid misunderstanding India in general, and Indian philosophy in particular, it is essential to appreciate three central tenets of the Indian way of thinking. These are:

Assimilation. In the Indian way of thinking, new experiences and ideas never replace old ones but are simply absorbed into, and made a part of, old experiences. Although some have characterized such thinking as static, in reality such thinking is both dynamic and conservative, since old experiences are preserved and new experiences are continually accumulated.

Belief in cycles. Another central tenet of the Indian character is the belief that all changes in the world take place through cycles, there being cycles superimposed on other cycles, cycles within cycles, and so on. Inherent in the concept of cycles is alternation, and the Upanishads speak of the two alternating states of all things being "potentiality" and "expression."

Acceptance of the coexistence of opposites. Early Western readers of the Upanishads were puzzled by the apparent inherent ability of the Indian mind to accept the coexistence of seemingly diametrically opposite concepts. Belief in, and acceptance of, contradictory ideas is a natural part of the Indian way of life, and the logical complement to the tenets already mentioned. It is an indisputable fact that birth (creation) must necessarily be eventually followed by death (destruction). Creation and destruction are inseparable alternations. Even concepts such as "good" and "evil" are complementary, as each of us may have within us the most lofty and divine qualities and at the same time the basest qualities. We ourselves and the whole world can be whatever we want to make of them.

These three tenets are responsible for the amazing continuity of the Indian civilization, its reverence for the elderly, and the acceptance of the aging process without a morbid fear of death.

Ironically, the culture that taught of the need to renounce materialistic desires also produced some of the most pleasurable things in life. The intricacies and highly developed nature of Indian art, music, dance, and cuisine are examples. And the Kama Sutra is perhaps the oldest, and best known, manual on the pleasures of love and sex.

FROM PYTHAGORAS TO KING

Throughout history, India's contributions to the Western world have been considerable, albeit during the Middle Ages they were often felt only indirectly, having been mediated by the Middle Eastern cultures.

After the early contacts between Greece and India in the sixth and fifth centuries B.C., many concepts that had been in use in India centuries earlier made their appearance in Greek literature, although no source was ever acknowledged. For example, consider the so-called Pythagorean theorem of a right triangle and the Pythagorean school's theory of the "transmigration of souls"; the former was in use in India (for temple construction) centuries earlier, and the latter is merely "reincarnation," a concept of Vedic antiquity. There was also a flourishing trade between the Roman Empire and the kingdoms in southern India, through which not only Indian goods but also ideas made their journey westward.

During the Middle Ages, the Arabs translated many classical Indian works into Arabic, and the ideas contained in them eventually made their way to Europe. A principal mission of the "House of Wisdom" that was established by the caliph in

Khorrum Omer/The World & I

Indian music has influenced Western artists, particularly in modern times. The beat of the tabla can be heard in pop music ranging from the Beatles to Michael Jackson.

In modern times, Indian music has had a considerable influence on Western music. Starting in the 1960s, the famous Indian sitar virtuoso Ravi Shankar popularized sitar music in the West, and now the melodic strains of the sitar, as well as the beat of the Indian drum known as tabla, can be heard in the works of many pop-music artists, ranging from the Beatles to Michael Jackson. The movies of the Indian filmmaker Satyajit Ray have also made a significant impact on the West.

The contributions of many modern Indian scientists have been important to the overall development of Western science. The mathematical genius Srinivasa Ramanujan, who died in 1920, has been called "the greatest mathematician of the century" and "the man who knew infinity." The discovery by the Nobel Prize-winning Indian physicist Chandrasekhara Venkata Raman of the effect (which bears his name) by which light diffusing through a transparent material changes in wavelength has revolutionized laser technology. The theoretical predictions by the Nobel Prize-winning astrophysicist Subrahmanyan Chandrasekhar on the life and death of white-dwarf stars led to the concept of "black holes."

In the literary area, the poetry of Nobel laureate Rabindranath Tagore and the philosophical interpretations of the scholar (and a former president of India) Sarvepalli Radhakrishnan have inspired the West. Albert Einstein was one of the admirers of the former and corresponded with him on the meaning of "truth."

In terms of our daily dietary habits, many vegetables such as cucumber, eggplant, okra, squash, carrots, many types of beans, and lentils were first domesticated in India. Rice, sugarcane, and tea, as well as fruits such as bananas and oranges, are of Indian origin. The name *orange* is derived from the Sanskrit word *narangi*. Chicken and cattle were also first domesticated in India, albeit the latter for milk production and not for meat consumption. Cotton was first domesticated in India. The process of dying fabrics also was invented in India. Indian fabrics (both cotton and silk) have been world renowned for their quality since antiquity. The game of chess was invented in India, and the name itself derives from the Sanskrit name Chaturanga.

India's most popular modern exports have been yoga and meditation. Hatha yoga, the exercise system that is a part of yoga, is now taught widely in America, in institutions ranging from colleges to hospitals. Many scientific studies on the beneficial effects of yoga practice are now under way. A similar state of affairs is true of Indian meditation techniques, which people under stress use for mental relaxation.

Finally the Rev. Martin Luther King, Jr., repeatedly acknowledged his debt to Mahatma Gandhi for the technique of nonviolent civil disobedience, which he used in the civil rights movement. For all India's material contributions to the world, it is its spiritual legacy that has had the widest impact. The ancient sages who wrote the Upanishads would have been pleased.

Baghdad in the eighth century was the translation of Indian works.

Among the major Indian ideas that entered Europe through the Arabs are the mathematical concept of zero (for which there was no equivalent in Greek or Roman mathematics) and the modern numerical system we use today. Until the twelfth century, Europe was shackled by the unwieldy Roman numerals. The famous French mathematician Laplace has written: "It is India that gave us the ingenious method of expressing all numbers by ten symbols, each receiving a value of position as well as an absolute value, a profound and important idea which appears so simple to us now that we ignore its true merit."

India's contributions to other areas of science and mathematics were equally important. The seventh-century Syrian astronomer Severus Sebokht wrote that "the subtle theories" of Indian astronomers were "even more ingenious than those of the Greeks and the Babylonians."

The scientific approach permeated other aspects of Indian life as well. For example, classical Indian music has a highly mathematical structure, based on divisions of musical scales into tones and microtones.

ADDITIONAL READING

A. L. Basham, *The Wonder That Was India*, Grove Press, New York, 1959.

Khorrum Omer/The World & I

Melodic inspiration: Performing traditional dance and music in Orissa.

——, *Ancient India: Land of Mystery,* Time-Life Books, Alexandria, Virginia, 1994.

Will Durant, *the Story of Civilization: Part I, Our Oriental Heritage,* Simon and Schuster, New York, 1954.

T. R. (Joe) Sundaram is the owner of an engineering research firm in Columbia, Maryland, and has written extensively on Indian history, culture, and science.

This article originally appeared in *The World & I,* October 1996, pp. 24-31. Reprinted by permission of *The World & I,* a publication of The Washington Times Corporation. © 1996.

THE JAIN DEITIES

Rev. E. Osborn Martin

The Jains, like the Buddhists, represent a revolt against *Brahamanism* which they regarded as a departure from the true primitive religion of India. But when *Buddhism* declined and finally died out, the Jains, though depleted by persecution, survived. They form a small but wealthy community of merchants and bankers. They have much in their religion that resembles Buddhism. Both reject the authority of the *Vedas,* both disregard caste rules, and profess to believe in the religious and social equality of man. The Jains are considered as heretics by orthodox Hindus, although they have so far departed from the tenets of Buddhism as to acknowledge in a general way the more common and modern Hindu deities, and their worship is very similar to that which prevails amongst the Hindus.

The origin of the sect is said to be accounted for in the following way: The innovations of the *Brahmans,* who introduced gradually into India such practices as *lingam*-worship, the worship of the cow and other sacred animals, the wondrous stories of the *avataras* of Vishnu, and certain sacrificial rites of *Puranic* times, were deeply resented for a long time by a number of influential Hindus of many castes. These men were unwilling to come to an open rupture, but their opposition to what they regarded as dangerous innovations and changes in the true primitive faith, handed down from remote times, never ceased.

A crisis, however, became unavoidable when the *Brahmans* introduced the sacrifice of *yajna,* in which a living offering, generally a ram, was sacrificed. This violated the most sacred principle, and the hitherto inviolable practice of the Hindus, and "the Jains" withdrew from association with the priestly castes, whom they regarded as corrupters of their primitive faith. The secession included men of all the four main castes, for, to some of the faithful *Brahmans,* were joined those from the warrior, merchant, and *Sudra* castes, who desired to maintain the purity of their ancient faith. The *Brahmans,* however, succeeded in imposing their will upon the body politic, and their innovations were adopted by the majority of the people. Consequently persecution arose and in many parts of the country, the places and objects of Jain worship were demolished, the Jains were deprived of their civil and religious liberty, and were reduced to such absolute subjection that in many provinces not a vestige of them remains.

There are two principal sects among the Jains, the *Jaina-Barsu* and the *Kashta-Sanghi-Swetambara* (white-robed Jains). The term Jain comes from *jina,* "he who has conquered" (i.e. human passions or infirmities). A *jina* is the deified saint, also called a Tirathankara, who is the object of Jain worship. Both Jains and Buddhists now worship a succession of deified saints in place of the many gods adored by the Hindus. The Jains divide time into three successive eras and assign twenty-four Jains to each era. They are now in the second era and the twenty-four saints of the first and second eras are the deities of modern Jainism.

"These twenty-four are represented in the temples as seated in an attitude of contemplation. In features they so resemble each other that in order to distinguish them they are painted in different colours and have their respective names engraved on their pedestals, or some distinguishing sign, commonly an animal, by their side. In the stories of their lives there is little of a distinctive character, but there is this noticeable fact that in height of stature and length of life there has been a steady decline." An example or two in support of the last remark may not be out of place. The first of the second series of twenty-four saints was Vrishabha. His stature was 500 poles in height, and he lived 8,400,000 great years. He was crowned king when 2,000,000 years old and reigned 6,300,000 years, and afterwards spent 100,000 years in the practice of austerities, by which he became qualified for sainthood. The last of the twenty-four saints, called "The Saint", because he is the best known of all, was Mahavira. He lost his father when twenty-eight years of age and became king, but resigned after two years' reign and entered upon a life of austerity. After forty-two years of preparation he became exempt from pain for ever. In other words he died at the age of seventy-two, obtaining "absorption". This, according to tradition, occurred twenty-five centuries ago!

The Jains, according to Abbe Dubois, have a lofty doctrine of God. They acknowledge but one Supreme Being. He is one, indivisible and invisible, a pure Spirit. He has four main attributes: wisdom, infinite knowledge, power, and happiness. This omnipotent Being is wholly absorbed in the contemplation of his own perfections and in the enjoyment of his own blessedness. Virtue and vice, good and evil, are equally indifferent to him.

"The adoration and worship which the Jains offer to their deified saints, the Tirathankaras, and to other objects of worship held sacred among them, does not detract from the worship of the Supreme Being, for these holy personages, in taking possession after death of the *moksha* or *mukti,* the supreme felicity, have become intimately united and inseparably incorporated with the Divine."

The Jains are firm believers in the doctrine of the transmigration of the soul from one body into another after death, and hold that the offender may suffer transmigration into the body of an insect, reptile, or bird, or quadruped, according to the degree of his offences. Naturally, therefore, they hold all life in honour, and their distinctive precent is "*ahimsa parama dharma*"—i.e. "non-killing is the supreme religion". They abhor the taking of life in any form, they show the greatest tenderness to animals, and are the best supporters of hospitals and asylums for sick or worn-out beasts.

From *Lord Mahavira in the Eyes of Foreigners* 1975, pp. 150-152 by Rev. E. Osborn Martin. © 1975 by Lord Mahavira in the Eyes of Foreigners.

Seeing the Sacred

A. Darsan

A COMMON SIGHT in India is a crowd of people gathered in the courtyard of a temple or at the doorway of a streetside shrine for the *darsan of the deity*. Darsan means "seeing." In the Hindu ritual tradition it refers especially to religious seeing, or the visual perception of the sacred. When Hindus go to a temple, they do not commonly say, "I am going to worship," but rather, "I am gong for *darsan*." They go to "see" the image of the deity—be it Krsna or Durga, Siva or Visnu—present in the sanctum of the temple, and they go especially at those times of day when the image is most beautifully adorned with fresh flowers and when the curtain is drawn back so that the image is fully visible. The central act of Hindu worship, from the point of view of the lay person, is to stand in the presence of the deity and to behold the image with one's own eyes, to see and be seen by the deity. *Darsan* is sometimes translated as the "auspicious sight"* of the divine, and its importance in the Hindu ritual complex reminds us that for Hindus "worship" is not only a matter of prayers and offerings and the devotional disposition of the heart. Since, in the Hindu understanding, the deity is present in the image, the visual apprehension of the image is charged with religious meaning. Beholding the image is an act of worship, and through the eyes one gains the blessings of the divine.

Similarly, when Hindus travel on pilgrimage, as they do by the millions each month of the year, it is for the *darsan* of the place of pilgrimage or for the *darsan* of its famous deities. They travel to Siva's sacred city of Vranasi (Benares) for the *darsan* of Visnu at Badrinath. Or they climb to the top of a hill in their own district for the *darsan* of a well-known local goddess. The pilgrims who take to the road on foot, or who crowd into buses and trains, are not merely sightseers, but "sacred sightseers" whose interest is not in the picturesque place, but in the powerful place where *darsan* may be had. These powerful places are called *tirthas* (sacred "fords" or "crossings"), *dhams* (divine "abodes"), or *pithas* (the "benches" or "seats" of the divine). There are thousands of such places in India. Some, like Varanasi, which is also called Kasi, are sought by pilgrims from their immediate locales.

Often such places of pilgrimage are famous for particular divine images, and so it is for the *darsan* of the image that pilgrims come. The close relationship between the symbolic importance of the image and the symbolic act of pilgrimage has been explored in a Western context by Victor and Edith Turner in *Image and Pilgrimage in Christian Culture*.[1] In the West, of course, such traditions of pilgrimage were often attacked by those who did not "see" the symbolic significance of images and who, like Erasmus, denounced the undertaking of pilgrimages as a waste of time. In the Hindu tradition, however, there has never been the confusion of "image" with "idol," and in India, pilgrimage is the natural extension of the desire for the *darsan* of the divine image, which is at the heart of all temple worship.

It is not only for the *darsan* of renowned images that Hindus have traveled as pilgrims. They also seek the *darsan* of the places themselves which are said to be the natural epiphanies of the divine: the peaks of the Himalayas, which are said to be the abode of the gods; the river Ganga, which is said to fall from heaven to earth; or the many places which are associated with the mythic deeds of gods and goddesses, heroes and saints.

In addition to the *darsan* of temple images and sacred places, Hindus also value the *darsan* of holy persons, such as *sants* ("saints"), *sadhus* ("holy men"), and *sannyasins* ("renouncers"). When Mahatma Gandhi traveled through India, tens of thousands of people would gather wherever he stopped in order to "take his *darsan*." Even if he did not stop, they would throng the train stations for a passing glimpse of the Mahatma in his compartment. Similarly, when Swami Karpatri, a well-known *sannyasin* who is also a writer and political leader, comes to Varanasi to spend the rainy season "retreat" period, people flock to his daily lectures not only to hear him, but to see him.[2]* However, even an ordinary *sannyasin* or *sadhu* is held in esteem in traditional Hindu culture. He is a living symbol of the value placed upon renunciation, and he is a perpetual pilgrim who has left home and family for a homeless life. Villagers are eager for the *darsan* of such a person, approaching him with reverence and giving him food and hospitality. In *The Ochre Robe*, Agehananda Bharati writes, "There is absolutely no parallel to the conception of *darsan* in any religious act in the West...."[2]

In popular terminology, Hindus say that the deity or the *sadhu* "gives *darsan*" (*darsan dena* is the Hindi expression), and the people "take *darsan*" (*darsan lena*). What does this mean? What is given and what is taken? The

Jagannath Deities

very expression is arresting, for "seeing" in this religious sense is not an act which is initiated by the worshiper.[3] Rather, the deity presents itself to be seen in its image, or the *sadhu* gives himself to be seen by the villagers. And the people "receive" their *darsan*. One might say that this "sacred perception," which is the ability truly to see the divine image, is given to the devotee, just as Arjuna is given the eyes with which to see Krsna in the theophany described in the Bhagavad Gita.[4]

The prominence of the eyes on Hindu divine images also reminds us that it is not only the worshiper who sees the deity, but the deity sees the worshiper as well. The contact between devotee and deity is exchanged through the eyes. It is said in India that one of the ways in which the gods can be recognized when they move among people on this earth is by their unblinking eyes. Their gaze and their watchfulness is uninterrupted. Jan Gonda, in his detailed monograph *Eye and Gaze in the Veda*, has enumerated the many ways in which the powerful gaze of the gods was imagined and expressed even in a time before actual images of the gods were crafted.[5] The eyes of Surya or Agni or Varuna are powerful and all-seeing, and the gods were entreated to look upon men with a kindly eye. In the later Hindu tradition, when divine images began to be made, the eyes were the final part of the anthropomorphic image to be carved or set in place. Even after the breath of life (*prana*) was established in the image, came the ceremony in which the eyes were ritually opened with a golden needle or with the final stroke of a paintbrush. This is still common practice in the consecration of images, and today shiny oversized enamel eyes may be set in the eyesockets of the image during this rite. The gaze which falls from the newly-opened eyes of the deity is said to be so powerful that it must first fall upon some pleasing offering, such as sweets, or upon a mirror where it may see its own reflection. More than once has the tale been told of that powerful gaze falling upon some unwitting bystander, who died instantly of its force.[6] Hindu divine images are often striking for their large and conspicuous eyes. The famous image of Krsna Jagannath in Puri has enormous saucer-like eyes.[7] Siva and Ganesa are often depicted with a third vertical eye, set in the center of the forehead. Brahma, inheriting the name "Thousand-Eyes" from Indra, is sometimes depicted with eyes all over his body, like leopard spots. While it would take us too far afield to explore the many dimensions of eye-power in the Hindu tradition, it is important for this study of the divine image to recognize that just as the glance of the inauspicious is thought to be dangerous and is referred to as the "evil eye," so is the glance of the auspicious person or the deity held to be profitable. When Hindus stand on tiptoe and crane their necks to see, through the crowd, the image of Lord Krsna, they wish not only to "see," but to be seen. The gaze of the huge eyes of the image meets that of the worshiper, and that exchange of vision lies at the heart of Hindu worship.

In the Indian context, seeing is a kind of touching. The art historian Stella Kramrisch writes,

> Seeing, according to Indian notions, is a going forth of the sight towards the object. Sight touches it and acquires its form. Touch is the ultimate connection by which the visible yields to being grasped. While the eye touches the object, the vitality that pulsates in it is communicated. ...[8]

Examining the words used in the Vedic literature, Gonda reaches the same conclusion: "That a look was consciously regarded as a form of contact appears from the combination of 'looking' and 'touching'. Casting one's eyes upon a person and touching him were related activities."[9]

Sanskrit poets and dramatists convey the subtleties of meaning expressed by the glances of the eyes, not only between lovers, but between husband and wife, whose public conversation was limited by rules of propriety.[10] They communicated in their glances. Writes Daniel H. H. Ingalls, "One must suppose that the language of the eyes was more advanced in ancient India than it is with us."[11] Gonda reflects on the "language of the eyes" as it may pertain to the religious context: "It is indeed hardly conceivable that the psychical contact brought about, in normal social intercourse, by the eye, should not, consciously or unconsciously, have been made an element in a variety of rites and religious customs, that the positive fascination of a prolonged look, fixed regard or other manners of looking should not, in ritual practice also, be a means of expressing feelings, of imposing silence, of signifying consent or satisfaction, or expressing will, love or reverence, a means also of participating in the essence and nature of the person or object looked at."[12]

Not only is seeing a form of "touching," it is a form of knowing. According to the Brahmanas, "The eye is the truth (satyam). If two persons were to come disputing with each other, ... we should believe him who said 'I have seen it,' not him who has said 'I have heard it.'"[13] Seeing is not only an activity of the eye, however. In India, as in many cultures, words for seeing have included within their semantic fields the notion of knowing. We speak of "seeing" the point of an argument, of "insight" into an issue of complexity, of the "vision" of people of wisdom. In Vedic India the "seers" were called rsis. In their hymns, collected in the Rg Veda, "to see" often means a "mystical, supranatural beholding" or "visionary experiencing."[14] Later on, the term darsana was used to describe the systems of the philosophy which developed in the Indian tradition. However, it is misleading to think of these as "systems" or "schools" of philosophical

thought. Rather, they are "points of view" which "represent the varied phases of the truth viewed from different angles of vision."[15]

B. The Visible India

Hinduism is an imaginative, an "image-making," religious tradition in which the sacred is seen as present in the visible world—the world we see in multiple images and deities, in sacred places, and in people. The notion of darsian calls our attention, as students of Hinduism, to the fact that India is a visual and visionary culture, one in which the eyes have a prominent role in the apprehension of the sacred. For most ordinary Hindus, the notion of the divine as "invisible" would be foreign indeed. God is eminently visible, although human beings have not always had the refinement of sight to see. Furthermore, the divine is visible not only in temple and shrine, but also in the whole continuum of life—in nature, in people, in birth and growth and death. Although some Hindus, both philosophers and radical reformers, have always used the terms nirguna ("qualityless") and nirakara ("formless") to speak of the One Brahman, this can most accurately be understood only from the perspective of a tradition that has simultaneously affirmed that Brahman is also saguna ("with qualities"), and that the multitude of "names and forms" of this world are the exuberant transformations of the One Brahman.

India presents to the visitor an overwhelmingly visual impression. It is beautiful, colorful, sensuous. It is captivating and intriguing, repugnant and puzzling. It combines the intimacy and familiarity of English four o'clock tea with the dazzling foreignness of carpisoned elephants or vast crowds bathing in the Ganga during an eclipse. India's display of multi-armed images, its processions and pilgrimages, its beggars and kings, its street life and markets, its diversity of peoples—all appear to the eye in a kaleidoscope of images. Much that is removed from public view in the modern West and taken into the privacy of rest homes, asylums, and institutions is open and visible in the life an an Indian city or village. The elderly, the infirm, the dead awaiting cremation—these sights, while they may have been expunged from the childhood palace of the Buddha, are not isolated from the public eye in India. Rather, they are present daily in the visible world in which Hindus, and those who visit India, move in the course of ordinary activities. In India, one sees everything. One sees people at work and at prayer; one sees plump, well-endowed merchants, simple renouncers, fraudulent "holy" men, frail widows, and emaciated lepers; one sees the festival procession, the marriage procession, and the funeral procession. Whatever Hindus affirm of the meaning of life, death, and suffering, they affirm with their eyes wide open.

So abundant are the data of the visual India, seen with the eye, that what one has learned from reading about

"Hinduism" may seem pale and perhaps unrecognizable by comparison. As E. M. Forster wrote of the enterprise of studying Hinduism: "Study it for years with the best of teachers, and when you raise your head, nothing they have told you quite fits."[16]

The medium of film is especially important for the student of Hinduism, for it provides a way of entering the visual world, the world of sense and image, which is so important for the Hindu tradition. Raising the eye from the printed page to the street or the temple, as conveyed by the film, provides a new range of questions, a new set of data. In India's own terms, seeing is knowing. And India must be seen to be known. While Hindu spirituality is often portrayed in the West as interior, mystical, and other-worldly, one need only raise the head from the book to the image to see how mistakenly one-sided such a characterization is. The day to day life and ritual of Hindus is based not upon abstract interior truths, but upon the charged, concrete, and particular appearances of the divine in the substance of the material world.

Many Westerners, for example, upon seeing Hindu ritual observances for the first time, are impressed with how sensuous Hindu worship is. It is sensuous in that it makes full use of the senses—seeing, touching, smelling, tasting, and hearing. One "sees" the image of the deity (*darsan*). One "touches" it with one's hands (*sparsa*), and one also "touches" the limbs of one's own body to establish the presence of various deities (*nyasa*). One "hears" the sacred sound of the *mantras (sravana)*. The ringing of bells, the offering of oil lamps, the presentation of flowers, the pouring of water and milk, the sipping of sanctified liquid offerings, the eating of consecrated food—these are the basic constituents of Hindu worship, *puja*. The presentation of such rites in film[3*] may be for the student an introduction to a view of Hindu culture which is not as evident nor as accessible in the textual traditions. For all of its famous otherworldliness, India is a culture that has also celebrated the life of this world and the realms of the senses.

C. Film Images

What do we mean by *image*? The term has been used variously in psychology, philosophy, religion, and the arts. For our purposes, there are two ways in which *image* is being used. First, there are the artistic images, the "icons" of the Hindu religious tradition, which are a primary focus of this essay. The creation of such images is perhaps the earliest form of human symbolization. People lifted out of the ordinary visible data of the world a shape, a form, which crystallized experience and, with its meanings and connotations, told a story. Long before people wrote textual treatises, they "wrote" in images. The term iconography means, literally, "writing in images." These visual texts, such as the great temples of Khajuraho or Konarak or the array of icons within a mod-

ern Hindu temple, constitute a considerable heritage of the human imagination for the scholar of religion. One must learn to "read" these visual texts with the same insight and interpretive skill that is brought to the reading and interpretation of scriptures, commentaries, and theologies.

Here, however, we are concerned with a second meaning of the term *image*—the visual images of India that are presented to us through the medium of film and photography. Rudolf Arnheim has noted what he calls the "widespread unemployment of the senses in every field of academic study."[17] Photographic images enable us to employ the senses in the process of learning. But they also give us pause to reflect on the role of this new, almost "magical," form of image-making in our own culture and in our efforts to know and understand another culture.

Photography and film have made possible the mass proliferation of images. In *On Photography,* Susan Sontag has reflected on the ways in which photography has become a way of defining, appropriating, and recycling "reality."[18] The image business has become an important part of modern consumerism and has turned all of us into the creators and consumers of images. People take photographs, buy photographs, go to films, watch television, glance at billboard advertisements. In short, photography has "greatly enlarged the realm of the visible."[19] Both Sontag's articulation and critique of the prominence of the image in modern society serve to underline our need to think seriously about the interpretation and use of film images. We can "see" such scenes as the Hindu pilgrims bathing in the River Ganga in Varansi or the Muslim mourners beating their chests with their fists. But what do we "make" of what we see? Seeing, after all, is an imaginative, constructive activity, an act of making. It is not simply the reception of images on the retina.

The term *hermeneutics* has been used to describe the task of understanding and interpreting ideas and texts. In a similar way, we need to set for ourselves the task of developing a hermeneutic of the visible, addressing the problem of how we understand and interpret what we see, not only in the classical images and art forms created by the various religious traditions, but in the ordinary images of people's traditions, rites, and daily activities which are presented to us through the film-image.

Rudolf Arnheim, in his extensive work on visual perception, has shown that the dichotomy between seeing and thinking which runs through much of the Western tradition, is a very problematic one. In *Visual Thinking,* he contends that visual perception is integrally related to thought.[20] It is not the case, according to Arnheim, that the eyes present a kind of raw data to the mind which, in turn, processes it and refines it by thought. Rather, those visual images are the shapers and bearers of thought. Jan Gonda, in writing on the Vedic notion *dhi-*, sometimes translated as "thought," finds similarly that the semantic field of this word in Vedic literature does not correspond as much to our words for "thinking" as it does to our no-

Siva Linga

tions of "insight," "vision," and "seeing."[21] Susanne Langer has also written of the integral relation of thought to the images we see in the "mind's eye." The making of all those images is the fundamental "imaginative" human activity. One might add that it is the fundamental activity of the religious imagination as well. She writes, "Images are, therefore, our readiest instruments for abstracting concepts from the tumbling streams of actual impression."[22]

Seeing is not a passive awareness of visual data, but an active focusing upon it, "touching" it. Arnheim writes, in language that echoes the Hindu notion of seeing and touching: "In looking at an object we reach out for it. With an invisible finger we move through the space around us, go out to the distant places where things are found, touch them, catch them, scan their surfaces, trace their borders, explore their texture. It is an eminently active occupation."[23]

According to Arnheim, the way in which we reach out for and grasp the "object we see, either in our immediate range of perception or through the medium of film, is dependent upon who we are and what we recognize from past experience." The visual imprint of an image, an object, or a scene upon the eye is not at all "objective." In the image-making process of thinking, we see, sort, and recognize according to the visual phenomenology of our own experience.[24] What people notice in the "same" image—be it an image of the dancing Siva or a film of a Hindu festival procession—depends to some extent on what they can recognize from the visual experience of the past. In the case of film, of course, it also depends on what the photographer has seen and chosen to show us. Arnheim writes that the eye and the mind, working together in the process of cognition, cannot simply note down images that are already there." "We find instead that direct observation, far from being a mere ragpicker, is an exploration of the form-seeking, form-imposing mind, which needs to understand but cannot until it casts what it sees into manageable models."[25]

As students, using the film-images of India, we are challenged to begin to be self-conscious of who we are as "seers." Part of the difficulty of entering the world of another culture, especially one with as intricate and elaborate a visual articulation, as India's, is that, for many of us, there are no "manageable models." There are no self-evident ways of recognizing the shapes and forms of art, iconography, ritual life and daily life that we see. Who is Siva, dancing wildly in a ring of fire? What is happening when the priest pours honey and yogurt over the image of Visnu? Why does the woman touch the feet of the ascetic beggar? For those who enter the visible world of India through the medium of film, the onslaught of strange images raises a multitude of questions. These very questions should be the starting point for our learning. Without such self-conscious questioning, we cannot begin to "think" with what we see and we simply dismiss it as strange. Or, worse, we are bound to misinterpret what we see by placing it solely within the context of what we already know from our own world of experience.

It has sometimes been claimed that the photograph is a kind of universal "language," but our reflections here make us question such a claim. Every photograph and film raises the question of point-of-view and perspective—both that of the maker and that of the viewer. And it raises the question of meaning. This "language," like speech, can obstruct as well as facilitate communication and understanding. Sontag writes that if a photograph is supposed to be a "piece of world," we need to know *what* piece of the world it is.[26] We need to inquire after its context. She cites Harold Edgerton's famous photograph of what appears to be a coronet, but is really a splash of milk, and Weston's photograph of what appears to be gathered cloth, but is a close-up of a cabbage-leaf. A picture, such as that of a brahmin priest decorating a Siva *linga* for the evening *arati,* or that of the Goddess Durga standing upon Mahisa may be worth a thousand words, but still we need to know which thousand words.

D. The Image of God

The vivid variety of Hindu deities is visible everywhere in India. Rural India is filled with countless wayside shrines. In every town of some size there are many temples, and every major temple will contain its own panoply of shrines and images. One can see the silver mask of the goddess Durga, or the stone shaft of the Siva *linga,* or the four-armed form of the god Visnu. Over the doorway of a temple or a home sits the plump, orange, elephant-headed Ganesa or the benign and auspicious Laksmi. Moreover, it is not only in temples and homes that one sees the images of the deities. Small icons are mounted at the front of taxis and buses. They decorate the walls of tea stalls, sweet shops, tailors, and movie theatres. They are painted on public buildings and homes by local folk artists. They are carried through the streets in great festival processions.

It is visibly apparent to anyone who visits India or who sees something of India through the medium of film that this is a culture in which the mythic imagination has been very generative. The images and myths of the Hindu imagination constitute a basic cultural vocabulary and a common idiom of discourse. Since India has "written" prolifically in its images, learning to read its mythology and iconography is a primary task for the student of Hinduism. In learning about Hinduism, it might be argued that perhaps it makes more sense to begin with Ganesa, the elephant-headed god who sits at the thresholds of space and time and who blesses all beginnings, and then

Durga as the Slayer of the Buffalo Demon
India, Pallava, 8th century
Height: 1.5 cm.

DENMAN WALDO ROSS COLLECTION, 27.171.
COURTESY, MUSEUM OF FINE ARTS, BOSTON

proceed through the deities of the Hindu pantheon, rather than to begin with the Indus Valley civilization and proceed through the ages of Hindu history. Certainly for a student who wishes to visit India, the development of a basic iconographic vocabulary is essential, for deities such as the monkey Hanuman or the fierce Kali confront one at every turn.

When the first European traders and travelers visited India, they were astonished at the multitude of images of

गणेश

Ganesa

the various deities which they saw here. They called them "idols" and described them with combined fascination and repugnance. For example, Ralph Fitch, who traveled as a merchant through north India in the 1500s writes of the images of deities in Varanasi (Benares): "Their chiefe idols bee blacke and evill favoured, their mouths monstrous, their eares gilded and full of jewels, their teeth and eyes of gold, silver and glasse, some having one thing in their hands and some another."[27]

Fitch had no interpretive categories, save those of a very general Western Christian background, with which to make sense of what he saw. Three hundred years did little to aid interpretation. When M. A. Sherring lived in Benares in the middle of the 1800s he could still write, after studying the city for a long time, of "the worship of uncouth idols, of monsters, of the linga and other indecent figures, and of a multitude of grotesque, ill-shapen, and hideous objects."[28] When Mark Twain traveled through India in the last decade of the nineteenth century, he brought a certain imaginative humor to the array of "idols" in Benares, but he remained without what Arnheim would call "manageable models" for placing the visible data of India in a recognizable context. Of the

"idols" he wrote, "And what a swarm of them there is! The town is a vast museum of idols—and all of them crude, misshapen, and ugly. They flock through one's dreams at night, a wild mob of nightmares."[29]

Without some interpretation, some visual hermeneutic, icons and images can be alienating rather than enlightening. Instead of being keys to understanding, they can kindle xenophobia and pose barriers to understanding by appearing as a "wild mob of nightmares," utterly foreign to and unassimilable by our minds. To understand India, we need to raise our eyes from the book to the image, but we also need some means of interpreting and comprehending the images we see.

The bafflement of many who first behold the array of Hindu images springs from the deep-rooted Western antagonism of imaging the divine at all. The Hebraic hostility to "graven images" expressed in the Commandments is echoed repeatedly in the Hebrew Bible: "You shall not make for yourself a graven image, or any likeness of anything that is in heaven above, or that is in the earth beneath, or that is in the water under the earth."

The Hebraic resistance to imaging the divine has combined with a certain distrust of the senses in the world of the Greek tradition as well. While the Greeks were famous for their anthropomorphic images of the gods, the prevalent suspicion in the philosophies of classical Greece was that "what the eyes reported was not true."[30] Like those of dim vision in Plato's cave, it was thought that people generally accept the mere shadows of reality as "true." Nevertheless, if dim vision described human perception of the ordinary world, the Greeks continued to use the notion of true vision to describe wisdom, that which is seen directly in the full light of day rather than obliquely in the shadowy light of the cave. Arnheim writes, "The Greeks learned to distrust the senses, but they never forgot that direct vision is the first and final source of wisdom. They refined the techniques of reasoning, but they also believed that, in the words of Aristotle, 'the soul never thinks without an image.'"[31]

On the whole, it would be fair to say that the Western traditions, especially the religious traditions of the "Book"—Judaism, Christianity, and Islam—have trusted the Word more than the Image as a mediator of the divine truth. The Qur'an and the Hebrew Bible are filled with injunctions to "proclaim" and to "hear" the word. The ears were somehow more trustworthy than the eyes. In the Christian tradition this suspicion of the eyes and the image has been a particularly Protestant position.

And yet the visible image has not been without some force in the religious thinking of the West. The verbal icon of God as "Father" or "King" has had considerable power in the shaping the Judeo-Christian religious imagination. The Orthodox Christian traditions, after much debate in the eighth and ninth centuries, granted an important place to the honoring of icons as those "windows" through which one might look toward God. They were careful, however, to say that the icon should not be "realistic" and should be only two-dimensional. In the Catholic tradition as well, the art and iconography, especially of Mary and the saints, has had a long and rich history. And all three traditions of the "Book" have developed the art of embellishing the word into a virtual icon in the elaboration of calligraphic and decorative arts. Finally, it should be said that there is a great diversity within each of these traditions. The Mexican villager who comes on his knees to the Virgin of Guadalupe, leaves a bundle of beans, and lights a candle, would no doubt feel more at home in a Hindu temple than in a stark, white New England Protestant church. Similarly, see the Moroccan Muslim woman who visits the shrines of Muslim saints, would find India less foreign than did the eleventh century Muslim scholar Alberuni, who wrote that "the Hindus entirely differ from us in every respect."[32]

Worshiping as God those "things" which are not God has been despised in the Western traditions as "idolatry," a mere bowing down to "sticks and stones." The difficulty with such a view of idolatry, however, is that anyone who bows down to such things clearly does not understand them to be sticks and stones. No people would identify themselves as "idolators," by faith. Thus, idolatry can be only an outsider's term for the symbols and visual images of some other culture. Theodore Roszak, writing in *Where the Wasteland Ends,* locates the "sin of idolatry" precisely where it belongs: in the eye of the beholder.[33]

In beginning to understand the consciousness of the Hindu worshiper who bows to "sticks and stones," an anecdote of the Indian novelist U. R. Anantha Murthy is provocative. He tells of an artist friend who was studying folk art in rural north India. Looking into one hut, he saw a stone daubed with red *kunkum* powder, and he asked the villager if he might bring the stone outside to photograph it. The villager agreed, and after the artist had photographed the stone he realized that he might have polluted this sacred object by moving it outside. Horrified, he apologized to the villager, who replied, "it doesn't matter. I will have to bring another stone and anoint *kunkum* on it." Anantha Murthy comments, "Any piece of stone on which he put *kunkum* became God for the peasant. What mattered was his faith, not the stone."[34] We might add that, of course, the stone matters too. If it did not, the peasant would not bother with a stone at all.

Unlike the zealous Protestant missionaries of a century ago, we are not much given to the use of the term "idolatry" to condemn what "other people" do. Yet those who misunderstood have still left us with the task of understanding, and they have raised an important and subtle issue in the comparative study of religion: What is the nature of the divine image? Is it considered to be intrinsically sacred? Is it a symbol of the sacred? a mediator of the sacred? How are images made, consecrated, and used, and what does this tell us about the way they are understood? But still another question remains to be addressed

before we take up these topics. That is the question of the multitude of images. Why are there so many gods?...

Footnotes

* See the use of the term in *An Indian Pilgrimage: Ramdevra* and *An Indian Pilgrimage: Kashi*. The word *auspicious (mangala, subha)* reminds us that there is no Sanskrit term which quite corresponds to what we mean by "sacred."

** Swami Karpatri is one of the *sadhus* profiled in *Four Holy Men: Renunciation in Hindu Society* by M. R. Binford, M. Camerini, and J. Elder (Contemporary South Asian Film Series). Seeking the *darsan* of *sadhus* is seen in a number of places in this film.

*** See H. Daniel Smith, *Bathing the Image of God* and *How a Hindu Worships at the Home Shrine* (Image India Series) for the best films of ordinary temple and home *puja*.

Notes

1. Victor and Edith Turner, *Image and Pilgrimage in Christian Culture* (New York: Columbia University Press, 1978). See especially Chapter 4, "Iconophily and Iconoclasm in Marian Pilgrimage."
2. Agehananda Bharati, *The Ochre Robe* (New York: Doubleday and Co., Inc., 1970), p. 161.
3. Charlotte Vaudeville, conversation, April 1980.
4. Bhagavad Gita 11.8.
5. Jan Gonda, *Eye and Gaze in the Veda* (Amsterdam: North-Holland Publishing Company, 1969).
6. Such an instance is cited in Margaret Stevenson, *The Rites of the Twice-Born* (1920, reprint ed., New Delhi: Oriental Books, 1971), p. 414.
7. In the Jagannath deities, Krsna is the black one on the right; his brother Balarama is white and is on the left; their sister Subhadra is yellow and is between them. See II.C below for a description of their creation and consecration.
8. Stella Kramrisch, *The Hindu Temple*, 2 vols. (1946, reprint ed., Delhi: Motilal Banarsidass, 1976), p. 136.
9. Gonda, *Eye and Gaze in the Veda*, p. 19.
10. Daniel H. H. Ingalls, *Sanskrit Poetry from Vidyakara's "Treasury"* (Cambridge: Harvard University Press, 1965), p. 138 ff.
11. Ingalls, p. 138.
12. Gonda, *Eye and Gaze in the Veda*, p. 4.
13. Cited in Gonda, *Eye and Gaze in the Veda*, p. 9.
14. Jan Gonda, *The Vision of the Vedic Poets* (The Hague: Mouton & Co., 1963), p. 28.
15. Gonda, *The Vision of the Vedic Poets*, p. 25.
16. E. M. Forster, *A Passage to India* (1924, reprint, Harmondsworth, England: Penguin Books Limited, 1974), p. 288.
17. Rudolf Arnheim, *Visual Thinking* (Berkeley: University of California Press, 1969), p. 3.
18. Susan Sontag, *On Photography* (New York: Farrar, Straus and Giroux, 1977).
19. Sontag, p. 115.
20. Arnheim, Chapter 2, "The Intelligence of Visual Perception."
21. Gonda, *The Vision of the Vedic Poets*, Chapter I, "Introduction" and Chapter II, "'Dhih' in the Rg Veda."
22. Susanne K. Langer, *Philosophy in a New Key*, 3rd edition (Cambridge: Harvard University Press, 1942), p. 145.
23. Arnheim, p. 19.
24. Arnheim, Chapter 5, "The Past in the Present" and Chapter 6, "The Images of Thought."

25. Arnheim, p. 278.
26. Sontag, p. 93.
27. William Foster, ed., *Early Travels in Indian 1583–1619* (London: Oxford University Press, 1921), p. 23.
28. M. A. Sherring, *The Sacred City of the Hindus* (London: Trubner & Co., 1868), p. 37.
29. Mark Twain, *Following the Equator* (Hartford, Connecticut: The American Publishing Company, 1898), p. 504.
30. Arnheim, p. 5.
31. Arnheim, p. 12.

32. Edward C. Sachau, ed., *Alberuni's India* (Delhi: S. Chand & Co., 1964), p. 17.
33. Theodore Roszak, *Where the Wasteland Ends* (Garden City, New York: Doubleday & Co., 1972), Chapter 4, "The Sin of Idolatry."
34. U. R. Anantha Murthy, "Search for an Identity: A Viewpoint of a Kannada Writer," in Sudhir Kakar, ed., *Identity and Adulthood* (Delhi: Oxford University Press, 1979), pp. 109–110.

The Hindu Ethic of
NONVIOLENCE

Mankind's survival is at risk. Our problems proliferate, our global predicament deepens daily. Humanity direly needs spiritual direction and new-found wisdom if it is to endure. Hinduism, Buddhism, and Jainism have for millenia been teaching noninjury, called *ahimsa,* as a spiritual principle and practical ethic. On these four pages we look at what Hinduism tells us about not causing others pain. Many are the sources of Hindu thought which inspire men and women to live the ideals of compassion and nonviolence. The *rishis* who revealed the principles of *dharma,* or divine law, in Hindu scripture knew full well the potential for human suffering and the path which could avert it. To them a one spiritual power flowed in and through all things in this universe, animate and inanimate, conferring existence by its presence. To them life was a coherent process leading all souls without exception to enlightenment, and no violence could be carried to the higher reaches of that ascent.

The rishis were mystics whose revelation disclosed a cosmos in which all beings exist in interlaced dependence. The whole was contained in the part, and the part in the whole. Based on this cognition, they taught a philosophy of non-difference of self and other, asserting that in the final analysis we are not separate from the world and its manifest forms nor from the Divine which shines forth in all things and all peoples. From this understanding of oneness arose the philosophical basis for the practice of noninjury and Hinduism's ancient commitment to it.

We all know that Hindus, who are one-sixth of the human race today, believe in the existence of God everywhere, as an all-pervasive, self-effulgent energy and consciousness. This basic belief creates the attitude of sublime tolerance and acceptance toward others. Even tolerance is insufficient to describe the compassion and reverence the Hindu holds for the intrinsic sacredness within all things. Therefore, the actions of all Hindus are rendered benign or ahimsa. One would not want to hurt something which one revered.

On the other hand, when the fundamentalists of any religion teach an unrelenting duality based on good and evil, man and nature or God and Devil, this creates friends and enemies. This belief is a sacrilege to Hindus because they know that the attitudes which are the by-product are totally dualistic, and for good to triumph over that which is alien or evil, it must kill out that which is considered to be evil.

In Sanskrit *himsa* is doing harm or causing injury. The "a" placed before the word negates it. Very simply, *ahimsa* is abstaining from causing hurt or harm. It is gentleness and noninjury, whether physical, mental or emotional. It is good to know that nonviolence speaks only to the most extreme forms of wrongdoing, while *ahimsa* (which includes not killing) goes much deeper to prohibit the subtle abuse and the simple hurt.

> Nonviolence, truth, freedom from anger, renunciation, serenity, aversion to fault-finding, sympathy for all beings, peace from greedy cravings, gentleness, modesty, steadiness, energy, forgiveness, fortitude, purity, a good will, freedom from pride—these belong to a man who is born for heaven.
> —BHAGAVAD GITA 16. 2-3

Beliefs, attitudes and actions interact to produce peace or violence. The *Brihadaranyaka Upanishad* (IV, 4, ii, 6) says: "Here they say that a person consists of desires. And as is his desire, so is his will. And as is his will, so is his deed; and whatever deed he does, that he will reap." Two thousand years ago South India's weaver saint Tiruvalluvar said it so simply, "All suffering recoils on the wrongdoer himself. Therefore, those who desire not to suffer refrain from causing others pain."

Because of the knowledge of reincarnation, the Hindu knows that he may one day be in the same position of anyone he might be inclined to harm or persecute. The Hindu who is consciously aware within his soul knows that he is the time traveller and may incarnate, take a body of flesh, in the society he most opposed, in order to equalize his hates and fears into a greater understanding which would result in the release of ignorance. The knowledgeable Hindu is well aware of all these possibilities. *Ahimsa* is certainly not cowardice; it is wisdom. And wisdom is the cumulative knowledge of the existing divine laws of reincarnation, *karma, dharma,* the all-pervasiveness and sacredness of things, blended together within the psyche or soul of the Hindu.

> **Here they say that a person consists of desires. And as his desire, so is his will. And as is his will, so is his deed; and whatever deed he does, that he will reap.**
> **—Brihadaranyaka Upanishad IV, 4, ii, 6**

There is a spiritual urge in every soul for peace. Even if a person is violent now, he or she inwardly yearns for peace. Man is essentially an instinctive, intellectual and superconscious, or soul, person. The instinctive nature is based on good and bad, mine and yours, up and down pairs of opposites. The soul nature is based on oneness, humility, peace, compassion, love, helpfulness. The intellectual nature is based on trying to figure both of these two out. It juggles knowledge from the lower nature to the higher nature and from higher nature to the lower nature. It works our formulas, finds solutions and processes knowledge.

The key is *yoga,* yoking the soul with the energies of the physical body (the instinctive nature) and yoking the energies of the soul with the energies of the mind (intellectual nature) and then, simply, one becomes consciously conscious in the soul. This is an experience to be experienced, and for the Hindu it is personal experience of God which is essential for liberation. The Hindu strives to be consciously conscious of his soul. When those soulful qualities are unfolded, he is filled with a divine love and would not hurt a flea if he could help it.

Scriptures Speak on Noninjury

To the heavens be peace, to the sky and the earth; to the waters be peace, to plants and all trees; to the Gods be peace, to Brahman be peace, to all men be peace, again and again—peace also to me!

Shukla Yajur Veda 36.17

If we have injured space, the earth or heaven, or if we have offended mother or father, from that may Agni, fire of the house, absolve us and guide us safely to the world of goodness.

Atharva Veda 6.120.1

Protect both our species, two-legged and four-legged. Both food and water for their needs supply. May they with us increase in stature and strength. Save us from hurt all our Days, O Powers!

Rig Veda 10.37.11

When mindstuff is firmly based in waves of ahimsa all living beings cease their enmity in the presence of such a person.

Yoga Sutra 2.35

O earthen vessel, strengthen me. May all beings regard me with friendly eyes! May I look upon all creatures with friendly eyes! With a friend's eye may we regard each other!

Shukla Yajur Veda 36.18

He who sees that the Lord of all is ever the same in all that is—immortal in the field of mortality—he sees the truth. And when a man sees that the God in himself is the same God in all that is, he hurts not himself by hurting others. Then he goes, indeed, to the highest path.

Bhagavad Gita 13:27–28

AHIMSA

Exploring Noninjury as a Way to Achieve Harmony with Our Environment, Peace Between Peoples and Compassion Within Ourselves.

What Is the Great Virtue Called Ahimsa?

Ahimsa, or noninjury, is the first and foremost ethical principle of every Hindu. It is gentleness and nonviolence, whether physical, mental or emotional. It is abstaining from causing hurt or harm to all beings. Aum.

To the Hindu the ground is sacred. The rivers are sacred. The sky is sacred. The sun is sacred. His wife is a Goddess. Her husband is a God. Their children are *devas.* Their home is a shrine. Life is a pilgrimage to liberation from rebirth, and no violence can be carried to the higher reaches of that ascent. While nonviolence speaks only to the most extreme forms of wrongdoing, *ahimsa,* which includes not killing, goes much deeper to prohibit the subtle abuse and the simple hurt. Rishi Patanjali described *ahimsa* as the great vow and foremost spiritual discipline which Truth-seekers must follow strictly and without fail. This extends to harm of all kinds caused by one's thoughts, words and deeds—including injury to the natural environment. Even the intent to injure, even violence committed in a dream, is a violation of *ahimsa.* Vedic *rishis* who revealed *dharma* proclaimed *ahimsa* as the way to achieve harmony with our environment, peace between peoples and compassion within ourselves. The Vedic edict is: "*Ahimsa* is not causing pain to any living being at any time through the actions of one's mind, speech or body." Aum Namah Sivaya.

What Is the Inner Source of Noninjury?

Two beliefs form the philosophical basis of noninjury. The first is the law of *karma,* by which harm caused to others unfailingly returns to oneself. The second is that the Divine shines forth in all peoples and things. Aum.

The Hindu is thoroughly convinced that violence he commits will return to him by a cosmic process that is unerring. He knows that, by *karma's* law, what we have done to others will be done to us, if not in this life then in another. He knows that he may one day be in the same position of anyone he is inclined to harm or persecute, perhaps incarnating in the society he most opposed in order to equalize his hates and fears into a greater understanding. The belief in the existence of God everywhere, as an all-pervasive, self-effulgent energy and consciousness, creates the attitude of sublime tolerance and acceptance toward others. Even *tolerance* is insufficient to describe the compassion and reverence the Hindu holds for the intrinsic sacredness within all things. Therefore, the actions of all Hindus living in the higher nature are rendered benign, or *ahimsa.* One would not hurt that which he reveres. The *Vedas* pronounce, "He who, dwelling in all things, yet is other than all things, whom all things do not know, whose body all things are, who controls all things from within—He is your soul, the Inner Controller, the Immortal." Aum Namah Sivaya.

What Is the Inner Source of Violence?

Violence is a reflection of lower, instinctive consciousness—fear, anger, greed, jealousy and hate—based in the mentality of separateness and unconnectedness, of good and bad, winners and losers, mine and yours. Aum. Every belief creates certain attitudes. Attitudes govern our actions. Our actions can thus be traced to our inmost beliefs about ourself and the world around us. If those beliefs are erroneous, our actions will not be in tune with the universal *dharma.* For instance, the beliefs in the duality of self and other, of eternal heaven and hell, victors and vanquished, white forces and dark forces, create the attitudes that we must be on our guard, and are justified in giving injury, physically, mentally and emotionally to those whom we judge as bad, pagan, alien or unworthy. Such thinking leads to rationalizing so-called righteous wars and conflicts. As long as our beliefs are dualistic, we will continue to generate antagonism, and that will erupt here and there in violence. Those living in the lower, instinctive nature are society's antagonists. They are self-assertive, territorial, competitive, jealous, angry, fearful and rarely penitent of their hurtfulness. Many take sport in killing for the sake of killing, thieving for the sake of theft. The *Vedas* indicate, "This soul, verily, is overcome by nature's qualities. Now, because of being overcome, he goes on to confusedness." Aum Namah Sivaya.

Is Vegetarianism Integral to Noninjury?

Hindus teach vegetarianism as a way to live with a minimum of hurt to other beings, for to consume meat, fish, fowl or eggs is to participate indirectly in acts of cruelty and violence against the animal kingdom. Aum.

The abhorrence of injury and killing of any kind leads quite naturally to a vegetarian diet, *shakahara.* The meat-eater's desire for meat drives another to kill and provide that meat. The act of the butcher begins with the desire of the consumer. Meat-eating contributes to a mentality of violence, for with the chemically complex meat ingested, one absorbs the slaughtered creature's fear, pain and terror. These qualities are nourished within the meat-eater, perpetuating the cycle of cruelty and confusion. When the individuals' consciousness lifts and expands, he will abhor violence and not be able to even digest the meat, fish, fowl and eggs he was formerly consuming. India's greatest saints have confirmed that one cannot eat meat and live a peaceful, harmonious life. Man's appetite for meat inflicts devastating harm on the earth itself, stripping its precious forests to make way for pastures. The *Tirukural* candidly states, "How can he practice true compassion who eats the flesh of an animal to fatten his own flesh? Greater than a thousand *ghee* offerings consumed in sacrificial fires is not to sacrifice and consume any living creature." Aum Namah Sivaya.

How Can Peace on Earth Be Achieved?

Peace is a reflection of spiritual consciousness. It begins within each person, and extends to the home, neighborhood, nation and beyond. It comes when the higher nature takes charge of the lower nature. Aum Namah Sivaya.

Until we have peace in our own heart, we can't hope for peace in the world. Peace is the natural state of the mind. It is there, inside, to be discovered in meditation, maintained through self-control, and then radiated out to others. The best way to promote peace is to teach families to be peaceful within their own homes by settling all conflicts quickly. At a national and international level, we will enjoy more peace as we become more tolerant. Religious leaders can help by teaching their congregations how to live in a world of differences without feeling threatened, without forcing their ways or will on others. World bodies can make laws which deplore and work to prevent crimes of violence. It is only when the higher-nature people are in charge that peace will truly come. There is no other way, because the problems of conflict reside within the low-minded group who only know retaliation as a way of life. The *Vedas* beseech, "Peace be to the earth and to airy spaces! Peace be to heaven, peace to the waters, peace to the plants and peace to the trees! May all the Gods grant to me peace! By this invocation of peace may peace be diffused!" Aum Namah Sivaya.

Ahimsa is the highest dharma. It is the highest
purification. It is also the highest truth
from which all dharma proceeds.
—Mahabharata XVIII: 1125.25

An individual can find total peace within himself, not through meditation alone—for peaceful actions must follow introspection—not through drugs, not through psychology or psychiatry, but through control. Peace is the natural state of the mind. It is there, inside, to be discovered in meditation and then radiated out to others. How do we bring individuals to this point? Of course, if the educational system promotes it, in every community the greatest potential for peace will be achieved. The educational system is controlled by the adults, so they have to come to terms with the fact that they must not be hurtful—physically, mentally or emotionally—and accept the basic principles of the Sanatana Dharma: all-pervasive energy, cause and effect and coming back in a physical birth until all scores are settled. Once the adults accomplish this, these basic principles of life will naturally be passed on to the next generation.

Ahimsa begins in the home, in the bedroom, in the kitchen, in the garden, in the living room. When *himsa,* harmfulness, arises in the home, it must be settled before sleep, or else those *vrittis,* those waves of the mind, which were disturbed by the creation of the situation, will go to seed to erupt at a later time in life. We cannot expect the children to control themselves if the parents do not control themselves. Those who attain a personal peace by controlling their instinctive nature become the spiritual leaders of human society. People who do become these leaders retroactively control the masses because of their spirit, their soul force—not because of the mind force, their cleverness, their deceptions, their political power, their money or contacts. Peaceful homes breed gentle people. Gentle people follow *ahimsa.*

From *Hinduism Today,* February 1996, pp. 11-14. © 1996 by Hinduism Today.

The Sacred Is the One True Reality of Brahman

Swami Nikhilananda

Swami Nikhilananda has written extensively about Hinduism in English and so helped bring a knowledge of this ancient religion to Western readers. Here he tries to explain the basic Hindu concept of "Brahman," the sacred reality that is the basis of all existence. Although Brahman can be spoken about in its "conditioned" aspect as a personal god one worships, this is only the way in which our minds seek to express this inexpressible reality. Brahman in itself—the absolute or "unconditioned" Brahman—is the "Being" which is presupposed in all beings, so we can never perceive Brahman except in the form of other beings. Brahman is the real within all of us, the same as the soul or inner true self (what Hindus call "atman") within human consciousness. It is the substance of all things and all people, and so can be seen everywhere—even though it is never seen in its pure unconditioned state. It is the universe as well as the mind by which we perceive the universe. In fact, there is only Brahman; no other reality exists but this One Reality. Hence the Sacred is not a God who is fundamentally different from us, ultimately; rather, what we call God and World are in fact the same reality. In rejecting the illusion of duality, one comes to see that all things are the one Brahman.

Questions

1. In what sense can Brahman be said to be infinite and yet "smaller than a mustard seed," according to Nikhilananda?
2. How is the "existence" of Brahman both like and unlike our own existence, in Nikhilananda's view?
3. Why does Nikhilananda believe that the nature of Brahman can be called "bliss" and "knowledge"?

As early as Vedic times, the Indo-Aryan thinkers investigated the nature of reality from two levels of experience, one of which may be called the absolute, acosmic, or transcendental level and the other the relative, cosmic, or phenomenal level. At the phenomenal level one perceives the universe of diversity and is aware of one's own individual ego, whereas at the transcendental level all differences merge into an inexplicable non-dual consciousness. Both of these levels of experience are real from their respective standpoints, though what is perceived at one level may be negated at the other.

In the Vedas, reality experienced at the transcendental level is called Brahman. This term denotes a non-dual pure consciousness which pervades the universe and yet remains outside it. Brahman is described as the first principle; from it all things are derived, by it all are supported, and into it all finally disappear. In Brahman alone the apparent differences of the phenomenal world are unified. According to the nondualistic Vedanta philosophy, Brahman is identical with the self of man, known as atman.

Etymologically, the word *Brahman* denotes an entity whose greatness, powers, or expansion no one can measure. The word *atman* signifies the consciousness in man which experiences gross objects during the waking state, subtle objects during the dream state, and the bliss arising from absence of the duality of subject and object in dreamless sleep.

Let us try to understand the nature of Brahman in both its aspects: transcendental and phenomenal. The Upanishads speak of the transcendental Brahman as devoid of qualifying attributes and indicative marks, and of the phenomenal Brahman as endowed with them. The attributeless Brahman is called the supreme or unconditioned Brahman, and the other the inferior or conditioned Brahman. The supreme Brahman, or pure being, is described by a negative method in such striking passages as: "Not this, not this," or "Where there is duality, as it were, one sees another, but when only the self is all this, how should one see another?" The conditioned Brahman, on the other hand, has been described by such positive statements as: "Whose body is spirit, whose form is light, whose thoughts are true, whose nature is like akasa, from whom all works, all desires, all odours proceed." The Upanishads generally designate the conditioned Brahman by the masculine *He* and the unconditioned Brahman by the neuter *it*.

"THESE RIVERS, MY DEAR, FLOW, the eastern toward the east, the western toward the west. They go just from the ocean to the ocean. They become the ocean itself. As there they know not 'I am this one,' 'I am that one'—even so, indeed, my dear, all creatures here, though they have come forth from Being, know not 'We have come forth from Being.' Whatever they are in this world, whether tiger, or lion, or wolf, or boar, or worm, or fly, or gnat, or mosquito, that they become.

"That which is the finest essence—this whole world has that as its self. That is Reality. That is *Atman*. That art though, Svetaketu...."

Chandogya Upanishad, VI.X.1–3
quoted in *A Source Book in Indian Philosophy*, 1957.

There is no real conflict between the two Brahmans; for Brahman is one and without a second, and can be regarded either from the phenomenal or from the transcendental point of view. When the sense-perceived world is regarded as real, Brahman is spoken of as its omnipotent and omniscient Creator, Preserver, and Destroyer. But when the world is not perceived to exist, as for instance a deep meditation, then one experiences Brahman as the unconditioned Absolute; the idea of a Creator, omnipotent and omniscient, becomes irrelevant. One worships the conditioned Brahman in the ordinary state of consciousness; but one loses one's individuality in the experience of the unconditioned Brahman. The transcendental Brahman appears as the cause of the universe in association with maya, and becomes known as the conditioned Brahman or Brahman with attributes, or by such other epithets as the Lord and the Personal God.

Let us consider the unconditioned Brahman. Indescribable in words, it is indicated by the Vedas as that "from which all speech, together with the mind, turns away, unable to reach it." Ramakrishna has said that all the scriptures and all the statements of holy men have been polluted, as it were, like food that has come in contact with the tongue; Brahman alone remains unpolluted, because it has never come in contact with any tongue. He used to say, further, that he had to come down three levels, so to speak, from the experience of non-duality before he could utter the word *Om*, a holy symbol of Brahman. Experienced as silence, the attributeless Brahman is described as "not that which is conscious of the external (objective) world, nor that which is conscious of the internal (subjective) world, nor that which is conscious of both, nor that which is a mass of sentiency, nor that which is simple consciousness, nor that which is insentient. It is unperceived [by any sense-organ], unrelated [to anything], incomprehensible [to the mind], uninferable, unthinkable, indescribable."

Sometimes the Upanishads ascribe to the unconditioned Brahman irreconcilable attributes in order to deny to it all empirical predicates and indicate that it is totally other than anything we know: "That non-dual Brahman, though never stirring, is swifter than the wind. Though sitting still it travels far; though lying down it goes everywhere." "It is subtler than an atom and greater than the great." The opposing predicates in these passages are ascribed to Brahman in such a manner that they cancel each other, leaving to the mind the idea of an indefinable pure consciousness free of all attributes. Though nothing definite can be predicated of Brahman, yet the search for it is not futile. The Upanishads repeatedly say that its realization is the supreme purpose of life, because it bestows immortality. When Brahman is known all is known.

The unconditioned Brahman is free from the limiting adjuncts of space, time, and causation. In describing Brahman as infinitely great and infinitely small, the Upanishads only point out that it is absolutely spaceless. It is "one and infinite: infinite in the east, infinite in the south, infinite in the west, infinite in the north, above and below and everywhere infinite. The east and the other directions do not exist for it—no athwart, no beneath, no above. The supreme Brahman is not to be fixed; it is unlimited, unborn, not to be reasoned about, not to be conceived." "It is my self within the heart, smaller than a corn of rice, smaller than a corn of barley, smaller than a mustard seed, smaller than a canary seed or the kernel of a canary seed. It is my self within the heart, greater than the earth, greater than the sky, greater than heaven, greater than all these worlds."

The timelessness of the unconditioned Brahman is indicated by the statement that it is free from the limitations of past, present, and future. Sometimes it is described as eternal, without beginning or end; sometimes as momentary, involving no time at all. Brahman is "what they say was, is and will be." It is that "at whose feet, rolling on, the year with its days passes by." "It is like a flash of lightning; it is like a wink of the eye."

Brahman is independent of causation. The law of cause and effect operates only in the realm of becoming, or manifestation, and cannot affect pure being. Brahman, according to the Vedas, is not born; it does not die. But from the level of relative experience Brahman is described as the cause of the universe.

Brahman is unknown and unknowable. To be known, a thing must be made an object. Brahman, as pure consciousness, is the eternal subject, and therefore cannot be made an object of knowledge. "You cannot see that which is the seer of seeing; you cannot hear that which is the hearer of hearing; you cannot think of that which is the thinker of thought; you cannot know that which is the knower of knowing." Brahman is unknowable for still another reason: it is infinite. What is the infinite? "Where one sees nothing else, hears nothing else, understands nothing else—that is the infinite. Where ones sees something else, hears something else, understands something else—that is the finite. The infinite is immortal; the finite, mortal."

Hindu philosophers often describe the unconditioned Brahman as Satchidananda, existence-knowledge-bliss pure and absolute. Existence, knowledge, and bliss are not attributes of reality; they are its very stuff. Pure existence is the same as pure knowledge and pure bliss. The word *existence* indicates that Brahman is not non-existence; the phenomenal universe, which is perceived to exist, cannot have been produced from nothing. But Brahman does not exist as an empirical object—like a pot or a tree, for instance—but as absolute existence, without which material objects would not be perceived to exist. Just as a mirage could not be seen without the desert, which is its unrelated substratum, so also the universe could not be seen if Brahman did not exist as its substratum. When the process of negation is carried on, step by step, there always remains a residuum of existence which cannot be negated. No object, illusory or otherwise, could exist without the foundation of an immutable existence—and that existence is Brahman. Therefore the term *existence*, as applied to Brahman, is to be understood as the negation of both empirical reality and its correlative, unreality. Whether the universe is seen or not seen, Brahman remains as the witness-consciousness. Brahman is often described as the "reality of reality," that is to say, the reality of the tangible world whose empirical reality is accepted.

Brahman is knowledge or intelligence. The identity of Brahman and atman, or the self, has been expressed in the well-known Vedic formula "that thou art." The very conception of atman in the Upanishads implies that it is the knowing subject within us. It is the inner consciousness and the real agent of perception, the senses being mere instruments. Perception, which is a conscious act, is impossible without the presence of a sentient principle, which is atman. "He who says: 'Let me smell this'—he is atman; the tongue is the instrument of speaking. He who says: 'Let me hear this'—he is atman; the ear is the instrument of hearing. He who says: 'Let me think this'—he is atman; the mind is his divine eye." "Into him, as eye, all forms are gathered; by the eye he reaches all forms. Into him, as ear, all sounds are gathered; by the ear he reaches all sounds." Because Brahman is identical with atman, Brahman is consciousness, knowledge, light. It is self-luminous and needs no other light to illumine itself. "It is the light of lights; it is that which they know who know the self." All material objects, such as trees, rivers, houses, and forests, are illumined by the sun. But the light that illumines the sun is the light of Brahman. "The sun does not shine there, nor the moon and the stars, nor these lightings, not to speak of this fire. When he shines everything shines after him; by his light everything is lighted." "The universe is guided by knowledge, it is grounded in knowledge, it is governed by knowledge; knowledge is its foundation. Knowledge is Brahman."

Brahman is bliss because it is knowledge. No real bliss is possible without knowledge. Needless to say, the bliss of Brahman is utterly different from the happiness that a man experiences from agreeable sense-objects; it is characterized by absence of the subject-object relationship. Worldly happiness is but an infinitesimal part of the bliss of Brahman. Again, Brahman is bliss because of the absence of duality in it; friction, fear, jealousy, secretiveness, and the other evils which plague a man's daily life arise from consciousness of duality. Brahman as bliss pervades all objects; that is why there is attraction between husband and wife, parents and children, creature and creature, God and man. Furthermore, Brahman is bliss because it is infinite. There is no real and enduring joy in the finite. The bliss of Brahman cannot be measured by any relative standard, human or other. Through the performance of religious rites and the fulfillment of moral obligations one may experience, after death, different measures of happiness in ascending degrees in the different heavenly worlds. But if a person is completely free from desire and possesses the knowledge of Brahman, he can attain here, before death, the measureless bliss of Brahman.

To summarize what has been said about the unconditioned Brahman, or pure being: Brahman is the negation of all attributes and relations. It is beyond time, space, and causality. Though it is spaceless, without it space could not be conceived; though it is timeless, without it time could not be conceived; though it is causeless, without it the universe, bound by the law of cause and effect, could not be conceived to exist. Only if one admits the reality or pure being as the unchanging ground of creation can one understand proximity in space, succession in time, and interdependence in the chain of cause and effect. Without the unchanging white screen, one cannot relate in time and space the disjoined pictures on a cinema film. Brahman is not a philosophical abstraction, but is more intimately known than any sense-object. It is Brahman that, as the inner consciousness, makes the perception of sense-objects possible. Brahman is the intangible reality that unifies all the discrete objects in the phenomenal universe, making it appear a cosmos and not a chaos. In the Vedas, Brahman is compared to a dike that keeps diverse objects asunder and prevents their clashing together, or again, to a bridge that connects the visible world with the invisible.

From the transcendental standpoint, there exists, therefore, no universe which is other than Brahman. Since Brahman is free from causality, the question of creation does not arise. Nothing is ever produced. Where, on account of ignorance, a man sees names and forms, substance and attributes, causal and other relationships, the knower of reality sees only pure being. To the illumined, nature itself is pure being. Duality being mere illusion, unconditioned pure being is the sole reality.

From *Enduring Issues in Religion*, 1995, pp. 121–128. © 1995 by Greenhaven Press, Inc.

UNIT 4
Buddhism

Unit Selections

Key Points to Consider

- What role does monastic life play in Buddhism? What role does it play in religion in general?

- What is the goal of Zen Buddhism and how do adherents attempt to attain it?

- What role does the teacher/discipline relationship play in Tibetan Buddhism?

- How do rituals for some Japanese Buddhists alleviate the pains of miscarriage and abortion?

- What are some of the major differences between Zen and Jodoshinshu Buddhism?

 **Links: www.dushkin.com/online/**
These sites are annotated in the World Wide Web pages.

Buddhist Studies WWW Virtual Library
http://www.ciolek.com/WWWVL-Buddhism.html

Koan Studies Pages
http://www.ciolek.com/WWWVLPages/ZenPages/KoanStudy.html

Pure Land Buddhism WWW Virtual Library: Jodo-Shinshu
http://www.pitaka.ch/shinshu.htm

Rissho Kosei Kai
http://philtar.ucsm.ac.uk/encyclopedia/easia/rissho.html

Zen Buddhism WWW Virtual Library
http://www.ciolek.com/WWWVL-Zen.html

Buddhism and Jainism (discussed in the previous unit) have a great deal in common. They both originated in the same time period and geographic location, and from similar philosophical roots. Their founders were both born to royal families and were destined to become kings. Each, in his own time, rejected the life of comfort and luxury, seeking instead to transcend the dualistic world of suffering and rebirth to find personal liberation. Consequently, both traditions placed an early emphasis on rejection of attachment to the material world, and their teachings focused on the means to gain eternal liberation. Unlike Jainism, however, Buddhism did not find lasting fertile ground for vitality and growth in its homeland of India, and its center of adherence and influence gradually shifted to East and Southeast Asia, where it became the dominant religion for most countries in these regions.

Because of its relatively early movement outside of India, the Buddhism of the time had not yet become weighted down with extensive tradition, doctrine, and dogma. As a consequence, it still had the ability to ameliorate itself into new cultural environments and adopt aspects of the existing cultural and religious framework of its new lands. Because of this movement and process of adaptation, Buddhism took on a rather unique character in each new place to which it spread. It became, in many ways, "indigenized," reflecting much of the previous religious culture and beliefs as the newly introduced beliefs and practices. This, in turn, helped facilitate its continued existence and growth.

Thus, in looking at Buddhism, one sees diverse cultural manifestations. Chinese Buddhism, for example, reveals definite Confucian and Taoist elements in ritual, beliefs, and practices. This can be seen in such things as its role in ancestor veneration, martial arts, and in temples in which deities from all three traditions are present. In Japan, Buddhist deities became associated with Shinto spirits (*kami*). Here, the two have become so connected that many Japanese see themselves as both Shinto and Buddhist, and many rituals and practices there reflect elements of both traditions. Buddhism in Tibet is an interesting case. The pre-Buddhist religion of Tibet was Bon, a highly ritualized and shamanistic tradition, and the Buddhism of the region is among the most ritualized and shamanistic forms of Buddhism. At the same time, however, it has been Bon that has been more deeply influenced by Tibetan Buddhism than vice versa. Finally, in America, many Buddhist schools and temples show the influence of Christian forms and ideas. In this way, Buddhism is arguably the most culturally diverse of all the major religious traditions today.

This unit takes a look at Buddhism both generically as well as in various cultural manifestations. The first article looks at the role of asceticism and monasticism in early Buddhism and the continuing appeal that the tradition has in the contemporary world. Japanese Zen has its main roots in early Chinese meditation Buddhism (Ch'an) and has become one of the more popular forms of the religion in the Western world. The second article is drawn from the teachings of a Japanese Zen master who lived and taught in America for many years, inspiring many to follow his practices of meditation and mind-stillness. The third article ponders the pivotal role of the spiritual teacher in Tibetan Buddhism and how the teacher-disciple relationship is fundamental to the learning and practice.

Jodoshinshu is a denomination of Pure Land Buddhism, the largest in Japan, and one of the largest worldwide. Its devotional approach and salvational nature make it distinct from many other Buddhist schools. "Shinran and Jodoshinshu" gives an overview of the tradition and its beliefs. The last article in this unit discusses the issue of abortion and the manner in which one Japanese Buddhist school addresses it.

The Beginnings of Buddhism

*Ian Mabbett considers how Buddhism, while preaching the rejection
of society, simultaneously became a popular religion.*

The venerable ascetic Mahavira for a year and a month wore clothes; after that time he walked about naked, and accepted alms in the hollow of his hand. For more than twelve years he neglected his body and abandoned the care of it; with equanimity he bore, underwent and suffered all pleasant or unpleasant occurrences arising from divine powers, men or animals.'

Mahavira (599–527 BC), the most celebrated teacher of the Jain religion in India, cultivated rigorous indifference to his surroundings. He silently endured stoning or dogs being set on him. He fasted, not even drinking, for long periods. He scrupulously harmed no living beings, and for long periods he sat motionless with heart pure and soul serene.

The early Jains like Mahavira were noted for their austerities. They believed that human actions (*karma*) generate a sort of field that controls the individual's later fate. Normally it compels the individual to be reborn after death into another form, human or otherwise; and as all forms of life are inherently unsatisfactory, it is better to withdraw from the world, ceasing to generate any karma; then one might hope not to be reborn but to achieve a transcendent spiritual state.

Mahavira was not unique in his day for this radical withdrawal from society. In the sixth century BC in northern India and Nepal, there were many holy men who had cut off ties with their families and lived rough. They sought spiritual advancement by meditation and ascetic practices, often undergoing severe forms of self-mortification. Some, despite their rejection of society, acquired social prestige.

The Buddha, like his older contemporary Mahavira, was a mendicant monk, and his teaching eventually became a great world religion. To understand its appeal properly, we need some knowledge of the way it worked in its original historical setting. How did a religion that preached the radical rejection of society become a popular movement and an accepted part of that society?

The story of Buddha's life as presented by the Buddhist scriptures (there is little other evidence) is essentially legendary. The scriptural tradition claims he was born as Siddhartha Gautama to a lordly family in the Himalayan foothills in what is now Nepal. 563 BC was long widely accepted as the date of his birth, but this has recently been challenged; it may be up to a century or so too early. As the story goes, it was foretold that he would become either a great ruler or a great holy man, and his parents surrounded him with luxuries to discourage him from any thoughts of a life outside the pleasure-loving court. As a young prince, Gautama became acquainted with the truth of unhappiness in human life only when he escaped the palace and saw for himself the reality of old age, sickness and death. The sight of a holy man, who seemed peaceful and content, finally inspired him to forsake palace, wife and family and become a wandering mendicant. At first he studied under teachers who prescribed rigorous fasting and self-mortification. Eventually, though, he rejected them all, realising that the way to salvation lay in peaceful meditation which could only be compromised by the distractions of physical discomfort. One night, meditating beneath a tree, he finally broke through all the barriers of ignorance and attachment and became enlightened. The title *Buddha*, meaning the Awakened One, applies to him from that moment in his life onward.

The story of the rest of his career represents him as constantly wandering from place to place, offering teachings to all—ordinary people, land-owners, priests and kings alike. It is difficult to distinguish authentic historical information from legends within the accounts given. People must have seen him in much the same way as they saw other mendicant teachers—as a man who cut off all ties with society and suppressed normal human desires, hoping thereby to eliminate the karma that carries normal people through this life and into the next one, and to make himself an empty vessel for some sort of superior spiritual power.

The Buddha accepted the belief in karma, and also the idea that spiri-

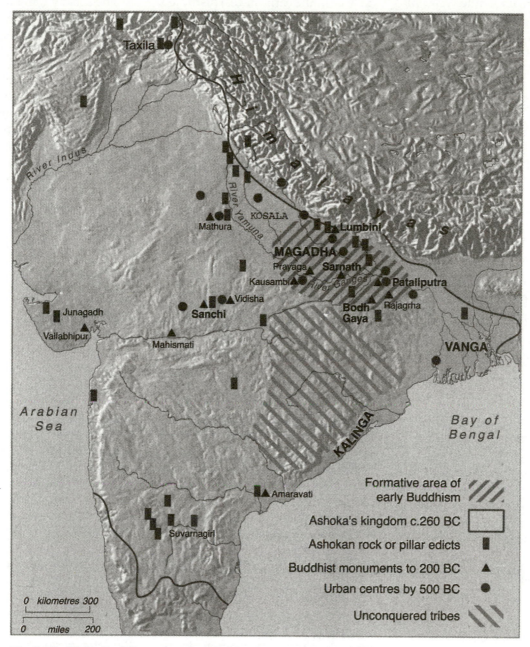

The India of the Buddha saw early urbanisation and the rise of significant kingdoms in the Ganges valley.

tual advance comes through the life of the wandering mendicant. He differed from the other religious leaders in two major respects. His path was called 'the Middle Way', between life in society (seeking pleasures) and the life of a rigorous ascetic (fasting and mortifying the flesh). And his understanding of karma was more psychological than those of other schools—to him, what mattered was not the action as such

but the intention behind it. Spiritual advance came from the cultivation of appropriate attitudes rather than outward behaviour. Buddhism introduced a dimension of morality.

The earliest Buddhist scriptures reflect a clear emphasis upon rigorous psychological self-discipline. Monks were supposed to kill all their emotional attachments, because any such attachment was a barrier to salvation. An early text urged:

Having torn the ties, having broken the net as a fish in the water, being like a fire not returning to the burnt place, let one wander alone like a rhinoceros.

A Buddhist monk must live outside society, putting behind him everything belonging to his old life. The monk was expected to own nothing, live simply, and travel about, meditating and preaching. His life was not meant to be easy.

The Buddha recommended that his followers live only on food scraps, wear only rags, sleep only at the foot of trees and use only urine as medicine. These principles were soon modified, but they represent the spirit of strict self-discipline.

The Buddha favoured lodging in the remote wilderness among woods and forests, where it was quiet, untainted by human presence, utterly secluded and suitable for solitary meditation. What counted above all was the elimination of all forms of attachment. An early text represented the Buddha as praising the life of the wanderer without possessions:

> He who has sons is made unhappy by sons. In the same way, he who has cows is likewise made unhappy by cows; for what gives support causes unhappiness, but he who has no support has no unhappiness.

A story told in another text makes vivid the fact that a monk was, in an important sense, dead to the whole world, including his former family. A monk's former wife comes to find him, hoping to win him back by showing him his baby son, but the monk refuses to take any notice of his wife or the child. He is held up as a model of dedication.

> Then, putting the child down in front of the venerable Sangamaji, she went off, saying, 'There's your child, samana [wandering monk]. Support him!' Then the venerable Sangamaji neither looked at that child nor said anything to him. Then Sangamaji's former wife, before she had gone far, looked back and saw the venerable Sangamaji neither looking at the child nor saying anything to him. On seeing that, she thought to herself: 'This samana is not desirous even of his child.' Then, turning back, she took up the child and went off.

The life of a Buddhist monk involved a strenuous mental discipline. Meditation practice was an elaborate science, serious commitment to which entailed a routine that (at least in the early stages) disrupted the normal pattern of sleeping and waking, producing dreamlike states. Monks devoted themselves to practices producing altered states of consciousness, they favoured isolation, ate and drank only minimally, and went without creature comforts. It is difficult at first to see why a religious movement like this should gain substantial popular support anywhere.

Such a lifestyle does have modern parallels. One example is the 'reeducation' process, popularly known as 'brain-washing', developed particularly in China in the 1950s in an attempt to change the personalities of individuals to fit the image of new Communist man. Another similarity is with the training undergone in modern armies by soldiers in special units. For example, the Ranger School programme at Fort Benning, Georgia, involves stress-producing physical demands, absolutely minimal diet, and prolonged sleep deprivation. All this produces altered states of consciousness, including hallucinations.

Monks in training might well have mistaken hallucinations for evidence of growing psychic powers, though eminent teachers have always cautioned against becoming attached to psychic powers, boasting about them, or regarding them as evidence of spiritual advancement. What the modern parallels help us to see is that, in different societies, some of the same techniques have been developed in order to transform people, eradicating the habits and attitudes that went with their old lives and setting them apart from ordinary people. This is precisely what the Buddhist order was supposed to do—even though it inevitably lost much of this character by becoming popular and growing back, as a respected institution, into the society that it had initially rejected. And despite that rejection of society, Buddhism had always to have enough dealings with society for members to be recruited in the first place, and to survive on the alms of supporters thereafter.

The society known to the Buddha was not primitive. By 600 BC, in the land between the Ganges and the Yamuna rivers, towns had appeared with administrative functions. Though many of the older communities north and west of the urban concentrations on the Ganges remained decentralised, with power residing in assemblies of dominant families (the Buddha himself appears to have come from one of these), but along the lower Ganges, kingdoms appeared, governed by monarchs intent on conquest. The two big kingdoms of Kosala and Magadha both figured in sacred texts as places traversed by the Buddha, who was consulted by their kings for advice. Many of his teachings are represented as having been first uttered while he was visiting their capitals—especially Vaisali, capital of Kosala.

The main advances in material culture became widespread later. By about the fourth century, money became a normal medium of exchange; commerce was expanding and caravans of merchants were risking the perils of the great wilderness areas in pursuit of profits from long-distance trade. By the time of Ashoka, India's first great emperor and proponent of Buddhism, in the late third century BC, writing had been introduced, baked bricks were widely used in construction, and iron tools had come into general use. Buddhism seems by then to have been particularly associated with commerce; in the later period vouched for by inscriptions, monasteries were often close to trading centres, and merchants figured prominently among lay supporters.

By the third century BC, the kingdom of Magadha had eliminated the competition and established an empire with outposts across most of the Indian subcontinent. This empire was founded by Ashoka's grandfather Candragupta (c.321–297 BC). According to tradition, the latter's minister Kautilya, who belonged to the hereditary brahman priesthood, was the author of a book on statecraft (the *Arthashastra*). In its extant form it is likely to date from much later, but what it envisages is an elaborate and centralised bureaucracy under the control of an absolute monarch.

Brahmans like Kautilya could serve kings in senior posts; they became a privileged stratum in society. Already in the Buddha's day, their position had become ambiguous. While Buddhist scriptures use the word *brahman* to denote an ideal holy man of advanced spirituality, at many points they also insisted that brahmans were often corrupt, small-minded, and superstitious or likely to trade on the superstitions of others. One text says that they were so greedy for their fees for assisting at a sacrifice that at the mere smell of one they ran up like dung-eating animals. The rank of brahman could be inherited and this no doubt generated a large class of people qualified as priests but compelled to make a living any way they could. The appeal of wandering mendicant religious teachers like the Buddha lay partly in the contrast between their message and that of the brahmans.

One explanation for the increasing appeal of the Buddha's teaching to the urbanised society of the rising states focuses on the central role of human unhappiness in the Buddha's teaching. The 'Four Noble Truths', said to encapsulate his doctrine, begin with the fact of unhappiness (or, more properly, the fundamental unsatisfactoriness of life, over which we have no control and in which no good things last). This unhappiness (secondly) has a cause (human grasping at impermanent things); the cause (thirdly) can be removed (by eliminating ignorance and grasping); and (last) there is a way to remove this cause by following the Buddha's teachings. This manifesto presupposes dissatisfaction with life, a type of dissatisfaction that is keenly felt and recognised as a problem to be solved. Following this explanation, the misery of poverty-stricken existence made people receptive to a teaching that portrayed life as a vale of tears.

There are problems, though, with this explanation. Why should people—even those who were anxious to do something about their unhappiness—be attracted to such an uncomfortable way of life? If they were poor to begin with, they would scarcely be better off as mendicants wholly dependent on the charity of poor householders. Furthermore, the period of the Buddha's life—in the sixth or fifth century BC—was not a time of misery, but one of expansion and urbanisation. Buddhism, with its prescriptions for an ascetic life outside society, is not the obvious choice for those experiencing urbanisation. And why should merchants, the agents of materialism, be natural allies of ascetics?

A second explanation for the rise of Buddhism uses an opposite argument. The new urban society in the Ganges Valley required a new culture and a new set of values appropriate to larger political units and to a more fluid economic system; Buddhism fitted the bill. This interpretation has become fairly standard among historians who argue that the old religion of the brahman priests, with its animal sacrifices and arcane rituals, was inappropriate to the cosmopolitan city-based kingdoms that were developing, and also to agricultural society, in which animals were scarce resources. By contrast, Jainism and Buddhism (both hostile to the taking of any form of life) offered universal values neutral towards different cultural groups.

There are no doubt elements of truth in these views, but we must not forget that Buddhism appears to have been intended, in its very earliest forms, not as a mass movement but for exceptional individuals who wished to forsake everything in order to seek salvation in solitary meditation. The problem remains—how could a movement that rejected life in society become a social force?

A third explanation for the appeal of Buddhism is put forward by those with an anthropological background. They argue that it did not really reject life in society, but from

the beginning favoured an active role for monks as counsellors, teachers and even priests, playing a full part in the life of the community. It is true that the Buddhist order acquired this sort of social role eventually, but it seems that this happened more as a result of Buddhism's popularity than its cause. It is impossible to overlook the evidence that this was a teaching for an elite of dedicated seekers of enlightenment who were prepared to forsake society and its comforts.

There is also the possibility that the arduous ascetic lifestyle was in fact an important feature of Buddhism's appeal. Recent research conducted by the present writer in collaboration with Dr G. Bailey suggests that ascetic monks who had detached themselves from society were perceived as trustworthy, impartial advocates by people in outlying communities who were suffering the political and economic encroachment of the urban kingdoms, but who lacked ways of coping with this encroachment.

Ultimately, there is no straightforward interpretation of the initial popularity of Buddhism.

There are indications within the scriptures that, almost from the outset, Buddhism began to involve itself more and more with the life of surrounding society. At first, monks were supposed to linger in one place only during the rainy season, but gradually the wandering decreased, so that eventually the retreats evolved into permanent monasteries, and the monks within them entered into a symbiotic relationship with the local lay supporters who supplied them with food and other goods. A large part of the scriptures, the *Vinaya*, sets out the rules that monks were to follow in their monastic life, and includes many details about relations with the laity.

In return for alms, the monks were originally supposed to offer only spiritual teaching, but they did many other things as well. One story cites the bad example of a monk who was supposed to have engaged in a spot of match-making. He made a practice of spying out eligible young men and women and singing their praises to the parents of possible spouses, describing them as beautiful, intelligent, energetic and so forth. In one case, he procured for a certain family a girl who was the daughter of a former prostitute. His efforts to put things right when the girl was mistreated were unavailing, and both the girl and her mother cursed him.

Such stories generally represent the Buddha as disapproving of the behaviour described, and instituting new rules to prohibit it. But the episodes of inappropriate behaviour show that monks must have allowed themselves to be drawn into roles that were not part of the original ascetic programme but which were expected by layfolk, who regarded them as wise men who could be trusted to help them in various ways.

Other examples are furnished by the monk's role as a physician. It is quite possible that the Buddhist order nourished a rich tradition of medical knowledge—perhaps for many centuries a stronger tradition than those of other religious groups; certainly people expected monks to prescribe antidotes and potions for various purposes. One story tells of a monk agreeing to prescribe for an abortion when the pregnant woman did not want her husband to discover her unfaithfulness; another tells of a monk prescribing a fatal concoction, when the patient's hands and feet had been cut off and his family did not want him to live. These acts earned severe reprimands from the Buddha.

The original ascetic impulse was revived from time to time, but the Buddhist order increasingly involved itself with the wider social concerns. In time, the monks became

domesticated as a functioning element in the community, much patronised by rulers. For the first couple of centuries after the Buddha's death (whether in c.483 BC, the traditional date, or up to a century later as is now believed possible), the story is obscure and the scriptures give little information about actual events. But in the third century BC the emperor Ashoka patronised the Buddhists and other schools of holy men lavishly, bestowing property upon them and encouraging all his subjects to respect them—an indication that by this time Buddhism had acquired popularity and social prestige.

Ashoka's reign, a major landmark in Indian history, was a turning-point in the fortunes of Buddhism. His inscriptions are the oldest surviving texts in India (apart from the still-undeciphered Indus Valley script of the third millennium BC) and they tell us much about his aspirations. He favoured brahmans and mendicant monks generally, but gave special favour to Buddhism, declaring himself an ardent lay follower.

> For two-and-a-half years I have been an open follower of the Buddha, though at first I did not make much progress. But for more than a year now I have drawn closer to the Order, and have made much progress.

The emperor assumed the authority to make rules for the communities of Buddhist monks. He promulgated a sort of code of public morality, called *dhamma*, consisting chiefly of harmonious co-existence, respect for elders and holy men, and the sanctity of all forms of life. Some have thought that this *dhamma* was identical with Buddhism but, though informed by Buddhist morality, it was essentially the emperor's own.

The subsequent evolution of Buddhism is much more richly attested by written sources. It is marked by various trends, some of which were probably present from early on—a growing tendency to treat the Buddha as a god, the building of monuments as ritual centres, the accumulation of myths about the Buddha's past lives, and developments in scholarly activity. The last of these was boosted by the practice of writing down Buddhist texts, which began in the first century BC.

Overall, Buddhism's early history is somewhat paradoxical: the first monks were solitary wanderers who absorbed spiritual merit and psychic powers by meditation in the wilderness; but as their fame grew, their services, both spiritual and practical, were solicited and they became caught up in a web of social relationships that made them functioning parts of the society they had left. The process is a natural one; it has taken place time and time again in the history of Buddhism and it is part of the way real life works.

FOR FURTHER READING
F.R. Allchin et al., *The Archaeology of Early Historic South Asia* (Cambridge U.P. 1995); H. Bechert and R. Gombrich, *The World of Buddhism* (Thames and Hudson 1991); Michael Carrithers, *The Buddha* (Oxford. U.P. 1983); R. Gombrich, *Theravada Buddhism: A Social History from Ancient Benares to Modern Colombo* (Routledge and Kegan Paul 1988); Romila Thapar, *A History of India*, volume 1(Penguin Books;1990, first ed. (1966)

Ian Mabbeth is professor of Indian and Buddhist Studies at Alchi Bunkyou University, Nagoya; this article is based on Research conducted jointly with Greg Bailey of La Trobe University, Melborne.

This article first appeared in *History Today*, January 2002, pp. 24-29. © 2002 by History Today, Ltd. Reprinted by permission.

The Marrow of Zen

by SHUNRYU SUZUKI

THE MARROW OF ZEN *"In the zazen posture, your mind and body have great power to accept things as they are, whether agreeable or disagreeable."*

In our scriptures (Samyuktagama Sutra, volume 33), it is said that there are four kinds of horses: excellent ones, good ones, poor ones, and bad ones. The best horse will run slow and fast, right and left, at the driver's will, before it sees the shadow of the whip; the second best will run as well as the first one does, just before the whip reaches its skin; the third one will run when it feels pain on its body; the fourth will run after the pain penetrates to the marrow of its bones. You can imagine how difficult it is for the fourth one to learn how to run!

When we hear this story, almost all of us want to be the best horse. If it is impossible to be the best one, we want to be the second best. That is, I think, the usual understanding of this story, and of Zen. You may think that when you sit in zazen you will find out whether you are one of the best horses or one of the worst ones. Here, however, there is a misunderstanding of Zen. If you think the aim of Zen practice is to train you to become one of the best horses, you will have a big problem. This is not the right understanding. If you practice Zen in the right way it does not matter whether you are the best horse or the worst one. When you consider the mercy of Buddha, how do you think Buddha will feel about the four kinds of horses? He will have more sympathy for the worst one than for the best one.

When you are determined to practice zazen with the great mind of Buddha, you will find the worst horse is the most valuable one. In your very imperfections you will find the basis for your firm, way-seeking mind. Those who can sit perfectly physically usually take more time to obtain the true way of Zen, the actual feeling of Zen, the marrow of Zen. But those who find great difficulties in practicing Zen will find more meaning in it. So I think that sometimes the best horse may be the worst horse, and the worst horse can be the best one.

If you study calligraphy you will find that those who are not so clever usually become the best calligraphers. Those who are very clever with their hands often encounter great difficulty after they have reached a certain stage. This is also true in art and in Zen. It is true in life. So when we talk about Zen we cannot say, "He is good," or "He is bad," in the ordinary sense of the words. The posture taken in zazen is not the same for each of us. For some it may be impossible to take the cross-legged posture. But even though you cannot take the right posture, when you arouse your real, way-seeking mind, you can practice Zen in its true sense. Actually it is easier for those who have difficulties in sitting to arouse the true way-seeking mind than for those who can sit easily.

When we reflect on what we are doing in our everyday life, we are always ashamed of ourselves. One of my students wrote to me saying, "You sent me a calendar, and I am trying to follow the good mottoes which appear on each page. But the year has hardly begun, and already I have failed!" Dogen-zenji said, *"Shoshaku jushaku."* *Shaku* generally means "mistake" or "wrong." *Shoshaku jushaku* means "to succeed wrong with wrong," or one continuous mistake. According to Dogen, one continuous mistake can also be Zen. A Zen master's life could be said to be so many years of *shoshaku jushaku.* This means so many years of one single-minded effort.

We say, "A good father is not a good father." Do you understand? One who thinks he is a good father is not a good father; one who thinks he is a good husband is not a good husband. One who thinks he is one of the worst husbands may be a good one if he is always trying to be a good husband with a single-minded effort. If you find it impossible to sit because of some pain or some physical difficulty, then you should sit anyway, using a thick cushion or chair. Even though you are the worst horse, you will get to the marrow of Zen.

Suppose your children are suffering from a hopeless disease. You do not know what to do; you cannot lie in bed. Normally the most comfortable place for you would be a warm comfortable bed, but now because of your mental agony you cannot rest. You may walk up and down, in and out, but this does not help. Actually the best way to relieve your mental suffering is to sit in zazen, even in such a confused state of mind and bad posture. If you have no experience of sitting in this kind of difficult situation you are not a Zen student. No other activity will appease your suffering. In other restless positions you have no power to accept your difficulties, but in the zazen posture which you have acquired by long, hard practice, your mind and body have great power to accept things as they are, whether they are agreeable or disagreeable.

When you feel disagreeable it is better for you to sit. There is no other way to accept your problem and work on it. Whether you are the best horse or the worst, or whether your posture is good or bad is out of the question. Everyone can practice zazen, and in this way work on his problems and accept them.

When you are sitting in the middle of your own problem, which is more real to you: your problem or yourself? The awareness that you are here, right now, is the ultimate fact. This is the point you will realize by zazen practice. In continuous practice, under a succession of agreeable and disagreeable situations, you will realize the marrow of Zen and acquire its true strength."

SHUNRYU SUZUKI is First Master of Zen Center, San Francisco and Carmel Valley.

From *Zen Mind, Beginner's Mind,* 1973, pp. 38-40. © 1973 by Weatherhill Inc.

An Essential Commitment

The teacher and the student share one inseparable mind

J. L. Walker

The compassion of the good lama,
And the disciple's perseverance in meditation,
These two interacting ensure the upholding of
     the Dharma.
And the essence of this interaction lies in their
     solemn commitment.

Initiation leading to a rapid transformation,
And invocation with intense trust and devotion,
These two interacting will bring us together
     soon.
And the essence of this interaction lies in
     blessings.

—Milarepa (1040–1123)[1]

IT IS TIBET, IN THE EARLY YEARS of the twelfth century. A monk in his middle years, dignified with knowledge and profound contemplative experience, walks along a path near his monastery. Once a famous physician, he lost his family to a disease he could not cure, and made a promise to his dying wife that he would become a monk and devote his life to the Dharma. The purity of his renunciation is complete.

On this particular day, he passes three beggars crouching beside the road. Predictably, they are discussing their next meal. One says that it would be nice to have a dish with vegetables. Another asserts that it would be better to be the king; then they'd have whatever they liked. The third, however, replies that best of all would be to be like the great yogin Milarepa, who needs neither food nor clothing, having attained transcendent wisdom. When Milarepa is hungry, the dakinis bring him cups of ambrosia.

Hearing Milarepa's name for the first time, the monk's heart spontaneously opens, and he is stopped in his tracks. Tears come to his eyes; for a time he cannot even walk. Returning to his room to meditate, he suddenly gains a deeper experience of clarity and emptiness than ever before. "Now what is happening?" he wonders. Inviting the three beggars to his room for a meal, he plies them with questions about Milarepa. As the

conversation unfolds, he realizes that he must leave the monastery and make the journey to find the teacher, wherever he may be, whatever the cost. This is the real beginning of his story, for without the union of learning with devotion the highest attainments cannot arise.

Tibetan Buddhism abounds with such tales, which appear in other traditions as well. The wandering dervish Shams of Tabriz spent years searching for his perfect disciple. Finding the learned teacher Rumi riding a donkey through the dusty marketplace of Konya, he asked Rumi a single question. Perceiving the depth of realization behind the question, Rumi fell unconscious from the donkey's back. Thus began one of the most famous and fruitful teacher-disciple relationships of all time. This Sufi poet of divine love once wrote that lovers do not suddenly meet somewhere, but they are in each other all along. The same is true of the spiritual teacher and disciple.

Whereas Shams traveled and prayed for years while seeking Rumi, the only one who could "endure my company," Milarepa waited in his mountains, teaching those who came to him. As he was getting old, his disciples begged him to choose a successor and pass on his entire teaching so the community would not lack a qualified leader when he was gone. In those days as Milarepa taught he would sometimes fall silent and smile, then resume speaking. His students inquired what the cause of this might be. He replied that the destined successor, one called "Physician," was even then approaching. Only this man had the capacity to receive Milarepa's complete transmission of his inner realization; only this person was the perfect vessel by virtue of his own excellent qualities.

THE INDIAN BUDDHIST sage Nagarjuna (second century C.E.) describes the ideal teacher thus:

Devote yourself to one possessing twelve
     qualities:
Much learning and great wisdom,
Not aspiring for material goods or possessions,

Possessing the Spirit of Awakening and great
compassion,
Enduring hardships and having little depression
or fatigue,
Having great practical advice, liberated from the
mundane path,
And possessing knowledge and erudition and
comprehension of the signs of warmth
[indication of success in spiritual practice].[2]

Those who have not had the opportunity of meeting the
Buddha face to face must rely on a qualified teacher who
embodies the enlightened qualities.

The qualities of the student are as important as those
of the teacher. These two, master and disciple, are essentially interdependent. Buddhist philosophy goes so far as
to say that the teacher arises only in dependence upon a
student. Only when one is chosen a teacher or spiritual
guide by another can one truly be called a teacher. This
interdependence is illuminated in the words of
Milarepa's great disciple Gampopa, the "Physician" he
had been awaiting:

If a spiritual mentor lacks realization, it does not
help even if his disciples act with reverence and
devotion. As an analogy, although the clay may
be good, if its mold has no indentations, it will
not form into a statue. If the disciples have no
reverence or devotion, it does not help even if
the spiritual mentor has realization. This is like a
cow having milk, but its calf having no plate.[3]

Even Gampopa, ablaze with devotion, found that
there are many difficulties to overcome in coming into
right relationship with the teacher. As Milarepa waited
on the mountain, on a distant plain Gampopa fell
suddenly ill and collapsed. As he lay alone and close to
death for three days beside the deserted road, he suppli-
cated Milarepa with absolute faith, praying that if he
were to die there he would have the good karma to meet
the master in a future life. Perceiving his devotion from
afar, Milarepa smiled and paused to bestow blessing on
the prostrate disciple. Recovered, Gampopa arrived at
last at Milarepa's encampment, only to be told that he
must retire to a nearby cave to meditate in order to
subdue the pride that had arisen in response to his rescue
and hearing of the master's prophecies concerning him.
Two weeks later, having pacified all his hope and fear, the
destined student was conducted at last into Milarepa's
presence.

Students must learn to abandon their faults and to
receive the teachings. Yet without the indispensible qualification of devotion, all the others that one may bring to
the relationship are useless. The Tibetans say that if the
sun of the disciple's devotion does not shine on the snow
mountain of the lama, the stream of blessings cannot
descend. At the same time, the quality of the one who

bestows the teaching is essential to the efficacy of its
transmission. The teacher imparts his or her being to the
student—not merely knowledge, however profound.

REFLECTING THIS central importance of the teacher,
an image variously known as a Refuge Assembly, a Merit
Field, or a Refuge Tree is ground in all schools of Tibetan
Buddhism. From the midst of a lake springs an enormous
tree, every branch of which is laden with beings: buddhas
and bodhisattvas, spiritual heroes and heroines, yogins
and yoginis, meditational deities, dakinis, and protectors
of the teachings. They sit in mediation, they stand, they
dance. Volume of texts representing the Dharma, each
wrapped in silk brocade, form a background for the main
figure. For Gelukpas, the Tree centers on the founder Je
Tsong-Khapa; for Nyingma practitioners, the center is
Padmasambhava. Sakyas may place the Sakya Pandita in
the middle, while for Kagyus the principal figure is
usually the Adhibuddha Vajradhara, who became the
source of the Kagyu teachings by direct mind transmission to the great yogin Tilopa. The student's own
personal teachers hold a special place in this assembly.

At the foot of the Refuge Tree, a figure kneels,
holding a golden offering mandala. This is the meditator,
the student who offers the *nyepa sum,* the three types of
delight owed to the master by every disciple: to bring
offerings to the teacher, to show respect in both body and
speech, and, most importantly, to practice according to
the teacher's instructions.

The Refuge Tree is used as a support for visualization, both for the meditation known as "Going for
Refuge" and for the Guru Yoga which is the foundation
of all Vajrayana practice. The interdependence of the
lama and disciple is not mere metaphor, but depends on
the principle of mind. In Buddhism, mind is the base of
both cyclic existence and nirvana—there is no Buddha
apart from the mind. If mind merges with lower things, it
will sink to that level, but if it can be merged with the
realized mind of the spiritual guide, it will lead to enlightenment. The teacher's mind holds the essence of
Buddhahood or awakened mind, the same mind that
exists, obscured by ignorance, in the student. When the
mind of the student and teacher are experienced directly
as one, this relationship becomes a living awareness.
Upon first meeting milarepa, Gampopa told the lama
the story of his long journey. Milarepa replied, "Our
connection is very profound and deep. Although you
have just arrived here, we have never been separate,
my son."

Having received empowerment and full training
from Milarepa, Gampopa returned to central Tibet. He
followed his guru's instructions to meditate in solitude
with great focus and discipline. One day he remembered
his teacher's instructions to return at a certain time, and
that he had let that time go by. Hurriedly he set out for the
appointed place, but on the way he met his fellow disciple

Gampopa (1079–1153), Kagyu Lineage master teacher

Rechungpa, who told him that Jetsun Milarepa had passed away. Anguished, Gampopa wept and then fainted. His friend revived him, and he made a song of prayer and supplication, which ends with these words of deep devotion on the ultimate union of the true spiritual guide and his disciple:

> Hold me close with your compassion, and
>   accept me.
> Even though I have no material gifts of
>   veneration to offer,
> I will practice
> Until we become one in the dharmakaya.

Do not cease your river of blessings.
Do not let me go from the book of your
    kindness.[4]

Notes

1. Lobsang Lhalungpa, *The Life of Milarepa* (New York: Penguin Arkana, 1979), p. 128.
2. Karma Chagme, with commentary by Gyatrul Rinpoche, translation by B. Alan Wallace, *A Spacious Path to Freedom: Practical Instruction on the Union of Mahamudra and Atiyoga* (Ithaca, New York: Snow Lion Publications, 1998), p. 18.
3. Ibid., p. 19.
4. Jampa Mackenzie Stewart, *the Life of Gampopa: The Incomparable Dharma Lord of Tibet* (New York: Snow Lion Publications, 1995).

"SHINRAN AND JODOSHINSHU"

Based on the Inaugural Lecture for the Numata Chair at Leiden University, The Netherlands on April 7, 1992 (Revised in July, 1998)

by Hisao Inagaki

Buddhism spread to the north-east beyond the borders of its homeland India, and reached China in the early centuries A.D. and from there Korea and Japan. The form of Buddhism which was introduced into those countries and enjoyed popularity was predominantly Mahayana, the Great Vehicle. Like other Pure Land schools, Shinran's Jodoshinshu belongs to Mahayana and shares the fundamental standpoint with various Mahayana systems, including Zen and Tibetan esotericism which have become popular in the west.

Jodoshinshu means 'the true essence of the Pure Land teaching'; originally it is not the name of the sect. Shinran had no intention of founding a new sect, but simply sought to reveal the essence of Pure Land teaching which had been transmitted and developed by the seven eminent masters in India, China and Japan. He compiled a collection of quotations from their works and those from Pure Land sutras and discourses, and thus formed a comprehensive system of the teaching of salvation, which has become known as Jodoshinshu, the True Pure Land sect, or Shinshu, the True sect. This branch of Pure Land Buddhism has come to be widely known by the name of 'Shin' ever since D.T. Suzuki first used this appellation. Although celebrated as the leading exponent of Zen, Suzuki in fact made a great contribution to the introduction of Shin to the west by writing articles and translating the first four chapters of Shinran's magnum opus, Kyogyoshinsho. From now on, I will use this abbreviation for Jodoshinshu.

All doctrinal and practical systems of Pure Land Buddhism center on a specific Buddha, called Amida, who is believed to be dwelling in the western paradise known as the Land of Utmost Bliss (Sukhavati) or, more popularly, the Pure Land. 'Amida' is the Japanese reading of the Chinese 'O-mi-t'o,' which represents the Sanskrit 'Amita', meaning 'immeasurable' or 'infinite'. 'Amita' is interpreted as standing for 'amita-abha' (infinite light) and 'amita-ayus' (infinite life). Amida, therefore, is better known in the west as Am-itabha, the Buddha of Infinite Light, and also Amitayus, the Buddha of Infinite Life.

Amida is the most popular Buddha in Japan, perhaps more popular than the founder of Buddhism, Shakyamuni. Being a transcendent Buddha beyond time and space, Amida saves those who have sincere faith in him and call his Name. He embraces such devotees in his Light and welcomes them to his Land of Utmost Bliss. His saving activity is assisted by Bodhisattvas, headed by Kannon (Kuan-yin, Avalokiteshvara) and Seishi (Shih-chih, Mahasthamaprapta). Statues of Amida flanked by those two Bodhisattvas are seen at many temples in Japan.

There are three basic scriptures of Indian and Central Asian origin which give full accounts of the history of Amida Buddha, his saving activity, glorious manifestations of the Pure Land and its essential nature, and so forth. They also describe how we can be born in the Pure Land and attain Enlightenment there.

Before we look into the contents of the three Pure Land sutras, there are a couple of basic principles in Buddhism, which need to be clarified. First is the theory of karma, which means 'action.' The law of karma is generally accepted in Hindu thought and is fully explained in Buddhism. According to this law, one's existence has continued from the beginningless past up to the present and, impelled by karma, will continue on and on into the indefinite future. One's life, therefore, does not end with death, but will be followed by another in a different form. According to the quality and quantity of our moral acts, our future destiny is determined. Simply stated, what we are is the result of what we have done in the past, and what we do now will create what we will be. And so, in Buddhism no creator god is conceived; our karma, including our thoughts and words, is responsible for our states of existence.

Secondly, such continuation of one's existence, called Samsara, is considered painful. Even though one attains a higher state of existence in the heavens, it does not last forever. It will be eventually followed by miseries in a lower state. Buddhism teaches us the way of emancipation from cycles of birth and death in Samsara. Such a state of emancipation is called Nirvana.

Thirdly, Buddhism does not simply encourage morally good acts. The quality of acts is important. However hard we may do good, if our acts are based on self-attachment, they produce only limited effect, short of attaining Nirvana. Truly good acts should, therefore, be free of self-attachment, and can only be successfully performed through intensive meditation.

Fourth is the Mahayana principle of dependent origination (pratitya-samutpada) and that of emptiness (shunyata). Briefly stated, all existing things are mutually related, and so are devoid of substantiality of their own. Based on this realization, the Bodhisattva seeks to cultivate pure merits without being attached to anything, to say nothing of his own self.

The last is that the pure merits obtained by selfless acts of love and compassion can be manifested as glorious bodies of the Buddhas and their Pure Lands. Such merit can also be shared by other beings. Those who partake of the pure merits of the Buddhas can quickly attain emancipation.

All living beings are potential Buddhas. Mahayana emphasizes that everyone has the Buddha-nature. One who believes in his Buddha-nature and seeks to realize it is a Bodhisattva. At the outset of the Bodhisattva's career, he makes vows, resolving to realize the highest wisdom (bodhi) and deliver all sentient beings from suffering. It is conceived in Mahayana that there are innumerable Bodhisattvas in the universe who are practicing the way to Buddhahood and also innumerable Buddhas who have already completed the Bodhisattva-course.

According to the Larger Sukhavativyuha Sutra (abbreviated to Larger Sutra), the longest and the most important of the three canonical scriptures, Amida was formerly a king. He met a Buddha and was deeply impressed by his personality. He renounced the world and became a Bodhisattva, a seeker of the Way, called 'Dharmakara' ('Store of Dharma or Truth'). He resolved to attain Buddhahood and save all suffering beings. At his request, the Buddha showed and explained to him all the glorious manifestations of the twenty-one billion Buddha-lands. Having seen them, Dharmakara meditated for five aeons (kalpas) on the Buddha-land he would establish and the way of saving beings from suffering. When the plan of his Buddha-land and his method of salvation became clear, he expressed them in his forty-eight Vows.

The Larger Sutra explains that Dharmakara's career as a Bodhisattva lasted for many aeons over innumerable lives. Vows alone do not automatically become reality; in order to realize the vows, one must do all kinds of meritorious deeds and also cultivate wisdom. When his wisdom reached the highest level and his virtues and merits were developed to the fullest extent, he became a Buddha, called 'Amida'. His supreme and boundless merits were then manifested as his majestic illuminating body and glorious Pure Land, as promised in his Vows.

Of all the Vows, the Eighteenth is most important for Pure Land Buddhists because it promises the salvation of those who maintain sincere Faith and call Amida's Name. This Vow provides a channel of contact between Amida and man. The devotee can partake of Amida's merit by repeating his Name, with which he will be able to be born in the Pure Land.

The Buddhas and their spheres of activity are beyond our ordinary sense-perceptions and concepts, but they can be visualized by specially trained minds. The second of the three Pure Land sutras, commonly known by the title 'the Contemplation Sutra', presents a method by which one can visualize Amida and his Pure Land with one's spiritual eye. Simply stated, there are thirteen steps of visualization, beginning with concentration on the setting sun. First, one faces west, gazes at the setting sun and imprints its image on the mind until one clearly sees it whether one's eyes are open or closed. When this is accomplished, one goes on to the next step, which is the meditation on water. One forms an image that the entire western quarter is flooded with water; in the next step, one visualizes that the water becomes frozen, and then the whole expanse of ice turns into lapis-lazuli. Since the earth of the Pure Land is made of lapis-lazuli, one who has seen it can now construct images of other aspects of the Pure Land and proceed to visualization of Amida himself. The Contemplation Sutra states that successful visualization of Amida and his Pure Land extinguishes one's evil karma and ensures birth in the Pure Land after death.

Throughout the history of the development of Pure Land Buddhism in India, China and Japan, recitation of the sacred Name of Amida has been the essential practice for attaining birth in the Pure Land. This practice, known as 'nien-fo' in Chinese, 'buddha-anusmriti' in Sanskrit and 'nembutsu' in Japanese, consists in repeating the six-character formula: na-mo-o-mi-t'o-fo in Chinese or namu amida butsu in Japanese. This formula literally means 'Adoration to Amida Buddha' or 'I take refuge in Amida Buddha.' In the Contemplation Sutra, after the thirteen visualizations, nine grades of aspirants are distinguished according to their moral and religious accomplishments and the gravity of transgressions they have committed. To the lower grades of those who have committed grave offenses, the Buddha recommends recitation of Amida's Name. According to the law of karma, those evildoers would be destined to hell, but their evil karma is cancelled by the merit of the Nembutsu which they repeat, and so they can be born in the Pure Land.

The Nembutsu is also exclusively recommended in the Amida Sutra, the shortest of the three Pure Land scriptures, where it is stated that by repeating the Name of Amida Buddha with singleness of heart for one to seven days, one can attain birth in the Pure Land. More importantly, in the 18th

Vow, which promises salvation of all beings, the Nembutsu is presented, along with deep faith, as the essential practice leading to birth in the Pure Land.

As compared with the meditative practice centering on visualization of Amida and his Pure Land, the recitative Nembutsu is an easy practice which anyone can perform at any time and anywhere. Its easiness, however, does not means that the Nembutsu is of poorer quality or earns smaller merit. All the Pure Land masters in the past, beginning with Nagarjuna of India, down to Shan-tao of China and Honen of Japan, placed great importance on the Nembutsu recitation.

Shan-tao (613–681) of T'ang Dynasty China, who was credited with organizing and propagating the Pure Land teaching, succeeded in visualizing the Pure Land and, based on his experience, wrote an extensive commentary on the Comtemplation Sutra and other works explaining the method of meditation and its doctrinal background. His system of practice, however, centers on recitation of the Nembutsu, while other practices, including meditation on Amida, serve as an aid.

Shan-tao's teacher, Tao-ch'o (562–645), is said to have chanted the Nembutsu as many as seventy thousand times a day. Shan-tao himself was dedicated to constant practice of the Nembutsu. His Nembutsu teaching spread far and wide, and was inherited by Honen (1133–1212) of Japan, who founded the Jodo sect based on the teaching that the exclusive practice of the Nembutsu alone is the sufficient cause for birth in the Pure Land. Honen's disciples, while following the Nembutsu practice, developed theories clarifying the doctrinal bases of the master's teaching. Shinran was one of them.

In Japan, before Honen founded the Jodo sect, the Nembutsu was already widespread even among the nobility, owing largely to the efforts of Genshin (942–1017) and other masters as well as such Nembutsu sages as Koya (903–972).

Genshin is particularly well-known as the author of the Ojoyoshu ("Collection of Essential Passages Concerning Birth in the Pure Land"). He describes in it details of sufferings in the evil realms of Samsara and those of the pleasure and happiness in Amida's Pure Land, and encourages us to seek birth there. Genshin also formed a society to practice the Nembutsu together on a fixed day of the month. The Regent Fujiwara Michinaga (966–1027) was one of those who died while holding one end of five-colored strings, of which the other end was tied to the hands of a statue of Amida. According to the Contemplation Sutra and Genshin's work, those who die mindful of Amida while reciting the Nembutsu will be welcomed by him with hosts of sages and escorted to the Pure Land. The five-colored strings were believed to ensure Amida's coming to welcome a dying person.

When we say Pure Land Buddhism, we do not merely mean Japanese Pure Land schools. In other parts of Asia, such as Korea, Taiwan and Vietnam, and also in the areas of Europe and America where Chinese, Japanese and Vietnamese communities exist, various forms of Pure Land faith and practice are maintained, often under the guidance of native Buddhist priests.

In Japan, Jodo and Shin have been the most popular forms of Buddhism. According to the government survey in 1987, the number of the temples of Pure Land Buddhism was 30,368, and that of its followers was 20,446,912, which was nearly a quarter of the total population of Buddhists in Japan. This figure compares more than favourably with Zen, which has only 9,481,011 followers. Although there is no way of knowing the exact number of the followers, the above figure gives us an idea of the extent of influence which Pure Land Buddhism still has in Japan.

If you begin your tour of Japan in Tokyo, you will not miss Kamakura on the way to Kyoto. Kamakura is a historically important place as the seat of shogunate government for 140 years and is also one of the centers of Zen Buddhism since the Kamakura period. By far the most popular tourist attraction is the huge sitting Buddha, 15 metres in height. This Buddha is Amida. He is sitting in meditation with his fingers formed in the Amida mudra. Erected in 1250, he has seen many vicissitudes of the world with compassionate eyes. He welcomes visitors from abroad as if wishing to say that Japan is the land of Amida Buddha.

When you get off the bullet train at Kyoto Station and walk a short distance to the north, you will find a majestic temple on your left. It is the head temple of one of the two largest Shin schools, called the Higashi or East Honganji. About ten minutes' walk to the west, you come to another temple of a similar scale, which is the Nishi or West Honganji. According to the survey in 1990, the number of temples belonging to Nishi Honganji is 10,369, and that of the priests is 27,238. The educational institutions are scattered throughout the country. Nine universities and junior colleges, including Ryukoku University where I used to teach, belong to Nishi Honganji, and the total number of junior and senior high schools is thirty-five. Besides those, Nishi Honganji has ninety-seven temples in the United States, fifty-nine in South America, and eighteen in Canada. In Europe there are two temples affiliated to this school, one in Antwerpen and one in Geneva, and a third has been built in Dusseldorf. There are also dojo, or Nembutsu centers, in various countries throughout the world.

Shinran, the founder of Shin, was born in Kyoto in 1173. Bereft of his parents when very young, he entered the priesthood at the age of nine. It was a turbulent age with the civil war between the two powerful clans, Minamoto and Taira, which ended in the defeat of the Taira clan and the establishment of the shogunate government in Kamakura in 1192 by Minamoto Yoritomo.

Shinran went to Mt. Hiei, the center of Tendai Buddhism, where he studied and practiced the Tendai teaching for twenty years. But failing to attain Enlightenment, he went down to Kyoto to seek a way of suitable salvation. At that time, Honen, who was forty years older than Shinran, was teaching the Nembutsu to men and women of all walks of life. Shinran went to see him and found the way of salvation in the Nembutsu.

When Honen's Nembutsu teaching invited the jealousy and criticism from the traditional sects and was finally persecuted, he and his leading disciples were exiled. Shinran was banished to Northern Japan in 1207, and later married there. After he was pardoned, he went to stay in Hitachi Province, north-east of Tokyo, where he taught Amida's law of salvation to local people, while he began to write the Kyogyoshinsho, the most comprehensive text of the Shin sect. After he passed sixty years of age, he returned to Kyoto and dedicated the rest of his life to literary activity until his death at ninety.

Shinran led a normal family life with a wife, a son and five daughters (according to another tradition, two sons and five daughters). According to the monastic precepts, Buddhist monks ought not to marry, because practicing the Buddhist Way in search of the transcendent Truth was considered incompatible with married life. When Shinran was exiled, he was stripped of priesthood and given a criminal's name, Fujii Yoshizane.

After that he was conscious of himself as being neither a priest nor a layman. Under the circumstances, he must have felt it natural to marry when he found a suitable wife, Eshin-ni. Through his entry into a matrimonial life, Shinran showed that Amida could save ordinary men and women.

Of all the Pure Land schools which arose in Japan after Honen, Shin has attained the most impressive institutional development. In its doctrinal aspect, too, Shin has offered wider perspectives in the re-interpretation of the Pure Land teachings. Shinran himself did not intend to found a new school, but as he states in the Kyogyoshinsho and other works, he merely followed the teachings of the Buddha and the Seven Patriarchs and sought to reveal their true meanings. His re-interpretation of the Pure Land teaching may seem to be based on his own personal judgement, but has actually served to clarify, through his insight and experience, the teachings developed and transmitted by Pure Land masters of the past.

Re-interpretation, by the way, is an indispensable element for any religious or philosophical advancement. In order for any religious theory and practice to keep its vitality, it needs to be interpreted and re-interpreted from new viewpoints based on deeper insights, personal experiences, and so forth. Re-interpretation is like digging up the earth to find new energy resources. The Dharma, or the Law, which the Buddha realized some twenty-five centuries ago, is like the earth. At first he taught a rather primitive way of digging and drilling and a method of processing the raw materials obtained. The term 'dharma,' which I have just translated as 'law,' had been widely used in India since early days. The Buddha used the same term for the truth he discovered

and for his theory and practice leading to its realization, but he did not use it with the same connotation as in the Hindu tradition. He gave it new dimensions of meaning and invested it with the connotations which were to be fully revealed a few centuries later, when Mahayana arose in India. From the Mahayana viewpoint, the Buddha's Dharma is meant to be re-interpreted over and over again with insightful wisdom and observations as historical, geographical and social circumstances change.

Re-interpretation in Buddhism, it must be emphasized, is closely linked with meditation. Mere intellectual re-interpretation does not go very far. From the beginning of its history, Buddhism has derived its spirituality and transcendent metaphysics from the experience of meditation. This applies to the Mahayana as a whole and to Pure Land Buddhism as well. As we have seen from the Contemplation Sutra, one can visualize the transcendent Buddha Amida and his Pure Land if one successfully practices according to the prescribed method. Whenever metaphysical speculations or theoretical analyses grow too complicated and threaten the life of spirituality, we can revert to meditation to remedy this tendency. But meditation is not always effective. In ages far removed from the time of the Buddha, good teachers of meditation are very rare. Even if you found one, it would be difficult to follow the prescribed method for a long time. Meditation on Amida and his Pure Land is easier than Zen, because we have objects of concentration and also we can count on Amida's spiritual power (adhisthana), which helps to accomplish the meditation.

Honen failed to attain salvation through the Tendai practices which he followed on Mt. Hiei for many years, and Shinran, too, practiced the same kind of meditation for twenty years, but without success. Honen found the way of salvation in the Nembutsu teaching expounded by Shantao of T'ang China, and then gave up all other Buddhist practices. Honen's conversion to the Nembutsu was accompanied by a deep awareness of his inability to save himself by his own power. He realized that Amida's power was working behind the Nembutsu. Based on this realization he re-interpreted the whole teachings of the Buddha, and placed the Nembutsu above all other practices.

Shinran is often compared to Martin Luther (1483–1546), and described as a renovator of Buddhism in much the same way as Luther is in Christianity. Shinran, however, did not stand up in open defiance of the ecclesiastical authority, nor did he intend to start a new movement. Like Honen and other Pure Land masters, Shinran's immediate concern was his own salvation, which was to be fully realized in the Pure Land. In this respect, his approach may be described as 'self-centered' and 'other-worldly'. But we note that his self-centeredness does not mean selfishness and that the other-worldliness is not an escapism or pessimism. For, through the acceptance of Amida's Compassion, he found close karmic relationships with other sentient beings, and also realized that, after transcending this world, i.e., going to the Pure Land, he would be able to come back and save other beings as he wished.

Shinran's deep self-reflection and his insight into Amida's law of salvation have brought about a complete reversal of the common-sense view and of ordinary Buddhist concepts. In the most popular Shin text, Tannisho ("Notes Lamenting Divergent Views"), Shinran is quoted as saying:

"Even a good person is born in the Pure Land; how much more easily an evil person! People of the world, however, usually say, "Even an evil person is born in the Pure Land, how much more easily a good person!" At first sight, this view seems reasonable, but it is contrary to the intention of the Primary Vow of the Other-Power.

The Buddha teaches that we can attain higher spiritual states by moral good and cultivation of wisdom through meditation. If we are unable to do any good, we will be destined to lower states of existence where we must receive suffering as the retribution of our wrongdoings. Although Shinran was actually capable of morally good acts, his reflective eye penetrated to the huge mass of evil karma in his unconscious realm, and so he recognized all acts as rooted in evil karma. He realized that he was hopelessly evil and not possessed of any stock of merit to count on for attaining salvation by his own power. The Tannisho quotes his saying as follows:

"Since I am incapable of any practice whatsoever, hell would definitely be my dwelling."

Shinran was, however, not despondent or desperate. Nor did he feel alienated from Amida's salvation. His realization of utter powerlessness is sure proof that he has been saved by Amida. On receiving through Faith Amida's boundless merit, wisdom and power, he was able to give himself up to Amida, along with his clinging to his limited power and stock of merit.

Shinran's re-interpretation of the Buddhist teachings comes from his experience of complete reliance upon Amida's Power, which is called 'the Other-Power'. He divided Buddhism into two: the Other-Power teaching and the teachings of self-power. Shin is entirely based on the Other-Power, but the other Buddhist ways are based on one's own efforts. Shinran did not even encourage the Nembutsu practice. For Shan-tao and Honen, the Nembutsu was the practice to be performed by one's utmost efforts. For Shinran, all that is required is Amida's saving activity which is to be received with sincerity of heart and deep faith; this faith is also Amida's free gift.

Shin Buddhism has produced many wonderful persons, called "myokonin". According to their biographies, those known as myokonin are usually men and women of little education, who have attained deep understanding of the Other-Power teaching. They are not simply devout practicers of the Nembutsu. Having realized the Other-Power and experienced oneness with Amida, they fully live up to his all-embracing Compassion. While keenly aware of their absolute powerlessness, they are always grateful to Amida,

and their daily life is full of spontaneous expressions of joy and selfless love.

Asahara Saichi (1851–1933) became interested in Buddhism in his late teens. After five or six years' serious pursuit of the Way, which mainly consisted of hearing sermons and thinking deeply on the law of salvation in relation to his own self, he gave it up. Ten years later his Buddhist aspiration arose again. While working as a ship's carpenter, he did not miss any opportunity to hear sermons. Seeking to understand the Other-Power salvation, he tried and tried again until, after he was 50, finally Faith was awakened in him. He changed his job and became a maker of wooden clogs. His overflowing joy in Faith found its expression in poems. Without any knowledge of Chinese characters, he wrote the poems on scraps of wood in Japanese syllabary while making clogs, and in the evening he copied them into notebooks. Out of a large number of poems, here are some examples showing his deep experience of Faith:

Namuamidabutsu and Amida
Are one and not two.
Namuamidabutsu is myself,
And Amida is my Parent;
Here is the oneness of Namuamidabutsu.
How happy I am for this favor!
Namuamidabutsu.

"O Saichi, where is your Land of Bliss?"
My Land of Bliss is right here."

How grateful I am—
your voice is Namuamidabutsu!
I, Saichi, have been saved by it.
You and I are one in Namuamidabutsu!

The Buddha's Name casually found on my lips—
It is indeed a wonderful Buddha!
It is our Parent Amida's call to us.
I, Saichi, am caught up in it!

This Faith is wonderful Faith;
The Buddha hears the Buddha's voice!
There is no room for me, Saichi, to meddle.
How grateful I am for his benevolence!
Namuamidabutsu, Namuamidabutsu.

For Saichi and other people of true Faith, the Nembutsu and Faith are inseparable. The Nembutsu is not a practice to be performed with diligence, but is the joyful, spontaneous expression of Faith. Namuamidabutsu symbolizes the oneness of Amida and the devotee, for 'namu' indicates his Faith, and 'amidabutsu' is Amida's universal and absolute saving power.

Ashikaga Genza (1842–1930), another myokonin, lived in the spirit of Amida's boundless Compassion, which was manifested in his acts of selfless love. One day he saw his persimmon tree in the garden tied round with thorny branches.

"Who did this?" he asked.

His son said, "I did. To protect persimmons from being stolen by children."

Genza said, "What will you do if someone gets hurt?" So saying, he removed thorny branches and, instead, stood a ladder against the tree.

The son protested, "Why, you make it easy for them to steal our persimmons."

Genza said, "Let them take what they want. We'll still have plenty more to eat."

On another occasion at dusk, a man was feeding his horse with beans in Genza's field. Genza saw this and cried, "Young man, beans on that spot are no good. Step further in, and you will find better beans for your horse." Hearing this, the man with the horse ran away.

Shoma (1799–1871) from Shikoku Island was a poor, illiterate man, hired for odd jobs or making straw ropes and sandals for a living, but had wonderful understanding of Amida's Compassion.

Someone asked him, "What is it like to have absolute Faith in Amida?" Shoma lay down comfortably in front of the family shrine.

When he went to a temple with his friend, he lay on his side relaxed in the Buddha hall. The friend reprimanded him, "You are impolite. Behave yourself."

Shoma replied, "This is our Parent's home. Don't be too ceremonious. Are you a son-in-law?"

Once he went on pilgrimage to the Honganji in Kyoto with his friends. On the homeward voyage, their boat was caught in a storm. All the passengers were frightened, but Shoma alone was sleeping peacefully on deck. When awakened by his friends, he exclaimed, "Haven't we come to the Pure Land yet?"

Many episodes and sayings of myokonin like those show that Shin followers who have attained the Other-Power Faith are like Zen adepts who have realized satori. They are completely free in their thinking and doing, and yet full of kindheartedness, gratitude and deep insight. They have transcended the boundaries of good and evil, and even those of this world and the Pure Land, but are not aloof in their attitudes towards their fellow-beings. They are understanding, ready to help others, and eager to lead them along the same Pure Land Way.

As we have seen above, Shin covers many aspects of human activity as well as the area beyond our day-to-day experience. Before anything else, Shin is the way of salvation through Amida's Power originating from his Vows.

Salvation in Shin has three implications: First, in the present life, we are enabled to attain unity with Amida, the Transcendent Buddha, and are freed from the bondage of karma; when our salvation is achieved through our endowment with Faith, we are filled with joy and gratitude to Amida.

Second, after death we will be born in the Pure Land, which is the Transcendent Realm beyond Samsara and is essentially the same as Nirvana. The Pure Land being the sphere of pure karmic energy, those born there can partake of it, enjoy life of utmost bliss, and perform activities as Bodhisattvas.

Third, in the Pure Land we will attain Nirvana and realize Enlightenment. This means that we will become Buddhas.

These three kinds of salvation can be conceived in temporal order, from the present to the future, but more importantly, the ultimate realization of Buddhahood is latent in the 'Here and Now' experience of Faith. Saichi says in one of his poems:

> O Saichi, who is the Buddha?
> He is no other than myself.
> Who is the founder of Shin Buddhism?
> He is no other than myself.
> What is the canonical text?
> It is no other than myself.

For Shinran, Faith is not only a free gift by Amida, but is essentially Amida himself, as he says in a hymn:

> One who rejoices in Faith, it is taught,
> Is equal to the Buddha;
> The Great Faith is Buddha-nature:
> Buddha-nature is the Buddha. (Jodo Wasan 94)

This means that Faith is everything. When one receives Faith, one is assured of birth in the Pure Land and attainment of Enlightenment. This is not simply Shinran's theoretical re-interpretation of the Pure Land teaching. Through Faith Shinran realized oneness with Amida, and Saichi and many other Shin followers share the same experience. Again, Faith is joy; it is joyful acceptance of Amida's saving Power. Amida approaches us in the form of Namuamidabutsu, and when this is received in our hearts, it becomes Faith. In other words, the Sacred Name is all that Amida is, and Faith, too, is Amida himself.

From *Inaugural Lecture for the Numata Chair at Leiden University*, April 7, 1992. © 1992. Reprinted with permission of the author, Hisao Inagaki.

Buddhism and Abortion: "The Way to Memorialize One's Mizuko"

William R. LaFleur

Mizuko, literally a "child of the waters," is the term used in modern Japan to refer to an aborted fetus or a stillborn. In today's Japan, Buddhist institutions feel uneasy about condoning abortion but are also reluctant to condemn it outright. Abortion has been legal in Japan since 1948 and there is no great interest in changing the law. Many Buddhist temples provide a ritual called a *kuyo* through which both "parents" of a *mizuko* can pray for its well-being in the "beyond," that is, in the "realm of the gods and Buddhas." The bodhisattva Jizo is prayed to as the powerful and compassionate figure who guides deceased children through the realm of the dead. Some observers hold that this ritual does much to relieve the so-called postabortion syndrome. In the public press as well as in some Buddhist periodicals, however, some temples have been criticized for being crassly commercialized in the provision of these rituals. Shiun-zan Jizo-ji (Purple Cloud Mountain Jizo Temple), a relatively new establishment on the outskirts of Chichibu, itself an object of such criticism at times, provides promotional brochures, one of which is translated below.

This translation of a brochure published by Shiun-zan Jizo-in first appeared as an appendix in William R. LaFleur, *Liquid Life: Abortion and Buddhism in Japan* (Princeton: Princeton University Press, 1992): 221–223.

The Way to Memorialize One's *Mizuko*

1. The *mizuko* resulting from a terminated pregnancy is a child existing in the realm of darkness. The principal things that have to be done for its sake are the making of a full apology and the making of amends to such a child.

In contrast to the child in darkness because of an ordinary miscarriage or by natural death after being born, the child here discussed is in its present location because its parents took active steps to prevent it from being born alive in our world. If the parents merely carry out ordinary memorial rites but fail to make a full apology to their child, their *mizuko* will never be able to accept their act.

Think for a moment how even birds and beasts, when about to be killed, show a good deal of anger and distress.

Then how much more must be the shock and hurt felt by a fetus when its parent or parents have decided to abort it? And on top of that it does not even yet have a voice with which to make complaint about what is happening.

It often happens that the living children of persons who have repeatedly had abortions will in the middle of the night cry out "Father, help!" or "Help me, Mommy!" because of nightmares. Uncontrollable weeping or cries of "I'm scared! I'm scared!" on the part of children are really caused by dreams through which their aborted siblings deep in the realm of darkness give expression to their own distress and anger. Persons who are not satisfied with this explanation would do well to have a look at two publications of the Purple Cloud Villa; these are entitled *Mizuko Jizo-ji's Collection of the Experiences of Departed Souls* and *The Medical Dictionary of Life*.

2. The next thing to do in remembering the *mizuko* is to set up an image of Jizo on the Buddhist altar in one's own home. That will serve as a substitute for a memorial tablet for the *mizuko*. Such a Jizo can do double service. On one hand it can represent the soul of the *mizuko* for parents doing rites of apology to it. Simultaneously, however, the Jizo is the one to whom can be made an appeal in prayer to guide the fetus through the realm of departed souls. Such Jizo images for home use can be obtained from the Purple Cloud Villa but can also be purchased at any shop specializing in Buddhist art and implements. As long as one performs this worship with a pure heart, it is bound to have a positive effect.

Some prices follow. Jizo images made of metal are either 3,000 yen for silver ones or 4,000 yen for gold. Add 1,100 yen to the price of either of these if home delivery is desired. These are prices as of September 1984.

3. Inasmuch as the Jizo image of the Buddhist altar also does double duty as a memorial tablet for a terminated fetus, it is allowable—after asking permission of the Jizo—to give it a place on the alter lower than the memorial tablets for one's parents and ancestors. Also it does not matter greatly whether it is to the right or the left on the altar.

4. The next thing of importance is to set up a stone Jizo image either in the cemetery of the Mizuko Jizo Temple or at one's own family temple. Such will serve as substitute for a gravestone for the aborted child and will constitute an eternal, ongoing ritual of apology and remembrance. Such action will undoubtably have a good effect—a fact shown in things published in our monthly periodical *The Purple Cloud*. The expenses involved in setting up a stone Jizo Buddha at our place are fully detailed in our publication *Concerning the 10,000 Jizos*. If requested, we will be pleased to send it.

5. The following pertains to the number of images needed if a person is the parent of more than one *mizuko*. One of each on the home altar and in the cemetery will suffice if all the *mizukos* were produced by a single couple—whether married or not. If, however, the father of a later *mizuko* was different from that of an earlier one—and, of course, also had a different family registry—separate Jizo images will be required. An exception to this could be made if a woman were to discuss this candidly with her second husband and get his permission. Then it would be just as in the case of a woman bringing along into her second marriage the children begotten in an earlier one. In such a case, if she requests that the deceased ancestors understand the situation, it is allowable for all her *mizukos* to be collectively remembered with a single image.

6. When at your home altar you are giving a daily portion of rice and water offering to your deceased ancestors, be sure to include the *mizuko* too—and let them know of their inclusion. Also pray for the well-being of your *mizuko* in the other world. Do this by standing before the Buddhas there and reciting either the *Heart Sutra* or the *Psalm to Jizo* used at the Jizo cemetery in Chichibu. In addition to that, if as an ongoing remembrance of your *mizuko* you write out in longhand a copy of the *Heart Sutra* once a day, you will at some point along the way receive the assurance that your child has most certainly reached Buddhahood. Until you receive such an assurance, you should continue to perform these rites of apology and remembrance.

7. To make amends for the fact that you never had to pay anything for the upbringing and education of a *mizuko*, you should give to the Buddha every day an offering of 100 yen for each of your *mizuko*. However, if you have had as many as ten terminated pregnancies, there may be hardship in laying out 1,000 yen every day; in such cases it is permissable to give only 300 or 500 yen—or even to give more or less depending on one's income. This is an expression of apology to the child for not having given it a love-filled upbringing. Therefore, you should put your love into these acts of remembrance, not being stingy with your time and resources. Once you get into the habit of thinking how much easier it would be

simply to make a 10,000-yen contribution once a month, you are missing the whole point. It is far better to put a daily offering on the altar every day and then on a special, designated day pay a visit to the Jizo Temple at Chichibu and make a contribution to the temple. Alternatively, you could do it while making the eighty-eight-temple pilgrimage on the island of Shikoku or the pilgrimage to the one hundred Kannon sites in western Japan.

8. When a person has awakened to the value and importance of remembering *mizuko*, one gains a much deeper faith and makes efforts to live as a bodhisattva, setting one's mind to performing at least one act of goodness each day. Also vowing to go on pilgrimage to Shikoku or the Kannon sites is an excellent way to be total and thorough-going in one's act of apologizing to and remembering the *mizuko*. It is important to be of a mind to do more than enough; to be of the opinion that one has already done plenty is just the kind of attitude that evokes a bad effect.

9. Children who are miscarried, born dead, or die shortly after being born differ, of course, from those whose lives are cut short by being terminated by their parents. Nevertheless, they too are *mizuko* and, when one gives consideration to his or her responsibility for the fact that these too did not enter life successfully, it would seem good to provide them too with *mizuko* rites, just as one would in the case of aborted fetuses.

10. Households whose members think about the seriousness of karmic laws related to abortion are also households that can take advantage of such occasions in order to deepen the faith of those within them. By continuing to perform adequate rites of apology and memorial, such persons later are blessed with the birth of fine, healthy children. Or, as an extension of good fortune, there are many instances of people really thriving. Some persons find that their own severe heart disease are cured or that the rebelliousness of children or neuroses go away. When on top of all that there is increased prosperity in the family business, there is good cause for lots of happiness.

Why not find out more about his by simply paying a visit to the Jizo Temple in Chichibu?

Further Reading

Samuel Coleman, *Family Planning in Japanese Society: Traditional Birth Control in Modern Urban Culture* (Princeton: Princeton University Press, 1983); Hoshino Eiki and Takeda Choshu, "Indebtedness and Comfort: The Undercurrents of *Mizuko Kuyo* in Contemporary Japan," *Japanese Journal of Religious Studies* 14, 4, (December 1987): 305–320; William R. LaFleur, *Liquid Life: Abortion and Buddhism in Japan* (Princeton: Princeton University Press, 1992).

UNIT 5
Religions of China and Japan (Non-Buddhist)

Unit Selections

Key Points to Consider

- Why is Confucianism gaining popularity in contemporary Chinese society?

- What is the role and importance of morality in Confucianism?

- How is the writing and copying of a text considered virtuous in China's religious culture?

- How did Taoist asceticism differ from Hindu and Buddhist asceticism?

- Why is Amaterasu so important to traditional Japanese culture?

- What role do matsuri play in the life of the Japanese?

 **Links: www.dushkin.com/online/**
These sites are annotated in the World Wide Web pages.

Internet Resources on China: Philosophy and Religion
http://newton.uor.edu/Departments& Programs/AsianStudiesDept/china-phil.html

New Religions
http://www.kokugakuin.ac.jp/ijcc/wp/cpjr/newreligions/index.html

Tenrikyo Official Home Page
http://www.tenrikyo.or.jp

The religious traditions of East Asia are ancient and deep and remain an integral part of nearly all the cultures of the region. This is especially true in the case of China and Japan, which are undoubtedly the two countries that have had the greatest influence on the development of religion in East Asia. In addition to being largely responsible for the great success of Buddhism, they have also given birth to popular and abiding indigenous traditions.

Because of various factors, including the early development of writing, China has the longest traceable history in the region, dating back nearly four millennia to the Xia Dynasty. Here, we can see the origins and earliest forms of beliefs and traditions that continue to thrive through to the present.

What has come to be called ancestor worship in Asia had its roots in the third millennium BCE Chinese Shang Dynasty. Here, rituals to gain the favor of ancestral spirits developed and became popular, especially with the royalty. Part of this was due to the growing desire for the perpetuation of life, as well as the importance placed on the family. As veneration of ancestors spread, each culture tended to modify the belief and practice to a varying extent.

Midway through the second millennium BCE, the Zhou Dynasty gave birth to Confucianism and Taoism. These two indigenous traditions, along with Buddhism (which is discussed in unit 4), comprise what have come to be called the "Three Ways of Thinking" in China. In order to understand the evolution of Chinese philosophy and culture, all three warrant study, for they have all played integral roles.

Kung Fu Tzu, the traditional founder of Confucianism, and Lao Tzu, the traditional founder of Taoism, were said to be contemporaries, and each elaborated a way of living and thinking that found a place in Chinese history. For his part, Kung looked to the past upon which to base his concepts. Respect, virtue, and righteousness are all woven in his philosophical approach to life and actions. The first article of the unit helps shed light on how his teachings and ideas have been interpreted throughout history and the role they still play. Like India, China also has a long and varied ascetic tradition. Stephen Eskildsen's article focuses on Chinese Taoist asceticism and its unique approach to the practice.

Since the Meiji Restoration of the late nineteenth century, there has been an expansion of new religious movements in Japan. This process mushroomed after World War II, with many Japanese seeking answers to the near destruction of their land, society, and way of life. In the last two decades, the role of these new movements has changed, but their prevalence remains.

The fifth article offers a look at the evolution, form, and diversity of religion in contemporary Japan. Lastly, Shinto (also discussed in the fourth article by Goro Kajimura) is one of the few existing world religious traditions in which a goddess has a central role. The final article of the unit shows the importance of Amaterasu, the Sun Goddess, in one of the new religious movements in Japan.

CONFUCIUS

Confucianism, once thought to be a dead doctrine, has made an astonishing comeback during the past 20 years. Cited as a major force behind East Asia's economic "miracles," it is now finding a renewed following among mainland Chinese grown disillusioned with communism. Yet what exactly Confucianism means is hard to say. All the more reason, Jonathan Spence urges, to return to the man himself—and to the little we know about his life and words.

Jonathan D. Spence

Across the centuries that have elapsed since he lived in northern China and lectured to a small group of followers on ethics and ritual, the ideas of Confucius have had a powerful resonance. Soon after his death in 476 B.C., a small number of these followers dedicated themselves to recording what they could remember of his teachings and to preserving the texts of history and poetry that he was alleged to have edited. In the fourth and third centuries B.C., several distinguished philosophers expanded and systematized ideas that they ascribed to him, thus deepening his reputation as a complex and serious thinker. During the centralizing and tyrannical Ch'in dynasty that ruled China between 221 and 209 B.C., the works of Confucius were slated for destruction, on the grounds that they contained material antithetical to the obedience of people to their rulers, and many of those who prized or taught his works were brutally killed on the emperor's orders.

Despite this apparently lethal setback, Confucius's reputation was only enhanced, and during the Han dynasty (206 B.C.–A.D. 220) his ideas were further edited and expanded, this time to be used as a focused source for ideas on good government and correct social organization. Despite the pedantry and internal bickering of these self-styled followers of Confucius, his ideas slowly came to be seen as the crystallization of an inherent Chinese wisdom. Surviving the importation of Buddhist metaphysics and meditative practices from India in the third to sixth centuries A.D., and a renewed interest in both esoteric Taoist theories of the cosmos and the hard-headed political realism of rival schools of legalistically oriented thinkers, a body of texts reorganized as "Confucian," with their accumulated commentaries, became the basic source for competitive examinations for entrance into the Chinese civil service and for the analysis of a wide spectrum of political and familial relationships: those between ruler and subject, between parents and children, and between husband and wife. In the 12th century A.D., a loose group of powerful philosophers, though differing over the details, reformulated various so-called Confucian principles to incorporate some of the more deeply held premises of Buddhism, giving in particular a dualistic structure to the Confucian belief system by separating idealist or universalist components—the inherent principles or premises, known as the *li*—from the grosser matter, or manifestations of life-in-action (the *ch'i*).

A final series of shifts took place in the last centuries of imperial China. During the 16th century elements of Confucian doctrine were deepened and altered once again by philosophers who emphasized the inherent morality of the individual and tried to overcome the dualism that they felt Confucians had erected between nature and the human emotions. In the 17th century Confucian scholars confronted the promise and challenge of newly imported scientific ideas from the West, brought by Jesuits and other Catholic missionaries. During the following century Confucian scholars embarked on a newly formulated intellectual quest for the evidential basis of historical and moral phenomena, one that led them cumulatively to peaks of remarkable scholarship. In the 19th century these scholars began to cope with Western technology and constitutional ideas and with the development of new modes of education. But in the 20th century Confucian ideas were attacked from within and without China as contributing to China's economic backwardness, myopic approach to social change, denial of the idea of progress, resistance to science, and a generally stultified educational system.

These attacks were so devastating that as recently as 20 years ago, one would have thought that the chances of Confucius ever again becoming a major figure of study or emulation were slight indeed, in any part of the world. In Communist China, where he had been held up to ridicule or vilification since the Communist victory of 1949, his name was invoked only when mass campaigns needed a symbol of the old order to castigate, as in the "Anti-Confucius and anti-Lin Biao Campaign" of 1973–74. But in that case the real focus of the campaign was Chairman Mao's former "closest comrade-in-arms," General Lin Biao, not the discredited sage of Lu. In Taiwan, though constant lip service was paid to the enduring values of Confucianism, the doctrine that lived on under that name was slanted in content and attracted few of the brightest young minds. It was a version of Confucian belief that followed along lines first laid down by Nationalist Party ideologues during the 1930s in an attempt to boost their own prestige and give a deeper historical legitimacy to party leader Chiang Kai-Shek. Although in Taiwan as in other parts of Asia there were great scholars who continued to explore the sage's inner meaning, in many Asian schools Confucius was also invoked in support of authoritarian and hierarchical value systems. In Europe and the United States, though Confucian texts were studied in East Asian and Oriental studies centers, they did not arouse much excitement, and the young—if they were interested in earlier Asian studies at all—were likely to be far more interested in Taoism or Buddhism.

Now, however, the revival is in full swing. Confucian study societies have sprung up inside the People's Republic of China, with government approval. In Taiwan, Confucianism is studied as a central aspect of philosophical inquiry, and so-called New Confucians are linking his ideas on conduct and the self to certain preoccupations in modern ethics. In the United States especially, many colleges now teach sophisticated and popular courses in "Confucian belief," and a distinguished stream of "Confucian" academics jet around the world as conference participants and even as consultants to foreign governments on the sage. Translations of Confucius's work, and that of his major followers, are in print with popular presses, often in variant editions. And "Confucian principles" are cited approvingly as being one of the underpinnings of the disciplined work habits and remarkable international economic success of a number of Asian states.

The renewed interest in Confucius is not the result of any rush of new information about him. There has been no newly discovered cache of intimate details about him or his family that could engage the public interest, no fresh sources that can be ascribed to him and thus deepen our sense of his achievement, or that could serve as the basis for new controversies. The scraps of information about Confucius are so slight that they barely give us an outline, let alone a profile, of the man. (The modern name Confucius is an early Western rendering of the sage's Chinese honorific name, "K'ung-fu'tsu.") We are almost certain that he was born in 551 B.C. We have a definite year of death, 479 B.C. He was born in the kingdom of Lu, one of the many small states into which China was then divided and which corresponds roughly to the area of modern Shandong province. His parents might have had aristocratic roots, but they were neither prominent nor wealthy, and though Confucius received a good education in historical and ritual matters, his parents died when he was young, and the youth had to fend for himself. He acquired a number of skills: in clerical work, music, accounting, perhaps in charioteering and archery, and in certain "menial activities" on which we have no other details. Sometime between 507 and 497 B.C. he served in the state of Lu in an office that can be translated as "police commissioner" and that involved hearing cases and meting out punishments. Before and after that stint of service he traveled to various neighboring states, seeking posts as a diplomatic or bureaucratic adviser but meeting with little success. Because of some feud he was, for a time, in mortal danger, but he handled himself with calmness and courage. He married and had one son and two daughters. His son predeceased him, but not before producing an heir. One of his daughters married a student of Confucius who had served time in jail. Confucius approved the match because he believed that the young man had in fact done no wrong. During his later years Confucius was a teacher of what we might now call ethics, ritual, and philosophy; the names of 35 of his students have come down to us.

To compound the problems caused by this paucity of biographical information, we have nothing that we can be completely sure was written by Confucius himself. What we do have is a record of what some of his disciples and students—or their students—said that he said. Usually translated as *The Analects of Confucius,* this collection is brief, aphoristic, and enigmatic. But the *Analects,* despite the problem of indirect transmission, remain our crucial source on Confucius's beliefs, actions, and personality. Not surprisingly, scholars disagree on how to interpret many passages and how much to believe in the authenticity of the different parts of this text. The best and perhaps the only gauges of authenticity are internal consistency, tone, and coherence. One can also look at the construction of each book—there are 20 in all, each running about five pages in English translation—and search for obvious distortions and later additions. The last five of the books, for example, have lengthy sections that present Confucius either as a butt to the Taoists or as an uncritical transmitter of doctrines with which he can be shown in earlier chapters to have disagreed. It is a fairly safe assumption that these were added to the original text by persons with a special cause to plead. Other books give disproportionate space to Confucius's praise of a particular student whom we know from other passages that he rather disliked. Perhaps in such cases we are witnessing attempts to correct the record by later followers of the student concerned. There does not seem to be any political censorship; indeed, one of the mysteries of the later uses of Confucianism concerns the way that the original text as we now have it has been preserved for two millennia even though it seems quite obviously to contradict the ideological uses to which it was being put. Interpretation and commentary, that is to say, carried more weight with readers than did the original words.

Given the bewildering array of philosophical and political arguments that Confucianism has been called on to support, and given, in particular, the generally held belief that Confucius was a strict believer in hierarchy and the values of absolute obedience to superiors, and that he lacked flexibility and imagination, it is an intriguing task to read the

Analects with open eyes and without any presuppositions drawn from later interpretative attempts. What was, in fact, the central message of the man Confucius himself?

Personally, almost two and a half millennia after his death, I find that Confucius is still especially valuable to us because of the strength of his humanity, his general decency, and the fervor of his belief in the importance of culture and the act of learning. He emphatically did not feel that he had any monopoly on truth. Rather, he was convinced that learning is a perpetual process that demands flexibility, imagination, and tenacity. He scolded students who would not get up in the morning, just as he scolded those who were unctuous or complacent. He said that he had no interest in trying to teach those who did not have the curiosity to follow up on a philosophical argument or a logical sequence of ideas after he had given them an initial prod in the right direction. He let his students argue among themselves—or with him—and praised those who were able to make moral decisions that might benefit humankind in general. But at the same time he adamantly refused to talk about the forces of heaven or to speculate on the nature of the afterlife, since there was so much that he did not know about life on this Earth that he was convinced such speculations would be idle.

It is clear that Confucius derived great pleasure from life. Once, one of his students could not think what to say to an influential official who had asked what sort of a person Confucius really was. Hearing of the incident, Confucius gently chided his student with these words: "Why did you not simply say something to this effect: He is the sort of man who forgets to eat when he tries to solve a problem that has been driving him to distraction, who is so full of joy that he forgets his worries and who does not notice the onset of old age?"

This brief exchange comes from *The Analects of Confucius*, book VII, section 19, and it is typical of words that Confucius left us, words through which we

can in turn analyze his character.* Another example could be taken from Confucius's views concerning loyalty to the state and the value of capital punishment. In later periods of Chinese history, it was commonplace to assert that "Confucian" bureaucrats and scholars should always put their duty to the state and the dynasty they served ahead of personal and family loyalties. Chinese history is also replete with grim details of executions carried out in the name of "Confucian" ideology against those who violated the state's laws. But in the most clearly authenticated books of the *Analects* that we have, we find completely unambiguous views on these central matters of human practice and belief. What could be clearer than this?

> The Governor of She said to Confucius, "In our village there is a man nicknamed 'Straight Body.' When his father stole a sheep, he gave evidence against him." Confucius answered, "In our village those who are straight are quite different. Fathers cover up for their sons, and sons cover up for their fathers. Straightness is to be found in such behavior." (XIII/18)

On executions, Confucius was equally unambiguous:

> Chi K'ang Tzu asked Confucius about government, saying, "What would you think if, in order to move closer to those who possess the Way, I were to kill those who do not follow the Way?" Confucius answered, "In administering your government, what need is there for you to kill? Just desire the good yourself and the common people will be good. The virtue of the gentleman is like wind; the virtue of the small man is like grass. Let the wind blow over the grass and it is sure to bend." (XII/19)

If it were humanly possible, Confucius added, he would avoid the law altogether: "In hearing litigation, I am no different from any other man. But if you insist on a difference, it is, perhaps, that

I try to get the parties not to resort to litigation in the first place." (XII/13) In the long run, the fully virtuous state would be forever free of violent death: "The Master said, 'How true is the saying that after a state has been ruled for a hundred years by good men it is possible to get the better of cruelty and to do away with killing.'" (XIII/11)

Since the words of Confucius have been preserved for us mainly in the form of aphorisms or snatches of dialogue—or the combination of the two—one way to find a coherent structure in his thought is to track the remarks he made to specific individuals, even if these are widely scattered throughout the *Analects*. Sometimes, of course, there is only one remark, especially in the case of those whose behavior Confucius considered beyond the pale. My favorite example here is his dismissal of Yuan Jang, allegedly once his friend: "Yuan Jang sat waiting with his legs spread wide. The Master said, 'To be neither modest nor deferential when young, to have passed on nothing worthwhile when grown up, and to refuse to die when old, that is what I call being a pest.' So saying, the Master tapped him on the shin with his stick." (XIV/43) That tapping on the shin, perhaps playful, perhaps in irritation, shows an unusual side of Confucius. Was he trying to add physical sting to his sharp words? More commonly with him, it was a laugh or a shrug that ended a potentially confrontational exchange.

With several of his students, Confucius clearly felt a deep rapport, even when they did not see eye to eye. One such student was Tzu-lu, who was more a man of action than a scholar. Confucius loved to tease Tzu-lu for his impetuosity. Thus, after telling his students that if he were on a raft that drifted out to sea, Tzu-lu would be the one to follow him, Confucius added wryly that that would be because Tzu-lu had at once more courage and less judgment than his teacher. On another occasion, when Tzu-lu asked if Confucius thought he, Tzu-lu, would make a good general, Confucius replied that he would rather not have as a general someone who would try to walk across a river or strangle a tiger with his bare hands. (V/7 and VII/11)

Different in character, but still very much his own man, was the merchant and diplomat Tzu-kung. Confucius acknowledged that Tzu-kung was shrewd and capable, and made a great profit from his business deals. He even agreed that Tzu-kung's type of intelligence was especially useful in the world of literature and thought: "Only with a man like you can one discuss the Odes. Tell such a man something and he can see its relevance to what he has not been told." (I/16) But Confucius did not like Tzu-kung's insistence on always trying to put people in a ranked order of priorities, as if they were so many objects—"For my part I have no time for such things," Confucius observed—and he was equally upset if he felt that Tzu-kung was skimping things that really mattered because of his private feelings: "Tzu-kung wanted to dispense with the practice of ritually killing a sacrificial sheep at the announcement of the new moon. The Master said, 'You love the sheep, but I love the Rites.'" (XIV/29 and III/17)

Most readers of the *Analects* feel that the student called Yen Yuan was clearly Confucius's favorite, and the one closest to the Master by behavior and inclination. Yen Yuan was poor but lived his life without complaining. He did not allow poverty to sour or interrupt his search for the Way, and his intelligence was truly piercing. As Tzu-kung, not a modest man, put it, "When he [Yen Yuan] is told one thing he understands 10. When I am told one thing I understand only two." To which Confucius sighed in agreement, "Neither of us is as good as he is." (V/9) In a similar vein, Confucius praised Yen Yuan's prudence, contrasting it with Tzu-lu's bravado. As Confucius phrased it, Yen Yuan was the kind of man who "when faced with a task, was fearful of failure," and who knew how "to stay out of sight when set aside;" furthermore, Yen Yuan was not above making mistakes, but more important, "he did not make the same mistake twice." (VII/11 and VI/3) When Yen Yuan died young, before being able to achieve his full promise, Confucius gave way to a conspicuous display of immoderate grief. When some of his

students remonstrated with him for showing such "undue sorrow," Confucius's answer was brief but powerful: "If not for him for whom should I show undue sorrow?" (IX/10)

Confucius lived to a fine old age, and not even regret over the loss of his favorite student and his own son could blunt the pleasures he felt at his own mounting experience and the attainment of something that might be approaching wisdom. He did not boast about the knowledge he had acquired—indeed he thought he was lucky to have got as far as he had. As he put it once to Tzu-lu: "Shall I tell you what it is to know? To say you know when you know, and to say you do not know when you do not, that is knowledge." (II/17) His own greatest ambition, as he once told Yen Yuan and Tzu-lu jointly, was "to bring peace to the old, to have trust in my friends, and to cherish the young." (V/26) On another occasion he went even further, telling his followers, "It is fitting that we hold the young in awe. How do we know that the generations to come will not be the equal of the present?" (IX/23) In the passage that is perhaps the most famous of his sayings, Confucius gave his own version of the stages of life, and it is as different as anything could be from Shakespeare's "Seven Ages of Man," with its heart-rending account of man's descent into the weakness and imbecility of old age after a brief phase of youthful vigor. Whereas according to the *Analects*, the Master said, "At 15 I set my heart on learning; at 30 I took my stand; at 40 I came to be free from doubts; at 50 I understood the Decree of Heaven; at 60 my ear was attuned; at 70 I followed my heart's desire without overstepping the line." (II/4)

Certainly we should not read Confucius as though he were always right. And as we read through the *Analects* we can find Confucius revealing a fussy and sometimes impatient side. Some of his vaunted arguments seem like quibbles, and he could be punctilious to the point of prudishness. His political motivations are often obscure, and he seems to appreciate various struggling rulers' foibles less than his own. But cleared of the ac-

cumulation of unsubstantiated details and textual over-interpretations that have weighed him down across the centuries, we find to our surprise an alert, intelligent, and often very amusing man.

How then did he get the reputation that he did, one at once more austere, more pompous, harsh even, and as a reinforcer of the status quo? Strangely enough, part of the reappraisal resulted from the efforts of the man who is undeniably China's greatest historian, Ssu-ma Ch'ien, who lived from around 145 to 89 B.C., during the Han dynasty. In his life's work, a composite history of China entitled simply *Historical Records*, which was completed between 100 and 95 B.C., Ssu-ma Ch'ien aimed to integrate the histories of all China's earlier states and rulers with the steady and inexorable rise to power of the centralizing Ch'in dynasty (221–209 B.C.), and he determined to give Confucius an important role in this process. Thus Ssu-ma Ch'ien paid Confucius the ultimate accolade by placing his story in the section devoted to the ruling houses of early China, as opposed to placing him with other individual thinkers and statesmen in the 70 chapters of biographies that conclude the *Historical Records*. In the summation of Confucius's worth with which he ended his account, Ssu-ma Ch'ien gave concise and poignant expression to his homage:

In this world there have been many people—from kings to wise men—who had a glory while they lived that ended after their death. But Confucius, though a simple commoner, has had his name transmitted for more than 10 generations; all those who study his works consider him their master. From the Son of Heaven, the princes, and the lords on down, anyone in the Central Kingdom who is dedicated to a life of learning, follows the precepts and the rules of the Master. Thus it is that we call him a true Sage.

To give substance to this judgment, Ssu-ma Ch'ien took all known accounts written over the intervening three centuries that purported to describe Confucius, following the principle that if there was no clear reason for discarding an item of biographical information, then he should include it, leaving for later generations the task of winnowing the true from the false. Thus was Confucius given courageous ancestors, his birth described in semi-miraculous terms, his own physical distinction elaborated upon. In one curious addition, Confucius's father was described as being of far greater age than the sage's mother: By one interpretation of the phrase used by Ssu-ma Ch'ien, that the marriage was "lacking in proportion," Confucius's father would have been over 64, while his mother had only recently entered puberty. Confucius's precocious interest in ritual and propriety, his great height and imposing cranial structure, the fecundity of the flocks of cattle and sheep that he supervised in one of his first official posts, his preternatural shrewdness in debate, his instinctive brilliance at interpreting unusual auguries—all of these were given documentary precision in Ssu-ma Ch'ien's account. The result is that Confucius not only emerges as a key counselor to the rulers of his native state of Lu, but the meticulousness of his scholarship and his flair for editing early texts of poetry, history, and music are presented as having attracted an ever-widening circle of hundreds or even thousands of students from his own and neighboring states.

Having constructed this formidable image of a successful Confucius, Ssu-ma Ch'ien was confronted by the need to explain the reasons for Confucius's fall from grace in Lu and for his subsequent wanderings in search of rulers worthy of his service. Being one of China's most gifted storytellers, Ssu-ma Ch'ien was up to this task, presenting a convincing scenario of the way the sagacity of Confucius's advice to the ruler of Lu made him both respected and feared by rival rulers in northern China. One of them was finally able to dislodge Confucius by sending to the ruler of Lu a gift of 24 ravishing female dancers and musicians,

along with 30 magnificent teams of chariot horses. This gift so effectively distracted the ruler of Lu from his official duties—most important, it led him to forget certain key ritual sacrifices—that Confucius had no choice but to leave his court.

In various ways, some subtle, some direct, the portrait of Confucius that Ssu-ma Ch'ien wove incorporated diverse levels of narrative dealing with the unpredictability of violence. This was surely not coincidental, for the central tragedy of Ssu-ma Ch'ien's own life had been his court-ordered castration, a savage punishment inflicted on him by the Han dynasty emperor Wu-ti (r. 141–87 B.C.). Ssu-ma Ch'ien's "crime" had been to write a friend a letter in which he incautiously spoke in defense of a man unjustly punished by the same emperor. Despite this agonizing humiliation, which placed the historian in the same physical category as the venal court eunuchs he so deeply despised, Ssu-ma Ch'ien refused to commit suicide; he maintained his dignity by making his history as grand and comprehensive as possible—his presentation of Confucius being a stunning example of his dedication to craft and content. Thus he describes Confucius as a man who had the bureaucratic power to make major judicial decisions but who did so only with care and consideration of all the evidence. When Confucius acted harshly, according to Ssu-ma Ch'ien, it was only when the long-term threat to his kingdom was so strong that leniency would have been folly. This explains one shattering moment in Ssu-ma Ch'ien's biography. One rival leader was planning to overthrow the ruler of Lu, but each of his ruses was seen through and foiled by Confucius. At last, in desperation, the rival ruler ordered his acrobats and dwarfs to perform wild and obscene dances at a ritual occasion that the ruler of Lu was attending. Confucius, according to Ssu-ma Ch'ien, ordered the dwarfs killed.

In another dissimilar but equally powerful comment on violence, Ssu-ma Ch'ien showed that even the descendants of a man of Confucius's integrity could not escape Emperor Wu-ti's willful power. Thus at the very end of his long biography, before the final summation, Ssu-ma Ch'ien lists all of Confucius's direct descendants in the male line. When he comes to the 11th in line, An-kuo, the historian mentions tersely that An-kuo had died "prematurely" under the "ruling emperor." Ssu-ma Ch'ien knew—and knew that his readers knew—that An-kuo had been executed on Wu-ti's orders for involvement in an alleged court coup. The line had not, however, been stamped out, because An-kuo's wife had borne a son before her husband was killed.

Ssu-ma Ch'ien's attempt to reconstruct a convincing psychological and contextual universe for Confucius was a brilliant one, and his version was elaborated upon and glossed by scores of subsequent scholars, even as suitable pieces of the Confucian legacy were seized upon by later rulers and bureaucrats to justify some current policy decision or to prove some philosophical premise. But after more than two millennia of such accretions, it seems time to go back to the earlier and simpler version of the record and try to see for ourselves what kind of a man Confucius was. The results, I feel, in our overly ideological age, are encouraging to those who value the central premises of humane intellectual inquiry.

---

*All citations of the *Analects* are from D. C. Lau's Penguin Books translation, *Confucius, The Analects*. In some cases I have made minor modifications to his translations.

Jonathan D. Spence is George B. Adams Professor of History at Yale University. His many books include The Death of Woman Wang (1978), The Gate of Heavenly Peace (1981), The Search for Modern China (1990), and, most recently, Chinese Roundabout (1992).

From *The Wilson Quarterly*, Autumn 1993, pp. 30-38. © 1993 by Jonathan D. Spence. Reprinted by permission of the author.

Stories from an Illustrated Explanation of the
Tract of the Most Exalted on Action and Response

Catherine Bell

Late imperial China (1550–1911) saw a remarkable proliferation of religious books written for nonelite social classes, which were growing in strength and status in conjunction with the economic expansion of the period. The availability of inexpensive mass printing at this time also promoted both widespread literacy or near-literacy and the broad marketing of books. In many of these popular religious works, Daoist, Buddhist, and neo-Confucian ideas were woven into a type of nonsectarian, heavily moralistic message concerning virtue, universal laws of cause and effect, and systems for calculating merit and demerit. Such works are generally known as "morality books."

The oldest and most famous morality book is the twelfth-century *Tract of the Most Exalted on Action and Response* (*Taishang ganying pian*). It is a relatively short work of about 1,200 characters that presents itself as the words of the Most Exalted, usually understood to be the Daoist deity, Laozi. His message is that food and bad fortune do not come into one's life without reason; rather, they follow as natural consequences of what people do, just as a shadow follows a form. Alluding to a complex cosmology in which a variety of deities oversee human behavior, the *Tract* teaches how the merit earned from good deeds will bring long life, wealth, and successful descendants, while the retribution that attends evil deeds ensures the eventual suffering of the wicked.

Within a century of its first published appearance in 1164, a Song dynasty emperor printed and distributed thousands of copies of the *Tract* in order to convey this message to his subjects, launching a long history of reprintings for didactic and meritorious purposes. The brief tract was republished with prefaces, commentaries, and stories to help illustrate its principles. Later editions added miracle tales, woodblock illustrations, proverbs, ledgers with which to calculate one's balance of merit and demerit, as well as lists of those who had donated to the printing of the text. In contrast to the direct message of the Most Exalted, which comprises the original short tract, many of these expanded editions began to call attention

to the physical text itself, urging the reader to venerate the book and disseminate it in every way possible. Such piety and enthusiasm gave rise to innumerable large- and small-scale devotional projects to reprint the text. When D. T. Suzuki and Paul Carus published one of several English translations in 1906, they suggested that more copies of the *Tract* had been published in China than any other book in all history.

An "Illustrated Explanation" of the *Tract* compiled by Xu Zuanzeng in 1657 was the basis for an expanded edition published by Huang Zhengyuan (fl. 1713–1755) in 1755. Huang's edition stresses two themes. First, he argues that the *Tract* contains the eternal wisdom of the Confucian sages, but in a form that even the most simpleminded can understand. With the easy commentaries and the selection of appealing stories that he has provided, he goes on, everyone can now read, appreciate, and profit from the message of the *Tract*. Second, Huang repeatedly declares that the most meritorious deeds of all are those activities that help to make the *Tract* available to others. Doing one good deed, such as setting free a caged animal, is certainly laudable, but how can it compare to making others aware of the consequences of their own actions? Hence, in the stories and segment from one of Huang's prefaces that follow, distributing the *Tract* is the height of virtue and sure to bring to anyone the formulaic rewards of prosperity, official position, and filial children.

The ideas of virtue and retribution expressed in these excerpts reflect the neo-Confucian idea that anyone, not just the educated elite, could become a virtuous sage. However, scholars have noted that this idea appears to be highly nuanced by a somewhat mercantile perspective: actions count over intentions; good and bad deeds not only add up or cancel each other out, they are also investments that bear fruit and testify to one's true character; and a practical, this-worldly orientation locates the causes and effects of morality and immorality in the here and now. At the same time, the goals of moral action include not only material prosperity, but also the time-honored goals of social prestige through official recognition by the emperor and a position in the government. It has been suggested that this particular vision of moral action flowered in an era marked by heightened social mobility and the social restructuring that attended urbanization and the expansion of commercial activity. Certainly, morality books like the *Tract* appear to have worked out a simplified and generalized Confucian moral ethos readily appropriated by major segments of the population. This achievement has been linked to the unity and traditionalism of Chinese culture in the late imperial period, on the one hand, and to the emergence of a modern style of moral individualism, on the other.

"On Distributing Morality Books"
by Huang Zhengyuan

It is said that those who do good deeds will obtain good fortune, while those who are not virtuous will experience misfortune. This is the reason for the blessings or calamities that befall the moral and the immoral. How clear it is! There is more than one road to virtue, but none can compare to distributing morality books. By transforming one person, a morality book can go on to transform ten million people. Spreading its teachings through one city, it can spread them through ten million cities. By exhorting one generation to virtue, it can effectively exhort ten million generations. This is different from all other means of virtue, which do things one at a time in only one direction.

If people can make use of this book, they will develop a virtuous heart; then they can be taught how to calculate their merits and demerits, thereby gradually extending their moral character until their virtue is complete. They will come from the towns and villages to advance the nation. The intellectuals will teach the ignorant. Preserving "the way" in this world, they will reverse the degenerate customs of our day. All depends on this book!

Although the book has a philosophy that divides things up into cause and effect, this is the only way to teach people to act virtuously. There is an old saying, "With upper-class people, one talks philosophy; with lower-class people, one talks of cause and effect." Now, it is difficult to exchange talk about philosophy, but there are many who can talk about auspicious or calamitous retribution. And such talk is enough to influence people's hearts. Therefore, while it is appropriate to have books on philosophy, there should be at least as many books on cause and effect.

Those who have composed, compiled, published, or donated to the printing of morality books and were subsequently saved from calamity and danger, amassing blessings and years of long life, both in the past and the present—well, they are too numerous to count!...These forebears attained high positions, prosperity, prestige, and longevity because they distributed morality books. These are just some of the good effects that distributing morality books has on the world and on people's hearts.

It is not a small thing and yet it does not burden people. Why then are there so few believers and so many unbelievers? People just do not know the truth within morality books. But if you want people to know the truth of morality books, you must first encourage them to be distributed. After they are disseminated, then one can hope that many will actually see the books. The greater the number of people who see it, then naturally the number who come to know its truth will also increase. Those who can sincerely grasp the truth in morality books will grow in virtue.

STORIES

A. Zhu Jiayou of the Qiantang District in Zhejiang Province was employed in the salt business and fond of doing good deeds. When Mr. Lin Shaomu was the General Surveillance Commissioner for Zhejiang, Zhu begged him to write out the two morality books, *Tract on Action and Response* and *Essay on Secret Merit (Yinzhi wen),* in handsome script in order to engrave the texts in stone. He also asked him to contribute more than ten thousand sheets of paper to make copies. All those who obtained a copy treasured the fine calligraphy. Night and day Zhu made copies. After a while, he gradually became able to understand the full meaning of the text, fortifying his body and soul. Both the one who wrote out the texts and the one who gave copies of them away received blessings in return. Zhu's son was given an eminent position in Anhui Province, while Lin was later appointed to an office with jurisdiction over the provinces of Hubei and Hunan. (Huang, 1:20b)

B. Once there was a man from the Wu Xi District in Jiangsu, named Zou Yigui, also called Xiaoshan (Little Mountain). At the time of the provincial examinations people were contributing to the printing of morality books and wanted him to donate also. Zou declined, saying, "It is not because I am unwilling to give money. Rather I fear that people will be disrespectful to the text and that would put me at fault." That night he dreamed that the god Guandi appeared to scold him, saying, "You study books and illuminate their basic principles, yet you also speak like this! If all people followed your example, virtue would practically disappear." Zou prostrated himself and begged forgiveness. He printed and circulated one thousand copies in order to atone for his fault. Moreover, by himself he painted a religious image on a board and devoutly chanted in front of it morning and night. Later, in the year 1727, he placed first in special examinations and entered the prestigious Hanlin academy, where he held a series of official positions, culminating in an appointment as Vice Minister in the Ministry of Rites. Zou always said to people, "One word is enough to incur fault. And among evil doers, no one is worse than the person who hinders the virtue of others." This story demonstrates that anyone who impedes contributions to morality books is guilty of the greatest fault and will be punished by Heaven. (Huang, Zushi shanshu bian section, 1:20a–b)

C. Shan Yangzhu lived at a small Buddhist temple. When he was born, he was weak and often ill. His mother prayed for him, vowing that if her son were cured, he would be a vegetarian for his whole life. In addition, she nursed him at her breast for six full years until he began to eat rice at the age of seven. When his mother died, he continued to live at the temple for forty-one years, yet he was in constant pain and suffering for half his life. One day he read the *Tract on Action and Response* and, thinking about his parents, suddenly repented of all his bad deeds. Thereafter, he collected different editions of the *Tract* and amended them with his own understanding of its meaning—revising, distinguishing and analyzing point by point. Altogether his study came to 330,000 words, divided into eight volumes and entitled *An Exposition of the Tract of the Most Exalted on Action and Response*. He did this in order to made amends for all his misdeeds, but also as an attempt to repay some small part of the boundless loving kindness of his parents. In 1655 he organized people to donate the money for publishing it. Because of these activities, everything that was painful and unhappy in his life gradually improved. (Huang, 1:28b)

D. At the end of the Yuan dynasty (1280—1368) there was a man named Chu Shaoyi, who not only diligently practiced the teachings of the *Tract on Action and Response,* but also printed and distributed it. He set each phrase to music so that his wife and the women in their quarters could understand it and be enlightened.

At that time the country fell into strife caused by rival warlords. One of them was Chen Youliang. When Chen was young and very poor, Chu had once helped him. Many years later, after Youliang and his army had occupied the provinces of Hubei and Guangdong, Youliang falsely proclaimed himself emperor of the country. He summoned Chu to come work for him and frequently gave him gifts of gold and silk. Chu did not dare refuse the gifts, but stored them in a bamboo chest and used them only to aid hungry families. Although he himself needed firewood and rice, he was not willing to use any of the gifts.

After the Ming emperor Taizu quelled the chaos and ascended the throne (1368), he sought out retired scholars of virtue throughout the empire. Civil authorities communicated the proclamation and recommended Chu, who was summoned to the capital. The emperor asked him: "Dear sir, what would give you the most pleasure?" Chu replied: "As for me, I am just an ordinary man who is pleased to live now in an age of great peace and prosperity. I only want the strength and diligence to plow and plant my fields. Virtue comes naturally that way. In addition, I want to instruct my children in virtue and teach my grandchildren. Nothing can give me more pleasure than these things."

Taizu then said: "The day that Chen Youliang usurped the throne, you sir did not join his side. Youliang honored and respected you, so we can see that even though he was an evil man, he was capable of rewarding virtue and righteousness. Virtue can influence anyone—you can trust that. The *Book of Chu* says that only virtue should be treasured. You sir will be called 'the treasure of the nation.'" Then the emperor himself wrote out those four characters, "regard as the treasure of the nation," and bestowed it on him. In addition, the emperor gave him elegantly spun silk and a special one-horse chariot to take him back home. By imperial order, each month the civil authorities were to provide Chu with grain and meat for the rest of his life. His son was appointed a provincial governor in Yunnan and his grandson entered the national university to study. As soon as the grandson's studies were completed, he received an official post in accord with his abilities. (Huang 3:6a)

E. Zhou Guangpu developed an upset stomach and became so ill that for more than twenty days he could not eat or drink. He was so sick that two deputies from the underworld arrived, put him in chains, and led him out the door. When they had traveled approximately ten miles, he saw a man off in the woods calling his name. He quickly went over to him and saw that it was none other than his dear old friend Ji Yunhe. The two men clasped hands and wept, greatly moved to talk with each other again after such a long separation. Then Ji drew close to Zhou's ear and whispered: "While I was alive, I was without fault because of all my education. I am trusted by the chief officers and judge of the underworld beneath Mount Tai. The fates of all the living and dead pass through my hands, so I can help you in the other world. The most important thing is the *Tract on Action and Response.* In a little while, when you come before the court, just say that you once made a vow to recite it ten thousand times. Beg to be released and returned to live in order to complete the vow. If the judge has any questions, I will plead for you myself." When he finished speaking, he left.

The two deputies escorted Zhou to a huge government office where he saw lots of people coming and going. Some were welcomed or sent off with drum rolls in their honor. Some wandered about freely, while others, manacled with chains, were led to and from the hells. Suddenly he heard his name called out as his case was summoned before the court. Zhou went up to the desk and kneeled. The judge spoke: "You are said to have been well-behaved and devout, but you were fond of eating animals and birds—even catching insects for food. If you please, are they not living things too? It is appropriate for you to be sentenced to the hell of the hungry ghosts for punishment."

Weeping and pleading, Zhou repeated what Ji had told him. The judge asked his officers if the story was true or not. Ji, who had been waiting on the side, cried out "It is true!" and presented his record book to the judge. When he had examined it, the judge smiled and said: "Because of this virtuous vow, it is proper to return him." Ji then spoke up again, saying, "This person was very sick. You should order a heavenly doctor to cure him." So the judge issued a command that Zhou be attended by a heavenly physician. The same two deputies escorted Zhou back home where he saw his body lying on the bed. The deputies pushed his soul back into its place and Zhou immediately regained consciousness.

Thinking that the heavenly doctor would be one of the Daoist immortals, Tao [Hongjing] (456–536 C. E.) and Xu [Mi] (303–363 C. E.), Zhou made a great effort to get up and with a cane started off for the Tao and Xu Temple across the river to pray. By the time he got to the middle of the bridge, he was doubled over and stumbling. A traveler from Shanxi stopped to help him. "I can see from your fatigue and the look on your face that you are troubled by a sick stomach. If it is not cured, you will surely die. I have some small skill and can cure you immediately. Why not follow me?"

They went together to a small house where they found a stove. The traveler started a fire to boil water for tea. From his side he pulled out a silver needle. He inserted it approximately an inch into the right side of Zhou's heart, and then twice lit some herbs on the end of it. Zhou cried out with pain. The traveler immediately stopped the burning, pulled out the needle, and applied a medicated bandage.

By this time the tea was ready. The traveler filled a small cup and asked Zhou to drink. Zhou declined, saying, "For many days I have not been able to consume even small amounts." The traveler replied, "This tea is not the same. Please try it." Zhou then drank two cups without any trouble. He felt his energy suddenly renewed. The traveler advised him, saying: "When you return home, it is best to drink rice soup at first, then eat only diluted rice gruel. After seven days you can eat and drink normally."

Zhou did as he had been told, and as a result he recovered in several days. He went to find the traveler in order to thank him, but there was no trace of him—even the house was gone. Only then did he realize that the stranger must have been the heavenly physician sent to cure him. Throughout his life Zhou faithfully recited the *Tract on Action and Response*, acquiring success, blessings, and long life (Huang, Lingyan section, 10a)

F. Li Dezhang was a middle-aged man whose wife had died. He had only one child, a fourteen-year-old son named Shouguan. Dezhang acquired some merchandise, one thousand carrying poles, and proceeded to the prov-inces of Hunan and Guangdong in order to sell them. Liyong, a man-servant with the household, accompanied the merchandise to keep an eye on it, while Li himself and Shouguan looked for a fast boat in order to take a trip on the Wujiang River. Father and son leisurely went ashore to visit the great royal temple there. Inside there was a Daoist priest with a book, who inquired of them, saying: "This temple prints the *Tract on Action and Response*. Would you be so kind as to make a contribution?" Dezhang hesitated without answering. Just then the boatman arrived to say that the wind was favorable and he wanted to set sail. So Li Dezhang put down the book and they hurried away to the depart in the boat.

When they came to the middle of the river, they suddenly encountered a storm that overturned the boat. Father and son both fell into the water, but the two were not able to find each other. Dezhang was rescued by a fishing boat, which let him off where he could meet his own cargo ship. He thanked and generously rewarded the fishermen. Then the master and his servant, Liyong, returned to the temple where they prayed for an explanation. The response was: "The *Tract on Action and Response* is a sacred text to save the world. Earlier you were not willing to make a contribution to it. Hence, you have come to this end." Dezhang replied: "If the Most Exalted has the divine power to enable my son and me to meet again, I will put up the whole cost of the project, and you will not have to use a cent that has been contributed." He ordered Liyong to fetch two hundred ounces of silver from the bank and hand it over to the temple as an offering.

Master and servant supervised the loading of the cargo on the ship and traveled to the city of Wuchang. On route they met an old traveling merchant named Fu Youcai who had lost money and was having trouble making his return trip home. This man was an engaging talker who could flatter people with his charm. Dezhang developed a close friendship with him. While they were traveling, the merchandise was greatly delayed, so Dezhang left half of it in Wuchang and half with Youcai. Liyong left them to go to Jingxiang. Less than a month later he received a letter from his master telling him that the merchandise had already been sold for two thousand ounces of silver. Since Liyong was in Jingxiang taking care of things and unable to get away, he arranged for the receipts to be given to Youcai, who would go to Wuchang and collect the money. When Youcai had the silver in his hands, however, he immediately rolled up his conscience and fled with the money. When Dezhang learned that Youcai had taken the money, he was grieved and depressed, losing all interest in returning home. He drifted for two years before he made any plans to go back. But Heaven helps virtuous people, and Dezhang had already contributed to the *Tract on Action and Response*. When there is virtue, there will be recompense.

When his son Shouguan fell into the water, he grabbed hold of a large piece of wood and floated to a village. There a widow took care of him as if he were her own son.

He studied and entered school. Unexpectedly one day at the bank of a stream he saw a young woman throw herself into the water. He immediately dove in to rescue her. When he asked her why she had done it, she answered: "My father's name is Fu Youcai. Years ago he left on business and arranged for me to stay with the family of my maternal uncle, who has no scruples at all. He wanted to sell me into a house of prostitution, so I tried to commit suicide." Suddenly there were lots of people all around. One of them was an old man who asked the young woman in surprise, "You, why are you here?" The woman looked at him and saw that it was her father. Father and daughter were reunited; you can imagine their happiness. Youcai was moved to gratitude by Shouguan's righteousness, so he gave his daughter to the young man as a wife and also arranged that the thousand ounces of swindled silver be entirely turned over to him as well.

Shouguan missed his father, and his heart pressed him to try to find him. So with his father-in-law he bought a boat and went to the Wujiang River to search for clues to his father's whereabouts. Not far from the royal temple, he saw the back of a boat with its sails set in readiness to depart. At the prow stood a man who looked just like his father. When they came up to each other, both father and son rejoiced in wild excitement, stopping only to question the other about what had happened since they had been parted. Shouguan told how he had taken a wife and obtained so much silver, recounting his story detail by detail. Dezhang asked to meet his new in-laws and entered the other ship's hold. He noticed that his son's father-in-law lay in bed with his face covered, not rising to get up. Dezhang lifted the cover and saw that it was Youcai. He laughed and said: "Once we were good friends. Now we are relatives by marriage and the thousand ounces of silver you have given to my son. What harm has there been? Let us be friends as we were before."

Together they went to the royal temple to fulfill Dezhang's vow. The carving of the blocks was completed, so they contributed another three hundred pieces of silver to print one thousand copies and have them distributed widely to exhort people to virtue. Families that were separated are brought back together again—is this not a reward for printing the *Tract on Action and Response?* (Huang, Lingyan section, 14a)

Further Reading

Catherine Bell, "Printing and Religion in China: Some Evidence from the *Taishang Ganying Pian*," *Journal of Chinese Religions* 20 (Fall 1992): 173–86; Judith A. Berling, "Religion and Popular Culture: The Management of Moral Capital in *The Romance of the Three Teachings*," in *Popular Culture in Late Imperial China*, ed., David Johnson, Andrew J. Nathan, and Evelyn S. Rawski (Berkeley: University of California Press, 1985), pp. 188–218; Cynthia J. Brokaw, *The Ledgers of Merit and Demerit: Social Change and Moral Order in Late Imperial China* (Princeton: Princeton University Press, 1991); Evelyn S. Rawski, *Education and Popular Literacy in Ch'ing China* (Ann Arbor: Center for Chinese Studies of the University of Michigan, 1979); Sakai Tadao, "Confucianism and Popular Educational Works," in Wm. Theodore de Bary, *Self and Society in Ming Thought*, ed. (New York: Columbia University Press, 1970); D. T. Suzuki and Paul Carus, trans., *Treatise on Response and Retribution by Lao Tze* (La Salle: Open Court, 1973).

Asceticism in Early Taoist Religion: Introduction

Stephen Eskildsen

The origins of the Taoist religion cannot be traced to a single founder or historical event. The religion emerged during the early centuries of the common era through the convergence of diverse elements of belief and practice. These elements were largely drawn from ancient immortality lore, macrobiotics, alchemy, Taoist philosophy, *yin-yang*/five agents cosmology, state cult, popular religion, and Confucian ethics. Buddhist beliefs and practices also were eagerly incorporated into the mix, particularly from the fourth century onward.

Immortality has always been a cherished goal in the Taoist religion, and many Taoists have practiced asceticism in the hope of gaining everlasting life. One of the most salient features of early Taoist asceticism was the great emphasis on fasting and the amazing variety of techniques devised to suppress hunger. Celibacy, self-imposed poverty, wilderness seclusion, and sleep avoidance also were practiced. Of course, not all early Taoists were ascetics. As has been the case in most other major religions, severe forms of self-discipline and self-denial were carried out primarily by a spiritual elite who made religious self-cultivation their exclusive vocation. This spiritual elite probably represented a distinct minority within the ranks of the faithful.

My working definition of "asceticism" is that proposed by Walter O. Kaelber in *The Encyclopedia of Religion*. While admitting that the word has no universally accepted definition, Kaelber states that it may be defined as follows when used in a religious context:

> a voluntary, sustained, and at least partially systematic program of self-discipline and self-denial in which immediate, sensual or profane gratifications are renounced in order to attain a higher spiritual state or a more thorough absorption in the sacred.

In most religions, the higher spiritual state and the absorption in the sacred are meant to help guarantee some form of salvation. For early religious Taoists, salvation meant not only a perfection or perpetuation of the spirit but also physical longevity and immortality. Their asceticism almost always purported to improve the strength and health of the human body. Even though Taoist ascetics sometimes taxed their bodies severely, they believed that their strength and health would eventually be restored if they courageously persevered in their austerities. Ultimately, their austerities were supposed to perfect them both spiritually and physically, finally transforming them into superhuman, divine beings with limitless longevity and extraordinary powers.

Many of the ascetic practices of the Taoists, in their basic forms, predate the emergence of the Taoist religion itself. The practices originated among ancient immortality seekers who perhaps were active as early as the fourth century B.C.E., if not earlier. Unfortunately, the scarcity of sources makes it difficult to adequately discuss the practices as they existed during such an early period. Our study focuses on roughly the first six centuries of the common era, a period for which a detailed examination of asceticism is feasible, due to a relative abundance of sources. A full exploration of the earliest roots of Taoist asceticism must be left for a future study. Nonetheless some points should be touched upon at the outset concerning some of the early precursors of the Taoist religion and the origins of its ascetic current.

The precursors that first come to mind are the Taoist philosophers of the late fourth or early third century B.C.E. whose wisdom is preserved in the *Laozi* (also known as the *Daode jing*) and the *Zhuangzi*. We do not know whether these philosophers pursued lifestyles or training methods of an ascetic nature. In the first place, we know little about who they were, what they did, and who they associated with. However, these texts do contain certain teachings that are compatible with an ascetic outlook and lifestyle. Prime examples from the *Laozi* would include the following:

The five colors make man's eyes blind;
The five notes make his ears deaf;
The five tastes injure his palate;
Riding and hunting
make his mind go wild with excitement;
Goods hard to come by
Serve to hinder his progress (Ch. 12)

Exhibit the unadorned and embrace the
    uncarved block,
Have little thought of self and as few desires as
    possible. (Ch. 19)
There is no crime greater than having too many
    desires;
There is no disaster greater than not being
    content;
There is no misfortune greater than being
    covetous.
Hence in being content, one will always have
    enough. (Ch. 46)

The *Laozi* conveys an apprehensive attitude toward stimuli that arouse the senses and enjoins its readers to decrease their self-centered desires and be content with what they have. Passages such as the aforementioned served as inspiration and justification for later Taoist ascetics. However, as we shall see, Taoist asceticism sometimes went well beyond what the *Laozi* recommends. Some religious Taoist texts teach one to eschew even the most basic necessities for a normal existence, such as food, rest, and companionship.

One of the most fundamental teachings of the *Zhuangzi* is that one should possess an outlook that "evens things out" (*qiwu*). While the profoundest subtleties of this outlook will not be explored here, it is relevant to point out that the *Zhuangzi* asserts that all things and circumstances that one may confront are of equal quality and desirability. Based on this outlook, one is to abandon all value judgments, desires, and worries. By doing so, one simply experiences the universe as it is and willingly accords with its flux. Such a person is described as follows:

The utmost man is daemonic. When the wide woodlands blaze they cannot sear him, when the Yellow River and the Han freeze they cannot chill him, when swift thunderbolts smash the mountains and whirlwinds shake the seas they cannot startle him. A man like that yokes the clouds to his chariot, rides the sun and moon and roams beyond the four seas; death and life alter nothing in himself, still less the principles of benefit and harm! (Ch. 2)

A person who "evens things out" would presumably not get wound up in pursuits of pleasure, wealth, and fame. His inner freedom would enable him to be content in any situation, however bleak. However, this does not mean to say that one should purposefully eschew the simple pleasures and bare necessities of life. In saying that the "utmost man" is impervious to fires, freezing, thunderstorms, and death, the *Zhuangzi* describes his inner equanimity and freedom. Later Taoist immortality seekers hoped to gain invulnerability at both the spiritual and physical levels, and sought to do so through self-imposed austerities. In their view, the inner virtue acquired through the austerities would somehow be accompanied by the attainment of physical immortality and supernormal powers. The *Zhuangzi*, however, makes no such promise. It teaches its readers to see death as a circumstance no less desirable than life and to willingly accept it as one of the marvelous workings of nature. Later religious Taoist texts similarly assert that Taoist adepts must overcome their yearning for life and fear of death. However, paradoxically, gaining such a state of mind was somehow supposed to enable them to evade bodily death. But in the view of the *Zhuangzi*, the acceptance of death brings no such tangible reward; it simply liberates people from their anxieties.

Similarly, the *Laozi* contains no clear statements affirming the possibility of physical immortality. In certain places it does present its wisdom as a means for surviving worldly perils and reaching a ripe old age. Certain passages could be interpreted as endorsements of yogic practices of a macrobiotic nature. Still, there is no clear indication that the author(s) believed in physical immortality.

However, immortality beliefs certainly existed by the time the *Laozi* and *Zhuangzi* were written. By the fourth century B.C.E., people were beginning to entertain ideas about immortal, superhuman beings who lived in remote, inaccessible mountains or islands. One such being is mentioned in the *Zhuangzi*, within a conversation (probably fictional) recorded between two men named Jian Wu and Lian Shu. Jian Wu tells Lian Shu about the following "wild extravagances" that he had heard from an eccentric named Jie Yu:

In the mountains of far-off Guyi there lives a daemonic man, whose skin and flesh are like ice and snow, who is gentle as a virgin. *He does not eat the five grains but sucks in the wind and drinks the dew* (emphasis added); he rides the vapour of the clouds, yokes flying dragons to his chariot, and roams beyond the four seas. When the daemonic in him concentrates it keeps creatures free from plagues and makes the grain ripen every year. (Ch. 1)

Most important for our purposes is the italicized portion. As we shall see, phrases like this commonly refer to severe fasting methods where the adept shuns solid foods while attempting to nourish himself or herself on air and saliva. During this period, superhuman beings with unusual eating habits may have merely been objects of fantasy and admiration. There still may not have been adepts who aspired to become like them. But if there were such adepts, they may have been practicing some of the fasting techniques that were later pursued by Taoist ascetics.

The deficiency of source hinders us from knowing much about the asceticism of the earliest immortality seekers. Most of the information on them is found in Sima Qian's (ca. 145–86 B.C.E.) *Shiji* (Chronicles of the Historian). There we are told about numerous court magicians (*fangshi*) from the kingdoms of Qi and Yan who offered their services to kings and emperors. Heeding their advice, several rulers during the fourth through the second centuries B.C.E. sent out expeditions to search for the legendary island dwellings of immortals. The court magicians also endorsed various cultic observances and macrobiotic techniques as aids toward immortality. It should be noted that Li Shaojun, active during the reign of Han Emperor Wu (Wudi, 140–87 B.C.E.), included what was probably a fasting method (*gudao* or the "method of grains") among his practices. However, even though fasting may have been included among the methods of the court magicians, the word "ascetic" would not seem to aptly characterize these men of worldly ambition. Still, it is not hard to imagine that there would have been some immortality seekers who observed their cults and honed their skills without seeking the patronage of the rich and powerful.

The *Xinyu*, written in 196 B.C.E. by the Confucian politician Lu Jia, contains an interesting criticism of immortality seekers.

> [If a man] strains and belabors his body, going deep into the mountains and seeking [to become a] Divine Immortal, [if he] abandons his parents, does away with his blood relatives (lit., "bones and flesh"), abstains from the five grains, and gives up the *Shi* [jing] and the *Shu* [jing] (i.e., classical learning), [thus] turning his back to what is treasured by Heaven and Earth in his seeking for the Tao of deathlessness; then he can no more communicate with [the people of] the world, or prevent what is not [right from happening].

This passage strongly suggests that immortality seekers had already acquired a reputation for their austerities and unworldly tendencies.

At some point, immortality seeking and Taoist philosophy came to be intimately linked. When and how this occurred is unclear. However, magicians of the kind previously mentioned may have been responsible for this phenomenon, as perhaps were the scholars of the Huang-Lao school (the line of demarcation between these two groups is blurry; they probably overlapped). The Huang-

Lao school originated in the Warring States kingdom of Qi—which covered most of present-day Shandong Province—and achieved its peak of influence during the early second century B.C.E. This school venerated two figures as its patrons; Laozi (the putative, most likely legendary author of the *Laozi* book) and the Yellow Emperor (a legendary emperor of remote antiquity). Its adherents interpreted and adapted the teachings of the *Laozi* to develop their own theories on statecraft and self-cultivation. They appear to have also promoted various macrobiotic measures such as alchemy, medicine, sexual yoga, light gymnastics, and dietetics. The findings unearthed in 1973 at the tomb of the Lady of Dai (d. ca. 186 B.C.E.) in Changsha (Hunan Province) attest to the fact that Taoist philosophy and macrobiotics simultaneously held the interest of many members of the early Han aristocracy. Numerous books were found in the tomb, including two copies of the *Laozi* (the earliest manuscripts of the book available), a Huang-Lao text called the *Huangdi sijing* (Four Canons of the Yellow Emperor), diagrams of macrobiotic light gymnastic postures, and a fasting manual entitled *Quegu shiqi pian* (Chapter on Getting Rid of Grains and Eating Air). Most amazingly, the corpse of the Lady of Dai was found preserved with skin and internal organs intact.

By the first century of the common era, immortality seekers had come to be known as "Taoists." This is apparent from evidence in the *Lunheng*, written by Latter Han skeptic Wang Chong (23–100 C.E.). In a chapter entitled "Taoist Untruths" (*daoxu*), Wang Chong endeavors to debunk the immortality beliefs and techniques of his time. In one passage, he writes,

> There is a belief that by the doctrine of Laozi one can transcend the world. Through serenity and non-desire one nurtures the essence (*jing*) and cherishes the vital force (*qi*). The longevity of people is based on their spirits. If their spirits are unharmed, they will live long and will not die. After accomplishing his affairs (his duties as royal archivist?), Laozi practiced this. After a hundred years he transcended the world and became a Perfected Being. (The text follows with Wang Chong's rebuttal of these beliefs.)

This passage not only attests to the linkage between Taoist philosophy and immortality seeking, but also reflects how the philosopher Laozi was revered as a great adept who attained immortality through serenity and non-desire.

The Latter Han Dynasty (25–220 C.E.) represents a critical juncture in the development of the Taoist religion. Immortality-seeking Taoists continued to develop their beliefs and techniques. While some of them only considered Laozi to be one of the many adepts who attained immortality, others went further in glorifying him. They deified him as being nothing less than a cosmic super deity, virtually equating him to the all-creating, all-embracing first principle (the Tao) described in the *Laozi*. They interpreted the *Laozi* along the lines of their own beliefs and utilized it to lend authority to their cosmology, macrobiotics, and mysticism.

The earliest known organized Taoist religious movements, the Great Peace School (*taiping dao*) and the Five Pecks of Rice School (*wudoumi dao*), emerged in the latter part of the second century C.E. The Great Peace School had a large following in the east, in portions of present-day Henan, Hebei, Shandong, Jiangsu, and Anhui provinces. The Five Pecks of Rice School—which later came to be known as the Heavenly Masters School (*tianshi dao*)—thrived in the west, in a region covering portions of present-day Sichuan and Shaanxi provinces. The discovery of the *Laozi bianhua jing* (Scripture on the Transformations of Laozi) from the Dunhuang manuscripts has provided evidence that there were other similar movements during this period. This text apparently belonged to a popular sect—distinct from the Five Pecks of Rice School—that existed in present-day Sichuan Province at the end of the second century.

The Great Peace and Five Pecks of Rice schools found most of their adherents among the peasantry. These schools emphasized ritual healing and rudimentary ethics based on the fundamental assumption that moral transgressions cause diseases. The Five Pecks of Rice School utilized the *Laozi* as its fundamental scripture, interpreting it along ethical lines to formulate moral precepts. Both groups entertained hopes of realizing a utopian age under an enlightened Taoist regime. To help usher in such a utopia, the Great Peace School took to armed revolt (the Yellow Turban revolt) against the Han dynasty in 184, only to be crushed. The Five Pecks of Rice School, situated at a remote distance from the seat of imperial power, enjoyed autonomous political control of its local area for roughly thirty years, before surrendering to military strongman Cao Cao in 215. Its cooperative stance toward its conquerors allowed it to survive as a religious body. An important, unresolved question is whether or not, and to what extent, the two schools propagated immortality techniques. While they may have included adepts of immortality techniques within their fold, it seems likely that most adepts functioned independently of these schools.

In the ensuing centuries, newer religious Taoist movements integrated immortality beliefs and techniques with the ethics and rituals of the Heavenly Masters School. At the same time, they increasingly imitated Buddhist doctrines and practices. Most influential among these movements were the Shangqing movement of the fourth century and the Lingbao movement of the fifth century. Each of these movements promoted new scriptures that they claimed to be revelations of supreme divine truth. By the fifth century, the Taoist religion and Buddhism had become bitter rivals, competing for the support of emperors and the souls of the people. Naturally, as the Taoist religion underwent this formative

process, its asceticism transformed significantly in its form, meaning, and purpose.

Ascetics in various religions have shared the inclination to view spirit (or soul) and matter as being mutually alien and antagonistic entities. Bodily mortification often has been carried out under the assumption that the flesh does little else but hinder one's progress toward salvation. For example, Christian ascetics have tended to view the flesh as the source of sinful impulses that hinder the salvation of the soul. The goal of Jain asceticism is to purify and liberate the soul from *samsara* by "burning away" the karmic matter that adheres to it. Manichaean ascetics considered the soul a particle of light issuing from the true God and aimed to liberate it from the evil prison of flesh.

However, Taoists sought to immortalize both mind and body, and they did not draw a stark contrast between spirit (or soul) and matter. This crucial fact strongly affected the content and nature of their asceticism.

Henri Maspero, the great Western pioneer in Taoist studies, adeptly argued that Taoist theories on souls dictated that Taoists seek eternal life through bodily immortality. To the Chinese, spirit and matter were different modes of *qi* (energy, ether, material force); spirit was a rarefied mode, matter a condensed mode. They thus saw the world as a continuum passing from void to material things. As a result, they had no concept of a soul that played the role of an invisible, spiritual counterpart to the material body. The Chinese view on souls was that every person possessed multiple souls. Although theories about the multiple souls varied in their specifics, a common view maintained that there were two groups of souls; the three *hun* souls and the seven *po* souls. The two groups of souls were believed to separate at death; the *hun* souls were thought to disperse into the skies, and the *po* souls were thought to seep out of the buried corpse into the soil. According to this theory, since the souls separated and dispersed at death, they did not perpetuate the deceased person's personality in an afterlife state that could be properly described as "salvation" or "immortality." Consequently, Maspero argued, the only means by which the Chinese could envision immortality was through the perpetuation of the flesh that kept the multiple souls together in their bodily habitat.

Yet it is possible that some early Taoist immortality seekers did not actually believe in the immortality of the flesh. To believe in it certainly requires a great leap of faith, since virtually all empirical evidence confronted in real life seems to contradict it. Some, in keeping with the spirit of the *Zhuangzi*, may have understood "immortality" strictly as being a metaphor for an inner freedom and peace of mind. Some may have believed only in the immortality of an entity more subtle than the flesh. Many Taoist texts of the Song dynasty (960–1279 C.E.) onward set forth as their highest ideal the immortality and heavenly ascension of the "internal elixir" (*neidan*), a divine, internal entity concocted from the pure, subtle forces latent in the body. When it ascends, this entity, which is also known as the *"yang* spirit" (*yangshen*) or the "body outside of the body" (*shenwai zhi shen*), is said to leave the mortal body behind. Rudiments of such later doctrines may have already existed in the minds of some Taoists during the period covered in this study.

However, while some Taoists probably understood "immortality" in such metaphorical or abstract ways, the immortality of the flesh is not explicitly rejected in any religious Taoist text of the first six centuries C.E. (as far as I am aware). Most early Taoist ascetics probably believed in the possibility of avoiding death and sought to achieve heavenly ascension in the immortal body.

Taoists also developed doctrines wherein hope was maintained for those who had died. First, there was the belief that some adepts had merely feigned their death by employing supernormal techniques of illusion. Even when death was not "feigned," it was believed that one could eventually gain the status of a lesser immortal after a lengthy sojourn in the subterranean realm of the dead, or become resurrected into the realm of humans. (It should be noted that in these scenarios the corpse does not decay and dissipate for eternity; it is somehow preserved, transformed, or regenerated). However, serious adepts who pursued ascetic practices generally aspired to the highest grades of immortality, which were to be attained only by bypassing death.

Because they believed that the body had to be kept intact for their goal to be realized, Taoist adepts usually avoided practices that they considered harmful to their health. They did not wound the body through self-flagellation. They usually emphasized cleanliness and took care of bodily hygiene. They did not malnourish themselves to the point of disease or death—at least not intentionally. Deviations from these norms were rare and tended to be met with criticism from fellow Taoists.

However, because the goal was to make the body immortal and superhuman, Taoist adepts needed to see tangible proof in the here and now that they were training and transforming it properly. The mental fortitude and physical durability to persevere in increasingly greater austerities were in themselves deemed as such proof, as were the trance experiences induced through painstaking measures. Thus practices such as fasting and sleep avoidance were carried out at an intensity comparable to, if not surpassing, the asceticism of other religions. In this sense, the Taoist mind/body view encouraged and intensified asceticism.

Severe forms of asceticism can thus occur even when the practitioner is not indifferent to the well-being of the body. Actually, this phenomenon is not unique to Taoism. For example, within the Christian ascetic tradition, attitudes toward the body have been both negative and positive. An interesting comparison can be made between attitudes expressed in accounts concerning two famous Christian ascetics, Ethiopian Moses and Simeon the Stylite. Ethiopian Moses (ca. 320–407 A.D.) was a monk active

in Egypt. He was a black man (hence the description "Ethiopian") of great physical size and strength who, prior to his conversion and monkhood, had been a slave and a robber and had committed every sort of imaginable sin. Throughout his monastic life, he was obsessed with overcoming his predisposition toward sinful acts and thoughts, which were blamed on his physical size and strength.

> Still, because he boiled with bodily vigor from his former way of life and was excited by pleasureful fantasies, he wasted his body with countless ascetic exercises. On the one hand, he abstained from meat and ate only a little bread, accomplishing a great deal of work and praying fifty times a day. On the other hand, for six years he prayed the whole night standing, never lying down or closing his eyes in sleep. At other times, he would go to the dwellings of the monks at night and secretly would fill the pitcher of each one with water. This was very hard work, for the place where some drew water was ten stades away, some twenty, some even thirty or more. For a long time he continued to have his former bodily strength, although he made every effort to conquer it with many ascetic exercises and oppressed his body with severe labors.

Here is an example where austerities were practiced for the precise purpose of weakening the body. Moses' bodily strength and vigor are described as things that had to be conquered, since they were the cause of his "pleasureful fantasies." The body is seen as the soul's adversary in its quest for salvation.

However, in the *Homily on Simeon the Stylite*, by Jacob of Serug (449–521 A.D.), a very different attitude toward the body is conveyed. Simeon (386–459) was a Syrian monk renowned for lengthy fasts and other austerities. He spent his last forty years praying, exposed to the elements atop a small platform on a pillar approximately sixty feet high. Jacob's homily vividly describes an occasion during Simeon's stay on the pillar when a gangrenous and putrescent ulcer developed on his foot, causing incredible pain. Jacob's account attributes the appearance of the ulcer to the work of the Devil, who was attempting to undermine Simeon's efforts. In spite of the pain, Simeon continued to pray, standing the entire time on his one good foot. The text tells us that while doing so, Simeon sang out the following words:

> My foot stands straight and does not bend. For its Lord will sustain it that it may stand and support the burden of the two. For lo, it bears the palace of the body like a pillar of the masterbuilder who fastens and supports it so that it will not be shaken. O Evil One, the hurt that you are causing does not hurt me since it is sweet for me;

you will tire yourself out as I am not going to leave my labor.

Eventually, when the condition of the bad foot had worsened to where it had rotted to tendons and bones, Simeon cut it off and said to it, "Go in peace until the resurrection. And do not grieve, for your hope will be kept in the kingdom."

Here the adversary is the Devil. The body is Simeon's ally. Even though Simeon's austerities tax the body severely, their purpose is not to weaken the body. Simeon trusts in God to strengthen and sustain the body so it can overcome the challenges of the Devil. He reassures his amputated foot that it will be reunited with him when his body is resurrected on the day of final judgment. Because of this belief in resurrection, the body is seen as bearing an equal stake with the soul in the battle with the Devil and the attainment of salvation.

Thus in the Christian tradition, asceticism has been accompanied by both negative and positive perceptions of the body. Simeon's concern for his body's sustenance and salvation bears a certain resemblance to the attitude of the Taoists. However, Taoism went a step further by asserting that austerities such as fasting and sleep avoidance, even when carried out to the point of bodily weakening and emaciation, would eventually strengthen the body and imbue it with powers previously unknown. Ultimately, in the best case scenario, the body was supposed to directly gain eternal life without undergoing death and resurrection.

For Taoist ascetics, becoming immortal meant redeeming the body from its mortal state. Also, most hoped to ascend to a heavenly realm beyond the ordinary world. Many believed the world itself was approaching inevitable destruction and was becoming increasingly evil in the process. These beliefs undoubtedly heightened their desire to transcend the world. In this sense, Taoist asceticism may have at times been motivated more by negative sentiments toward the mundane world than by positive aspirations toward higher goals. This pessimistic mood is particularly understandable in light of the widespread social strife that existed throughout the period of the late Han and Six dynasties. The end of the Han dynasty was marked by political intrigue and corruption that engendered widespread hardship and dissatisfaction among the populace. The culminative result was the aforementioned Yellow Turban Revolt of 184 C.E. Political and social stability rarely existed throughout the ensuing centuries. Wars persisted during the Three Kingdoms period (220–280) when the Wei, Shu and Wu kingdoms battled for supremacy. After a brief reunification under the Western Jin dynasty (265–316), the north was conquered by non-Chinese peoples who fought incessantly among themselves. During the fleeting intervals of peace, the political scene was rife with corruption, intrigue, and danger, rendering the benefits of social power and status dubious. For the peasantry and aristocracy alike, it must

have often been difficult to be pleased with what the world had to offer.

On the other hand, it can be argued that one's outlook toward the world and society is determined more on a personal, psychological level. Under virtually all circumstances, there are always people who by temperament can only perceive the human condition in a negative light. Nonetheless, one must not disregard the impact the historical context can have in dictating the extent and degree to which an antiworldly mentality can find its expression.

At both the physiological and cosmological levels, Taoist asceticism can be understood as a struggle between the forces of good (yang) and evil (yin). The good forces, at the physiological level, are the body's pure qi and the multitude of internal bodily deities that are activated through austerities. The austerities also serve to subdue the evil forces. The evil forces include the body's impure qi, along with its internal demons that try to undermine the adept's progress. At the cosmological level, the adept endeavors to communicate with divine beings (gods and immortals) and gain their support, while resisting the temptations of the mundane world and the demons that dwell in it. The enlightened mind and heightened spirituality of the ascetic are identified with qi in its refined, subtle forms that belong to the yang principle and possess a divine quality. The ordinary untrained flesh is seen to be full of gross, profane qi of the yin principle that hinders spiritual progress by obscuring the divine qi in the body. The uniqueness of this dualism lies in how the two sides of the duality are not completely alien to each other. Everything, regardless of which side it belongs to, is originally the same thing (qi) that has issued from the primordial state of non-being. The distinction between the things of the two sides lies not in their basic nature but in their degree of purity and refinement. This means that the untrained flesh, even though it is gross and impure, has the potential for transformation. Austerities act as the agent for this transformation.

Taoists fasted to purge the body of its impure qi. Because they considered all ordinary foods impure, they tried to eat as little as possible. To suppress their hunger they ingested special drug recipes and carried out techniques such as breath holding, air swallowing, saliva swallowing and talisman swallowing. The pure qi contained in the air and in their own saliva was thought to nourish the body in the best way possible, activating its latent divine forces in the process. Celibacy was practiced to retain seminal fluid. The vital forces that sustain life were thought to be concentrated in the semen, meaning that ejaculation could lead directly to the shortening of life.

Through their austerities, Taoists hoped to reach a higher spiritual state. By shedding all worldly desires and single-mindedly seeking immortality, they hoped to evoke the sympathy and assistance of gods and immortals. The elimination of sexual desire was considered particularly important in this regard. By employing meditation techniques that usually involved special visualizations, adepts entered trances, thereby hoping to encounter divine beings or gain a foretaste of heavenly realms. These trances also were partially induced and heightened by fasting and sleep avoidance.

Even though Taoist ascetics placed paramount importance upon health, it appears that overzealousness occasionally may have led to bodily harm and even death. The *Zhouyi cantongqi*, an alchemical text ascribed to Wei Boyang of the second century, contains a passage that criticizes the excesses of ascetics.

> [Adepts] eat air and make their intestines
> and stomach growl,
> Exhaling the proper [*qi*] and inhaling the
> evil [*qi*] from the outside.
> They never sleep during the daytime or
> night time,
> And never rest from morning till
> evening.
> Their bodies become more and more exhausted by the day.
> With their consciousness obscure, they
> look like idiots.
> [The blood in] their 100 blood vessels
> boils like water in a kettle,
> Making them unable to reside in pure
> clarity.
> They build walls and erect altars and
> shrines,
> To engage in reverent worship from
> morning till evening.
> Demonic entities manifest their forms to
> them in dreams,
> And they become emotionally moved.
> In their hearts and minds they rejoice,
> And say to themselves, 'My life span will
> definitely be extended!'
> Suddenly they die prematurely,
> And their rotting corpses are exposed.
> (*Zhouyi cantongqi jie* [HY1004/TT628],
> 1/2lb–22a)

It is difficult to determine how often ascetic excesses lead to premature death. Usually, in most such cases, adepts probably fully intended to benefit—not harm—their health. The failure of such adepts could be rationalized by fellow adepts on the grounds that the failed adepts had pursued their methods incorrectly or had lacked inner devotion and moral virtue.

As we shall see, certain "immortality techniques" were tantamount to religious suicide. Theoretically, however, such methods were designed not to destroy the body but to create the illusion of death. The idea, particularly in instances where deadly quantities of poison were ingested, was that the corpse of the adept was merely an illusion fabricated for people to see. While creating this illusion of a corpse, the adept supposedly concealed himself from society to live on elsewhere as an immortal. However, it seems possible that in some cases ascetics may have abused and killed themselves as a result of more negative ideas and feelings. Some of them may have hated their bodies for the impurity of their untrained states. Some may have simply wanted to flee the agonies of worldly existence at all costs.

By the fourth century, and especially the fifth century, Taoists were eagerly incorporating Buddhist doctrines and practices into their religious system. Buddhist doctrines presented the Chinese with new and exciting possibilities for attaining spiritual perfection and transcendence. Taoists adopted the belief in *karma* and reincarnation and came to equate heavenly immortality with the liberation from *samsara*. The doctrine of *karma* accentuated the importance of suppressing and eliminating desires more than ever before. The doctrine of reincarnation caused Taoists to infer the existence of an individual spirit that survives successive bodily deaths. (This directly contradicted the Buddha's doctrine of no soul, or *anatman*. Ironically, however, even Chinese Buddhists were initially unable to avoid drawing this inference from the doctrine of reincarnation.)

As Buddhist influence became greater, there seems to have arisen an increased tendency among Taoists to emphasize spiritual enlightenment and transcendence more than physical longevity and immortality. Furthermore, the newly derived notion of an eternal, transmigrating spirit may have caused some to understand the ultimate salvation solely as the liberation of the spirit. This in turn may have caused some to abandon the ideal of physical immortality altogether. Among such Taoists, there may have arisen a tendency to devalue and abuse the body intentionally, in the hope of expediting the liberation of the spirit.

Apparently due to an awareness of such a problem, the *Yuqing jing* (HY1301/TT1022–102431), an anonymous Taoist scripture of the sixth or seventh century, vehemently criticizes ascetic abuses. The *Yuqing jing* asserts that salvation must be realized within "this body," and insists that one must seek to perpetuate the life of the body, since the body is "the basis of the Tao." However, at the same time, the scripture does equate immortality with liberation from *samsara*. It also describes the ultimate salvation as an ascension and a union with a formless Non-Being. In other words, while vehemently asserting the need to keep the body intact, the *Yuqing jing* describes the greatest salvation as being a noncorporeal state. It thus presents us with an apparent contradiction and causes us to wonder what was supposed to happen to the flesh when the adept merged with the formless nonbeing. However, the idea seems to be that a good Taoist immortalizes the physical body by refining it into a formless state.

Over the centuries, historical writing—particularly that of traditional Confucian scholars, but also that of modern historians—has tended to cast a shadow of doubt upon the integrity of the Taoist religion. Prior to the latter half of this century, the Taoist religion had been a topic of little interest to historians, and mention was rarely made of Taoist religion aside from when it somehow affected political events. The Taoists mentioned in the standard histories have tended to be dubious characters; they include insurrectionists like Zhang Jue and Sun En, fawning political opportunists like Wang Qinruo and Lin Lingsu, and quack alchemists like Liu Mi. The infamy of such characters has caused many to ignore or lose sight of the fact that most Taoists have practiced their religion in good faith. Historians of religion are now finally beginning to gain a more complete view through the texts of the Taoist Canon. We no longer rely solely on the accounts of those who were indifferent or hostile to the religion. This study focuses on a phenomenon that bears testimony to the earnestness with which Taoists practiced their religion. Taoist ascetics were willing to deny themselves the most basic worldly needs and comforts for the sake of their religious perfection.

THE MYTHS OF IZUMO

IZANAGI-NO-MIKOTO AND IZANAMI-NO-MIKOTO

THE CREATION OF HEAVEN AND EARTH

Once upon a time, some ages ago, when this world began to be made, Heaven and Earth were created. First, Ame-no-minakanushi-no-kami was born in *Takamagahara* (The Plain of High Heaven) and then both Takamimusubi-no-kami and Kamimusubi-no-kami saw the light of day.

In those days, Heaven and Earth were not yet solid but just drifting about like jellyfish, in the liquid condition of floating oil. From this, like the buds of a reed emerging from the mud, Umashiashik-abihikojo-no-kami, and after him Ame-no-tokotachi-no-kami were born. These five Gods died respectively as *Hitorigami* (A Single God). And after two Hitoriagamis, two Gods and two Goddesses were born, Izanagi-no-mikoto (God) and Izanami-no-mikoto (Goddess) saw the light of this world.
—The Kojiki—[1]

THE PRODUCTION OF ISLANDS AND GODS

Ame-no-minakanushi-no-kami gave a splendid halberd to Izanagi-no-mikoto and Izanami-no-mikoto, saying "Put that floating country into order and make it solid and stable." So, they soon stood on *ame-no-ukihashi,* a bridge floating in the clouds, and after thrusting the halberd down and stirring up this world, he lifted it up and the salt water on the edge of the halberd fell drop by drop, and became a small island. This is *Onokorojima.*[105]

After flying down to that island, the God and the Goddess built a splendid palace and lived there. So, Izanagi-no-mikoto asked the Goddess, Izanami-no-mikoto, "How is your body constructed?" "I have one part that is complete and yet still incomplete in my body," she answered. And he, Izanagi-no-mikoto said, "I have one part that is complete and yet too much complete in my body. How about inserting mine into yours in order to produce islands?". "That will be a splendid thing", answered Izanami-no-mikoto.

He continued, "Then let's get married by the act of our turning around this big pillar", and he said "You, do it from the right side. I'll meet you by going from the opposite side".

While they began to turn, Izanami-no-mikoto said "You're a fine man, indeed", and after that Izanagi-no-mikoto said, "You're a beautiful girl, indeed."

After they thus spoke to each other, he said to the Goddess, "It is no good for you, the female, to have started talking before I did."

But they got married and *Mikohiruko* was born. The baby was put into a boat made of reeds and put on the stream. Then they talked with each other and after that, they went up together to Heaven to seek the advice of the God in Heaven, saying, "Let's tell Him that that bad baby was born." In Heaven, following the order of the God there, burning the bone of part of the shoulder of a deer, a fortune-teller said "Your baby was not a good one, because one of you, the female, spoke first. You had better go down to earth again and next time the male should speak first".

And they went down again and turned around the column just as they had done before. This time, Izanagi-no-mikoto spoke first, saying "You're a pretty girl indeed, aren't you?" And Izanami-no-mikoto followed him saying, "You're a nice young man, aren't you?"

After finishing saying this, they got married and Izanami bore another baby, Awajishima Island. And they then produced, one island after another: Shikoku Island, Oki Islands, Tsukushi Islands (Kyushu today), Iki Islands, Tsushima Islands, Sado Island, and finally Oyamato-toyoakitsushima (Honshu).[2]

These eight islands are called *Oyashima-no-kuni* (the land of Oyashima) or *Toyoashihara-no-mizuho-no-kuni* (that of Toyoashihara-no-mizuho). After the production of the islands was completed, they produced many more Gods, such as the God of the sea, that of the land, that of the river, and that of the field, which were the Gods of the world of nature and finally when the God of fire was born, the Goddess was burned on her private parts and died.

—The Kojiki—

YOMI-NO-KUNI[3] (the land of the dead)

Izanangi-no-mikoto grieved very much, saying, "I'm very sorry that I've lost my beloved wife on account of a child," and he buried the dead body of the Goddess, with much tears in his eyes, in Mt. Hiba, situated between the border of Izumo[4] and Hoki.[5] She had gone away to Yomi-no-kuni, an intensely dark land visited only by the dead. After that, he (Mikoto) soon pulled out a long sword called Totsuka-no-tsurugi (See Notes No. 6) and with one blow, cut to death the God of Fire who was the origin of the Goddess' misfortune. But he wanted to meet her again, and followed her to the very dark land, Yomi-no-kuni. Thus he knocked at the closed door of the palace where his wife was, and after a little while the Goddess came out. He called her name from the darkness, and said, "My dear, the establishment of the country we tried together is not yet completed, so, would you please come back to me once more?" Then the Goddess answered regretfully, "You should have come to see me earlier. I've already eaten the food of this land, Yomi-no-kuni, because you were so late in coming here. But now that you've come all the way to see me, I'd like to go back with you by all means. Anyhow I shall consult with the Gods here. During that time, never never look at my body. Do you agree to that condition?"

After insisting so strongly, she entered into the depth of the palace, but she did not appear for a long time, so he became intolerably impatient and proceeded into the depth of the palace, illuminating the interior of darkness, pulling out the comb put into the left side of the hair of his head, which was in the Mizura style,[7] and breaking off a big tooth of one end of the comb to burn it as a torch. Lying there was the Goddess, whose body, much decayed and in horrible condition, was entirely putrid and covered with maggots. There were Oikazuchi (the Great Thunder) around her head, Ho-no-Ikazuchi (the Fire Thunder) on her chest, Sakiikazuchi (the Female Thunder Spirit) on her private parts, Waka-Ikazuchi (the Young Thunder) on her left hand, Tsuchi-Ikazuchi (the Thunder of The Earth) on her right hand, Nari-Ikazuchi (the Clap Thunder) on her left leg, and Fushi-Ikazuchi (the Lying Flat Thunder Spirit) on her right leg. There were eight kinds of thunders in all. They were squatting there with terrible looks.

They frightened Mikoto so much that he ran away. Soon after that, the Goddess got up slowly and said with much anger, "Although I strongly prohibited you from looking at me, you've put me to shame very much", and she ordered her servants, female Onis (demonesses), to run after him. Mikoto threw back the black leaves of the black vine, one after another which were inserted in his hair as accessories, running away from her. Almost instantly wild grapes grew up at the place where each leaf fell.

While those female Onis[8] were eating them, Mikoto was able to escape from their pursuit. After they finished eating them, the female Onis pursued him again. Mikoto, this time, picked up his comb from the right side of his hair and threw off the broken teeth one by one. Each tooth turned into Takenoko, bamboo shoot, one after another and they gracefully shot up. The female Onis picked them up and began to eat them. That time too Mikoto was able to run away farther. This time, the eight thunders who were around the Goddess pursued him violently accompanied by a lot of armies of their comrades, the demons.

That time, he… hurriedly pulled out a Totsuka-no-tsurugi and swung it backward as he came with much trouble to the foot of the slope, Yomotsuhirasaka, that was located on the border between this world and Yomi-no-kuni.

He wrenched three peaches off the peach tree that stood beside him, and threw them back as strongly as he could. His pursuers, surprised and confused, ran for their lives, and were all scattered.

Mikoto named that peach tree Okamuzumi-no-mikoto, saying, "Please help all people in Japan whenever they are in suffering, just as you helped me".

Finally, the Goddess by herself began to run after him. Mikoto has already gone over the slope of Yomotsuhirasaka, but on catching sight of her, he covered the mouth of the slope with a big stone that he had hurriedly brought and that could be moved only with the power of a thousand men.

The Goddess had much difficulty in going forward even one step farther, hindered by the great stone, so that they exchanged the words of farewell with the boulder between them facing each other.

"My darling, after today, I'll make them strangle a thousand people to death every day all over Japan, in revenge for this violence", said the Goddess. Then Mikoto said, "My darling, if you dare to do so, I'll build babies' huts for one thousand five hundred babies a day," and he then went back at a stretch to his home. That name, Yomotsuhirasaka signifies the slope called Ibuyazaka in Izumo.

—The Kojiki—

MISOGI[9]

Izanagi-no-mikoto came back from Yomi-no-kuni and after saying, "Alas, what a dirty and offensive country I was in! I'll quickly purify myself and remove impurities from my body", he went to Awagihara that was in Hyuga (Tsukushi)[10] to purify himself in the clean water of the river flowing there.

As he stood by the riverside and took off his clothes piece by piece, one God after another was born from each piece and finally seventeen Gods were born in all. Looking at the water flowing in the river, he said, "The stream is swifter in its upper course, and slower in the lower course," and going down in the middle course, he poured the water upon himself, washed every side of his body whereupon fourteen more gods were born. Finally, when he washed his left eye, a beautiful and noble Goddess was born, so he named her Amaterasu Omikami. And then when he washed his right eye, a God (Tsukiyomino-mikoto) was born. Finally when he washed his nose, another God, Susano-no-mikoto, was born. Feeling lucky he said, "I've born many children and finally I have been able to bear the three best children." Thus after taking off his necklaces of Tamas,[11] and handing it to Amaterasu Omikami, he enjoined to her, "Go up to Heaven and govern *Takama-gahara*", then he said to Tsu-kiyomi-no-mikoto, "Govern *Yoru-no-kuni,* the land that is always dark." And last of all, he commanded Susano-no-mikoto to govern the ocean.

—The Kojiki—

Notes

1. Records of Ancient Matters.
2. The mainland of Japan.
3. The country into which the souls of humans go after the death of their bodies.
4. Shimane Prefecture today.
5. Tottori Prefecture today.
6. It means the sword whose blade is ten times as long as one firm hold.
7. Japanese hair style of a man in ancient times.
8. Female fiends.
9. In another words, those whose bodies are dirty or sinful go to the river to purify themselves.
10. Fukuoka Prefecture today.
11. *Magatama* (variously colored and sized jewel of agate).

From *The Myths of Izumo,* 1978, pp. 1-9. © 1978 by Hokosho Printing Company, Inc.

Japanese Religions in the New Millennium

"New-New" Religious Sects

The rapid economic development that took place in Japan in the 1960s and beyond was not made without the sacrifice of a rich, humanistic, cultural and spiritual tradition. Unlike the people of the Meiji period, most Japanese in the postwar period have been too busy to reflect on moral and religious questions. Meanwhile, society has became highly competitive and people's lives stress-ridden—a situation that has elicited the formation, since the late 1970s, of yet more new religious sects, including Suko Mahikari (1978), Agonshu (1981), and Aum Shinrikyo (1984). These "new-new religions," as they are sometimes called, share certain general characteristics. For one thing, their doctrines are highly eclectic, incorporating elements from various religious traditions and spiritual systems of the world, just like the new-age movements in the West. These new-new religions generally guarantee the followers some sort of mystical experience and healing. Their messages are aimed largely at individuals rather than at the family unit.[1]

The Rise and Fall of Aum Shinrikyo

The Aum Shinrikyo sect, founded by Asahara Shoko in 1984, reveals a troubling aspect of religious cults. Exotic and mystical elements of Asahara's teaching appealed to isolated, lonely, aimless youngsters. Asahara opened up a new world of spiritual life and mysticism to them. Borrowing from Transcendental Meditation, Asahara, calling himself a "guru," claimed that adept followers gained the ability to levitate. He also promised followers mystical trips, which were induced by hallucinogenic drugs, an overdose of which killed a number of "initiates." Under Asahara's manoeuvering, misguided followers became "robots" whose function was to bring about their teacher's prophecy of the end of the world. Still fresh in the memory today is the atrocity committed by certain members of Aum Shinrikyo, who in March 1995 killed twelve people and injured more than five thousand in a gas attack on the Tokyo subway.

With the arrest of the culprits, criminal malpractices of the sect were unearthed, and subsequently most followers left. On January 18, 2000, Aum Shinrikyo reemerged with a new name, "Aleph," the first letter of the Hebrew alphabet, which means "infinity." Today, the sect has some eight hundred followers.

Statements by former members of Aum Shinrikyo testify that they were looking for a way to better the world, or to affirm their spirituality, or that they simply sought a community of like-minded idealists.[2] These innocent needs were subverted by the founder. Placing the Aum incident in the context of Japan's modern history, the historian and critic R. J. Lifton has argued that Japanese society's experience of two radical transformations—the Meiji Restoration and the defeat in World War II—caused deep trauma in the national psyche, and that this "psychohistorical dislocation" underlies the Aum incident.[3]

The Religious Phenomenon of *Mizuko Kuyo*

Somewhere in the mid-1970s, a new religious phenomenon of offering Buddhist memorial services (*kuyo*) for unborn fetuses and stillborn babies, known as "mizuko kuyo," became popular. "Mizuko" literally means "water-child." It is said that about two-thirds of Japanese women have to resort to abortion to practice family planning, mainly for financial reasons because children's education is very expensive in today's Japan. Certainly, abortion is not a light matter and can leave psychological scars on young mothers. Many of these women turn to Buddhist temples to have memorial services performed. Such ceremonies seem to originate from the feeling of anxiety or guilt on the part of these women, but some scholars argue that they are prompted by fear of "revenge of an angry spirit" (*tatari*). Still others find feminist issues in the debate around abortion and *mizuko kuyo*, which they see as a social phenomenon that reflects a heavily male-dominated society.[4] No doubt, there is no one answer that explains *mizuko kuyo* in its totality. Be that as it may, the women perceive memorial services as a means of allowing the spirits of the unborn to rest in peace and of sending them off to heaven; in turn, they feel that their own sense of guilt is removed. Most women purchase from the temple a small stone statue of Bodhisattva Jizo, the protector of children, and place it on the temple ground, a practice analogous to erecting a gravestone. Often a knitted cap is placed on the head of the statue and a bib hung around its neck; these little extras express the mother's concern that a bare statue, somehow identified with the baby, would be cold without the cap and could not eat without the bib. *Mizuko kuyo* is performed not only in popular Buddhist temples but also by many Buddhism-based religious sects.

Japanese Religions Today

If asked their religion, two out of three Japanese people today would answer that they have no personal religious faith. Two things may account for this. One is that religious activities have become cultural activities, so ingrained in the lives of the Japanese people that their religious origin is no longer recognized. This would explain the fact that on the first three days of the New Year, 2001, more than 88 million Japanese (about 70 percent of the population) crowded into Shinto shrines and Buddhist temples throughout the country to usher in the new millennium—but they consider this a nonreligious act. The traditional year-end general cleaning, whose origin goes back to the Shinto proclivity for cleanliness, continues to be performed in most households; and these days, small cleaning businesses advertise their availability to do the job.

The other reason for the apparent lack of a need for religious affiliation is the fact that Buddhist temples have long been social institutions. Many families still belong to Buddhist temples—the legacy of the *danka* system but individual family members are not conscious of that formal affiliation on a day-to-day basis. Only at the time of a funeral do they discover it. Over 90 percent of Japanese funerals are conducted according to Buddhist rites.

Most of the Buddhist schools and sects of the past still thrive to this day; the monasteries of Mt. Hiei, Mt. Koya, and Eiheiji are still the major training centers of monks, and there are nunneries for female aspirants. The Aum Shinrikyo incident provoked much soul-searching among the more orthodox faiths; here was evidence that they were not meeting many of people's spiritual needs. Accordingly, some reforms were adopted. For example, the Japanese Association of Buddhism issued a statement in January 2000 that Buddhist temples would no longer charge for their service of conferring a Buddhist name and a title (*kaimyo*) on the dead—a kind of "passport to paradise." Until then, bereaved families had been paying the priest about $2,000 as a token of thanks for the *kaimyo* conferred on the deceased. Japanese Buddhist institutions are now making an effort to bring themselves up to date and be socially meaningful.

Understandably, many Japanese still find Shinto intellectually repugnant because of its prewar association with the ultra-nationalistic State Shinto. But on the popular level, people flock to Shinto shrines to gain the protection of the *kami* deities, these worshippers include students facing entrance exams, single people looking for marriage partners, expectant mothers, people worried by illness in their family, merchants praying for good business, and fishermen and farmers praying for a good catch or a rich harvest. Where there are wishes, there will always be Shinto shrines for the Japanese.

Looking Toward the Future

On August 9, 1999, conservative politicians, who held a majority in the Japanese Diet, voted to adopt the "rising sun" (*hinomaru*) as the official national flag and the song "Ours is Your Majesty's Reign" (*kimigayo*) as the national anthem, in preparation for Japan entering the new millennium. Before the passage of the bill, the government insisted that displaying the national flag and singing the anthem were "optional" at school ceremonies, but in 2001 the Ministry of Science and Education unilaterally adopted the position that they were mandatory. Also in 2001, domestic concerns were raised by the declared intention of newly elected prime minister Koizumi to worship as head of state at the Yasukuni Shrine, with all its imperial connotations, on August 15—the day that commemorates the end of World War II; this also elicited criticism from both the South Korean and the Chinese governments. In order to avoid international friction, the prime minister's advisors shifted forward the date of his visit to the shrine by two days.

The dramatic collapse of the Japanese economy in the early 1990s impacted on all sectors of the nation's life. In the wake of corporations' downsizing and restructuring, large numbers of workers lost their jobs. Many of these workers had devoted everything to their companies, for their entire life. Now, at a relatively advanced age, they found themselves with no sense of direction, which prompted them for the first time to question the meaning of their lives. Crushed by financial burden, a number of owners of small businesses committed suicide—a phenomenon that persists to this day. For other workers, religion, as the carrier of fundamental values or the source of spiritual healing, is once again becoming meaningful. In this atmosphere, established religions continue to adapt themselves to the new needs of the people, while many more "new" religions will no doubt arise.

Ecological crises, too, have made many people embrace a holistic worldview, which a number of new religions advocate. The ethical aspects of biotechnology and the use of nuclear energy are also among the concerns that some religious sects are beginning to address. Environmental protection movements are rediscovering the ecological merit of the ancient Shinto view of the organic relationship between humans and nature.

A Japanese newspaper article of June 2000 reported that some Japanese are breaking away from the traditional Buddhist funerals and are having their ashes returned to nature rather than placed in a graveyard.[5] The article described how the ashes of thirty-six people, including those of eleven Japanese, were launched in a rocket from Vandenberg Air Force Base in California on December 20, 1999, and noted that the funeral company that arranges the "space burial" had been receiving telephone inquiries daily concerning the next rocket launch, scheduled for the spring of 2001. For the Japanese, this option is not only much less expensive than the traditional Buddhist funeral (around $8,500, compared to an average of $25,000) but also because they found it romantic to think of the ashes of their loved ones in the sky. The rocket orbits the earth for eighteen months before it crashes into the atmosphere and burns up. A young woman whose husband's ashes were on the rocket two years after his death was reported as saying that whenever she looked up into the sky, she felt that her husband was present, and that she would like to think that he had "become a star in the sky."

Over the centuries, religious practices have changed and will continue to do so, but the religious sentiments that are expressed in these practices remain timeless.

Notes

1. Shimazono, "New Religious Movements": 227–28.
2. Kanariya no kai, ed., *Oum o yameto watakushtiachi (We Who Quit Aum Shinrikyo)* (Tokyo: Iwanami Shoten, 2000).
3. R. J. Lifton, *Destroying the World to Save It: Aum Shinrikyo, Apocakyptic Violence, and the New Global Terrorism* (New York: Henry Holt, 1999): 236–37.
4. For a concise coverage of this debate see "Articles, Review Essays, and Response on the Theme of 'Abortion and *Misuko kuyo* in Japan,'" *Journal of the American Academy of Religion,* 67,4 (December 1999): 737–823.
5. "New funerals emerging: Burials at sea and space," *Asahi Evening News,* 29 June 2000: 1–2.

From *Japanese Religious Traditions,* March 2002, pp. 109-113. © 2002 by Prentice Hall.

The Goddess Emerges from her Cave: Fujita Himiko and her Dragon Palace Family

CARMEN BLACKER

FUJITA HIMIKO, or Ryúgú Otohime (the Dragon Palace Princess) as she is also called, is the foundress of the religious group known as Ryúgú Kazoku, or the Dragon Palace Family. She founded the group in October 1973, soon after a dramatic initiatory vision revealed to her the task she was destined to perform in life, and the message she was to bring to the world. The Ryúgú Kazoku should, therefore, be counted among the *shin-shin-shúkyó*, or 'new, new' religions, which made their appearance during the 1970s and 1980s, and which are readily distinguishable from the older 'new' religions which arose after 1945.[1]

Himiko's group is of particular interest today insofar as her message is, unbeknown to herself, curiously consonant with much that is occurring in the West. This message for mankind is clearly centred on the coming Age of the Goddess, *megamisama no jidai*. This kairos she claims to be close at hand, despite all appearances to the contrary. The goddess is about to come at last into her own. Having been for centuries quenched by hard, war-like, masculine divinities, who are accorded paramount status beyond their deserts in monotheisms throughout the world, the goddess will once more arise and bathe the world in the millennial joys of her light and love.

While proclaiming such a message, Himiko seems for the most part unaware of the recent surge in the West of literature about the goddess. The remarkable spate of books, papers, conferences and workshops on the goddess and her myth, the work of Maria Gimbutas, Robert Graves, Anne Baring, Miranda Green and many others, has so far neither influenced nor interested her. Her own supernatural revelation has taught her all she needs to know.

This dramatic initiation took place at 11.30 a.m. on 7 October 1973. She was standing outside a large cave near Kumamoto, in company with a woman ascetic called Shioyama, when with extraordinary suddenness the goddess Amaterasu Ómikami appeared to her in the unusual form of a mermaid. With her fish tail, the goddess gave Himiko a slap on the cheek, and announced that now was the moment of her true arrival, her true emergence from the cave. The myth recounted in the *Kojiki* of her *iwatobi-raki* (emergence from the cave) some two thousand years ago was a mere rehearsal of what was now to take place. She emerged now from the dark cave to bring the joyful news that the world would soon be suffused with the light and love of the Mother Goddess. Here was *megamis-ama no yomigaeri*, the resurrection of the goddess; the world was soon to become *nyoi-hóju*, a wish-fulfilling jewel.

Her companion, Shioyama, heard the sound of the slap, and of the goddess's voice, but was not sufficiently advanced to see the mermaid avatar. Only Himiko both saw and heard the full revelation.

From that moment she felt herself imbued with the tremendous supernatural power of the goddess, and lost no time in proclaiming her message to the world. She also lost no time in having a bronze statue of the mermaid erected inside the cave, where it stands even now for all to see, with an inscription recording the event in 1973 as a turning point in history.

Likewise, from the moment of her initiation, Himiko found that her spiritual powers were greatly enhanced. Before this event she had displayed minor psychic powers, experiencing encounters with divinities both in dream and waking vision. Near the Nachi waterfall, for example, in the course of a pilgrimage from Yoshino to Kumano, she had seen the Thirty-six Boys of Fudó Myóó. Now she found that she could both see and converse with all kinds of spiritual beings, both benevolent and troublesome. In consequence, she was now able to heal all types of sickness, both physical and mental, which are caused by invisible spiritual beings. She was able to see the unhappy ghost, or the neglected divinity, who was causing the headaches, the arthritis, the depression, the lethargy, and after listening to its story she could perform the correct ritual for bringing the entity to its due salvation.

At the same time, she realized that it was not only Amaterasu Ómikami who had chosen her to be the vehicle of revelation. A number of ancient goddesses and queens had at the same time elected to reincarnate themselves in her body and transmit to her their powers. The powerful and mysterious Queen Pimiko, mentioned in the Chinese *Wei Chih* of the third century, was one of those who conferred her name and power upon her. Ryúgú Otohime, the daughter of the Dragon King, was another; hence her spiritual cognomen Otohimesama. Armed with this identity she feels herself in touch with the network of symbolic correspondences, in Japanese myth and legend, which radiate from the feminine figure—water, dragons, fish, the water world in general. Yet another figure with whom she declares a conscious identity is Happyaku Bikuni, the girl from Wasaka who accidentally ate mermaid's flesh and was condemned in consequence to wander mysteriously over the country for 800 years.

Lastly, she claims identity with the great queen of the lost continent of Mu, which sank below the sea not far from Japan many thousands of years ago.[2]

With this powerful combination of ancient and august feminine figures congregating inside her, with her timely message of an imminent golden age, and with her practical ability to heal sickness and solve troubles, she was admirably qualified to found a new religious group.

The Ryúgú Kazoku is now nearly twenty years old. It is not a large group by Japanese standards, its membership totalling not more than 1500. Most of the members come from the Kansai area, where she has established her headquarters in a flat in Higashi Yodogawa near Osaka. But there is also a flourishing branch in Tokyo, and her mailbag every day contains letters and pleas for help from all over Japan. Living with her in her headquarters is Kawami Yoshiharu, a young man who performs many invaluable tasks for her, not least of which is the editing of a monthly journal.

This journal, the *Ryúgú Otohime*, which has now reached its one hundred and thirtieth issue,[3] gives news of Himiko's latest visions, revelations and travels over Japan and the rest of the world; it contains articles interpreting current events in the light of the imminent advent of the goddess age, and examples of her successful cures of cases of melancholy, asthma, paralysis of the legs, insomnia and terrible fears of death and the end of the world. Patients from all over Japan describe their sufferings, and their fervent gratitude to Himiko for removing the spiritual cause of the malaise.

The journal furthermore reminds its readers every month that with Himiko as their guide and leader, the following services are available to them. First, *reisa* or spirit investigation. We are all overshadowed by spiritual beings, who are usually benign and protective, but which can be displaced from time to time by malicious entities which sap our vital energy and cause sickness and mis-

fortune. Or by unhappy entities who are trying by these means to call attention to their plight. By the technique of *reisa*, Himiko will give you a spiritual check-up to investigate the entities overshadowing you, and will deal appropriately with any which need to be cleared or moved on to other destinations. Second, *mitama-matsuri* a rite which will purify, comfort and placate the molesting spirit, so that its aggressive inclinations are removed. Third, *shukufuku* or the blessing of the Mother Goddess, which acts as a spiritual tonic, enabling you to recuperate from the depletion you have suffered.

Members of the Ryúgú Kazoku are further encouraged to apply to Himiko for regular check-ups, whether they feel ill or not. If you cannot get to her Osaka flat in person, you can send a recent photograph with name, sex, date of birth and a clear statement of the trouble. It is also important to have a *reisa* carried out for any *old* objects in your house; old books, old trees or wells, any antique objects, even an old used car, are all subject to dangerous spiritual infestation which can cause malaise to their owners. A further service of blessing, *petto-kuyó*, is offered for your dogs, cats or birds, which are also vulnerable to spiritual attack.

Her work with photographs is very systematic, and she showed me several large albums in which she has preserved records of former cases. Her method is to inspect the photograph with her psychic eye, which will immediately see the figure of the molesting or overshadowing entity. She then makes a quick sketch of the entity, speaks to it, listens to its story, and performs the necessary rite to purify it and bring it to its proper salvation. The patient thereupon quickly recovers.

The albums contain the photographs, each with its accompanying sketch of the molesting entity, together with notes for further treatment. Many of the unhappy spirits whom she has saved prove to be centuries old. There are many cases of samurai killed in the wars of the sixteenth century who have lingered without proper absolution for three hundred years. Cases, too, are not uncommon of warrior spirits of even older date, remaining unhoused from the Gempei wars at the end of the twelfth century.

An interesting example of her work with photographs is the *reisa* she performed on a newspaper photograph of Saddam Hussein in November 1990. Overshadowing the face of the tyrant were three sinister figures: a bull, a king riding a horse and a terrifying old woman. The bull she knew by her psychic powers to be Apis, and the king to be Nebuchadnezzar, with whom Saddam Hussein had already identified himself. But the old woman eluded her. She therefore addressed the visionary figure, 'Who are you?'

'I am the Old Woman of the Desert', was the reply. Her insight told her that the figure was a depleted, starved, enraged remnant of the ancient goddess Ishtar, once worshipped all over the Middle East but long suppressed and insulted by Islam. She and the other two figures were all *maibotsujin*, buried gods, suppressed by Islam but now reasserting themselves and demanding due nourishment. Many of them dated back to Sumer and Babylon, on the sites of which Iraq now stood, and were accustomed to receiving offerings of blood sacrifices. To obtain their usual fare they therefore possessed a ferocious chieftain like Saddam Hussein and forced him to invade Kuwait. From the slain in the war they could derive the vital nourishment needed for their revival.[4]

Himiko's work of spirit diagnosis and healing thus occupies most of the time she spends at home. There is another and no less important commitment, however, which takes her away from her headquarters on travels of an adventurous and apparently indefatigable kind. She claims first to have visited every nook and cranny of Japan, every mountain, bay, lake, temple and shrine, and to know every prefecture better than people who have lived there all their lives.

But her journeys are by no means confined to Japan. Her travels abroad have taken her to at least fifty foreign countries. She spent six months wandering over India; she has visited Turkey, Greece, Israel, Tibet, and even Easter Island. She has been to almost every State in America. In the summer of 1989 she made one trip to the United States, and another to England and Scotland, during which she spared an afternoon to visit Cambridge.

When I first became acquainted with her, I imagined that her passion for travel was due simply to a powerful kind of natural wanderlust. I soon understood that the reasons were more complex. The journeys were often undertaken, not simply of her own volition, but at the insistent command of various *kami*. They were themselves *kamiwaza*, actions wrought by a *kami*. She would hear a voice in the middle of the night, ordering her to go at once to a certain place. If she did not instantly obey, the *kami* would harry and nag her until she had no alternative but to do its bidding. The funds for these journeys would invariably be provided for her by a miraculous source, *kamisama no o-hakarai*.

There were two reasons why she should receive supernatural commands to travel to certain places. First, because in the places she is ordered to visit there were miserably unhappy ghosts who have been unable to achieve their proper *jōbutsu* or salvation, whom she can bring to a joyous release. And second, because in these places she is able to make contact with the benign tutelary divinity, converse with them and make sure they are doing their job properly. She thus establishes a spiritual network, *reiteki-nettowáku*, with the local *ubusunagami* or genius loci, so that they agree to cooperate in the great work of the goddess.

Of her work in saving unhappy and neglected ghosts she has many dramatic tales to tell. In 1990, for example, she visited the group of islands off Nagasaki. On Himejima she found a tablet commemorating 130 Japanese Christians who in the seventeenth century had fled to the island for safety, and taken refuge in a cave with only seaweed to eat. They were discovered before long, captured,

put to the water torture and eventually killed. Himiko was at once aware that for three hundred years none of these poor souls had been able to attain proper salvation because no one had performed the correct obsequies for them. They rushed towards her, their faces haggard and woebegone, begging her to rescue them. Within a few minutes she had saved them all, and had the satisfaction of seeing them rise upwards, their faces filled with joy and gratitude.[5]

While travelling in Shikoku in 1990, she found many spirits of the defeated Heike family, who had fled there from the battle of Yashima and the battle of Dan-no-ura in 1185. They, too, for eight hundred years, had been unable to find peace, and had been waiting for someone to perform the correct ritual for them. These also Himiko was able to save; a poor Heike lady, who had been waiting eight hundred years, was rapturously grateful.[6]

Again, during her trip to America in May 1989, she visited the Grand Canyon. There she had the strange experience of seeing large numbers of very ancient ghosts, *kodairei*, gazing at her intently. She asked them who they were.

'We are the spirits of people who died in a war long ago, and for centuries have been awaiting your coming. Please release us from this valley.'

At once she performed the necessary rite, and was delighted to see them turn into black butterflies and fly upwards to the sky released from their bondage. She later discovered that they were the ghosts of Hopi Indians who were the original inhabitants of the valley.[7]

Of her work with the spirit network of local divinities there are likewise many examples. When she visited the island of Kinkazan in October 1987, after a rough crossing, she went straight to the shrine. There the goddess Kanayamabime-no-mikoto, wearing a tunic of pale green, scarlet sleeves and a Nó woman's mask of incredible beauty, appeared to her visionary eye. The goddess danced with exquisite grace, holding a golden fan, and Himiko composed a suitable *uta* to confirm the encounter.

On the island of Chikubushima likewise, the goddess Benten, guardian of the island, appeared to her visionary eye and danced. And on 15 January 1991 Himiko led a party of her followers on a pilgrimage to the Ise shrine. There the goddess Amaterasu Ōmikami appeared to her in fiercely embattled array, wearing armour laced with red lacing. This vision, she prophesied to her disciples, was a clear omen of coming war. And sure enough, that very night, the Gulf War broke out.

These friendly contacts with local genii are also carried outside Japan. During her journey to Scotland in July 1989, she was anxious to communicate with the Loch Ness monster, or Nesshi-chan as she called him. She stood for some time on the lakeside, murmuring a secret spell which might summon him, aware that near at hand were tourist buses and souvenir shops which might impede his appearance. She was nevertheless disappointed to see no sign of Nesshi-chan.[8] But that night he appeared to her in a dream and said, 'I must apologise for not coming to see you earlier this afternoon. There were too many people around for me to show myself.'

This greeting was communicated to her by some telepathic means which was neither English nor Japanese. In her dream she patted him on the head and said, 'You're the guardian spirit of Scotland, and so mind you do the job properly.' Nesshi-chan looked very pleased, and with the single word 'Hai' (Yes!), vanished from sight.[9]

From these examples it will be readily seen that Himiko's work is an interesting combination of old and new, of the traditional work of the holy, empowered person, and a message which is new in so far as it has few parallels among the new religions.

Her indefatigable travelling, for example, the salvation she brings to unhappy lost spirits, the friendly relations she establishes with local *kami*, what are these but an updated version of the work of the old *yúgyó-hijiri*—the wandering holy men, or the *tabisó*, the travelling priest who figures in so many of the Nó plays? Their task was precisely to rescue unhappy souls and to celebrate the local *kami*, so that blessings would in consequence pour down on the village or island. Indeed, some of her stories of visits to old battlegrounds are reminiscent of the Nó plays of Zeami. Unhappy warrior ghosts are brought to final peace through her powers and charismatic gifts. The *uta* too, which she composes as a final capping for a successful rescue, are thoroughly traditional in spirit and inspiration.

Traditional also, or at least common to a good many other new religions, is her partnership with a man. In many cases the woman Foundress is able to expand her group thanks to the organising ability of a man. She is the vessel for the divine revelations. He translates them into action. Himiko is aided in this manner by Kawami Yoshiharu, who edits the monthly magazine, writes a good deal of it himself, looks after the headquarters while she is away on her travels, and does a good many household tasks for which the Great Mother has no time.

Her emphasis on the diagnosis of sickness as spirit possession, and her consequent healing through the divine powers accorded to her at her initiation, is likewise to be found in many of the New Religions. But in other respects her message is remarkably new. She is unusual in the first place in claiming identity exclusively with supernatural feminine figures, with Amaterasu Ómikami, with Queen Pimiko and the Great Queen of Mu. Also from time to time with the World Mother. Other Foundresses are usually possessed by a male divinity, as was Ógamisama the Foundress of Tenshó Kótai Jingukyó, the Dancing Religion.

She is also unusual, if not unique, in claiming that the coming millennium will be brought about by the revival of the Goddess, Megamisama. Millennarianism is not uncommon among the New Religions, but to my knowledge none except the Dragon Palace Family see it as the re-emergence of the goddess from her dark cave.

Like other 'new, new religions', she puts Japan firmly at the epicentre of the coming New Age of the Goddess. Others in the West may write and speak of the goddess and propound her myth, but it is Himiko's revelation in 1973 which will prove to be the turning point in history. The second bronze statue of the mermaid which she erected in 1990 at the north end of Lake Biwa will serve to confirm the accelerating process.

FOOTNOTES

1. Two articles have appeared in *Monumenta Nipponica* describing Himiko and her teachings. Ben-Ami Shillony, 'The Princess of the Dragon Palace: a New Shinto Sect is Born', vol. 39, 1984, and Richard Fox Young, 'Little Lad Deity and the Dragon Princess', Vol. 44, 1989. Since becoming acquainted with Himiko in 1988 and making several journeys in her company, I have come to feel that neither of these articles adequately describe her work, particularly her work of spirit diagnosis and healing.
2. Personal communications from Himiko herself, and to be found *passim* in *Ryúgú Otohime*.
3. As from July 1993.
4. *Ryúgú Otohime*, No. 98, November 1990.
5. *Ibid.*, No. 90, March 1990.
6. *Ibid.*, No. 95, August 1990.
7. *Ibid.*, No. 81, May 1989.
8. *Ibid.*, No. 102, March 1991.
9. *Ibid.*, No. 84, August 1989.

From *Japanese New Religions in the West,* 1994, pp. 23-32. © 1994 by Japan Library.

MATSURI

They are, perhaps, the ultimate celebrations. Amid a spectacular display of costume, color, and age-old ritual, participants summon the gods down to earth to mingle and rejoice with them. A most eloquent form of worship, Japanese festivals are intimate, joyous encounters with the divine.

Japan may well enjoy more festivals than any other country in the world. On almost any day of the year, at least one festival is sure to be under way somewhere on the archipelago, and on certain days, the whole nation seems to be in the thick of celebration. varying in size and grandeur, some *matsuri* may involve no more than a single part-time priest and the handful of residents of a tiny farming village modestly celebrating spring planting; others may engage a cast of more than a thousand to thrill tens of thousands of onlookers with their pageantry. They encompass celebrations both rural and urban, traditional and modern, solemn and fun.

Originally, and still predominantly, Shinto observances, *matsuri* came also to include certain calendrical rites of Chinese Buddhist origin. But whether Shinto or Buddhist at heart, elements of both are often present at any one event.

Prevailing images of modern Japan tend to minimize the significance of these ancient religious practices. Yet they have long provided the people with a strong spiritual identity and continue to hold an honored place in Japanese life. Considerable insight into contemporary Japan can be gained from a knowledge and understanding of these spiritual roots which continue to sustain the nation through its technological, political, and social changes.

Although many Japanese people are inclined to declare to foreigners that they have no religion at all, that conviction seems to arise from a difference in terms. Japanese interpretation of the term "religion" generally presupposes a founder, a doctrine which excludes all others, a holy book, a weekly holy day—elements which certain other religions possess but theirs, largely, do not. Simply put, the Japanese consider Buddhism more a philosophy than a religion, and Shinto, a spiritually integrated way of life.

Shinto (the way of the gods) is an indigenous and animistic faith with its origins deep in the mists of time. Its central theme is the veneration of the life force, which is nature, and of Amaterasu Omikami, nature's creator and the progenitor of the Japanese imperial line. She is the Great Divinity Illuminating Heaven, goddess of the sun.

Shinto gods, the divine forces, are called *kami*. Existing in immense numbers, they are manifest in all things, animate and inanimate, and pervade all aspects of human life. It is believed that the world functions through the cooperation of the *kami* and their believers and strives toward the social harmony in which the gods rejoice. The *kami* are linked inextricably to the Japanese psyche, so much so that it has been said that without Japan there would be no Shinto, and without Shinto, no Japan. In the distant past, it helped the Japanese to define their role in the immediate world. Today it serves as a grounding force for a people who, in times of great change, are trying to hold on to their identity, as well as to redefine their relationship with a far broader and more complex world. Inseparable from daily life, Shinto is observed in a multitude of acts, ceremonies, and festivals throughout the year.

Although *kami* faith stretches far back into Japanese history, it was given the name Shinto in the eighth century, and then only to differentiate it from the growing popularity of Buddhism and other imported beliefs and philosophies. Buddhism, although born in India, arrived in Japan from China by way of Korea in the sixth century. Introduced as only one part of the vastly superior Chinese culture that so awed the Japanese, it was enthusiastically taken up by the imperial court as a faith with possible greater divine powers than those of their native gods. It took several centuries for Buddhism to reach the Japanese commoner but when it did, it flourished. In a form more Japanese than Chinese or Indian, Buddhism has been a substantial force in Japan for a millennium.

After an initial rivalry, Shinto and Buddhism settled into a largely peaceful coexistence, with Shinto gods often viewed as local manifestations of Buddhist deities, rather than competitors. Indeed, Buddhism has a history of accommodating itself to local faiths. The religions mingled and even at times merged, so that the line between the two can still often be a little blurred. However, the two belief systems are very different from one another, so each has its own niche to fill. The realm of Shinto is the cycle of nature, the seasons, and everyday life, while Buddhism's domain is death and afterlife.

Although a relatively small nation, Japan supports some 75,000 Buddhist temples and 100,000 Shinto shrines, both small and large, modest and grand. These remarkable numbers say much about the respect given to the spiritual side of life in Japan. The vast majority of people call upon each religion as needed and without any sense of personal conflict, for their gods are not jealous gods. In a mutually beneficial relationship, the gods serve the people, and the people serve the gods, giving them their due at the proper time, at the proper place, and in the proper way. These various acts of worship culminate in the celebration of *matsuri*. Derived from the verb *matsuru* (to worship), *matsuri* serve as a means for the people to offer the divine world their prayers, gifts, reverence, and joy.

The festival is many things to the Japanese people: an opportunity for communion with their gods and ancestral spirits; an avowal of their common past, which reaches far back into mythical times; a celebration of nature and the renewing cycle of the seasons; and, not least of all, an excuse for exuberant merrymaking with family and neighbors, thereby reaffirming communal bonds and providing welcome relief from the work and regimentation of daily life.

A great many of the *matsuri* are related to rice growing, the very foundation of Japanese culture. Others honor the guardian deities of clans, villages, towns, and districts. Still others range from celebrations of national history and culture to more individual and family-oriented festivals.

As primary as is the cultivation of rice to the Japanese people, so are the festivals which guard and celebrate that process. Rites connected to the agricultural cycle are held throughout most of the country and span all four seasons. The gods are petitioned for a favorable growing season, to drive away pests and natural disasters which could harm the burgeoning grain, while later in the year, thanks are given for a bountiful harvest. Extremely varied in form and accouterment, these festivals are bound by their common purpose.

In winter, farming communities all over Japan begin to enact primeval rites to invoke the favor of the deities upon their upcoming labors. Every February, in the northern prefecture of Aomori, for example, the farmers of Hachinohe gather to perform a dance of fertility, stomping the snow-covered earth to call it to life. Splendid headdresses worn by these Emburi Matsuri dancers bear the painted images of Inari, the god of grains, and Ebisu, a god of prosperity.

Spring brings numerous ceremonies to seek continued fortune for the cultivation process. Typical of events undertaken elsewhere, the rice planting around Nara is preceded by a spring festival at Kasuga Shrine, where *miko* (sacred shrine maidens) enact the planting process in stylized dance. Their virginity symbolizes the fertility which is sought for the young rice shoots. In this act of imitative magic, all stages of growth are represented and ritually

brought to fulfillment, thereby petitioning the same auspicious denouement for the actual crops.

With the rains of early summer, followed by the intense, sometimes enervating, midsummer heat, community festivals continue to beseech the *kami* for heedfulness to their precious crops. Kawase Matsuri in Chichibu exemplifies that season's celebratory supplications which seek not only the continued growth and safety of their rice crops, but heavenly protection for the health of the people. The spirit of the deity, ordinarily enshrined at Chichibu Shrine, is ceremonially transferred to the *mikoshi* (portable shrine). After carrying it in parade to the river, its bearers immerse it and boisterously splash around in the water to give the god a ritual bath and, at the same time, to entertain him. He returns the favor soon, when golden autumn brings paddies heavy with grain. Meanwhile, the people revel with their god and take pleasure in this brief but welcome break in their workaday routine.

When the abundant harvest is in, it is again time to remember the gods. Autumn festivals abound, and some of the best of them are at the ubiquitous Inari shrines, where the deity of grains is worshiped. In Shinto, certain animals are regarded as messengers of the gods, and at Inari shrines, it is the white fox. In an interesting syncretic observance, the Buddhist temple Hojoji in Yamaguchi Prefecture celebrates an annual autumn Kitsune-no-Yomeiri (Foxes' Wedding Procession). A costumed and masked fox-bride and fox-groom are ritually married in celebration of a long-ago miracle, when a pair of old foxes died and attained buddhahood. In honor of the foxes' long, faithful life together, young women take part in the procession, hoping that it will lead them to long and faithful marriages, too. But this is rice country, and the Shinto association with foxes is unmistakable, particularly with a small Inari shrine right on the temple grounds. With harvest prayers and an altar laid with offerings of new rice, the event's supplementary dedications are those of a Shinto harvest festival.

Other livelihoods are not forgotten. The deities are implored to provide fishermen with abundant catches by means of *matsuri* held in many coastal fishing towns and villages. In Ohara on the Pacific coast of the Boso Peninsula, this plea takes the form of Hadaka Matsuri, the so-called Naked Festival, in which the area's fishermen, dressed only in *fundoshi* (loincloths), bear eighteen god-dwelling *mikoshi* into the ocean waves.

Festivals may focus on other elements of nature, too. The beauty of nationally revered blossoms, the advent of the autumnal full moon, or the continued rest of the sleeping volcano Mount Fuji, for example, are celebrated in *matsuri* around Japan.

Life's milestones may also be observed in festival form. Celebrated nationwide on November 15 is the beloved childhood festival Shichi-Go-San (Seven-Five-Three). On that day, or on a near weekend, boys of age five and girls of ages three and seven are taken to their local shrines to be blessed with the divine protection of their guardian deity or, as has recently become fashionable, to a grander shrine of particular importance to make the event even more memorable. The tots are dressed in their finest. For girls that often means a diminutive but spectacular kimono with all the required accessories—a major parental investment for the sake of beauty, tradition and, again, memories.

Major among the family-oriented festivals celebrated nationwide is the summer Festival of the Dead, O-Bon. An event of the ancient Chinese Buddhist calendar, it has been celebrated in Japan since the seventh century. With lanterns or fires to light their way, the spirits of ancestors are welcomed home from the world beyond for a three-day visit. Family members return to their hometowns to reunite with one another and to honor their ancestors. In villages, towns, and urban neighborhoods, outdoor folk dances called *bon odori* are performed by residents who are often charmingly attired in the colorful cotton *yukata* and wooden *geta* of summer evenings of old. Originally intended as entertainment for the visiting spirits, today this ancient custom has become more an enjoyable social event for the living. It nevertheless still embodies the essence of O-Bon, a happy time for families in their continuing and satisfying relationship with the spirits of their ancestors and departed loved ones.

Reenactments of legends and historical moments dear to the people comprise yet another category of the countless festivals celebrated each year throughout Japan. One of the grandest, Kyoto's Gion Matsuri sprang from a plea by Emperor Seiwa to the *kami* enshrined at Yasaka Shrine to bring to an end the devastating plague of the summer of 869. When it duly abated, the city held a great festival of thanksgiving to the deity, featuring a hand-drawn wheeled pavilion topped with medieval halberds.

In the year 970, that festival was instituted as an annual event, in praise and continuing petition of the illustrious *kami* who had brought the land salvation a century before. Year by year, century by century, the event gained in splendor, with more numerous pavilions acquiring ever more features and embellishments. Today these floats are of the finest construction and bear a wealth of treasured antique art objects, mechanical historical figures, and elaborated scenes, as well as bands of musicians playing the hypnotic flute, drum and *shamisen* music called Gion-bayashi. Over thirty majestic floats are drawn by teams of straining, *happi*-coated men and accompanied in procession by many hundreds of gloriously costumed men, women, and children.

Riding high on the lead float is the *chigo* (the celestial child), a prepubescent boy carefully selected and ritually sanctified to be acceptable to the god. Indeed, it is the *chigo* who will embody the *kami* spirit during this festival. And it is his ritual act of perfectly severing the sacred rope (*shimenawa*) to formally open the procession which will ensure the god's blessings upon the city for the coming year.

For the sightseeing multitudes who have come from across Japan to view this spectacle, the procession *is* the festival. But for citizens of Kyoto, natives of the city for generations upon generations, that is only one grand element in a month-long choreographed drama of history, religion and, not least of all, community pride. Something more than a festival, Gion Matsuri with all its rites and trappings has become a true symbol of the city.

Kyoto, the cradle of Japanese culture, is also home to the oldest festival in Japan and, some say, in the world. Aoi Matsuri dates from the sixth century, when floods compelled the citizens to petition for relief the goddess of water (Tamayorihimeno Mikoto) and her son, the god of thunder (Kamo Wakeikazuchino Kami). Almost every year for the past fourteen centuries, a spring procession has been led from the Kyoto Imperial Palace to Shimogamo Shrine and Kamigamo Shrine, where they are respectively enshrined. Prayers are offered, as well, for an abundant rice harvest, so dependent on fickle nature. Leaves of *aoi* (wild ginger), a legendary deterrent to thunder, adorn eaves along the procession route, as well as the costumes of the participants. An imperial messenger on horseback leads the way, followed by an ox-drawn, lacquered cart heavily hung with wisteria. Although the festival's origins are much earlier, the accompanying retinue wear the deep-sleeved brocade robes typical of the late Heian era, the tenth and eleventh centuries when Japanese cultural refinement was at its apogee.

The small mountain city of Nikko in Tochigi Prefecture presents a comparable spectacle of its own, but with a marital theme. The resplendent Toshogo Shrine is the final resting place of the Edo era shogun and unifier of Japan, Tokugawa Ieyasu. In 1617 his remains were brought to Nikko in a grand procession befitting his rank. There he was enshrined, deified, and worshiped as a *kami*, as is customary in Japan for exceedingly great personages. Every year in the months of May and October when spring and autumn are in their glory, this Thousand Man Procession (Sennin Gyoretsu) is reenacted.

Offerings are placed on the altar, sacred Shinto dances are performed, and a spirited and skillful exhibition of ancient-style equestrian archery (*yabusame*) is given, all seeking to please and entertain the deities. The procession begins with parish dignitaries on horseback leading companies of samurai soldiers and guardsmen, fitted out in authentic military manner of that bygone time: armored, helmeted, and bearing spears, halberds, bows and arrows, or matchlock guns. There are falconers and flag-bearers, masked lions, monkeys and fairies, with Shinto priests, sacred shrine maidens, pages, and traditional musicians adding to the numbers. Last of all come three *mikoshi*, the portable shrines which house the deities, including the sacred spirit of Ieyasu, for the duration of the festival. Crowded up and down the avenue are many thousands of spectators who, for a short time, feel their nation's illustrious history come to life.

Japanese festivals have always changed with the times. While those no longer relevant adapted or disappeared, new ones developed to meet certain spiritual and community needs. In 1989 Tokyo established an elaborate procession of its own, Jidai Matsuri (Festival of the Ages), patterning it after a great event of the same name in Kyoto. In the name of Tokyo's cultural renaissance, the parade reviews history from the days when the city was called Edo. Here in this great metropolis, where three out of four residents have their roots elsewhere, an event of this nature endeavors to engender a greater sense of community. Although not religiously inspired, like several other city festivals of recent genesis around Japan, religion is not forgotten here, either. The procession is tied to other events at Sensoji, Tokyo's oldest Buddhist temple, thereby bringing many worshipers among the spectators to temple precincts. In proper *matsuri* tradition, mercantile interests are also satisfied, for on that day the shops and stalls on temple grounds and in the neighborhood do exceedingly fine business.

At any festival, both place and intermediaries must first undergo ritual purification before seeking the favor of the divine world. The deity is invited to descend to the festival site, where glorious praises are offered in prayer (*norito*). Generous offerings must be made in the course of the festival's events—from the best of food and drink placed on shrine altars to sacred music, dance, drama, and other entertainments performed within the sacred boundaries of the shrine. The parading of the *mikoshi*, the elaborate and weighty portable shrine and momentary home of the honored deity, is frequently the festival highlight. With the *mikoshi* borne through the neighborhood on the striving shoulders of a multitude of somewhat intoxicated celebrants, this is no solemn procession. The unrestrained, nearly ecstatic, drum-beating, chanting, cheering, and jostling are thought to be pleasing to the gods. Sharing the burden of this tremendous weight is considered a privilege by the bearers, and the feat is cathartic, effecting physical and spiritual renewal of both bearers and their enthusiastic observers.

Official festival participants meet the gods wearing the proper garments, showing the careful attention to form demonstrated in all aspects of Japanese life. Only the finest materials and workmanship are evident, with garments most often of pure silk in the richest weave and made in traditional ceremonial style. No expense is spared in the veneration of the deities, particularly in these quite affluent times.

Matsuri are the happiest and most optimistic of occasions, when personal cares are momentarily forgotten. Customarily extremely reserved, the Japanese people then appear at their sociable best, emboldened by joy, the strength of numbers, and perhaps by some sanctified *sake*, too. Festival visitors, including foreigners, are unquestionably welcome, and their sincere interest in the proceedings often generates a quiet pride among the celebrants. These are not secret rites for believers or initiates only, but celebrations for all who care to partake.

An indivisible part of Japanese life, festivals evolve with the times, embodying the concerns of the people. Constant throughout the thousands of festivals is the ardent appeal for good luck, health, and prosperity. In the past when life was difficult for most, well-being seemed wholly at the mercy of the *kami*, yet even today, the protection and sense of security they offer maintain their appeal.

Matsuri are a visually compelling admixture of ritual, symbol, costume, and color. Anchoring the present to the past and the secular to the religious, they play a notable part in the spiritual, cultural and social life of the nation.

Gorazd Vilhar and Charlotte Anderson

UNIT 6
Judaism

Unit Selections

Key Points to Consider

- How is sacred space defined and utilized in Judaism?

- Describe Theodor Herzl's dream of Zionism. How close have Jews come to the reality of a homeland?

- How have politics affected the history of Jerusalem?

- What is the importance to Jewish tradition of teachings such as those attributed to Rabbi Nachman?

- What relationship does Messianic Judaism have to other forms of Judaism?

- What were some of the religious aspects of the Holocaust?

 **Links: www.dushkin.com/online/**
These sites are annotated in the World Wide Web pages.

Judaism and Jewish Resources
http://shamash.org/trb/judaism.html
Judaism
http://www.religioustolerance.org/judaism.htm

Judaism is the oldest surviving religion of the Western world. An ethnic religious tradition, it provided essential theological roots for the two largest prophetic traditions in the world today, Christianity and Islam. Judaism's own roots go back nearly 4,000 years to a group of nomadic peoples known as the Habiru. During the first two millennia, the religious beliefs and practices of the people became gradually concretized geographically, in the land of Israel, as well as theologically, doctrinally, and mythologically, in the form of the Tanak, the Jewish Bible. However, the land and the people experienced multiple challenges to their independence and individuality. The Babylonians, Persians, Greeks, and Romans all sought to control and possess them. Finally, in the first century CE, the Jews lost their homeland, and once again became a nomadic people, of sorts, for nearly 2,000 years. It is in this environment that Judaism has taken shape and developed its distinctive character.

Without a homeland in which to freely practice their faith, Jews turned to each other, to their culture, and to their scripture as their means of survival. This process created in them a deep sense of unity and oneness with each other and with their divinity, but it also often led to limited interactions with others around them. This separateness has led them to be, as a group, marginalized, and even despised, where they have lived. Yet, their tradition and their faith have endured, and the determination and unity that was necessary to do so have become strong influences in the evolution of Judaism, both as a people and as a religion.

Judaism is the second largest religious tradition in America. Until recent decades, however, very few Americans knew anything substantial about the tradition, yet many maintained feelings of suspicion, resentment, and outright hatred for its followers. Fortunately, times are changing, and as Judaism gradually gains acceptance as a "legitimate" religion, a better understanding of its role and place in the fabric of world traditions is becoming possible.

Because of its lack of a homeland and access to sacred geographic spaces, Jews have had to develop a means of creating their own sacred spaces. The opening article of this unit relates this process and the importance it plays in Judaism. The next article looks at Theodor Herzl's dream of Zion—a homeland for the Jewish people. Then Bernard Wasserstein examines how politics has affected the city of Jerusalem. Since their exile from the land of Israel, rabbis have been the preservers and promoters of their religious culture, and one of the most important means to do this has been through storytelling. The next two articles present examples of the kinds of stories that have been used as vehicles to preserve and pass on their traditions and their beliefs. The final article remembers the Holocaust, known in Hebrew as Shoah: It also reflects on the countless other innocent victims of hatred and the courage that many have faced in standing up to such oppression.

The Sacred Space of Judaism

By Irving Friedman

"… but the Lord was not in the wind; and after the wind an earthquake; but the Lord was not in the earthquake; and after the earthquake a fire; but the Lord was not in the fire; and after the fire a still small voice."

(I Kings XIX-11 and 12)

The history of Judaism can be regarded as its changing relationship with sacred and profane space.

In the beginning there was no space, and God was a breath blowing on the waters of a spaceless abyss. It was only when He withdrew into Himself that primordial space could appear, sanctified by a dilute ray of His light. Within this space He created heaven and earth, and He made His habitation in one of the seven heavens.

The Garden of Eden was sacred earth (Adamah) for Adam was formed of dust from its four corners. Into him God breathed the breath of life and with it His own image. But man was banished from this sacred soil which shared the curse upon him and became further polluted with the blood of Abel spilled on it by Cain.

Finally the earth and all the life it contained were condemned because of the iniquity of man. Terrestrial space had to be purified by a flood which returned it to its beginning in the waters. The seed of life was preserved by a three-story ark, which housed the three divisions of mankind descended from Noah's three sons, as well as the three subhuman categories of animals, reptiles and birds.

After the flood the earth began to conduct the current of life again, yielding its fruit to Noah and his progeny.

Abraham, the tenth generation after Noah, abandoned the profane space of Mesopotamia to wander southward into Canaan with his nomadic flock in search of the sacred pastures promised him by God. But he found famine there, and had first to go down into Egypt, a symbol of material wealth and wisdom, before he could find his spiritual heritage in the promised land. Three generations later, Joseph also had to "go down into Egypt," and the sacred seed which he represented took root there in suffering and grew into a nation away from its sacred land. The pastoral embrace of endless space by the Hebrew shepherds who brought their flocks into Egypt was lost forever.

After the exodus, God commanded the construction of a mobile tabernacle or tent of meeting with Him. This was a portable prototype of Solomon's temple, half its size, and embodied an outer chamber for public worship and an inner one containing God's presence and the ark of the covenant to house the tablets of the ten commandments.

Around this tabernacle as a center, which was guarded by the priestly tribe of the Levites, the entire host of the Hebrews was arranged by tribe according to the four points of the compass. The tent-tabernacle was covered by a cloud indicating the presence of God. When it moved, a pillar of cloud covered it by day and a pillar of fire by night.

The Ark of the Covenant was carried in a wooden tent throughout the desert. When it was captured by the Philistines, David recovered it and conveyed it to Jerusalem, but he was forbidden by God to build a lavish sanctuary. It remained for Solomon to erect the first and most glorious temple, a permanent habitation for the sacred in the center of a nation of farmers which had abandoned the mobile sacred space of nomads.

The temple maintained the distinction between outer and inner chambers initiated by the desert tabernacle. An outer porch, ten-cubits-square, opened on the forty- by twenty-cubits Holy Place, where the main service took place. This led into the twenty-cubits-square Holy of Holies, the innermost chamber where the Ark of the Covenant was kept but no rites were performed. Two Cherubim with outstretched wings hovered over the ark, portraying the protective presence of God in the inner sanctuary.

The symbolism of this seventy-cubit-long temple, which reflected the composition of the universe as well as the nature of man, was recognized by the rabbis of the Talmud as well as Josephus. It was obviously designed as a three-stage passageway from the outer to the inner world. In the universe this transition is from ocean to land to heaven. In man it progresses from his feet, to his chest, to his head.

Two pillars stood in front of the temple, and between them the light streamed in each morning, for the entrance was oriented to the sun. They were variously interpreted as symbolizing the sun and moon, the pillars of cloud and fire, or endurance and continuity.

In the outer Holy Place, a square altar of brass represented the four corners of the earth, which was the source of food for the body of man. Within the Holy of Holies, the golden altar for incense symbolized the soul of man and its food.

While a table of shewbread consecrated human toil to the divine, a seven-branched candlestick symbolized the light of the seven planets, as well as the seven openings in the head of man.

This twofold symbolism uniting man and god in the temple was accepted even by the prophets and ascetic Essenes who criticized the conduct of the priesthood but did not reject the cult of the temple. Nevertheless, in 586 B.C. the temple lay in ruins and the nation was banished from its sacred land to Babylon.

This exile was only one in a series which had begun with the banishment of Adam and Eve from Eden. The cycles of spiritual exile alternating with redemption were externalized in the recurring banishment from and return to sacred space. Slowly the people adjusted to separation from land and temple by developing the synagogue which was a perennial place of worship cut off from any permanent attachment to the land. The religious wandering of the tabernacle in the desert was resurrected in the ubiquity of the synagogue and its wandering people.

The preservation of their sacred character was ensured by the tradition that the spirit of God, the Shechinah, had gone into exile with His people. It yearned for reunion with the divinity just as the Hebrews yearned to return to the sacred land, perpetually intoning, "Next year in Jerusalem."

But the failure of a Messiah to appear and attest the sacred character of their return only emphasized that land could no longer embrace man in a natural sanctity. His redemption from exile now required him to create his own inner space to let the sacred in, just as God, at the creation, had made room to let the world in.

The Hebrews who first found their God in special places and later saw Him everywhere, now ask themselves where is the place of the soul.

From *Parabola*, 1978, pp. 20-23. © 1978 by Parabola, The Magazine of Myth and Tradition, www.parabola.org. Reprinted by permission.

A BLUEPRINT OF ISRAEL

Dreaming of Altneuland

Nearly a century ago, the founder of modern Zionism imagined an "old-new" land much like today's Israel. Much like, but also much unlike

IF ONLY it could have come true. By 1948, many thought it had: after two millennia of exile, the Jewish people had a homeland, in the land where its ancestors had lived. But it was not the homeland dreamed of by Theodor Herzl, the founder of modern Zionism, in his visionary novel "Altneuland", published in 1902. Herzl had made the mistake that many Zionists have made, or chosen to make, after him. His "old-new land" was not "a land without a people for a people without a land". A century ago, Palestine, part of the Turkish empire, was indeed thinly populated. But people there were, and most were not Jews. In Herzl's dream, the existing Arabs welcomed the vigorous newcomers whom he imagined settling there in the 1920s, and the new society they created. Even before that decade, in the real world, was over, he was to be proved bloodily wrong.

His mistake was less obvious in 1902 than it looks now. Europe still believed in its right to colonise the world, and the benefits it brought by doing so; within the past 20 years, the British had taken control of all Egypt, not just a sliver of the Levant. Besides—though it is hard to spot in the book— Herzl's future Altneuland was not independent, but still under Turkish rule, part of an empire in which, in 1902, people of umpteen nationalities and faiths did in fact co-exist. Bulgars, Anatolian Greeks, Armenians, Syrians and sundry other Muslims: they all had their place, not always comfortable, but, on the whole, theirs, and they had learned to live with their different neighbours. Why not a Jewish place, and a people living in harmony with its neighbours, indeed its fellow-citizens? Herzl, after all, had just been trying to negotiate that very thing with the Turks.

A Jewish land, or just a land of Jews?

At the time, the criticism directed at his book was quite different. To the many non-Zionist Jews, this was just another flight of a fantasy that threatened their position in West European societies. To many others, especially in Eastern Europe, the trouble was that Herzl's place was more new than old, and not especially Jewish. They were half right. Seen from today, Altneuland is essentially a bit of comfortable, cultured, bourgeois 1900-ish Vienna transplanted to the Levant by people who happen to be Jews.

It's true that at a Passover supper Herzl's hero, Friedrich Loewenberg, a Jew who had found that condition in Vienna a curse, not a blessing,

> pronounced the *Haggadah* with a penitent's zeal, his throat often tight with emotion. It was almost 30 years... Then had come "enlightenment", the break with all that was Jewish, and the leap into the void. At this Seder table, he seemed to himself a prodigal son returned to his own people.

But this is not every family's Seder. One guest is Friedrich's friend, the older, wealthy Adalbert Kingscourt (by origin, von Koenigshoff, a German nobleman), with whom he set out 20 years earlier on the travels that brought them to Altneuland. There are three Christian clerics. And, amid the harmony of faiths, the guests listen to an account, on a phonograph roll, of the achievements of the New Society for the Colonisation of Palestine. Altneuland is a land of town planning, engineering, lively commerce, industry, mechanised farming. It has a mixed economy, with many co-operatives. It is run by a benevolent technocracy. There is voting, but little politics: "our courts have repeatedly ruled that the term 'professional politician' is an insult". And Jewish culture, Jewish faith? The common tongue is Yiddish. The Temple has been rebuilt. But the book's most visible rabbi, one Dr Geyer, heads not a synagogue, but a faction within the New Society.

He is hostile to further immigration, and non-Jewish membership in the New Society. The book's second hero—in truth, its real one—David Littwak, son of an ex-peasant street pedlar in Vienna, proclaims, in contrast, that

> the New Society rests on ideas that are the common stock of the whole civilised world… It would be unethical to deny a share in our commonwealth to any man, wherever from, whatever his race or creed.

One of Littwak's friends is Reschid Bey, a Berlin-educated Muslim whose father

> was among the first to understand the beneficent character of the Jewish immigration… Reschid himself is a member of our New Society.

Reschid is very clear about it. "Were not the old inhabitants ruined by the Jewish immigration. Didn't they have to leave?" Kingscourt asks. No, he replies:

> It was a great blessing for all of us. Naturally the landowners gained most, because they were able to sell to the Jewish society at high prices… [But] those who had nothing stood to lose nothing, and could only gain. And they did gain: opportunities to work, prosperity. Nothing could have been more wretched than an Arab village at the end of the 19th century. The peasants' clay hovels were unfit for stables. The children lay naked and neglected. Now everything is different. They benefited from the progressive measures of the New Society whether they joined it or not… These people are better off than at any time in the past.

"You're queer fellows, you Muslims," Kingscourt goes on. "Don't you regard these Jews as intruders?"

> You speak strangely, Christian. Would you call a man a robber who takes nothing from you, but brings something? The Jews have enriched us, why should we be against them?

But do ordinary Arabs think the same?

> They more than anyone, Mr Kingscourt. Excuse me, but it was not in the West that I learned tolerance. We Muslims have always got on better with the Jews than you Christians.

As for centuries was true. And the members of the New Society think likewise. In the vote for its congress, the prejudiced Dr Geyer comes nowhere, Littwak triumphs and then becomes the society's new president, the obvious candidate, the older man who built Altneuland, having stood down in his favour.

It's a classic secular-Zionist vision. There were moments in the real 1920s when some serious people believed it possible. But it was always utopian, probably even in the conditions of 1902. Even by the 1930s—long before the anti-colonial upsurge after 1945, or the mass Jewish migration to Israel—the Arab Revolt in British-mandate Palestine was to prove this bit of Herzl's dream a pipe-dream: you can't flood foreigners, however deserving or skilled, into a region and expect that they'll be welcome.

Here is the missing element in "Altneuland": except that the New Society runs a farm penal colony, there's not a hint of force, not even Turkish force. In reality, some Jewish settlers, quite early, had at times to carry guns. And today's Israel, though it doesn't say so too loudly, owes its creation and survival no more to Herzl than to the harsh realists of Zionism, men like Avraham Stern or the young Menachem Begin, who argued that if Jews were to have their state, or indeed a future, they would do so with a rifle at their sides or not at all. In Herzl's dreamland, all is done by worth, thought, skill and civilised decision.

Indeed, having defeated malaria in Palestine, one scientist dreams of doing the same in Africa, thus making "vast areas available for the surplus populations of Europe", and for black Americans too:

> I have lived to see the restoration of the Jews, I should like to pave the way for the restoration of the Negroes.

Life should be that simple. Visionary as he was, when Herzl wanders off his main point in this novel, he is a child of his time. He depicts harshly the anti-Jewish hostility that pushed Friedrich to leave Europe. But, with mass emigration to Altneuland, and thereby less "Jewish competition", that hostility, avers one recent migrant, "has ceased to exist". Still less does Herzl foresee (any more than did others, far later) even a hint of the Nazi horrors that were to come.

Greening the desert

In some other ways, though, Altneuland is not too far from the real Israel, at least in its early decades.

The first step to it was to buy land, before the New Society's plans became public knowledge; then, having asked the Turks for the time being to maintain controls on immigration, to select suitable immigrants. Prefabricated housing was bought from France, timber from Sweden, iron from Germany, all this, and the shipping, being centrally organised. Supply of the countless everyday items, however, was put out to tender by European department stores, carefully scrutinised for any hint of a cartel. These set up branches, and as the new markets flourished, manufacturing sprang up. Railways were built right and left, with

American and (improbably) Russian capital, interest payments being guaranteed by the New Society. And hey presto, at Swiss Family Robinson speed, Altneuland's economy was born.

Not without dispute. Its main organiser

> was reproached for enriching the businessmen. I did not mind… If firms made large profits, I was content. Our own cause was served. People will rush to a place where gold grows out of the earth. How it grows does not matter.

Yet, though the economy is mixed, the New Society itself is "a syndicate of co-operative societies, a syndicate that comprises industry and commerce [and] keeps the welfare of the workers in mind." Shades of early Israel's Histadrut. No pure kibbutzim are visible, but farming is mainly done by co-ops. One may farm for oneself, but actual members of the New Society cannot own land; Reschid Bey has sold his orange groves to it, then leased them back, on the 49-year lease later used by the Jewish National Fund.

And sure enough the newcomers have made the desert bloom. Indeed, they are even smarter than the real Israelis. For a start, they have dug a canal from the Mediterranean to the Dead Sea, and use its final falls for hydro-power, enabling them to employ electric ploughs, instead of the draught cattle that they first planned to import. More than that, from the Dead Sea they draw "great quantities of fresh water" for irrigation—a miracle of chemistry that Herzl wisely (or not noticing, one suspects) does not further explain.

His real lesson, though, was for the Jews of his day. In Altneuland "religion had been excluded from public affairs", and its extremely vigorous cultural life rings more of Vienna than Jerusalem. But there, in the Old City, are two new buildings. One, oh dreams, is the Palace of Peace, the other—site unspecified—the new Temple. Seated in this, Friedrich reflects:

> What a degraded era that was, when Jews had been ashamed of everything Jewish… They need not have been surprised at the contempt shown them; they had shown no respect for themselves.
>
> And out of those depths they had raised themselves. Jews looked different now, because they were no longer ashamed of being Jews. Other nations were grateful to them when they produced some great thing; but the Jewish people asked nothing of its sons except not to be denied.

That part of Herzl's dream has been wholly achieved. One can wonder what he would have thought of another people trying today—albeit by worse methods, because the world paid no attention to good ones—to achieve a land and an identity.

The Politics of Holiness in Jerusalem

By Bernard Wasserstein

Jerusalem, we are often told, is a holy city to three world religions. But the holiness of Jerusalem is neither a constant nor an absolute. It may be conceived of as divinely inspired or as a human attribution. What is undeniable is that, considered as a historical phenomenon, the city's sanctity has waxed and waned according to social, economic, and cultural conditions, and, perhaps above all, political influences.

Judaism, Christianity, and Islam claim to venerate Jerusalem as holy—and no doubt the adherents of each make the claim with full sincerity and zeal. But, in the case of the first, religious devotion did not carry with it, until very recently, a demand for restoration of sovereignty. As for the two successor faiths, of each it can be demonstrated that the holiness of Jerusalem was a late historical development rather than present *ab initio*. In all three cases, the dispassionate observer is compelled by the evidence to conclude that the city's sanctity arose as much from political as from purely spiritual sources.

What is at stake here is not merely the destiny of one medium-sized city, nor even the resolution of the Israeli-Palestinian conflict, but nothing less than the future relationship of the Islamic, Christian, and Jewish worlds. Each has invested the Jerusalem question with emotional freight deriving from the attribution of holiness to specific areas of the city. Scholars of all three religions have been mobilized to verify the authenticity of proprietorial claims. As the Palestinian writer Edward Said has conceded, "We must also admit that Jerusalem, in particular, and Palestine, in general, have always provoked extraordinary projections that have combined distant though reverential assertion with rude grabbing."

Thus we find Elie Wiesel, in the summer of 2000, opposing the right of an elected Israeli government to cede Palestinian control over the greater part of the Old City of Jerusalem, which he said was far more central to Jewish identity and consciousness than to Islam. The late A.L. Tibawi, a Palestinian historian who worked in exile in Britain, wrote as if Jerusalem were sacred only to Muslims and Christians, denying Jews any legitimate place there at all.

Such denials continue today. On a recent visit to Jerusalem, I listened to a Palestinian scholar earnestly insisting that any Jewish religious interest in the Temple Mount was bogus, since the ancient Jewish Temple could be proved to have been sited elsewhere. There is nothing new in all this. Under Muslim, Christian, and Jewish rulers, generations of scholars have acted as handmaidens of power, embroidering history to justify exclusive political pretensions.

Two Jewish voices. The first is that of Ananus, the oldest of the priests of Jerusalem on the eve of the destruction of the Second Temple 70 years after Christ. According to the account of his contemporary Josephus, Ananus, in tears and casting his eyes toward the Temple, which had been seized by the party of Jewish extremists known as Zealots, said: "Certainly it had been good for me to die before seeing the house of God full of so many abominations, or those sacred places that ought not to be trodden upon at random filled with the feet of these blood-shedding villains." The second voice is that of the proto-Zionist Moshe Leib Lilienblum. Writing in 1882 of the future Jewish state in Palestine, he declared: "We do not need the walls of Jerusalem, nor the Jerusalem temple, nor Jerusalem itself."

Two Jewish voices; two Jewish views of Jerusalem.

The Jewish presence in the Holy Land may, as we are often told, have remained continuous throughout the period between the end of the second Jewish Commonwealth and the rise of Zionism. The contention is sometimes extended to an allegedly continuous Jewish presence in Jerusalem. For example, the first president of Israel, Chaim Weizmann, in a speech in Jerusalem in 1948, referred to "the unbroken chain of Jewish settlement in this city." Whatever the truth of such a claim for Palestine in general, the evidence for it in the case of Jerusalem is questionable. Jews were forbidden to live in the city under Roman and Byzantine rule. Although some Jewish pilgrims appear to have visited it, there is no evidence of a Jewish community there between the second and the seventh centuries.

Jews resumed residence in Jerusalem after the first Arab conquest of the city, in 638. A number of documents in the Cairo *Geniza* (a store of old manuscripts uncovered at the end of the 19th century) record financial contributions by Jews in Egypt, Syria, and Sicily toward the support of poor Jews and the maintenance of a synagogue next to the Western ("Wailing") Wall in Jerusalem. When the Crusaders conquered Jerusalem in 1099, Jews were once more thrown out of the city. Only after 1260, under the government of the Mamluk sultans, based in Egypt, did they slowly return, although they came into conflict with Christians, particularly over Mount Zion.

The conquest of the city by the Ottoman Turks, in 1516, created conditions for secure Jewish settlement and slow demographic growth. But in the 17th century, the estimated Jewish population was still only one thousand souls, perhaps 10 percent of the total. In that period, the main center of Jewish life in Palestine, certainly of Jewish intellectual life, was not Jerusalem but Safed. For a long time in the 18th century, Jewish bachelors and persons under 60 were forbidden by the Jewish "Istanbul Committee" to live in Jerusalem. The object of the ban was to limit the size of the Jewish population, which, it was feared, would otherwise be too large to support. The earliest community records of the Jews in Jerusalem, as distinct from records elsewhere about them, date from no earlier than the 18th century. As the Israeli historian Jacob Barnai has written, "the lack of material reflects the lack of organic continuity in these communities during the late Middle Ages and the Ottoman period."

Yet if Jewish settlement in Jerusalem for much of the pre-modern period was sparse and patchy, Jerusalem has nevertheless always been central to the thought and symbolism of Judaism: the resting place of its holy tabernacle, the site of its Temple, the capital of its monarchy, the subject of lamentation from the year 70 down to our own time. Jews faced Jerusalem when they prayed. They called it "the navel of the earth." Biblical literature, halakha (Jewish law), aggada (nonlegal rabbinic teaching), tefilla (liturgy), kabbala (mystical writings), haskala (the Hebrew enlightenment of the 18th and 19th centuries), and Jewish folklore all celebrated Jerusalem's ancient glory and mourned its devastation. In medieval Spain, Yehuda Halevi and Shlomo ibn Gvirol wrote poignant verses expressive of yearning for Jerusalem. In Eastern Europe, a picture of Jerusalem traditionally hung on the eastern wall of the Jewish house. In our own day, Shmuel Yosef Agnon rejoiced in the renewal of Jewish creativity in the city whose "hills spread their glory like banners to the sky." Throughout the ages, Jerusalem remained the foremost destination of Jewish pilgrimage. Above all, Jerusalem carried for Jews an overwhelming symbolic significance as the focus of messianic hope and the locus of the imminently expected resurrection.

At the same time, Judaism differentiated between the heavenly Jerusalem (Yerushalayim shel ma'lah) and the earthly, or everyday, one (shel matah). Religious devotion to the city was not regarded as involving any duty to regain Jewish sovereignty over it. Indeed, when the idea of such a restoration first began to be discussed, in the 19th century, the dominant strain of religious opinion was strongly opposed. That remained true until the destruction of the religious heartland of Jewry, in Eastern Europe, between 1939 and 1945. At least until then, most Orthodox Jewish authorities opposed Zionism as a blasphemous anticipation of the divine eschatological plan. And on this point they found common cause with most early leaders of Reform Judaism—though the two groups would have shrunk with horror from any thought of commonality. Orthodox Zionists were a relatively insignificant stream within the Zionist movement—and equally so within Orthodox Judaism. Zionism, until long after the establishment of the State of Israel, in 1948, remained predominantly and often aggressively secular.

Early Zionist thinkers generally avoided attributing special importance to Jerusalem. The exponent of "spiritual" Zionism, Ahad Ha'am, was repelled by his first encounter with the Jews of Jerusalem, in 1891; later, when he moved to Palestine, he chose to settle in Tel Aviv. The founder of political Zionism, Theodor Herzl, was shocked by Jerusalem's filth and stench when he first visited, in 1898. When Arthur Ruppin set up the Zionist Organi-

zation's first Palestine Office, in 1908, he did so in Jaffa, not Jerusalem. The early Zionist settlers in Palestine, from the 1880s onward, and particularly the socialist Zionists, who arrived in large numbers after 1904, looked down on Jerusalem and all it stood for in their eyes—obscurantism, religiosity, and squalor. In particular, they despised what they saw as the parasitism of Jerusalem's Jews and their dependence on the halukah (charitable dole) from co-religionists in Europe and North America. David Ben-Gurion, who was later, as Israeli prime minister, to declare Jerusalem the capital of Israel, did not bother to visit it until three years after his own immigration to Palestine.

> **The early Zionist settlers in Palestine, particularly the socialist Zionists, looked down on Jerusalem and all it stood for in their eyes—obscurantism, religiosity, and squalor.**

Modern Hebrew literature also contained deeply contradictory tendencies regarding Jerusalem: In the last two decades of the 19th century, writers of the ahavat Zion (love of Zion) school tended to extol Jerusalem and sing its praises; modernist poets and novelists, from Haim Nahman Bialik onward, took a more harshly realistic view. In the first half of the 20th century, a stream of writing (Yosef Haim Brenner, Nathan Alterman, Avraham Shlonsky, the early Uri Zvi Greenberg) that was hostile to Jerusalem—loathing it, demystifying it, even stressing its irrelevance—shaped a profoundly negative view of the city in the Hebrew literary imagination. Of course, that was only one stream of thought—but, in its time, perhaps the most influential and truly expressive of the Zionist revolution against Jewish traditionalism.

Thus spiritual values exalting Jerusalem competed with, and were overshadowed by, other religious, social, political, and intellectual forces in forming the ambivalent modern Jewish view of Jerusalem.

T WO CHRISTIAN VOICES. First, St. Jerome (c. 342-420), who went on pilgrimage to the Holy Land and spent the last 34 years of his life in a monastery in Bethlehem. He argued that it was part of the Christian faith "to adore where His feet have stood and to see the vestiges of the nativity, of the Cross, and of the passion." The second voice is that of St. Gregory of Nyssa (4th century), who wrote to a disciple, "When the Lord invites the blest to their inheritance in the Kingdom of Heaven, he does not include a pilgrimage to Jerusalem among their good deeds."

Two Christian voices; two Christian views of Jerusalem.

For Christians, the sanctity of Jerusalem derives wholly from the events associated with the life, death, and resurrection of the Savior in that city. Historically speaking, however, there is no evidence of any particular sanctity attached to Jerusalem by Christians until the 4th century, and it is only then that we encounter the first recorded account of a Christian pilgrimage to Jerusalem.

Squabbling Christian sects were compelled by the Muslim authorities to hand over the keys to the Church of teh Holy Sepulchre—the reputed tomb of Jesus—to a Muslim family for safekeeping.

Recent scholarship has focused on the ecclesiastical struggle in 4th-century Christianity between those who affirmed the holiness of Jerusalem and those who tended to play it down. As P.W.L. Walker writes, "Jerusalem and the 'holy places' showed from the outset that, despite their capacity to be focuses for Christian unity, they also had great potential for division." Walker lays stress on the "largely negative and dismissive" views of Eusebius, bishop of Caesarea, in Palestine (c. 260-340), regarding Jerusalem's holiness. Eusebius's opinion may have derived in part from competition between his episcopal see and that of Jerusalem. Beyond that, it has been argued, his view was born of a desire to combat an incorrect emphasis on the physical, earthly Jerusalem—an error he attributed to the Jews.

By contrast, and in opposition to Eusebius, Bishop Cyril of Jerusalem (c. 320-386) maintained that the "prerogative of all good things was in Jerusalem." That became, indeed, a dominant view in the church. Just as Eusebius's somewhat negative view of Jerusalem has been connected to his attitude toward Jews, the more affirmative Christian attitude to Jerusalem in the early Middle Ages was also bound up with hostility to the Jews. According to Amnon Linder, of the Hebrew University of Jerusalem, "The complete destruction of Jewish Jerusalem and its transformation into a Christian city, with the resultant expulsion, dispersion, and subjugation of the Jews, was seen as a Divine punishment and as an essential stage on mankind's road to complete salvation." The triumph of the Christian theological view of Jerusalem's holiness was, however, an outcome not only of debate among the church fathers, but also of the political triumph of the emperor Constantine, who ruled Jerusalem from 324 to his death in 337. The celebrated journey of his mother, Helena, to Jerusalem to identify the sites of the crucifixion and resurrection marked a turning point in the Christian history of the city. The Anastasis (later known as the Church of the Holy Sepulchre), erected over the reputed tomb of Jesus at Constantine's command and dedicated in 335, replaced a temple to Aphrodite at the same location. Like so many other holy places and shrines in Jerusalem, the Anastasis thus, from its very outset, gave physical expression to competitive religious spirit—in this case, between Christianity and paganism.

With Helena's visit, Jerusalem became firmly established as a center of veneration and pilgrimage for Christians. The *Itinerarium Burdigalense*, an account of a pilgrimage to Jerusalem from Bordeaux in 333, is one of the earliest examples of what became a common literary genre. Christian glorification of Jerusalem was briefly challenged in 363, when the pagan emperor Julian the Apostate proposed to rebuild the Temple in Jerusalem. But after his death in battle that year, the process resumed with even greater momentum. It was in full flood by the last two decades of the century, when Egeria, probably a Spanish nun, wrote a narrative of her pilgrimage to Jerusalem—still widely read today.

External financial support for Christian institutions in Jerusalem, as for Jewish ones, is a longstanding feature of the city's history, in the case of the Christians extending back to the Byzantine period. During the first period of Muslim rule over the city, non-Muslims almost certainly still formed a majority of the population of the city. At one point in the early Arab period, there is even said to have been a Christian governor of the province. On Christmas Day 800—coronation day of Charlemagne in Rome—the new emperor is reported to have received the key to the Church of the Holy Sepulchre and the flag of the holy city as tokens of respect from the Patriarch of Jerusalem (or, according to another account, from the Muslim Caliph Harun al-Rashid). Charlemagne and his son Louis built a number of new Christian institutions in Jerusalem. That construction work gave rise to some conflict. In 827, for example, Muslims complained that Christians had built a bigger dome over a church than that over the Muslim shrine of the Dome of the Rock. Similarly, competition in pilgrimages, a feature of religious and commercial life in the city throughout the ages and into modern times, is recorded very early. The pilgrimages and the holy days with which they were associated were frequently occasions of communal violence. On Palm Sunday in 937 or 938, a Christian procession was attacked and the Church of the Holy Sepulchre was burned to the ground. On Pentecost in 966, a number of churches were pillaged. And on September 28, 1009, the Holy Sepulchre was again destroyed, by order of the mad Caliph al-Hakim. It was not rebuilt until 1048—and then only partially.

The conquest of Jerusalem by the Crusader forces of Godfrey de Bouillon, on July 15, 1099, inaugurated a new period of terror against Muslims and Jews, all of whom were driven out of the city, their mosques and synagogues destroyed. The Muslim shrines on the Temple Mount were turned into Christian churches. The Crusader kings carved the city into separate districts based on the nationality of the Christian settlers, the knightly orders, and the various eastern Christian communities. The Orthodox Patriarch was packed off to Constantinople, and the Latins (Roman Catholics) assumed the *praedominium* (right of pre-eminence) over the holy places.

After the final ejection of the Crusaders from Jerusalem, in 1244, Christians were compelled to translate their conception of Jerusalem from an earthly to a heavenly sphere. Christian pilgrimages, however, continued: Chaucer's Wife of Bath went to Jerusalem three times. And books of *Laudes Hierosolymitanae* (praises of Jerusalem) were produced in large quantities. The Christian struggle for Jerusalem now assumed a new form. Having lost the war against the Infidel, Christians embarked on a war against each other.

Now began in earnest the great contest between the Eastern and Western churches for control of the holy places, above all the Church of the Holy Sepulchre, in Jerusalem, and the Church of the Nativity, in Bethlehem. Unable to agree among themselves, the squabbling Christian sects were compelled by the Muslim authorities, in or before 1289, to hand over the keys of the Church of the Holy Sepulchre to a Muslim family for safe-keeping. When the last Crusader fortress in Palestine, at Acre, fell in 1291, the only remaining Latin institutional presence in Palestine was that of the Franciscans, who had arrived in 1217. In the early 14th century, Pope Clement VI appointed them to the "Custody of the Holy Land" (*Custodia Terrae Sanctae*). That little outpost of Roman Christianity saw as its primary task the battle against the pretensions of the Eastern churches to pro-prietorship of the holy places. It fought by every means to up-hold the enduring rights in Jerusalem of the true Rome. The fight carried on into modern times and, in modified form, en-dures still. It has colored every aspect of Christian life in Jerus-alem, as well as the diplomacy of the Christian powers in relation to the holy city.

Thus for Christians, as for Jews, though in different ways, Jerusalem was both a symbol of unity and a fault line of pro-found internal schism.

Two MUSLIM TRADITIONS. The first is a statement attributed to the Prophet Muhammad, according to which he said, "He who performs the pilgrimage to Mecca and visits my grave [in Medina] and goes forth to fight [in a holy war] and prays for me in Jerusalem—God will not ask him about what he [failed to perform of the prescriptions] imposed on him."

> **The Crusaders' conquest of Jerusalem was greeted by Muslim indifference. The heightening of religious fervor for its recapture may be explained largely by political necessity.**

The second tradition concerns Umar, the second Muslim ca-liph, who reigned at the time of the first Muslim conquest of Jerusalem, in 638. Umar, it is said, was in a camel enclosure when two men passed by. He asked where they came from and they said Jerusalem. Umar hit them with his whip and said, "Have you performed a pilgrimage like the pilgrimage to the Kaaba [in Mecca]?" They said, "No, O Commander of the Faithful, we came from such and such a territory and passed [Jerusalem] by and prayed there." To which Umar said, "Then so be it," and let them go.

Two Muslim voices; two Muslim views of Jerusalem.

For Muslims, the holiness of Jerusalem derives primarily from its identification with the "further mosque" (*al-masjid al-aqsa*), mentioned in the Koran as the place to which the Prophet was carried on his "night journey" from Mecca. From Jerusalem he ascended to the seventh heaven.

There is some evidence, however, to suggest that the attribu-tion of sanctity to Jerusalem was, at least in part, connected to the city's central position in the two precursor religions that Islam claimed to supersede. According to Muslim tradition, Jerusalem was the first *qibla* (the direction of prayer) before it was changed to Mecca in 624. The practice is not attested to in the Koran, but it is ingrained in Muslim tradition—and has sur-vived within living memory in the practice of some elderly wor-shippers in the Dome of the Rock.

In the earliest period of Islam, there appears to have been a tendency to emphasize the holiness of Mecca and Medina and to stress the importance of pilgrimages to those cities rather than to Jerusalem. There were also, however, some contrary views, and it was not until the second Islamic century (719–816 of the Christian era) that there developed a general acceptance of the holiness of all three cities. A decisive point came during the ca-liphate of Abd al-Malik b. Marwan (685–705). He was engaged in conflict with a rival caliph, Abd Allah b. al-Zubayr, who was installed at Mecca. Abd al-Malik built Jerusalem's most im-pressive surviving religious monument, the Dome of the Rock—often wrongly called the "Mosque of Umar": It is, in fact, a shrine, not a mosque, and has nothing to do with Umar. One authority, Richard Ettinghausen, an Islamic-art historian, has argued that the Dome of the Rock was not merely a memo-rial to the ascension of the Prophet: "Its extensive inscriptions indicate that it is a victory monument commemorating triumph over the Jewish and Christian religions." The great Hungarian orientalist Ignaz Goldziher argued that Abd al-Malik's motive in building the shrine and reaffirming the city's sanctity was to compete with the rival Meccan caliph and divert the pilgrim trade to his own dominions. That view has been widely ac-cepted, although S.D. Goitein, the distinguished scholar of Is-lamic-Jewish relations, who worked at the Institute for Advanced Study in Princeton, N.J., disagreed, suggesting that Abd al-Malik's object was to create a structure that could match the magnificent churches of Jerusalem and other towns in geo-graphical Syria. What unites all those interpretations is the attri-bution of an underlying competitive motive to the caliph. The Arabic name of the city, al-Quds ("the Holy"), first appears only in the late 10th century.

Surprisingly, the conquest of Jerusalem by the Crusaders was greeted, at first, by Muslim indifference rather than fervor for its recapture. Even those Muslims who called for a holy war against the invading Franks refrained, with few exceptions, from stressing the sanctity of Jerusalem—which seems in that period to have been neither widely diffused nor deeply im-planted in Muslim thought. A change of attitude emerged only in the mid-12th century. As so often in the history of Jerusalem, heightened religious fervor may be explained in large measure by political necessity. In the 1140s, Zenki, ruler of Mosul and Aleppo, with his son and successor Nur al-Din, called for an all-out war against the Crusader state. Their official propagandists consequently placed a sudden emphasis on the holiness of Jerusalem in Islam. That tendency was further accentuated under the leadership of Saladin, who used the sanctity of Jerus-alem as a means of cowing potential opponents. In the late 12th century, the idea of the holy city was invoked no less in internal Muslim quarrels than in the external conflict with Christendom. The Muslim reconquest of Jerusalem, on October 2, 1187, was greeted with an outburst of enthusiasm and rejoicing in the Is-lamic world. Saladin's victory was hailed in letters, poems, and messages of congratulation. During the following years, the lit-erature in praise of Jerusalem (*Fadail Bayt al-Maqdis*) was hugely amplified and extended. Muslims were encouraged to resettle there or to go on pilgrimage. Returning pilgrims carried to their homes the concept of the sanctity of Jerusalem.

Henceforth, Muslim rule over the city came to be regarded as a veritable act of faith. In 1191, Saladin wrote to Richard the Lion-Hearted, in the course of armistice negotiations, that even if he (Saladin) were personally disposed to yield the city, the crusading English king "should not imagine that its surrender would be possible; I would not dare even to utter the word in front of the Muslims." Jerusalem was nevertheless returned to the Christians by the Treaty of Jaffa in 1229. Under that agreement, Jerusalem, Bethlehem, and Nazareth were handed over to the Holy Roman Emperor, Frederick II, though the Muslims were permitted to retain their holy places there. At the same time, the walls of Jerusalem were demolished so that it would no longer serve as a fortified point. The result was that, for many years, the city was vulnerable to military attack and to raids from nomads. The treaty was to last for 10 years. After that, fighting broke out again, and, in 1244, the city was sacked by invading Kharezmian Tartars. Only after 1260 was order restored under the Mamluks.

Under Mamluk rule, Jerusalem was not a place of any political importance. The division of the city into four quarters—Muslim, Christian, Jewish, and Armenian—had its origins in this period. Islamic institutions were established and the Muslim character of the city enhanced, though, unlike the Christians, Muslims tolerated the presence of other faiths. Religious groups tended to settle around their most important shrines and holy places: Muslims north and west of the Haram al-Sharif (literally "noble sanctuary"—the name given to the Temple Mount); Armenians in the southwest, near their Cathedral of St. James; the other Christians in the northwest, near the Holy Sepulchre; and the Jews in the south, near the Western Wall. By the dawn of the modern era, divided Jerusalem was a geographical as well as a spiritual fact.

So WE SEE that within Judaism, Christianity, and Islam there have been countervailing positive and negative tendencies regarding Jerusalem—and that, in each case, political considerations have played a significant part in the affirmation or qualification of Jerusalem's holiness. Competition among the faiths has repeatedly focused on Jerusalem. Each has tried to outbid the other two in claiming Jerusalem as a central religious symbol, often by means of hyperbolic special pleading. Yet each religion has been ambivalent or fractured in its relationship to Jerusalem—in how it has seen the city's degree of holiness, its holy places, and its function in this world and the next. These lines of division have determined the history of the earthly city in the modern period.

This cautionary tale should serve as a warning to those who would invoke religious fervor in support of political claims to Jerusalem. Of course, any settlement must make provision for the legitimate spiritual interests of all three faiths. But those can be met without impairing the longstanding principle of the "status quo," traditionally applied to Jerusalem in religious disputes. Muslims already control the Haram al-Sharif. Every Israeli government since 1967 has recognized their right to do so; none has sought to impose direct Israeli control; none has permitted Jewish extremists, hoping to prepare for the rebuilding of the Temple, to establish a foothold. Christians control all of their holy places and no longer seek to use them as stalking-horses for claims of sovereignty over Palestine. Nor does the Vatican any longer seek the internationalization of Jerusalem (a euphemism for what would, in effect, have been Christian control of the city). As for the Jewish holy place, the Western Wall: That is securely in Israeli hands, and Palestinian representatives, in talks with Israelis in recent years, have accepted that it should remain so.

At his final meeting with Israeli and Palestinian negotiators, on December 23, 2000, President Clinton proposed the application to Jerusalem of "the general principle that Arab areas are Palestinian and Jewish ones are Israeli." That, he suggested, should apply to the Old City. In subsequent discussions at the Egyptian Red Sea resort of Taba, the negotiators made significant progress toward agreement on the outstanding issues regarding a permanent settlement both of the Arab-Israeli dispute, in general, and of the problem of Jerusalem, in particular.

That progress has been cast aside as a result of the continuing Palestinian intifada and the Israeli response. But sooner or later, since neither side can totally defeat the other, the two will have to return to the negotiating table. Jerusalem will once more be on the agenda for discussion. Israel has claimed since 1967 to have "unified" the city. Yet no city in the world today is more deeply divided—politically, socially, religiously. Neither side wishes to see a wall re-erected between Jewish and Arab areas, as existed from 1949 to 1967. The population of the city today, including Arab and Jewish areas beyond the city limits but within its sociogeographic region, is approximately half-and-half Jewish and Arab.

Somehow, a way must be found to enable people to live together—but the task is not helped by the *trahison des clercs* of those scholars who help stir up religious emotions to assert political claims. "The religious mind will not easily relinquish its hold on the sacred ground of mystery and miracle," Edward Gibbon warned in a passage on the Crusades in his *Decline and Fall of the Roman Empire*. "But the holy wars which have been waged in every climate of the globe, from Egypt to Livonia, and from Peru to Hindostan, require the support of some more general and flexible tenet." Of course, the tenet to which Gibbon, a child of the Enlightenment, referred was reason. The faithful may scoff. But does not reason's still, small voice, even in this unreasonable age, have some place in the search for a solution to this most intractable of conflicts?

Bernard Wasserstein is a professor of history at the University of Glasgow and president of the Jewish Historical Society of England. This essay is adapted from Divided Jerusalem: The Struggle for the Holy City, *being published this month by Yale University Press.*

SAYINGS OF RABBI NACHMAN

The World

The world is like a revolving die, and everything turns over, and man changes to angel and angel to man, and the head to the foot and the foot to the head. So all things turn over and revolve and are changed, this into that and that into this, what is above to what is beneath and what is beneath to what is above. For in the root all is one, and in the transformation and return of things redemption is enclosed.

Beholding the World

As the hand held before the eye conceals the greatest mountain, so the little earthly life hides from the glance the enormous lights and mysteries of which the world is full, and he who can draw it away from before his eyes, as one draws away a hand, beholds the great shining of the inner worlds.

God and Man

All the troubles of man proceed from himself. For the light of God continually pours over him, but man, through his all too physical life, makes himself a shadow so that the light of God cannot reach him.

Faith

Faith is an immensely strong thing, and through faith and simplicity, without any subtleties, one becomes worthy of attaining the rung of grace, which is even higher than that of holy wisdom: abundant and powerful grace of God is given to him in holy silence until he can no longer endure the power of the silence and cries aloud out of the fullness of his soul.

Prayer

Let everyone cry out to God and lift up his heart to Him, as if he were hanging by a hair and a tempest were raging to the very heart of heaven so that he did not know what to do, and he had almost no more time left to cry out. And in truth there is no counsel and no refuge for him save to remain alone and to lift up his eyes and his heart to God and to cry out to Him. One should do this at all times, for a man is in great danger in the world.

Two Languages

There are men who can utter words of prayer in truth so that the words shine like a jewel that shines of itself. And there are men whose words are only like a window that has no light of its own, but only shines forth out of the light that it admits.

Within and Without

Man is afraid of things that cannot harm him, and he knows it, and he craves things that cannot be of help to him, and he knows it; but in truth the one thing man is afraid of is within himself, and the one thing he craves is within himself.

Two Kinds of Human Spirit

There are two kinds of spirit, and they are like backward and forward. There is one spirit that man attains in the course of time. But there is another spirit that overwhelms man in great abundance, in great haste, swifter than a moment, for it is beyond time and for this spirit no time is needed.

Thinking and Speaking

All thoughts of man are speaking movement, even when he does not know it.

Truth and Dialectic

Victory cannot tolerate the truth, and if one displays a true thing before your eyes, you reject it for the sake of victory. He, then, who wants the truth in himself drives away the spirit of victory, for only then is he ready to behold the truth.

The Aim of the World

The world was created only for the sake of the choice and the choosing one.

Man, the master of choice, should say: The whole world has been created only for my sake. Therefore, man shall take care at every time and in every place to redeem the world and fill its want.

Joy

Through joy the spirit becomes settled, but through sadness it goes into exile.

Perfection

One must perfect oneself to unity until one is perfected in creation as he was before creation, so that he is wholly one, entirely good, thoroughly holy, as before creation.

One must renew oneself every day in order to perfect oneself.

The Evil Urge

The evil urge is like one who runs about among men, and his hand is closed and no one knows what is in it. And he goes up to each and asks, "What do you suppose I have in my hand?" And each imagines that just what he most desires is in that hand. And everybody runs after it. And then he opens his hand, and it is empty.

One can serve God with the evil urge if one directs his passion and his fervor of desiring to God. And without the evil urge there is no perfect service.

In the righteous the evil urge is transformed into a holy angel, a being of might and destiny.

Ascent

No limits are set to the ascent of man, and to each the highest stands open. Here your choice alone decides.

Judging Oneself

If a man does not judge himself, all things judge him, and all things become messengers of God.

Will and Obstacle

There is no obstacle that one cannot overcome, for the obstacle is only there for the sake of the willing, and in reality there are no obstacles save in the spirit.

Between Men

There are men who suffer terrible distress and they cannot tell anyone of it, and they go about full of suffering. But if one meets them with laughing countenance, he may cheer them with his joy. And it is no small thing to cheer a man.

In Concealment

There are men who have no authority at all when they reveal themselves, but in concealment they rule the generation.

The Kingdom of God

Those who do not walk in loneliness will be bewildered when the Messiah comes and they are called; but we shall be like a man who has been asleep and whose spirit is tranquil and composed.

The Wandering of the Soul

God never does the same thing twice. When a soul returns, another spirit becomes its companion.

When a soul comes into the world, its deed begins to ascend out of the hidden worlds.

There are naked souls who cannot enter into bodies, and for them there is great compassion, more than for those that have lived. For these latter were in bodies and have procreated and produced; but the former cannot ascend, and also they cannot descend to clothe themselves with bodies. There are wanderings in the world that have not yet revealed themselves.

The righteous must be unsettled and transient because there are fugitive souls who only thereby can ascend. And if a righteous man resists and will not wander, he becomes unsettled and transient in his house.

There are stones, like souls, that are flung down on the streets. But once the new houses are built, then one will fit into them the holy stones.

From *The Tales of Rabbi Nachman*, 1956, pp. 35–41. © 1956. Reprinted with permission of BRILL NV.

He Who Was Caught in His Own Trap

Do you know who love tales the most? Children! They would leave their favorite and most entertaining game if you started to tell them a tale. The zaddik of Kálló was very fond of children. On Sabbaths he would allow them to gather around him, and their innocent hearts jumped with joy when he looked at them with his kind, smiling eyes.

It was going to be a beautiful tale. Purim was approaching, and it was at that time that the rebbe would customarily tell his most beautiful tales. The children fastened their faithful, glistening eyes on the zaddik, whose eyes looked as if they could penetrate the thick walls of his house.

He began his tale quietly and seriously:

Once, far, far away there lived a mighty king. His realm was great and his wealth was immense. An army of servants surrounded him, waiting for his commands. Many strangers came to his city and among them a Jewish builder arrived one day. He stopped in front of the king's palace and he was taken aback by what he saw. "It is amazing," he murmured, "that a king so powerful and wealthy should live in such an old and unpretentious palace. If he only commissioned me, I would build him such an enchanted palace that the whole world would marvel at it."

At that moment the king leaned out of one of the many windows of his palace and his gaze fell upon the stranger who had been watching his palace. "Bring him to me," he commanded, for he wanted to know why the stranger had been standing there for so long.

The builder came and stood respectfully in front of the king.

"Does your king live in a more magnificent palace?" asked the king upon hearing the builder's explanation.

"Your Majesty," replied the Jew, "do not take offense at my amazement, but this unpretentious palace befits neither your power nor your wealth. I could build you a great and truly majestic palace if you would provide me with the tools and workers I need."

The king agreed. "Let it be."

For many weeks, hundreds of workers, machines, and beasts of burden toiled until the magnificent palace was finished. The king's beaming face revealed his feelings; he could not even dream of anything more beautiful.

"Master," he said, "I want to thank and honor you properly for this masterpiece. Remain in my kingdom."

The Jewish builder became a prominent and respected man. The king respected his knowledge and grew so fond of him that not a day passed without the Jewish builder's coming to the palace twice, where his opinion was asked even on matters of state.

Small wonder that some people began to envy the builder. At first, they whispered only among themselves, but soon malicious rumors reached the king's ears too, but he was so deeply convinced of the honesty of his Jewish favorite that he quickly dismissed them. The enemies of the builder, however, did not rest. One day, when the ruler was in a bad mood, one of his counselors said to him, "My lord, the Jewish builder is not worthy of the many favors you have bestowed upon him. The palace has one great defect. I have recently observed a group of strangers who viewed the palace snickering. When I asked them the reason for their behavior they laughed and said, 'Who could build such an ugly palace? The builder who designed such unattractive windows has made fun of the king.' Your Majesty, this proves that the Jew is unworthy of the high position to which you have raised him."

Gradually the king began to give credence to those who conspired against his favorite. "Indeed," he thought, "the windows are ridiculously shapeless. The Jew has made fun of me. New windows must be installed immediately."

The king entrusted the conspiring counselor to carry out his orders.

"And what should become of the impudent Jew, Your Majesty?" inquired the counselor. "For he who arouses the ruler's wrath is deserving of death."

The king, however, was reluctant to give a quick decision in the matter. "Tomorrow," he replied. "Tomorrow we shall decide."

The conspirators were victorious, it seemed.

On the following day, the king sent a sealed letter and a note of instruction to the Jewish builder. The message read, "One of my ships has just anchored by the seashore.

Go to it and give this letter to the captain. You will be informed of the rest there."

"Throw the bearer of this letter overboard," it read. The captain read the unusual order with surprise. He looked at the builder with pity. After a moment of hesitation he spoke quietly to the builder, "I shall not obey the king's order. It is cruel and unjust. You will put on a cook's uniform and remain on board in secret. We shall see what the future brings."

In a few days the ship set out on a worldwide voyage.

The evil counselor rejoiced that the hated rival no longer stood in his way. Even the king forgot about him. After some time had passed the ship returned to its home port. When the king was informed of the arrival of the ship he sent a message to the captain that he wanted to inspect all the wonderful things the ship had brought from faraway lands.

"Your opportunity is here," said the captain to the builder. "The king will be on board tomorrow. You will put on your old clothes, and when you see the king approaching, jump into the sea from the other side of the ship. I know you are a good swimmer so you will have no difficulty. By the time the king steps on board, you will have swum around the ship and suddenly you will stand in front of him in wet clothes. I shall leave the rest to you."

Thundering music signaled the king's arrival. He stepped aboard, followed by a magnificent entourage. Walking at the king's side, the haughty counselor looked around proudly. Suddenly his countenance grew pale. He turned to the king and whispered with quivering lips, "Look, Your Majesty!"

The astonished king recognized the builder, who now stood dripping wet before him. "How did you come here? What happened to you?"

"Your Majesty," replied the builder, "it is a miraculous story. They cast me into the sea, but I did not perish as you can see. A huge fish swallowed me and took me straight to the King of the Seas. When he learned of my profession he commissioned me to build him a palace. The huge enchanted palace is finished, and only the windows are missing. I did not dare to accept responsibility for them—I have already had bad luck with them. But can anyone imagine a palace without windows? I told the King of the Seas that here in your realm, Your Majesty, there was a famous builder who could make beautiful windows. 'I shall borrow that skillful man from my royal brother on land,' said the King of the Seas. 'One of my servants will help you swim to the ship so you may deliver my message.' And now, Your Majesty, the envoy of the King of the Seas is standing before you requesting that you fulfill this wish. The giant fish is waiting at the side of the ship."

Streams of cold sweat poured down the face of the evil counselor. He could only stammer, as the king's gaze rested on him, "My lord—have mercy on me!"

The king, however, showed no mercy. He turned to the Jewish builder, "My friend, you will stay here, and the counselor will leave to finish my royal brother's palace."

Thereupon the king's men grabbed the trembling counsel and threw him into the sea.

From *Rabbi Eizik: Hasidic Stories About the Zaddik of Kallo*, 1978, pp. 41-45. © 1978. Reprinted with permission of the Fairleigh Dickinson University.

Holocaust Remembrance Day brings memories of evil, courage

Abstract: *Yom ha-Shoah (Holocaust Remembrance Day) provides an occasion to remember (1) the Holocaust itself, (2) numerous cases of genocide and state-sanctioned homicide in the 20th century, (3) the courageous individuals who helped intended victims.*

Ann Marie Bahr

Yom ha-Shoah (Hebrew for "Holocaust Remembrance Day") is celebrated on 27 Nissan, which in 2002 coincides with Tuesday, April 9. Certainly, there is much to remember on this day.

First, there is the Holocaust itself. Approximately 6 million Jews were intentionally and systematically annihilated by the Nazi government during World War II.

Jews were herded into ghettos surrounded by walls or fences. The Nazis confiscated nearly all their belongings.

Severe overcrowding, lack of hygiene, starvation and denial of basic medicines led to widespread epidemics in many ghettos.

In addition, Jews were forced to endure long hours of forced labor. No wonder, then, that in Warsaw, the largest of the ghettos, approximately 85,000 Jews (about 20 percent of the ghetto population) died from the conditions before the Nazis began to deport them to a death camp.

The first death camp was at Chelmno, Poland. It began to function on Dec. 8, 1941, when Jews from the surrounding area were brought there. Eventually, approximately 320,000 people, mostly Jews, were murdered there before the Nazis abandoned the camp on Jan. 17, 1945.

About 1.5 million children were murdered by the Nazis between 1933 and 1945. The overwhelming majority of them were Jewish. Some were shot. Many were asphyxiated with poisonous gas in concentration camps or subjected to lethal injections. Others perished from disease, starvation, exposure, torture or severe physical exhaustion from slave labor. Still others died as a result of medical experiments conducted on them by German doctors in the camps.

By 1945 two out of every three European Jews had been killed. Although Jews were the primary victims, they were not the only victims. Close to 500,000 Gypsies and at least 250,000 mentally or physically disabled people were also victims of genocide.

More than 3 million Soviet prisoners of war were killed because of their nationality. Poles and other Slavs were targeted for slave labor, and almost 2 million perished.

Homosexuals and others deemed "anti-social" were also persecuted and often murdered. In addition, thousands of political and religious dissidents, including communists, socialists, trade unionists and Jehovah's Witnesses, were persecuted for their beliefs, and many of them died as a result of maltreatment.

Second, this date can be a day to remember all victims of genocide and state-sanctioned homicide. The first significant genocide of the 20th century was directed against the Armenian residents of Asia Minor by the Turkish government. The slaughter began on April 24, 1915; April 24 is still commemorated by Armenians around the world as Martyrs' Day.

The Soviets under Stalin put to death nearly 62 million between 1917 and 1953; these were mostly individuals who disagreed with the communist state. Between the years 1945 and 1976 Mao Zedong and his communist regime oversaw the death of between 44 million and 72 million people, both ethnic Chinese and large numbers of the ethnic minorities within China and on its borders.

The Tutsi made up about 9 percent of the population of Rwanda for a total of about 1 million people. Nearly 80 percent of them were killed during a three-month period of civil war and genocide in 1994, and 5 percent died as a result of disease and starvation afterward.

Even without mentioning the Cambodians killed by the Khmer Rouge army, the Chinese exterminated at the hands of the Japanese during World War II, the approximately 400,000 Hungarians who died at the hands of Romanians, the civil war in Sudan, or the ethnic cleansing aimed primarily at Muslims in the former Yugoslavia, we can see that mass murder, much of it sanctioned or supported by governments, was scrawled large across the face of the 20th century.

Third, Yom ha-Shoah is an occasion for remembering the "Righteous Among the Nations," those who helped Jews escape the Holocaust. Among them was Chiune Sugihara, a Japanese consul in Lithuania.

Against the order of the Japanese government, Sugihara issued 2,500 transit visas to Jews. Upon his return to Japan, he was dismissed from the Japanese Foreign Service and had to do odd jobs to make a living.

Ellen Nielsen, a widow, supported her six children by buying fish directly from fishermen on the docks of Copenhagen, Denmark, and selling it to passersby. She had no interest in politics.

Yet when she discovered that two young men who were regular customers were Jews, she sheltered them.

Thus began a process by which over 100 refugees passed through her home on their way to Sweden. Mrs. Nielsen was caught by the Gestapo in December 1944 and sent to Ravensbruck concentration camp.

There were many others, too numerous to mention, who demonstrated a similar courage. It is they who allow the human race to enter the 21st century with at least a small amount of humanity and dignity clinging to its footprints.

From *The Brookings Register*, February 21, 2002, p. A7. © 2002 by The Brookings Register, Brookings, SD. Reprinted by permission.

UNIT 7
Christianity

Unit Selections

Key Points to Consider

- Why has the ethnic and racial demography of Christianity changed so much in the last several decades?

- What are the factors that make someone a "Catholic" today?

- Why do some conservative Catholics resent contemporary public education?

- What are some of the limits put on freedom of religion?

- What role does Mary, the mother of Jesus, play in contemporary Christianity?

- How has the practice of Christianity changed over the last several decades?

 **Links: www.dushkin.com/online/**
These sites are annotated in the World Wide Web pages.

ATLA World Christianity Website
http://www.yale.edu/adhoc/research_resources/wcig.htm

History, Beliefs, Practices, Deeds, etc., of the Roman Catholic Church
http://www.religioustolerance.org/rcc.htm

Mark A. Foster's Religious Studies Resource Links: Christianity
http://old.jccc.net/~mfoster/christian.html

Special Report: American Catholics Survey
http://www.natcath.com/NCR_Online/archives/102999/web/index.htm

Wikipedia: Christianity
http://www.wikipedia.com/wiki/Christianity/

World Religions: Comparative Analysis
http://www.comparativereligion.com

Christianity is arguably the most successful religion in the world, in terms of numbers and influence. Christian missionaries have preached to and converted people in nearly every country and culture and have established their indelible presence almost everywhere. For most people in the Western world, and even many others around the world, Christianity has defined religion, what it is and what it is not. Yet, the tradition itself has gone through countless changes since its inception two thousand years ago, and circumscribing its beliefs and practices remains an elusive task.

Christianity started out as a small group of Jewish individuals following a teacher they believed to be a saviour for their people, their culture, and their nation. Within a century of the death of Jesus, however, there were already vastly different interpretations of who he was, what his teachings were, and what it meant to be a Jesus-follower. Early Church leaders sought to clearly define who and what a "true" Christian believes with the Nicene Creed in the mid-fourth century, and for centuries Roman Christian elders continued to work toward establishing firm parameters around the faith. Over time, Christianity became relatively definable in doctrine and philosophy and remained so, for the most part, until the sixteenth century. It also stayed primarily within the Roman Empire and environs, with very little expansion elsewhere. Then, everything began to change.

The catalyst for this change was the Protestant Reformation, which began in the early sixteenth century. Over the next several decades, there were increasing challenges to the established hierarchy of the Church, as well as to its doctrines, definitions, and practices. As individuals, groups, and even nations broke away from the Roman Catholic interpretation of Christianity, a proliferation of diversity in doctrine and practice ensued. Soon, there were multiple new forms and new denominations of Christianity, some following relatively close to the established traditions of the past, and some pursuing an entirely new reconceptualization of the religion. This process has continued unabated, with the result that there are currently an estimated 33,000 denominations of Christianity, making it easily the most diverse of all religious traditions in the world today.

Many of the changes and challenges that Christianity is currently facing are the direct result of our rapidly changing world, filled with new ideas, aspirations, and values. In confronting these, the religion is responding in a myriad of ways. Some Christians see the need to insulate themselves and their families from what they perceive as negative contemporary social influences, while others see this as an opportunity to move the tradition in new directions. The opening article of this unit looks at this continuing phenomenon of change in the Church, and the new forms that are manifesting, geographically, racially, and culturally. The next few articles address some of the ways in which Christians are responding to secular and pluralistic sentiments of contemporary popular culture and society. "A Child's Death Raises Questions About Faith" brings up the question of religious freedom and its limits in the face of secular values. The last two articles consider some of the new ways in which Christianity is seeking to appeal to contemporary Americans, both in terms of religious practice and in terms of belief. The last of these focuses on Mary, the mother of Jesus, and how her power and presence in the Church is attractive to many, while suspect and questioned by others.

The Changing Face of the Church

How the explosion of Christianity in developing nations is transforming the world's largest religion

By Kenneth L. Woodward

IT IS SUNDAY MORNING IN AGBOR, A REMOTE VIL-lage in southwest Nigeria, where chickens peck at rutted roads and bicycles outnumber cars. All morning long women in brightly colored dresses, wide-eyed children holding hands, men in white Sunday shirts and dark pants stream toward the churches. There are more than 20 of them within a square kilometer. Some are clearly Roman Catholic, Anglican and evangelical Protestant—the fruit of Western missionaries. But most are of purely African origin like the Celestial Church of Christ, Miracle Apostolic Church and The Winners Chapel. And so it goes all across the African subcontinent, where Christianity is a 24/7 experience. On decaying asphalt highways the backs of trucks and buses proclaim Christian slogans: IN HIS NAME, ABIDE WITH ME, and GOD IS GOOD. Inside urban malls, the lilting pop music carries an upbeat Christian message in Ibo, Twi or Swahili. Even the signs above storefronts bear public witness: THY WILL BE DONE HAIR SALON, THE LORD IS MY LIGHT CAR WASH and TRUST IN GOD AUTO RE-PAIR, SPECIALISTS IN MERCEDES BENZ.

This is the heart of contemporary Africa. And south of the Sahara, at least, that heart is proudly Christian. Pope John Paul II has visited Africa 10 times—more than any continent outside Europe—and for good reason. Here among the Ashanti and Baganda and the thousand other tribes who occupy the world's second largest continent, Christianity is spreading faster than at any time or place in the last 2,000 years. Among the most prom-inent African Christians is an Ibo from Nigeria, Cardinal Francis Arinze, a Vatican official now regarded as a prime candidate to become the first black pope.

In 1900, the beginning of what American Protestants christened as "the Christian Century," 80 percent of Christians were either Europeans or North Americans. Today 60 percent are citizens of the "Two-Thirds World"—Africa, Asia and Latin America. "The center of Christianity has shifted southward," says Andrew Walls, an expert in the history of Christian missions, at the University of Edinburgh, Scotland. "The events that are shaping 21st-century Christianity are taking place in Africa and Asia." Europe itself is now a post-Christian society where religion is essentially an identity tag. In Scotland less than 10 percent of Christians regularly go to church, but in the Philippines the figure is nearly 70 percent. In Nigeria alone there are seven times as many Anglicans as there are Episcopalians in the entire United States. The Republic of Korea now has nearly four times as many Presbyterians as America.

Not only is the flood tide of non-Western Christians altering the map of world Christianity, it is also reversing the flow of influence within the Catholic and Protestant worlds. A month ago the presiding bishops of the worldwide Anglican Communion met in North Carolina amid a rift between the liberal churches of the West and the eruption of more conservative churches in Africa and Asia. On Feb. 21, the pope expanded the College of Cardinals to a record 184; of the 135 eligible to elect the next

Christianity's March Through the World

The vitality of Christianity is fading in the West, especially in Europe, where most Christians rarely cross the threshold of a church. The center of Christianity is shifting to the developing world—to Nigeria and India—and people are embracing the faith in thousands of ways. As it has since the beginning, the religion continues to evolve, depending on who's doing the worshiping.

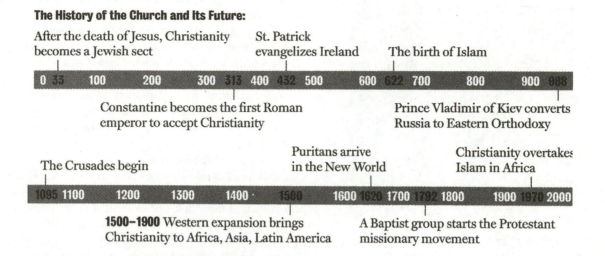

The History of the Church and Its Future:

After the death of Jesus, Christianity becomes a Jewish sect

St. Patrick evangelizes Ireland

The birth of Islam

0 33 100 200 300 313 400 432 500 600 622 700 800 900 988

Constantine becomes the first Roman emperor to accept Christianity

Prince Vladimir of Kiev converts Russia to Eastern Orthodoxy

The Crusades begin

Puritans arrive in the New World

Christianity overtakes Islam in Africa

1095 1100 1200 1300 1400 1500 1600 1620 1700 1792 1800 1900 1970 2000

1500–1900 Western expansion brings Christianity to Africa, Asia, Latin America

A Baptist group starts the Protestant missionary movement

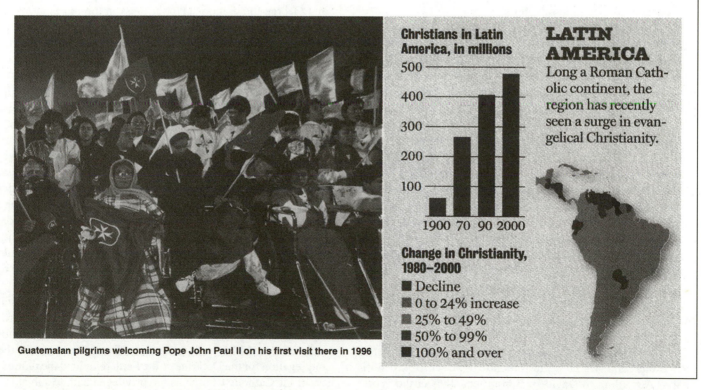

Guatemalan pilgrims welcoming Pope John Paul II on his first visit there in 1996

Christians in Latin America, in millions

500
400
300
200
100

1900 70 90 2000

LATIN AMERICA

Long a Roman Catholic continent, the region has recently seen a surge in evangelical Christianity.

Change in Christianity, 1980–2000

- Decline
- 0 to 24% increase
- 25% to 49%
- 50% to 99%
- 100% and over

pope, 41 percent are from non-Western nations. And as Christianity becomes a truly global religion, theologians from India and other parts of Asia are developing new and often controversial interpretations of the faith based on their contacts with Hindu and Buddhist traditions.

The emergence of non-Western Christianity has many converging causes. In Latin America, the faith that arrived with the conquistadors in the 16th century is now expanding in part because the population is exploding. In India, the growth is mainly among the outcasts, who find in Christianity hope and dignity denied them by the rigid caste system. In China, Christianity answers problems of meaning that Marxism fails to address. But wherever it spreads, Christianity is also seen as the religion of the successful West—a spiritual way of life that is compatible with higher education, technology and globalization. American missionaries have never been more active in the developing

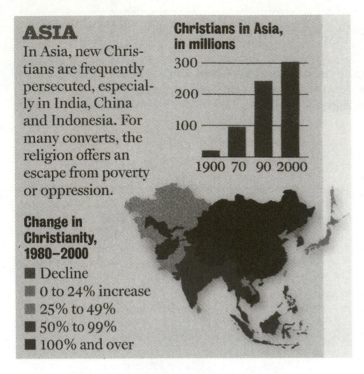

ASIA

In Asia, new Christians are frequently persecuted, especially in India, China and Indonesia. For many converts, the religion offers an escape from poverty or oppression.

Christians in Asia, in millions

300
200
100

1900 70 90 2000

Change in Christianity, 1980–2000
■ Decline
■ 0 to 24% increase
■ 25% to 49%
■ 50% to 99%
■ 100% and over

world, providing health and education for the poor and—through television—reaching into the most humble homes with messages of miracles and salvation.

As a result, for the first time in its history, Christianity has become a religion mainly of the poor, the marginalized, the powerless and—in parts of Asia and the Middle East—the oppressed. Its face has also changed. "Christianity is no longer a white man's religion," says Larry Eskridge of the Institute for the Study of American Evangelicals at Wheaton College in Illinois. "It's been claimed by others."

Christians in the West are already experiencing the effects of this massive demographic shift. Countries that were once considered Christian homelands have become the mission territories of the new millennium. Evangelists from Latin America and Africa now hold crusades in cities like London and Berlin. The effects on Catholicism are especially pronounced. One in six priests serving in American Catholic parishes is now imported from abroad, and among native-born Catholic seminarians a disproportionate number are of Asian background. In Rome, seminarians from former mission countries are now as numerous as those from Europe and North America. The United States used to be the Jesuits' primary source of new recruits. Today India is the largest supplier.

But to millions of Christians in Africa and Asia words like "Protestant" and "Catholic" inspire little or no sense of identification. According to David B. Barrett, coauthor of the World Christian Encyclopedia, there are now 33,800 different Christian denominations. "And the fastest-growing are the independents, who have no ties whatsoever to historic Christianity," he says. In Africa alone, the collapse of European colonialism half a century ago saw the wild proliferation of indigenous Christian cults inspired by personal prophecies and visions. Throughout Nigeria, there are thousands of "white garment" congregations like those of the Celestial Church of Christ—a name that

founder Samuel Bibewu Oshoffa saw written in the sky in 1947. In the vision, God told Oshoffa what true believers should wear and why they should go barefoot during services—as Moses was commanded to do when he approached the burning bush.

As in the past, today's new Christians tend to take from the Bible whatever fits their needs—and ignore whatever fails to resonate with their own native religious traditions. The Chinese have no tradition of personal sin—much less the concept of an inherited original sin—in their bedrock Confucian background. But they have a lively sense of "living ancestors" and the obligation to do them honor. On the Chinese New Year, says Catholic Bishop Chen Shih-kwang of Taichung, Taiwan, "we do mass, then we venerate the ancestors"—a notion that is totally foreign to Western Christianity. In India, where sin is identified with bad karma in this and previous lives, many converts interpret the cross to mean that Jesus' self-sacrifice removes their own karmic deficiencies, thus liberating their souls from future rebirths.

In parts of Africa where urbanization has dissolved the old tribal morality, many new Christians have replaced it with the rigorous "purity code" governing personal behavior they find outlined in the Book of Leviticus. On the other hand, in officially Catholic Brazil, many Christians still appease the old tribal deities brought from Africa by slaves four centuries ago—albeit under different names. Thus in Bahia they may honor Saint George the dragon-slayer at mass in the morning and at night venerate the same patron of the hunt as the Afro spirit-deity Oxósi. "I don't think there has been a more dramatic moment of trying to define Christ since the fourth century, when the Council of Nicaea was convened to decide what was orthodox and what was not," says Martin Palmer, director of the International Consultancy on Religion, Education and Culture, in Manchester, England.

From the very beginning Christianity has been a migratory religion, seeking to plant the Gospel at the center of whatever foreign culture its missionaries could penetrate. In the process, the Gospel has not only been transplanted but also repeatedly reinterpreted. But in its developed forms (especially the Roman Catholic), Western Christianity has also emphasized the importance of maintaining doctrinal orthodoxy. Now that Christianity is becoming a truly global religion, the problem is how to decide which elements of Western thought and culture are essential to the faith.

Just last fall, the Vatican published a highly controversial document aimed at curbing what the pope considers compromising attitudes among some Asian bishops and theologians toward other world religions. In "Dominus Iesus" the Congregation for the Doctrine of the Faith reiterated the uniqueness of the Catholic Church as the privileged path to salvation. But the main concern of the 9,000-word document was the Vatican's fear of syncretism—mixing religions—among Catholic missionaries influenced by Asian spirituality. All religions are not equal, the Congregation insisted: "Catholics must be committed to announcing the necessity of conversion to Jesus Christ."

"Dominus Iesus" was immediately criticized—even in Rome —by mission scholars who have labored long to find a

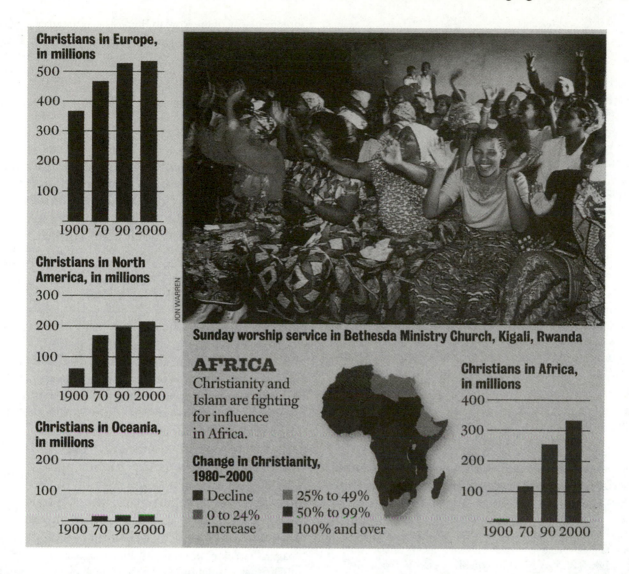

Christians in Europe, in millions
500, 400, 300, 200, 100
1900 70 90 2000

Christians in North America, in millions
300, 200, 100
1900 70 90 2000

Christians in Oceania, in millions
200, 100
1900 70 90 2000

JON WARREN

Sunday worship service in Bethesda Ministry Church, Kigali, Rwanda

AFRICA
Christianity and Islam are fighting for influence in Africa.

Change in Christianity, 1980–2000
- Decline
- 0 to 24% increase
- 25% to 49%
- 50% to 99%
- 100% and over

Christians in Africa, in millions
400, 300, 200, 100
1900 70 90 2000

way of presenting Christ in terms that Hindus and Buddhists can understand. "The church cannot disregard the Spirit of God working in other people, in all cultures and religions," insisted Father George Karakunnel of the Pontifical University in Aluva, India.

Rather than demand that Indian converts accept Jesus as Westerners conceive of him, some missionaries today offer a Christ who is congruent with native spiritual traditions. Thus, in many Indian churches, as well as various Christian ashrams, priests have adopted the dress and rituals of the Hindu majority. The mass may begin with "Om," the sacred sound of the Vedas, and at communion the priest sometimes distributes traditional Hindu *prasad* (consecrated fruits and sweetmeats) along with the Eucharistic bread. But the identification of Christianity with Indian traditions often goes beyond externals. At the Jeevan Dhara Ashram in the Hindu holy city of Rishikesh, Vandana Mataji, a Catholic nun, sings *bhajans* (devotional songs) in praise of Jesus and of Krishna four times a day, eats strictly vegetarian and meditates in silence with retreatants. "Christians do not have a monopoly on Christ," Vandana Mataji teaches. "Nor is their knowledge of him exhaustive of his full reality."

For most Asians, however, what makes Jesus attractive is his identification with the poor and the suffering. "If you're an untouchable in India, meeting this Jesus for the first time is powerful stuff," says former Protestant missionary Scott Sunquist, of Pittsburgh Theological Seminary. But more important, says Father Karakunnel, Asian Christians themselves must witness to Christ through "the liberation of the impoverished and downtrodden." That, in fact, was precisely what the late Mother Teresa of Calcutta did—let Christ speak through her own works of mercy instead of proselytizing others.

What many U.S. Christians fail to realize is that when Asians convert to Christ it requires enormous courage. Converts typically are ostracized by family and neighbors—and often targeted for persecution. Over the last six months, Chinese communists have demolished some 1,500 houses of worship—most of them Christian—whose members refused to accept direction from the state. In officially secular India, scores of Christians have been murdered and their churches trashed since the rise of militant Hindu groups. On Christmas Eve, churches in nine Indonesian cities were bombed, killing at least 18 believers and wounding about 100 more. An additional 90 Christians were murdered for refusing to convert to Islam, and some

The Next Pope?

IF GOD ANSWERS THE CONSTANT prayers of the people of Onitsha, Nigeria, the city will soon be known as the town that gave the Roman Catholic Church its first black pope. It was here that Francis Arinze presided as archbishop for 18 years, before he arrived at the Vatican in 1985 and became Nigeria's first cardinal. And it is where, every year, Arinze returns to worship in the Holy Trinity Cathedral. "No one wants to talk about his chances—to do so could work against him," says Father Martin Omikumls, the cathedral's pastor. " But everyone is praying that it be God's will."

At 69, Arinze is the right age for a pope. In ceremonial appearances he flashes a winning smile and displays a self-deprecating sense of humor. Since his name first appeared on journalistic lists of *papabali* four years ago, Arinze has avoided reporters as a matter of policy—a sure sign that he is taking the talk of his candidacy seriously. But his experience at the Vatican has been limited to a single post: as president of the Pontifical Council for Interreligious Dialogue, he has been the pope's contact man with Muslims, principally, but also with Hindus and Buddhists. His early pastoral letters, as well as his more recent pronouncements, show Arinze to be old-fashioned in his theology, and reluctant to venture much beyond quotations from John Paul II.

Arinze averages three visits a year to the United States, yet his profile is so low that few African-Americans claim to know him. His most frequent American host is a wealthy white Catholic, Thomas Monaghan, founder of Domino's Pizza and financial backer of conservative Catholic causes. Nonetheless, the possibility that Arinze might become the first black pope has generated considerable buzz within the nation's small circle of elite black Catholics. "It would be a symbol that the church is color blind," says Dr. Norman Francis, president of Xavier University in New Orleans.

Arinze has strong competition. There are 27 Latin American cardinals, and they may well feel that the time is ripe for one of them to occupy the papal throne. What's more, John Paul II is known to regard the churches of Africa as still rather new to the faith. But Arinze, an Ibo, has an extra cachet. The Ibos claim to be descended form the Biblical patriarch Jacob. This would make Arinze not only the first black pope, but the first to claim a Hebrew lineage as well.

With ROBERT KAISER BLAIR in Rome

after the decay of the Roman Empire, so Africans are embracing Christianity in face of the massive political, social and economic chaos. Plagued by corrupt regimes, crushing poverty, pandemic AIDS and genocidal wars—as in Rwanda and Sudan—Africans find the church is the one place they can go to for healing, hope and material assistance from more fortunate Christians in the West.

But there are cultural factors operating, too. Africans have always recognized a spiritual world within the empirical, and there is much in tribal religions that makes adaptation to Christianity easy. But the traditional African world view also includes witches and spirits of every kind—especially those of the tribal ancestors. All these presences have power to work good or evil on the living, and so must be placated or warded off through fetishes. Even today, says Buti Tlthagale, Catholic archbishop of Bloemfontein, South Africa, "African Christians are closer to their cultural roots than they are to Christianity. If there is a death in the family, even priests and nuns will cut their hair and wash their faces in the bile of an animal slaughtered for that purpose. What this says to me is that we are still living in both worlds."

But many African theologians insist their tribal heritage is part of a Biblical tradition. They say there were black Africans among Jesus' disciples at Pentecost, when the church was founded, and that they carried Christianity to Africa long before it arrived in Northern Europe. "The problem," says Catholic Archbishop Peter Sarpong of Kumasi, Ghana, "is not how to Christianize Africa"—the old missionary approach—"but how to Africanize Christianity."

In fact, much of what Western missionaries once opposed as tribal witchcraft and idol worship more tolerant churchmen now regard as the spadework of the Holy Spirit—a tilling of the soil for the planting of an authentically African church. The idea isn't new: some early fathers of the Western church saw "pagan" Greek philosophy as divine preparation for the truths of Christian revelation. In the same way, many African theologians insist that the old tribal religions are more Christian because they are less skeptical of the supernatural than the post-Enlightenment Christianity of the modern West. "Africans are much closer to the world of Jesus" than are Western Christians, argues Protestant theologian Kwame Bediako of Ghana. What is really happening in Africa today, he believes, is "the renewal of a non-Western religion." Yet from the evidence of what actually goes on in local churches, something very different is taking place. When Africans read the Bible or hear it preached, they see that Jesus was a healer and an exorcist, and controlling evil spirits has always been a primary function of tribal shamans. As a result, the most powerful and pervasive form of African Christianity today is Pentecostal faith healing—imported directly from the West. Last November, for example, nearly 6 million Nigerians jammed a park in Lagos to experience the miraculous healings of Reinhard Bonnke, a Florida-based evangelist. Those are numbers even Billy Graham might envy. Every night in cities like Accra, Ghana, thousands of Africans seek out evening Pentecostal "prayer camps." Most are women who can't find husbands or wives suffering from infertility, but others come because they've found no job. The diagnosis in every case is past association with tribal witchcraft. One by one,

600 more are still being forcibly detained on the island of Kasiui.

If any continent holds the future of Christianity, many mission experts believe, it is Africa. There they see history doing a second act: just as Europe's northern tribes turned to the church victims are sent rolling and moaning on the floor as freelance Pentecostal preachers "deliver" them from evil spirits in the name of Jesus.

Even the Catholic Church—still the largest body of Christians in black Africa—now provides healing services that are indistinguishable from the Pentecostal. It's a defensive measure: "These churches are getting most of their members from us," says Archbishop John Onaiyekan of Abuja, Nigeria, the young leader of Nigeria's Catholic Church.

Africans also embrace Pentecostalism because—again like tribal religions—it promises material abundance in *this* life. The best-attended churches are supported by relatively well-off, educated Africans who do not want to lose their precarious prosperity. "In the U.S., people can get a mortgage to buy a car," says Michael Okonkwo, founder and self-appointed bishop of the Redeemed Evangelical Mission in Lagos. "But in Africa, if I want a car, I have to pray to God to give me the money to pay cash."

Indeed, throughout sub-Saharan Africa the Christian ministry is now regarded as the fastest career path to upward mobility. Catholic priests are better educated—and better recompensed—than other members of their families. Moreover, since anyone can claim anointing by the Holy Spirit, anyone with a charismatic personality can start a church. In this way, an estimated 1,200 new churches are launched each month—many of them with literature and instructions provided by evangelical organizations in the West. "Christian missions are perhaps the biggest industry in Africa," says British scholar Paul Gifford, who is currently teaching at a new Pentecostal university in Ghana. And given the political and economic chaos of most African countries, they are often the best conduits of Western influence and financial investment.

Although Christianity's future may lie outside the West, Western influence is still decisive wherever the Gospel is preached. In religion, as in other international affairs, globalization means that superpowers remain dominant. For the world's poor, Christianity often appeals just because it is seen as the religion of the most successful superpower, the United States. Nonetheless, as the world's most missionary religion, Christianity has a history of renewing itself, even in the most culturally inhospitable places. That is the hope that hides behind the changing face of the church.

With ANNE UNDERWOOD *in New York*, ROBERT BLAIR KAISER *in Rome*, SUDIP MAZUMDAR *in New Delhi*, MAHLON MEYER *in Hong Kong* MAC MARGOLIS *in Rio de Janeiro*, LARA SANTORO *in Nairobi and* UCHE EZECHUKWU *in Abuja*

Pluralism and the Catholic University

Alan Charles Kors

The decline of Catholic higher education in our country should concern all Americans, regardless of their religious affiliation. (I am not myself a Catholic.) The Catholic tradition, preserved and revitalized by its own institutions, has made and will continue to make truly indispensable contributions to the intellectual and moral vitality of American life.

At the most basic level, Catholic higher education is vital to the meaning of American pluralism, which does not entail homogeneity, but a variety of lived differences. From well before the time of its founding as a nation, America has allowed distinctive voluntary communities to flourish in peace. We have created a unique society, in which we not only learn from each other—either deeply or marginally, substantively or as objects of mutual curiosity—but in which we also learn from the very possibility of that learning. If you had told our forebears, who came here from cultures all over the world, that their heirs would be living and working harmoniously with the sons and daughters of every inhabited continent, they would have found it to be beyond possibility. If you had told them, further, that their heirs would be living and working harmoniously with the sons and daughters of Catholics, Jews, Lutherans, Unitarians, Calvinists, atheists, Hindus, Muslims, and Buddhists, they would have thought you quite mad. The irenic pluralism of the American experiment in religious liberty is historically unprecedented, and, where understood, a political and social inspiration.

Two things underlie the beauty and wonder of this variety. First, it is based on a voluntary act. Whatever the effect of family and early educational influence, the reality of voluntary choice is an ineluctable part of the American experience. The Amish may choose to remain in their community or to define themselves in other ways. Jews may choose to remain in the traditions and laws of their fathers, or they may choose to redefine their beliefs and their identities. Catholics may choose to remain in the church and faith that received them, or they may choose to seek their beliefs and obligations elsewhere. We are what we are, in this astonishing land, by personal acts of the will for which we are individually responsible. Your creed, religious identity, and witness are not dictated by the state or by the absence of other real choices. In America, our pluralism itself makes us conscious, vivid, and truly volitional embodiments of our choices about ultimate things.

The precondition of making such choices, however, is the existence of the means to actualize them. The choice of an orthodox Jewish life, for example, depends upon the existence of higher Jewish education. The choice to be Amish depends upon the existence of a rich Amish cultural life. Likewise, the choice to be Catholic depends upon the existence of the depth and fullness of Catholic higher learning and education.

We have all chosen to live in pluralistic America, with people who have made private choices quite different from our own. This does not mean, however, that we choose to live only in pluralistic communities and institutions within that pluralistic society. Indeed, our society would cease to be genuinely pluralistic if we transformed all institutions and traditions within it into pluralistic ones. Most individuals thus choose to live in somewhat pluralistic neighborhoods, and most, though not all, to work in pluralistic businesses or enterprises. Virtually none among us, however, chooses to attend pluralistic churches and places of worship; in that domain of life, almost everyone wishes to participate in a community of individuals who accept one set of beliefs and liturgies and who reject others. When it comes to universities, some of us see them as more analogous, within limits, to neighborhoods, while others of us see them as more analogous to communities of belief and value. From religious Americans who make the latter choice with regard to universities there arises the rich tapestry of credal higher education.

In terms of the deepest meaning of American pluralism, those who make the latter choices enrich us all because they allow individuals to realize the fullest potentials of their choices. Where would Judaism be without its Talmud Torahs and its Yeshivas? Where would secular humanism be without its Harvard? Where would American Catholicism be without its truly Catholic institutions of higher education?

The preservation and vivification of distinct traditions of belief and value benefit American pluralism immeasurably. This gives us the ability to learn from each other at our most coherent and best informed, which means the ability to discover claims of truth in traditions into which we were not born. American pluralism not only profits incalculably from vital centers of non–pluralistic education, but, indeed, ultimately depends upon them for its cultural vitality.

John Stuart Mill, in *On Liberty*—a work, I fear, too casually dismissed by many Catholic thinkers—observed that if one wished to learn a belief, it was not enough to be taught it by someone who was not an adherent. One needed to hear a belief in its most forceful, persuasive form—that is, from a believer. If Protestants wish to understand Catholicism, they need to hear more than Protestant exposition of what it is that Catholicism supposedly teaches. They need to hear it articulated and defended by a Catholic mind alive to its faith and belief.

In addition to the benefits that flow from keeping pluralism alive, the philosophical and theological tradition of Catholicism enriches the life of the American mind. In particular, the Catholic tradition embodies the very foundation of the civilization of the West, the meeting of Athens and Jerusalem.

We live in an age of willful blindness and willful forgetfulness. Philistines do not know that virtually every thrust that they make against Christian belief was anticipated and articulated in the *sed contra* objections of the doctors of the Church themselves. They do not know that the debates of which the moderns are so proud ultimately resolve into arguments that arose in past ages among Catholic philosophers and theologians—realism versus nominalism, the limits of natural human knowledge, the tension between philosophical skepticism and rational dogmatism. To cite one example among so many, in seventeenth-century France one found scholasticism of vari-

ous philosophical stripes, Thomist and Scotist revivals, an Augustinian revival, Cartesian, Aristotelian, and Malebranchist schools of Catholic natural philosophy, a flowering of mysticism as well as debates about the dangers of mysticism. There were deep disputes between Jansenists and Jesuits. Dominicans, Franciscans, and Jesuits debated each other over the nature of non-Christian cultures and the scope and limits of natural law and natural reason. Montaigne, Charron, Mersenne, Gassendi, and the singular Aristotelian Barbay; Pascal, Arnauld, Fenelon; devotees of Suarez, Salamanca, Louvain, the Sorbonne, and Port Royal—all living and flourishing within the bosom of the Catholic Church.

Never, in the history of all creeds, has there been more intellectual dynamism, vitality, philosophical diversity, mutual criticism, and natural philosophical liberty than in the history of the Catholic Church. Every century's or generation's rediscovery of or encounter with Augustine and Aquinas, for example, is productive of profoundly creative thought and debate and forces anew a consideration of the deepest issues known to the human mind. Think of the rediscovery in recent times of the genius of the Catholic University of Salamanca, and of its insights, creativity, and analytic rigor on issues of natural law, economics, and politics. I do not trust the secular universities to cherish this heritage, let alone to keep it alive. If Catholic universities will not sustain in both learned and living form the immeasurable legacy and demonstrable relevance of the Catholic intellectual and theological inheritance, who will? Harvard? The University of Minnesota? My own University of Pennsylvania, which could barely be persuaded to preserve the study of religion, theology, and spirituality as an academic discipline?

The students in my courses are excellent, with minds open to thoughtful consideration of everything presented to them. Through no fault of their own, they know nothing about the following: Arius, Athanasius, the Nicene Creed, Patristics, Augustine, Boethius, the contribution of the Irish Church to Western Civilization, the Investiture Controversy, Aquinas, Suarez, or the Catholic

Reformation. I have to explain, de novo, all of these references. I must explain to them the difference between an apology in the modern sense and apologetics. They have never heard of natural law. They cannot name a single Catholic pope, cardinal, archbishop, or theologian of the seventeenth, eighteenth, or nineteenth centuries. Should one care about Catholic higher education? The question answers itself.

This ignorance is rendered even more disturbing by the manifest and uninformed hostility of the secular academic world to Catholicism. At the curricular level, the truly serious study of Catholicism, let alone the recognition of the intellectual vibrancy and legitimacy of a distinctly Catholic perspective, is virtually limited to underfunded Medieval Studies programs, and even in that domain, their place is slipping fast.

Consider, if you will, the varying career trajectories of scholars at our secular universities who make the following statements about their commitments: I am a Foucauldian; I am a Thomist. I am a deconstructionist; I am an Augustinian. I am a gender feminist; I am a neo-Scholastic. I am a political and cultural radical; I am a Catholic. Colleagues at secular universities say with pride, and are rewarded for, such statements as, "My teaching and scholarship are an extension of my radical politics." Now, imagine the reaction to a professor at the same institutions who said, "My teaching and scholarship are an extension of my Catholic faith."

If one looks at the university in loco parentis, the situation is even bleaker. Speech codes protect feminists from any creation of "a hostile or offensive environment," but gender feminists may say whatever they choose about the Catholic Church, its pontiff, its clergy, and its beliefs. The sign, "Keep Your Rosaries Off Our Ovaries," is a commonplace of pro-choice rallies. Catholic-bashing hate speech is a staple of most so-called Women's Centers. The very universities that ban antifeminist speech in the name of civility and sensitivity to the culture of "others" proclaim Catholic-bashing to be a mark of their devotion to freedom of expression. Catholic students must bear the insults of Serrano's *Piss Christ*, a crucifix immersed in the artist's urine, and Serrano is invited to university after university to exhibit his work and give speeches on art. At Carnegie Mellon University, a Resident Advisor, Patrick Mooney, asked to be excused from wearing a pink triangle during Gay and Lesbian Awareness Week on grounds of his Catholic conscience, while reiterating his contractual obligation not to discriminate in any way against gay and lesbian students. He was fired. There are many such examples of double standards.

The so-called "multicultural" agenda that dominates freshman orientations and residential programming presents itself as inviting the deep study, appreciation, and celebration of all cultures. I can guarantee that this feigned inclusiveness does not extend to Catholic culture. Indeed, multiculturalism has come to mean that the culture of which Catholicism is a part must be diminished and overcome. For many academics, multiculturalism simply means that there is one dominant, hegemonic, wicked culture that prevails in the West; Greek and Christian in its origins, it spreads arbitrary injustice everywhere. Only those voices that speak against and vitiate Western, Christian culture are deemed "multicultural." That is why only Liberation Theology, among the full spectrum of Catholic voices, is "multicultural." That is why the Sandinistas are "multicultural," while the Catholic Cuban entrepreneurs of Dade County are not. It is up to faithful Catholics to break this monopoly on academic moral witness, and to demonstrate, by lived experience and vivid sincerity, the absurdity of the "multiculturalist" claim to have demystified their cultural contribution to humanity.

It is once again time for Catholic universities to serve as monasteries, preserving the deepest things, in the midst of the current barbarian ravages. They are uniquely qualified to preserve the most precious of legacies: the Western intellectual tradition, which is linked to an openness to the human condition wherever it is found. Against social constructionism, this tradition recognizes that there is a reality independent of the human will. Against the crude current academic categories of race, ethnicity, and sexuality, it affirms the moral truth of a common humanity based upon our existence as beings with rational and responsible souls. Perhaps most importantly, in an academic culture that no longer affirms individual freedom, responsibility, accountability, and dignity, Catholic universities must preserve the belief that freedom and dignity have an ontological status that is a precondition of our full humanity. They must bear witness to the belief that freedom is a gift that distinguishes us from the beasts.

ALAN CHARLES KORS *is Professor of History at the University of Pennsylvania and President of the Foundation for Individual Rights in Education. This essay is adapted from his Cardinal Newman Lecture, given at the annual meeting of the national Cardinal Newman Society held at Georgetown University.*

Raising Christian children in a pagan culture

by Ellen T. Charry

CHRISTIANS HAVE always had to reflect on their relationship to the dominant culture. St. Paul urged his fledgling converts to reject vestiges of paganism and cling instead to the identity given them by being baptized into the death and resurrection of Christ. In this he was followed by the Church Fathers, who carefully sifted the culture to see what would faithfully and fittingly correspond with Christian claims and what would corrupt them.

Raising children in our culture has forcefully reminded me of how crucial this act of discernment and resistance is. It has also persuaded me that the intentional formation of young Christians is the most important ministry contemporary churches can undertake. Modern liberal education, stemming from Rousseau, assumes that children flourish when given the freedom to select among many options in developing their own unique gifts and talents. This approach can succeed with Christian children, but probably only in a culture that is sympathetic to Christian practices and beliefs. That is no longer our situation. Becoming a Christian today is, as it was in the earliest centuries, an intentional choice made in the face of other options. While children do need freedom, they also need to be deliberately shaped by Christian practices so that they may have a genuine chance to understand and respond to the gospel.

In the Middle Ages ascetical disciplines strengthened character, cultivated independence from physical and emotional needs, and encouraged self-control. Today money, sex and power, not the classical theological virtues, set the standards for achievement and status. Expression of emotion, not its control, is encouraged. Self-development rather than self-control is the goal. Accepting guidance from any source but the self—and especially looking for guidance from God—is looked upon as a sign of weakness, or simply as an eccentricity. Yet while youngsters think they are creating themselves, they are in reality being formed by television; by the sports, entertainment and advertising industries; by the shopping malls and by the streets. The market forces behind these institutions are not interested in children's moral, social and intellectual development.

Intentional Christian nurture is necessary because our culture shapes children for a world shorn of God.

Intentional Christian nurture is necessary because our culture shapes children for a world shorn of God. Christians see power in the crucified Jesus; popular culture defines power as winning in athletic or commercial combat. A Christian learns about hope from the resurrection; our culture sees hope in a new-car showroom. The church is again called upon to rescue people out of paganism.

Against the dehumanizing currents in popular culture, the church stands for a decision to find one's dignity in Jesus Christ. A discipled Christian life expresses itself in every interaction with other people and the creation. Each person and object is a gift from God, protected by the love of Jesus Christ. We must face Jesus Christ every time we touch another person's mind, feelings or body. Unless our children know Jesus, what will protect them from hurting themselves and others?

The church is perhaps the only institution with the beliefs, literature, liturgy, practices, social structure and authority (diminished though it be) necessary to rescue children from the violence and other deforming features of late 20th-century life. But it cannot accomplish this by simply laying the faith before young people and inviting them to choose it. Nor can it impose Christian identity by force and indoctrination. It can only prepare the setting for the Holy Spirit slowly to nurture children into Christian faith and practice. Churches need to think creatively about how to assist the Spirit in this process of formation.

THE CHURCH is well positioned for forming Christian children. First of all, it is one of the few institutions with access to the whole family. Both parents and children can be brought into the church's social and intellectual orbit, where they can publicly interact with one another and find support for their life together. Furthermore, the pulpit offers perhaps the only remaining locus of personal and public edification and exhortation.

Of course, religious education must begin at home and at an early age. Well-intentioned parents may encounter an immediate obstacle: they themselves do not feel comfortable speaking about God. Parents who are unable to articulate their faith will find it difficult to raise Christian children. These adults may gain some credibility with their children by entering with them into a process of study, prayer and reflection. Otherwise, children will quickly discern the shallowness of their parents' faith. Perhaps nothing makes a stronger impression on children than to be invited to study scripture with parents who are studying not to indoctrinate the child but for their own spiritual nourishment. To prescribe a program of scripture study for children alone, when parents do not participate, can seem like punishment, and can be the source of yet another power struggle between parents and children. Indeed, parents who rigidly impose their Christian beliefs in an attempt to exert authority over their children will be seen as more concerned with their own power than with their children's life with God. We should trust that adolescents will recognize and respect reasoned religious convictions.

PARENTS NEED to ask some hard questions about their own faith and their relationship with their children. Some may hope that their children will be instructed in the faith during the 45 minutes a week of church school, but this scant instruction cannot compete with the powerful influences that bombard the child the rest of the week. Furthermore, church school teachers are often untrained and poorly educated in the faith. And though church may provide an important social milieu for youngsters, the content of faith may never be clearly articulated there.

Parents need to talk to one another, other parents and church staff, and plan how to raise their children. Christian education should be the province of men as well as women. Children need fathers who can talk to them about God, about humility as honor, about Jesus' self-sacrifice on the cross, and about dignity as servanthood. Fa-

thers may be eager to get their sons onto the ballfield or artillery range, but they must learn to be even more eager to get down on their knees with children and teach them to pray.

Prayer is crucial. It teaches children to reflect on their own lives and on the world around them. It provides breathing space from the overstimulation of our society. Attending to how to pray and for whom to pray trains children to focus on the welfare of others and on world events. Prayerbooks are wonderful resources; they contain prayers for travelers, for those far away, for the sick, for those living alone, for government leaders, for an end to civil strife, for proper use of natural resources. We should also teach children to pray for virtues like compassion, courage, cheerfulness and charity.

The activity of godparenting has enormous potential for forming Christian children; the resources for godparents are limited only by one's imagination.

While there are good books of prayers for children, the newspaper is probably our best source for learning to pray for others. Helping children to select a focus for prayer from a newspaper article and then to write their own prayers is excellent training—in prayer and also in thinking and writing. Some children might want to keep a scrapbook of their prayers and the articles that inspired them, so that they can look back and recall the people and events for which they have prayed.

Of course, one also learns to pray by being prayed for. Parents would do well to bless their children, perhaps when they leave for school in the morning, and to pray for them when they are facing special stresses, and at times of celebration. This means that parents must be comfortable praying aloud and spontaneously—a daunting thought for those accustomed to having the minister do the praying.

THE ACTIVITY of godparenting—which, like family prayer and study, has been all but abandoned in many contexts—has enormous potential for forming Christian children. (Grandparents can also exercise a godparenting role.) The resources for godparents are limited only by one's imagination. I suggest the following guidelines:

• Place your concern for the child's spiritual and moral development in the context of a wider involvement in her whole life. Building a genuine relationship with a child takes effort, time and energy. It requires a regular structure so that your presence in the child's life is reliable. Visits to and trips with children expand their world and build trust. If distance makes this context impossible, phone calls can underscore the importance of the relationship.

• Consult with the child's parents so that your godparenting supports their theology and educational approach. Parents can tell you about the child's intellectual and social maturity level so that your exchanges will be appropriate. Do not be daunted by distance.

• Letters are a wonderful way to express your faith thoughtfully. A pattern of writing regularly gives the child something to look forward to. I write to my goddaughter about God and Jesus, prayer, moral discernment, sin, death (when her grandfather died) and the need for times of quiet and reflection to listen for God. Sometimes I write about the liturgical season, a special feast or biblical characters and stories; sometimes I suggest projects in preparation for a holiday. She keeps my letters in a folder and rereads them when she says her evening prayers and reads her Bible. Inviting a child to send back pictures of her favorite biblical stories or characters and eventually to write return letters brings the relationship to a level of mutuality that dignifies the child.

Any suggestions for Christian parenting and godparenting may come to naught if congregations do not take Christian formation seriously.

Churches need to realize that all baptized Christians are responsible for forming one another in Christ. True, parents and teachers are very important. But every time one participates in the covenant of baptism one renews one's own baptismal covenant and promises (in the words of the Book of Common Prayer) to "do all in [one's] power to support these persons in their life in Christ." This public vow is the proper starting point for the formation of Christians.

This task requires the energy of every parish member. Even skilled parents cannot raise children alone; the authority of popular culture is too strong. They need the support and advice of the church. Also, children need to learn to relate to a variety of people—both other children and adults, both friends and strangers—in order to develop a proper range of social skills. They need to see themselves as part of a community larger than their immediate families, and to have their growing knowledge and love of God nurtured by people other than their parents. This is especially true as adolescents explore the world beyond the family, and the authority of the peer group and the general culture increases.

Congregations need, first of all, to support the work of parents and godparents. Groups might be set up for sharing ideas, materials and experiences in these areas. Capable, experienced parents might mentor new parents. Groups of families might join for prayer, study and support. A fathering group might encourage men to become more involved in children's religious development.

Though it is important to minister to single people, this should not be done at the expense of meeting the increasing needs of families, especially single mothers with children. Some childless singles might be enriched by supporting youngsters. Some congregations may want to set up foster godparenting programs that pair adults with children with whom they share common interests, or with children who have special needs or stresses from illness, divorce, relocation or a death in the family, or to whom they can teach a skill. Adults might be asked to speak with youth about tensions between Christian faith and the world of business, the professions or competitive sports, or simply to witness to their faith. Local service projects might be undertaken involving children and adults. Whatever the project, careful screening, training and ongoing support for those undertaking such ministries is crucial.

Beyond this, churches must attend to youth ministry and ways of incorporating children into the liturgy. In some churches Christian education is a stepchild of congregational programming. Christian educators are rarely honored and are often underappreciated. (I once taught a ten-week Bible class for church-school teachers in a congregation that was raising $100,000 for a new organ but had no budget for teacher-training materials.) Some may want to consider establishing training requirements for church-school teachers, and rethink the voluntary status of much of Christian education.

Though it is important to minister to single people, this should not be done at the expense of meeting the increasing needs of families.

Enlisting congregational energy, especially from men, for the raising of children is crucial. Attracting more men to Sunday school teaching and youth ministry would help. Inviting adults to relate to other people's children is difficult but important, especially for adolescents, since other adults may have more credibility with adolescents than do adults in the family. Adolescence is the time when most children disappear not only from church, but from adult company. Teenagers can easily withdraw into or be abandoned to the adolescent subculture, and become distrustful of adults. Many feel awkward, embarrassed and bored around adults, and older adults may feel just as uncomfortable around teenagers. This standoff can lead to adolescents' isolation. Young people do need space to develop their own identities, and pressuring them to interact with adults when they are socially clumsy can be humiliating to them. Yet warm, trusting relationships with adults are required if moral and spiritual guidance is to be reclaimed.

Many congregations already successfully integrate children into worship through children's sermons, a children's procession, folk or family services, special youth days and pageants. Churches might also consider celebrating liturgically children's growth and development. Christian children should come to see their growth not simply as a celebration of self but as a celebration of their growth in Christ within the church. Baptismal birthdays might be celebrated through prayers offered by the whole congregation, reminding children and adults that they are bound together as the body of Christ. This would also remind the adults of their vows to the children.

These suggestions for forming Christian children merely scratch the surface of what needs to be done. We need churches to turn their full attention toward children, not simply to applaud them, but to lead them gently and steadily to God. Other forces in our culture are extremely strong, and they may well win our children's hearts eventually. How can churches do anything less now than to surround children with the light of Jesus Christ and the company of seasoned pilgrims?

Ellen T. Charry is a professor of theology at Southern Methodist University's Perkins School of Theology in Dallas.

From *The Christian Century,* February 16, 1994, pp. 166-168. © 1994 by The Christian Century Foundation. Reprinted by permission. subscriptions: $49/yr. from PO Box 378, Mt. Morris, IL 61054, 1-800-208-4097.

Child's Death Raises Questions

Courts: A couple who prayed instead of seeking medical care for their daughter face charges of involuntary manslaughter.

By TINA DIRMANN
TIMES STAFF WRITER

Although 11-month-old Julia Wiebe struggled for days with a raging fever before dying of meningitis last summer, authorities say the true cause of death was neglect by her mother and father.

Richard and Agnes Wiebe of Rancho Cucamonga face charges of involuntary manslaughter for failing to get the simple antibiotics that would have saved Julia's life. They have pleaded not guilty.

The Wiebes—members of a small, tightknit church in Upland whose members claim branches around the world—say they did not realize how sick their daughter was. But they acknowledge religious convictions prevented them from seeking medical attention. Instead, they relied on prayer.

"The parents made a decision not to seek medical care, which could have treated the child and prevented the death," pathologist Stephen Trenkle testified during a preliminary hearing that began last month and continues today. "They chose another form of healing. They made that choice—and from my position, they made the wrong choice."

The case bears striking parallels to another unfolding in Boston, where authorities put a woman suspected of religiously motivated medical neglect in custody to protect her unborn fetus.

In the Wiebe case, county child welfare officials took custody of another baby born to the couple after the death of Julia.

Several members of their church, the Church of God Restoration, have silently supported the couple. At one recent hearing, about a dozen women in ankle-length skirts and long-sleeved shirts under waist-length vests and jackets appeared in court.

And watching everything from his seat in the back of the courtroom was Daniel Layne, the white-bearded founder of the Restoration Church.

Critics of the church say that under Layne's direction, members have moved away from their families, shunned friends, and avoided medical care for themselves and their children.

But Layne, 58, sharply denies these charges. Church members are free to act as they choose and are not punished, he said. Critics, he said, are either relatives who never took the time to understand the church or former members bearing grudges.

"Our members are not brainwashed, they are not zombies, they are not under any mind control," Layne said in an interview this week. "This is a voluntary association of freethinking people."

Although Layne declined to discuss the Wiebe case, he did say a strong belief in divine healing is one of the tenets of the church. He, in fact, would decline modern medical help if he were ill, Layne said.

"But if someone here were sick and wanted to go to a hospital," Layne said, "I would take them to the hospital myself, stay with them, pray with them, and then welcome them back with open arms into our service."

Church Rejects Much of Modern Society

Layne, a self-described transient and recovering heroin addict from Los Angeles, said he found God 22 years ago. He belonged briefly to the Church of God, but quickly became frustrated with what he

considered a lax interpretation of the Bible. So in 1981 he broke away and started his own conservative church, now located in Upland.

Members reject much that is integral to modern society: rock music, movies and television. The church subscribes to strict standards of dress and behavior that includes modest dress, much like the Amish, and favors use of prayer over medicine, he said.

"I wanted to go back to the year of the reform, around 1880, and stick to what our pioneer brethren taught," Layne said.

Eventually Layne's church in Upland—which now has about 55 members, he says—sprouted satellite congregations in Louisiana, Ohio, Canada, Mexico and Germany, with a total membership that investigators estimate at more than 800 people.

Layne maintains that members are not forced to follow the church's teachings, but follow out of their own free will. But some former church members and an expert who has been tracking the group say Layne's grip on his followers has become increasingly intense in recent years.

One former Church of God Restoration minister said Layne attracted him and his wife about 10 years ago with his "seriousness about Christianity." At the time, "We didn't see the control he has now," said David Kauenhowen, a Canadian resident. "He was a humble man back then. And we enjoyed the church, until he got so personally involved in people's lives."

After a few years, however, Layne began dictating the way parishioners should dress, Kauenhowen said. Long pants and shirts for men, T-shirts always underneath. Women couldn't show their legs or even

143

their ankles. Jewelry of any kind, including wedding rings, was forbidden.

In time, Layne required parishioners to seek his approval to date, to marry or to move, Kauenhowen said. Children were subject to strict discipline and physical punishment from an early age and were to be home-schooled or sent to small schools run by the church. And if relatives became critical of the new guidelines, Layne advised shutting them out, he said.

And although prayer was always emphasized over medical treatment, in recent years Layne began shunning members who sought help from a doctor, calling it a sign of weakness in their faith, Kauenhowen and others said.

Rick Ross, a New Jersey-based consultant and paid expert witness who writes and lectures nationally on small sects, said that in the last six months he's gotten more than a dozen calls from former church members or relatives alarmed by Layne's teachings. Some are concerned that relatives are not getting proper medical care. Others say loved ones have cut them off because they questioned the group's beliefs, he said.

"They see a situation [in which] the person they care about has a lessening control over their lives," Ross said. "And they are fearful of what that's leading to."

Another Case of Trouble With the Law

The Wiebe case is not the first time that Restoration followers have gotten into trouble with the law.

On July 4, Canadian authorities removed seven children from the home of a Church of God Restoration family in Aylmer, Ontario. Authorities were responding to complaints that the children had been beaten, in some cases with belts and sticks, and that at least one child suffered a severe burn and was denied medical care. The children were returned to their parents by the court with conditions for their treatment while a trial is pending.

Kauenhowen, the former minister, said he told Layne he was alarmed by the direction of the church, a criticism that got him thrown out in February 2000, he said. Current members, he added, no longer speak to him.

> *'Faith is not a guarantee that we will be healed. [It is] believing that God's way will be done.'*
> **Richard Wiebe** to investigators

Layne, who has never been married and has no children, said Kauenhowen is simply bitter over his falling out with the church. And relatives who complain are doing so because they refuse to understand their loved one's faith. Some interpret the church as extreme because of its rejection of all that modern society has to offer. But that does not make it a cult, he said.

"There's a pressure from society to conform to the norm," Layne said. "And that's difficult for us because we have a doctrine that teaches separation from what society teaches us—immorality, rock music, divorce, sexually explicit material, television. To us, all of that is horrible."

He denies being the church's only leader. Five other elder ministers join him in overseeing its teachings, he said.

"I wouldn't deny I have an influence on the church," Layne said. "But I would deny that anyone has to accept [my influence].... We don't run people's lives."

Courts Draw the Line at Hurting Children

Ross said there are thousands of small sects across the country not affiliated with Restoration that follow similar beliefs regarding medical treatment. And though the courts try to respect the fundamental right to religious freedom for adults, they draw the line when edicts of the church hurt children.

Prosecutors routinely charge parents with offenses ranging from child neglect to manslaughter for denying medical care.

In one of the boldest moves yet by a court, a Massachusetts judge ordered Rebecca Corneau into protective custody to ensure the safety of her unborn fetus. Corneau belonged to a fundamentalist sect called The Body, which rejects all medicine, including prenatal care.

Last July, the Wiebes' 11-month-old daughter began vomiting. Over the next few days, she became sicker, eventually developing a fever and suffering seizures that lasted more than two hours at a time, Richard Wiebe told investigators. Wiebe and his wife fervently prayed over the little girl. They covered her tiny body with wet rags. As she weakened, they fed their daughter chamomile tea through an eyedropper. The Wiebes said they didn't know how sick their daughter was. They thought she just had the flu.

But by July 6, the little girl stopped breathing.

The Wiebes tried to perform CPR, but Julia never recovered. Wiebe called their pastor, Layne, who directed the couple to call paramedics, according to court testimony. Investigators believe the baby had been dead more than two hours by the time they arrived.

Under questioning by San Bernardino County Sheriff's investigators, Richard Wiebe, a draftsman for an Upland company, said he and his wife never considered taking Julia to the hospital.

"That was not something that I had an option for," Wiebe told investigators during a taped interview played in court Thursday. "I'm settled with the Lord and I was going to trust him."

Wiebe added he still believes he made the right decision. He was prepared to accept God's will.

"Faith is not a guarantee that we will be healed," Wiebe told investigators. "Faith is just believing that God's way will be done."

Agnes Wiebe was pregnant at the time of Julia's death and has since given birth to a boy. Sheriff's officials seized the baby in January and placed him in protective custody. A trial in that case is also pending.

The Wiebes remain free on bail. The judge in Rancho Cucamonga Superior Court will decide whether to order them to stand trial.

From the *Los Angeles Times*, March 12, 2002, p. B1. © 2002 by the Los Angeles Times. Reprinted by permission.

Resuscitating Passion

A new breed of pastors relies less on formal training and more on Jesus. The American religious scene increasingly is filled with independent churches and entrepreneurial clergy

By Julia Duin

A call to worship: *Bickle, above right, founded the International House of Prayer in 1999. At top left, visitors to the church pray while staffers work.*

It is Sunday morning on a cool March day in downtown Kansas City, Mo., and Bartle Hall is rocking. "I have an unashamed desire to be great in the eyes of God!" declares the Rev. Mike Bickle, a casually dressed baby-boomer preacher, to 3,000 boisterous evangelical Christians inside the convention center. Speaker after speaker during the weekend conference has urged the faithful to strive for a radical, "prophetic" Christianity. "Even the dedicated are half-compromising," Bickle tells the throng. "If you have the pain of an unsatisfied heart, this propels you into the heart of God. Don't let anyone get rid of that pain for you."

Since the birth of itinerant evangelism in colonial America, self-taught and freewheeling preachers have come and gone. "The new breed is really the old breed," says the Rev. Louis Weeks, president of Union Theological Seminary in Richmond, Va., noting that many revivalist ministers prefer on-the-job training to the seminary. Whatever their background, however,

ministers face the same challenge: retaining the interest of baby boomers and younger Americans who embrace personal experience, egalitarianism and dress-down informality.

One such congregation, Southwest Community Church of Palm Desert, Calif., grew from 300 members to about 7,000 within a few years of hiring a 33-year-old pastor. The Rev. David Moore wore sport shirts in the pulpit and preached how-to sermons on improving relations with children, spouses and friends rather than verse-by-verse expositions of Scripture.

Such new methods are good, but they may not be enough to stir a "spiritually stagnant" America where churchgoers "have traded in spiritual passion for empty rituals," says George Barna, an evangelical Christian pollster. Although the number of committed Christians—those holding to orthodox beliefs—grew from 35 percent of the faithful in 1995 to 41 percent this year, the pollster says, weekly church attendance dropped the same amount: from 49 percent to 42 percent.

PHOTO BY MAYA ALLERUZZO/INSIGHT

Making a joyful noise: *The Harvest Worship Band leads the congregation in song at Calvary Chapel.*

The 41 percent of the population who call themselves born-again Christians amount to roughly 114 million. But the numbers enrolling in Bible study and adult Sunday school or volunteering for religious activities have shrunk. "The challenge to today's church is not methodological," Barna says. "It is a challenge to resuscitate the spiritual passion and fervor of the nation's Christians."

Leadership Network, a nonprofit Christian group formed in Dallas in 1984, has embraced the challenge. Styling itself a "network of innovative church leaders," it offers publications and advice from outside-the-box clerics such as the Rev. Kirbyjon Caldwell, who delivered the closing prayer during President George W. Bush's inauguration.

Good ideas are catching, according to the Leadership Network, which scans the country for spiritual leaders who recognize the changing social landscape. Some exist within denominations; others have started their own. Aided by a $3 million annual grant from the Buford Foundation and endowed by Dallas cable TV executive Bob Buford, the Leadership Network sponsors one-day conferences around the country. The organization also sends out an in-depth teaching, "Explorer" to 1,800 subscribers over the Internet, plus an additional 7,000 *Reader's Digest* versions.

The Leadership Network readily acknowledges that megachurches—full-service "worship centers" complete with gyms and restaurants—resemble multilevel corporations more than village parishes. In the process, some have lost that personal touch. "It used to be that churches employed a senior pastor, a youth pastor and a children's worker," says the Rev. Bruce Miller, 39, pastor of the 1,300-member McKinney Fellowship Bible Church in McKinney, Texas. "Now you have people on staff who do marketing."

The American scene increasingly is filled with independent churches that belong to denominations founded in the last 20 years. The clergy who lead them are spiritual entrepreneurs—mostly men who are dissatisfied with traditional denominations.

Many come from the ranks of the Assemblies of God, a Pentecostal denomination that boasts abundant clergy: 18,000 ordained ministers for 12,000 congregations, according to the Rev. Russell P. Spittler, an Assemblies of God minister and academic provost at Fuller Theological Seminary in Pasadena, Calif. "Some who grew up in the Assemblies of God eventually felt strictures by the denomination, so they bailed out," Spittler says. "We were like a farm for ideas and practices, and they want to do more."

The 1998 National Congregations Study of 1,236 houses of worship of all faiths, conducted by University of Arizona sociologist Mark Chaves, estimated that 19 percent of roughly 325,000 congregations are independents. About 150 of these are megachurches (churches with more than 2,000 worshippers, as defined by the Megachurch Research Center in Springfield, Mo.). Sixty percent of independent mega-churches are charismatic.

Entrepreneurial clergy, moreover, often may be found among the 30 percent of American ministers whose highest training is Bible college, or the 10 percent with only a high-school education. Bypassing seminary is no shame in many church traditions. The Assemblies of God bylaws, for example, say "no certain amount of education shall ever be required for ordination."

The entrepreneurial boom is making its mark on black pastors and churches as well. Though formal theological education is more than ever available to blacks, many opt for on-the-job training. This worries leaders in historically black denominations such as the African Methodist Episcopal Church, where higher education was a hard-fought achievement.

But it's tough to argue for seminary study when preachers such as Bishop T.D. Jakes can go from a storefront in West Virginia to a $32 million sanctuary in Dallas. Jakes, 43, became "bishop" of his own nascent denomination, which boasts 26,000 local members, a TV show and best-selling books.

"The 1950s was not a boom time for the black church, but it grew dramatically from the 1970s to 1990s," says Lawrence Mamiya, professor of African studies at Vassar College. Between 1983 and 1996, for example, the census recorded a jump in black males who identified their occupation as clergy. Their number nearly tripled, from 14,357 to 39,649, while the black population as a whole rose less than 10 percent. Few of these men had time to go to seminary. Instead, they trained under a clergy-apprenticeship system. Its leading example is the Church of God in Christ, a Pentecostal and entrepreneurial tradition with 5 million members—but only one seminary.

Entrepreneurs in the predominantly white evangelical culture see graduate-school seminaries as part of the problem. "A lot of seminary training is academic," says Brad Smith, 42, president of the Leadership Network. "But learning Hebrew and Greek don't fit real-life needs. There is a new kind of clergy driven by the question our culture is asking: What is the usefulness of our church to society? The older clergy don't think that's a valid question. The newer clergy think it is."

What do people want? "People want experience," Smith says. "So worship is everything." Hence the 90 to 105 minutes of worship at the Kansas City gathering, the singing and music punctuated by individuals who shake tambourines, dance in the aisles or wave banners.

University of Southern California religion professor Donald E. Miller, a leading researcher of new-breed ministers and churches, calls the phenomenon "new-paradigm" churches. "The pastors of 'new-paradigm' churches tend to be extremely bright, close to the age and experience of their boomer congregations and unfettered by seminary educations that instruct them on how to run a church," Miller writes in his book *Reinventing Protestantism*.

Mainline churches are too bureaucratic, he says, while "their message is ambiguous, lacking authority and their worship is anemic." The professor studied three trendsetting charismatic denominations—Calvary Chapel, Hope Chapel and Vineyard Christian Fellowship—that originated with the Southern California beach scene and hippie culture of the 1960s. Lack of seminary training among leaders did not hurt the denominations' exponential growth, he found. Nearly all mainline Protestant and Roman Catholic clergy have graduate-level seminary training. By contrast, only 38 percent of clergy leading Calvary's 600 churches have an undergraduate degree.

On Monday nights, music and youth ministry prevail at Calvary's mother church in Costa Mesa, Calif., a sweeping complex that suggests a hacienda-style shopping center. Sunday morning is more traditional. And in the midst of preaching three sermons that day, the Rev. Chuck Smith, the founder, explains what a church can do.

"Our feeling is that if a church is all that a church should be, then seminaries would be unnecessary," Smith says. "The churches should be teaching the Bible. We go from Genesis to Revelation."

In fact, Smith's tape series—encompassing the entire Bible on several hundred tapes over several years of Sunday services—serve as a core curriculum. Members of his congregation listen to the tapes while commuting or on the job; they also take courses in the morning or on Sunday or Wednesday nights.

"On the road, they are in a seminary of sorts," Smith says. "After a few years here, they are ready to go out and share with others the things they've learned."

Calvary's worship is casual and what some label "soft charismatic," with an openness to—but not a heavy use of—"gifts of the Holy Spirit" such as healing, prophecy and speaking in tongues. Only men are pastors. And Dave Rolph, an associate Calvary pastor, is a rare case: He earned a master's of divinity at Talbot Theological Seminary in Los Angeles. But he says men inspired by ministry don't have to study for 10 years or plunk down $40,000 for a seminary degree.

"Today, the information is all out there, thanks to computers," Rolph says. "You can buy a CD-ROM now for $60 that has as much theological material on it as my whole education."

This contrast between a spontaneous ministry and formal training is one more issue that divides Christian clergy, already split over the Bible, the role of women, morals and politics. Yet scholars such as the University of Southern California's Miller stress that formal mainline clergy could learn from the "new paradigm." Meanwhile, most successful pastors surely know one thing: The daily needs of both the saved and the lost, especially in a society where institutions such as the family are in flux.

Handmaid Or Feminist?

More and more people around the world are worshipping Mary—and it's led to a holy struggle over what she really stands for

By RICHARD N. OSTLING

When her womb was touched by eternity 2,000 years ago, the Virgin Mary of Nazareth uttered a prediction: "All generations will call me blessed." Among all the women who have ever lived, the mother of Jesus Christ is the most celebrated, the most venerated, the most portrayed, the most honored in the naming of girl babies and churches. Even the Koran praises her chastity and faith. Among Roman Catholics, the Madonna is recognized not only as the Mother of God but also, according to modern Popes, as the Queen of the Universe, Queen of Heaven, Seat of Wisdom and even the Spouse of the Holy Spirit.

Mary may also be history's most controversial woman. For centuries Protestants have vehemently opposed her exaltation; papal pronouncements concerning her status have driven a wedge between the Vatican and the Eastern Orthodox Church. Conflict surrounds the notions that she remained ever a virgin, that she as well as Jesus was born without sin and that her sufferings at the Crucifixion were so great that she participated with her son in the redemption of humanity.

Yet even though the Madonna's presence has permeated the West for hundreds of years, there is still room for wonder—now perhaps more than ever. In an era when scientists debate the causes of the birth of the universe, both the adoration and the conflict attending Mary have risen to extraordinary levels. A grass-roots revival of faith in the Virgin is taking place worldwide. Millions of worshippers are flocking to her shrines, many of them young people. Even more remarkable are the number of claimed sightings of the Virgin, from Yugoslavia to Colorado, in the past few years.

These apparitions frequently embarrass clerics who have downplayed her role since the Second Vatican Council of 1962–65. "It's all the fashion," sniffs Father Jacques Fournier of Paris, reflecting skepticism about the populist wave of sightings. The hierarchy is wary about most of the recent claims of miraculous appearances; only seven Marian sightings in this century have received official church blessing.

Church concern has served to highlight the most interesting aspect of the growing popular veneration: the theo-logical tug-of-war taking place over Mary's image. Feminists, liberals and activists have stepped forward with new interpretations of the Virgin's life and works that challenge the notion of her as a passive handmaid of God's will and exemplar of some contested traditional family values. "Mary wants to get off the pedestal," says Kathy Denison, a former nun and current drug-and-alcohol counselor in San Francisco. "She wants to be a vital human being."

Whether they hold to those views or not, people the world over are traveling enormous distances to demonstrate in person their veneration of the Madonna. The late 20th century has become the age of the Marian pilgrimage. Examples:

At Lourdes, the biggest of France's 937 pilgrimage shrines, annual attendance in the past two years has jumped 10%, to 5.5 million. Many new visitors are East Europeans, now free to express their beliefs and to travel. Despite the inevitable attraction of Lourdes for the ill and aged, one-tenth of the faithful these days are 25 or younger. "We also have new kinds of pilgrimages," reports Loïc Bondu, a spokesman at the site. "They dance, they sing, they praise out loud. They're more exuberant."

In Knock, Ireland, where 15 people saw the Virgin a century ago, the lines of the faithful lengthened dramatically after Pope John Paul II paid a visit to the shrine in 1979. Since then, attendance has doubled, to 1.5 million people each year. To handle the influence, a new international airport was opened at Knock in 1986.

At Fátima, Portugal, the shrine marking the appearance of Mary before three children in 1917 draws a steady 4.5 million pilgrims a year from an ever widening array of countries. One million devotees turned out last May when John Paul made his second visit.

In Czestochowa, Poland, attendance at the shrine of the Black Madonna has increased to 5 million a year, rivaling Fátima and Lourdes, since John Paul's visit in 1979. Last August the Pope spoke there to 1 million Catholic youths.

In Emmitsburg, Md., attendance has doubled in the past year, to 500,000, at one of the oldest of 43 major Marian sites in the U.S., the National Shrine Grotto of Our Lady of Lourdes.

MOTHER OF GOD

The traditional view, taken from the Bible and ancient church creeds, is that Mary was a virgin when she conceived, so that Jesus did not have a human father and was truly the Son of God. Thereafter, Rome teaches, she retained virginal status.

The view of modern Catholic and Protestant liberals is that that account should not be taken literally. One feminist thinker contends that Jesus had a human father and that the main point is Mary was "not identified by her relationship with men."

The boom at such long-established sites is almost overshadowed by the cult of the Virgin that has developed through new reports of her personal appearances, most spectacularly at Medjugorje, Yugoslavia. Before Yugoslavia's civil war erupted and travel became much more difficult last September, more than 10 million pilgrims had flocked to the mountain village since the apparitions began in 1981. Six young peasants there claim that the Virgin has been imparting messages each evening for 10 years. Hundreds of ailments have been reported cured during visits to the region where the visitations take place. None of them have been verified, however, by the meticulous rules applied at Lourdes.

Paradoxically enough, the Medjugorje apparitions are a headache for the local Roman Catholic bishop, Pavao Zanic. He flatly asserts that "the Madonna has never said anything at Medjugorje." Our Lady, he snaps, has been turned into "a tourist attraction" and "a bank teller." The Vatican has intervened to determine whether Medjugorje is a fraud. Rome is officially noncommital while the case remains open but advises bishops not to sponsor pilgrimages to the site.

Less spectacular appearances by the Virgin have attracted streams of the faithful in locales from Central America to the Slavic steppes. In Nicaragua, President Violeta Barrios de Chamorro is a strong believer in a series of visitations by the Madonna in the small town of Cuapa, where Mary was witnessed by a church caretaker several times from May through October of 1980. During a 1981 Mass celebrated at the spot by the Archbishop of Managua, with some 30,000 people in attendance, believers say the sun changed colors. In Hrushiw, Ukraine, tens of thousands of people gathered in 1987 after a 12-year-old claimed to see the Madonna hovering over a church that had been shut down by the ruling communists.

More recently, the Madonna has been seen in the U.S. Devotees by the thousands have been flocking to the

HANDMAID OF THE LORD

When the angel Gabriel brought the news of God's plan for the birth of the Messiah, says the Gospel of Luke, the young Nazarene girl said, "Let it be." Her response thus provides believers with the perfect model of humility and submissiveness.

Mary's submission was to God alone, not to Joseph or other male authority figures, feminists argue. Contemporary women can be inspired because Mary was a strong person who acted independently when she affirmed the course of her life.

Mother Cabrini shrine near Denver, where Theresa Lopez, 30, says the Virgin has appeared to her four times in the past seven weeks. Marian apparitions were reported by parish coordinator Ed Molloy at St. Dominic's Church in Colfax, Calif., for 13 weeks in a row last year, and there was a surprise reappearance six weeks ago. In Our Lady of the Pillar Church of Santa Ana, Calif., Mary's image has been seen by Mexican immigrant Irma Villegas on the mosaics each morning since October, boosting attendance at 7 a.m. Mass enormously. Says Villegas: "Mary told me to talk to people about it so I did."

This being the late 20th century, Americans participating in these epiphanies are doing something about it: networking. Says Mimi Kelly of Louisiana's Mir [Peace] Group: "People come back with a burning desire to do something good for mankind." Some 300 groups of medjugorje believers exist across the U.S., publishing at least 30 newsletters and holding a dozen conferences a year. There are 70 telephone hot lines that feature the Virgin's messages from Yugoslavia: in Alabama dial MOM-MARY. Over the past 16 months a Texas foundation has put up 6,500 billboards inspired by Medjugorje. The huge signs say the Virgin appeared "to tell you God loves you."

No one can take more satisfaction in the growth of faith in the Virgin—or feel more unease at some of the pathways it has taken—than John Paul II. Devotion to Mary was ingrained in the Pope in his Polish homeland, where over the centuries the Madonna has been hailed for turning back troops of the Muslim Turks, Swedish Lutherans and, in 1920, Soviet Bolsheviks. The previous Black Madonna icon was a mobilizing symbol for the country's efforts to throw off communism, and is still a unifying image for the entire nation.

When he was made a bishop in 1958, John Paul emblazoned a golden M on his coat of arms and chose as his Latin motto "Totus Tuus" (All Yours)—referring to Mary, not Christ. Once he put on St. Peter's ring, John Paul made Mary's unifying power a centerpiece of his papal arsenal. He has visited countless Marian shrines during his globe trotting, and invokes the Madonna's aid in nearly every discourse and prayer that he delivers. He firmly believes that her personal intercession spared his life when he was shot at St. Peter's Square in Rome in 1981; the assassination attempt occurred on May 13, the exact anniversary of the first Fátima apparition.

Moreover, John Paul is firmly convinced, as are many others, that Mary brought an end to communism throughout Europe. His faith is rooted in the famed prophecies of Mary at Fátima in 1917. According to Sister Lucia, one of the children who claimed to see her, the Virgin predicted the rise of Soviet totalitarianism before it happened. In a subsequent vision, she directed the Pope and his bishops to consecrate Russia to her Immaculate Heart in order to bring communism to an end.

According to Lucia, papal attempts to carry out that consecration failed in 1942, '52 and '82. John Paul finally carried out Mary's directive correctly in 1984—and the very next year Mikhail Gorbachev's rise to power inaugurated the Soviet collapse. Says Father Robert Fox of the Fatima Family Shrine in Alexandria, S. Dak.: "The world will recognize in due time that the defeat of communism came at the intercession of the mother of Jesus."

With such a powerful institutional presence behind the effort to revive Mary's influence, it was to be expected, at least to some degree, that her popularity would grow. What was far less predictable was the outpouring of new interpretations of the Virgin's message for believers. In his writings, the Pope has given a conservative tilt to the meaning of Mary's life. The Pontiff's 1988 apostolic letter *Mulieris Dignitatem* (On the Dignity and Vocation of Women), citing positions taken at Vatican II, declared that the Blessed Virgin came first as an eminent and singular exemplar of both virginity and motherhood." He extolled both states as ways women could find their dignity.

John Paul's traditionalist leanings find their most pointed expression in the Pope's continued refusal to consider the ordination of women as priests. The Vatican's argument is that if Christ had wanted women priests or bishops, Mary above all would have become one. On the other hand, John Paul does not argue that women must shun careers just because Mary was a homebody. Although the Pope lauds Mary for her submissiveness, it is in relation to God, not to male-dominated society.

But a much more aggressive view of Mary is emerging from feminist circles within the church, emphasizing her autonomy, independence and earthiness. Old-fashioned views of the Virgin, complains Sister Elizabeth Johnson, a Fordham University professor of theology, "make her appear above the earth, remote and passive," with "no sex and no sass." She adds, "There's still a strong element of that in the present hierarchy."

The revisionist views of the Madonna claim her as an active heroine who was variously an earth mother and a crusader for social justice. Mary, says Sister Lavinia Byrne, who works with non-Catholic groups in Britain, stood by loyally during her son's crucifixion while all but one of his male disciples ran away. Her agreement to bear the Son of God, argues Ivone Leal of Portugal's Commis-

sion on the Status of Women, was the act of "a strong woman. She followed her son's adventurous life, which was known to be doomed to failure, and always sustained him." Says French writer Nicole Echivard: "The Mother of God is the one from whom women are created in their preference for love and for people, rather than for power or machinery. Mary is the most liberated, the most determined, the most responsible of all mothers."

MOTHER OF BELIEVERS

The traditional view is that Mary led a perfect life on earth and now reigns as Queen of Heaven. There she continues to pray to help believers. Mary is the most powerful of the saints in interceding with God and dispensing gifts to supplicants.

Modernists argue that the notion of the woman who was free of original sin and rules as a heavenly monarch detaches Mary too much from the rest of humanity. She should be taken off her pedestal and understood as a flesh-and-blood woman.

Others emphasize the political dimension. "Mary stood up for the poor and oppressed," says Sister Mary O'Driscoll, a professor at the Dominican order's Angelicum university in Rome. She and others point out that in the Magnificat (*Luke 1*), the pregnant Mary declared that God "has put down the mighty from their thrones and exalted those of low degree; he has filled the hungry with good things, and the rich he has sent empty away."

The activist interpretations do not necessarily run counter to Vatican teaching. Back in 1974 Pope Paul VI portrayed Mary as a "woman of strength who experienced poverty and suffering, flight and exile." John Paul II has said much the same thing, referring to Mary's "self-offering totality of love; the strength that is capable of bearing the greatest sorrows; limitless fidelity and tireless devotion to work."

But some other views strike dangerously close to fundamental Catholic truths. Among them:

Virginal Conception. The Gospels of *Matthew* and *Luke* state that Mary was a virgin and that Jesus was conceived miraculously without a human father. This belief is also included in the ancient creeds, and traditional Christians insist upon it. Some liberal Catholic scholars, however, increasingly follow liberal Protestant thinkers and doubt that this was literally true. Father Raymond Brown, the leading U.S. Catholic authority on the Bible, has declared the issue "unresolved." Jane Schaberg, who chairs the religion department at the University of Detroit, goes further. She contends, to traditionalist scorn, that the unwed Mary was impregnated by a man other than fiancé Joseph and that she was a liberated woman who was "not identified or destroyed by her relationship with men."

LADY OF SORROWS

In the past, Popes have deemed Mary's maternal sufferings at the Crucifixion to be so profound that she took part with Jesus in the mystery of salvation and that therefore she should be recognized as the Co-Redeemer of humanity. Catholicism now avoids the term Co-Redeemer, which offends other churches, Feminists note that Mary stayed by Jesus' side at the Crucifixion while male disciples fled. Liberationists see her sufferings in terms of political injustice.

Perpetual Virginity. A Catholic and Orthodox tradition 15 centuries old holds that Mary was ever virgin, meaning that she and Joseph never had sex and that the "brothers" of Jesus mentioned in the Bible were cousins. This idea consolidated the tradition of celibacy for priests and nuns. Protestants reject the belief as antisexual and lacking in biblical support. Liberal Catholic theologian Uta Ranke-Heinemann of Germany contends that the notion of a celibate clergy demeaned women by robbing Mary of sexuality and normal motherhood. This is, Ranke-Heinemann declares, "a monstrous product of neurotic sexual fantasy." Responds a Vatican official: "The church doesn't have problems with sex. The world does."

Immaculate Conception. This tenet holds that Mary was conceived without original sin. The concept was popular for centuries but was not defined as Catholic dogma by the papacy until 1854, partly in response to popular pressure stirred up by Marian apparitions. Unofficial belief adds that Mary lived a perfect life. Protestants insist the Bible portrays Jesus as the only sinless person. Marina Warner, author of *Alone of All Her Sex: The Myth and Cult of the Virgin Mary*, contends that Rome's dogma artificially sets Mary apart from the rest of the human race.

There is yet another kind of rethinking of Mary going on. Protestants see no biblical basis for praying to her for favors, and they believe veneration of her can slide into worship that is due to God alone. They also reject the idea that human beings, Mary included, can contribute to humanity's salvation. Nonetheless, some Protestants are softening aspects of their hostility. Church of England theologian John Macquarrie has proposed revisions of such dogmas as the Assumption of Mary into heaven, which could then be seen as a symbol of the redemption that awaits all believers. Theologian Donald Bloesch of the University of Dubuque says fellow conservative Protestants "need to see Mary as the pre-eminent saint" and "the mother of the church." Similar convergences will receive a thorough airing in February, when U.S. Catholic and Lutheran negotiators issue an accord, years in the making, on Mary's role.

The shift in the debate over Mary represents a delayed backlash against the influence of the Second Vatican Council, which made Mary emphatically subordinate to her son in church teachings. Prior to Vatican II, Popes had proclaimed Mary the Co-Redeemer with Jesus. During the council, bishops were under pressure from the faithful to ratify the Co-Redeemer doctrine; instead they issued no decree on Mary at all. Rather she was incorporated into the *Constitution on the Church*, a move that placed the Virgin among the community of believers in Christ rather than in anything resembling a co-equal position.

The effects of that downplaying have rippled through the observances of the church to the point that Mary's statues have been removed from some sanctuaries and Catholic parishes have gradually reduced the traditional novena devotions to the Virgin. John Paul clearly thinks the reconsideration went too far, and his fellow venerators of Mary agree. In Eastern Europe, says Warsaw priest Roman Indrzejczyk, enthusiasm for Mary is no less than a "a reaction to the matter-of-fact religiousness of the West."

Behind Vatican II's reconsideration of the Virgin and some of the uneasiness expressed over her populist revival, say feminists, is a concern over making Mary into a competitive divinity, a tradition common to many of the pagan religions that Christianity superseded. Remarks Warner: "The great terror is that she will be worshipped above her son."

Even for feminists who have no desire to go that far, the idea of a return, however marginal, to that notion of supernatural feminine power is alluring. Says Sandra Schneiders, a professor at the Graduate Theological Union in Berkeley: "There has been a stupendous upsurge in goddess research and the feminine divinity as an antecedent to the male god. It's not unrelated that the Virgin Mary's popularity has also increased. Judeo-Christianity has been exclusively male, leaving a gap that cries out for feminine divinity."

It seems clear, though, that the world is crying out for many things from Mary, and in some fashion is receiving them. Devoted mother or militant, independent female or suffering parent, she remains one of the most compelling and evocative icons of Western civilization. Renewed expressions of her vitality and relevance are signs that millions of people are still moved by her mystery and comforted by the notion of her caring. Whatever aspect of Mary they choose to emphasize and embrace, those who seek her out surely find something only a holy mother can provide.

—With reporting by Hannah Bloch/New York, Greg Burke/Medjugorje, Robert T. Zintl/Rome, and other bureaus

UNIT 8
Islam

Unit Selections

Key Points to Consider

- Why do recently discovered manuscripts of the Koran (Qur'an) pose a problem for othodox Muslims?

- How is violence dealt with in the Bible and the Koran?

- What is the significance of the Dome of the Rock to Judaism, Christianity, and Islam?

- Can Islam and contemporary secular society coexist? Explain.

- How important is family life to Islam?

 **Links: www.dushkin.com/online/**
These sites are annotated in the World Wide Web pages.

Muslim Scientists and Islamic Civilization
http://cyberistan.org/islamic/

The Western world has produced three of the major world religions, Judaism, Christianity, and Islam. Although Americans have gradually come to better understand Judaism, until September 11, 2001, most were content in their lack of knowledge about Islam, even though there are currently more than 5 million Muslims living in the country. Since 9/11, however, it has become one of the most discussed, yet still misunderstood, non-Christian religions in contemporary America. The World Trade Center disaster immediately thrust Islam into a bright, and critical, light, causing many Americans to view the religion and its followers with fear, distrust, and even hatred. Yet, Islam shares numerous similarities with Christianity, both theologically and practically. Moreover, the two religious traditions are the most prevalent traditions in the world today.

As a prophetic religion, Islam is primarily based on the words of its sole prophet, Muhammad. These teachings are contained in the Koran (Qur'an), and are believed to have originated directly from Allah, the divine, and to have been given to Muhammad by the angel Gabriel. Somewhat uniquely, Islam accepts many of the teachings and beliefs of its predecessor traditions, Judaism and Christianity, while at the same time viewing Muhammad as the last and greatest prophet of God.

In Christianity, the highest value is placed on the belief in the saving power of Jesus as the only way. In Islam, not only is the profession of faith necessary, but a strict adherence to religious law is also seen as necessary. It is for this reason that the Koran, like the Hebrew Bible, elucidates specific punishments for specific transgressions. Christianity dispensed with many of the rituals and dietary restrictions imposed on Jews. Islam, adopts many of these once again, making Islam and Judaism similar in many of their beliefs and practices.

The first two articles in this unit deal with scripture. "What Is the Koran?" introduces students to the orthodox Muslim view of their sacred scripture, and it also tells of recent discoveries that raise questions about its historical development. Because of Islam's historical connections with Abraham, the patriarch of Judaism, the two traditions share many theological and philosophical similarities. However, this has not prevented the two religions from having a great deal of enmity toward each other. Considering this, the next article compares the Koran with the Bible, finding themes in both scriptures that justify violence as well as hope for reconciliation.

In the third article, Walid Khalidi presents an article on a site sacred to Islam, Judaism, and Christianity alike. The author suggests that Muslims have viewed the place as sacred since the time of Muhammad. Then, a Muslim writer presents his religion's view of Allah as "the one true God." He attempts to show how the secular and materialistic aspects of the contemporary world are inherently at odds with Islam. In the process, he offers insights as to why so many Muslims have disdain for Western society and the Western world.

Like religious traditions around the world, Islam is going through a period of change and challenge in its engagement with the values and ways of the contemporary world. In the final article in this unit, a Muslim professor discusses the diversity of thinking in Islam, and he searches for scriptural sources to support his belief that Islam can accommodate modernity and democracy.

What Is the Koran?

Researchers with a variety of academic and theological interests are proposing controversial theories about the Koran and Islamic history, and are striving to reinterpret Islam for the modern world. This is, as one scholar puts it, a "sensitive business"

By Toby Lester

IN 1972, during the restoration of the Great Mosque of Sana'a, in Yemen, laborers working in a loft between the structure's inner and outer roofs stumbled across a remarkable gravesite, although they did not realize it at the time. Their ignorance was excusable: mosques do not normally house graves, and this site contained no tombstones, no human remains, no funereal jewelry. It contained nothing more, in fact, than an unappealing mash of old parchment and paper documents—damaged books and individual pages of Arabic text, fused together by centuries of rain and dampness, gnawed into over the years by rats and insects. Intent on completing the task at hand, the laborers gathered up the manuscripts, pressed them into some twenty potato sacks, and set them aside on the staircase of one of the mosque's minarets, where they were locked away—and where they would probably have been forgotten once again, were it not for Qadhi Isma'il al-Akwa', then the president of the Yemeni Antiquities Authority, who realized the potential importance of the find.

Al-Akwa' sought international assistance in examining and preserving the fragments, and in 1979 managed to interest a visiting German scholar, who in turn persuaded the German government to organize and fund a restoration project. Soon after the project began, it became clear that the hoard was a fabulous example of what is sometimes referred to as a "paper grave"—in this case the resting place for, among other things, tens of thousands of fragments from close to a thousand different parchment codices of the Koran, the Muslim holy scripture. In some pious Muslim circles it is held that worn-out or damaged copies of the Koran must be removed from circulation; hence the idea of a grave, which both preserves the sanctity of the texts being laid to rest and ensures that only complete and unblemished editions of the scripture will be read.

The effort to reinterpret the Koran, thus far confined to scholarly argument, could lead to major social change. The Koran, after all, is currently the world's most ideologically influential text.

Some of the parchment pages in the Yemeni hoard seemed to date back to the seventh and eighth centuries A.D., or Islam's first two centuries—they were fragments, in other words, of perhaps the oldest Korans in existence. What's more, some of these fragments revealed small but intriguing aberrations from the standard Koranic text. Such aberrations, though not surprising to textual historians, are troublingly at odds with the orthodox Muslim belief that the Koran as it has reached us today is quite simply the perfect, timeless, and unchanging Word of God.

The mainly secular effort to reinterpret the Koran—in part based on textual evidence such as that provided by the Yemeni fragments—is disturbing and offensive to many Muslims, just as attempts to reinterpret the Bible and the life of Jesus are disturbing and offensive to many conservative Christians. Nevertheless, there are scholars, Muslims among them, who feel that such an effort, which amounts essentially to placing the Koran in history, will provide fuel for an Islamic revival of sorts—a reappropriation of tradition, a going forward by looking back. Thus far confined to scholarly argument, this sort of thinking can be nonetheless very powerful and—as the histories of the Renaissance and the Reformation demonstrate—can lead to major social change. The Koran, after all, is currently the world's most ideologically influential text.

LOOKING AT THE FRAGMENTS

THE first person to spend a significant amount of time examining the Yemeni fragments, in 1981, was Gerd-R.

Puin, a specialist in Arabic calligraphy and Koranic paleography based at Saarland University, in Saarbrücken, Germany. Puin, who had been sent by the German government to organize and oversee the restoration project, recognized the antiquity of some of the parchment fragments, and his preliminary inspection also revealed unconventional verse orderings, minor textual variations, and rare styles of orthography and artistic embellishment. Enticing, too, were the sheets of the scripture written in the rare and early Hijazi Arabic script: pieces of the earliest Korans known to exist, they were also palimpsests—versions very clearly written over even earlier, washed-off versions. What the Yemeni Korans seemed to suggest, Puin began to feel, was an *evolving* text rather than simply the Word of God as revealed in its entirety to the Prophet Muhammad in the seventh century A.D.

Since the early 1980s more than 15,000 sheets of the Yemeni Korans have painstakingly been flattened, cleaned, treated, sorted, and assembled; they now sit ("preserved for another thousand years," Puin says) in Yemen's House of Manuscripts, awaiting detailed examination. That is something the Yemeni authorities have seemed reluctant to allow, however. "They want to keep this thing low-profile, as we do too, although for different reasons," Puin explains. "They don't want attention drawn to the fact that there are Germans and others working on the Korans. They don't want it made public that there is work being done *at all*, since the Muslim position is that everything that needs to be said about the Koran's history was said a thousand years ago."

To date just two scholars have been granted extensive access to the Yemeni fragments: Puin and his colleague H.-C. Graf von Bothmer, an Islamic-art historian also based at Saarland University. Puin and von Bothmer have published only a few tantalizingly brief articles in scholarly publications on what they have discovered in the Yemani fragments. They have been reluctant to publish partly because until recently they were more concerned with sorting and classifying the fragments than with systematically examining them, and partly

because they felt that the Yemeni authorities, if they realized the possible implications of the discovery, might refuse them further access. von Bothmer, however, in 1997 finished taking more than 35,000 microfilm pictures of the fragments, and has recently brought the pictures back to Germany. This means that soon von Bothmer, Puin, and other scholars will finally have a chance to scrutinize the texts and to publish their findings freely—a prospect that thrills Puin. "So many Muslims have this belief that everything between the two covers of the Koran is just God's unaltered word," he says. "They like to quote the textual work that shows that the Bible has a history and did not fall straight out of the sky, but until now the Koran has been out of this discussion. The only way to break through this wall is to prove that the Koran has a history too. The Sana'a fragments will help us to do this."

Puin is not alone in his enthusiasm. "The impact of the Yemeni manuscripts is still to be felt," says Andrew Rippin, a professor of religious studies at the University of Calgary, who is at the forefront of Koranic studies today. "Their variant readings and verse orders are all very significant. Everybody agrees on that. These manuscripts say that the early history of the Koranic text is much more of an open question than many have suspected: the text was less stable, and therefore had less authority, than has always been claimed."

COPYEDITING GOD

BY the standards of contemporary biblical scholarship, most of the questions being posed by scholars like Puin and Rippin are rather modest; outside an Islamic context, proposing that the Koran has a history and suggesting that it can be interpreted metaphorically are not radical steps. But the Islamic context—and Muslim sensibilities—cannot be ignored. "To historicize the Koran would in effect delegitimize the whole historical experience of the Muslim community," says R. Stephen Humphreys, a professor of Islamic studies at the University of California at Santa Barbara. "The Koran is the charter for the commu-

nity, the document that called it into existence. And ideally—though obviously not always in reality—Islamic history has been the effort to pursue and work out the commandments of the Koran in human life. If the Koran is a historical document, then the whole Islamic struggle of fourteen centuries is effectively meaningless."

The orthodox Muslim view of the Koran as self-evidently the Word of God, perfect and inimitable in message, language, style, and form, is strikingly similar to the fundamentalist Christian notion of the Bible's "inerrancy" and "verbal inspiration" that is still common in many places today. The notion was given classic expression only a little more than a century ago by the biblical scholar John William Burgon.

The Bible is none other than *the voice of Him that sitteth upon the Throne!* Every Book of it, every Chapter of it, every Verse of it, every word of it, every syllable of it... every letter of it, is the direct utterance of the Most High!

Not all the Christians think this way about the Bible, however, and in fact, as the *Encyclopaedia of Islam* (1981) points out, "the closest analogue in Christian belief to the role of the Kur'an in Muslim belief is not the Bible, but Christ." If Christ is the Word of God made flesh, the Koran is the Word of God made text, and questioning its sanctity or authority is thus considered an outright attack on Islam—as Salman Rushdie knows all too well.

The prospect of a Muslim backlash has not deterred the critical-historical study of the Koran, as the existence of the essays in *The Origins of the Koran* (1998) demonstrate. Even in the aftermath of the Rushdie affair the work continues: In 1996 the Koranic scholar Günter Lüling wrote in *The Journal of Higher Criticism* about "the wide extent to which both the text of the Koran and the learned Islamic account of Islamic origins have been distorted, a deformation unsuspectingly accepted by Western Islamicists until now." In 1994 the journal *Jerusalem Studies in Arabic and Islam* published a posthumous study by

Yehuda D. Nevo, of the Hebrew University in Jerusalem, detailing seventh- and eighth-century religious inscriptions on stones in the Negev Desert which, Nevo suggested, pose "considerable problems for the traditional Muslim account of the history of Islam." That same year, and in the same journal, Patricia Crone, a historian of early Islam currently based at the Institute for Advanced Study, in Princeton, New Jersey, published an article in which she argued that elucidating problematic passages in the Koranic text is likely to be made possible only by "abandoning the conventional account of how the Qur'an was born." And since 1991 James Bellamy, of the University of Michigan, has proposed in the *Journal of the American Oriental Society* a series of "emendations to the text of the Koran"— changes that from the orthodox Muslim perspective amount to copyediting God.

Crone is one of the most iconoclastic of these scholars. During the 1970s and 1980s she wrote and collaborated on several books—most notoriously, with Michael Cook, *Hagarism: The Making of the Islamic World* (1977)—that made radical arguments about the origins of Islam and the writing of Islamic history. Among *Hagarism*'s controversial claims were suggestions that the text of the Koran came into being later than is now believed ("There is no hard evidence for the existence of the Koran in any form before the last decade of the seventh century"); that Mecca was not the initial Islamic sanctuary ("[the evidence] points unambiguously to a sanctuary in northwest Arabia... Mecca was secondary"); that the Arab conquests preceded the institutionalization of Islam ("the Jewish messianic fantasy was enacted in the form of an Arab conquest of the Holy Land"); that the idea of the *hijra*, or the migration of Muhammad and his followers from Mecca to Medina in 622, may have evolved long after Muhammad died ("No seventh-century source identifies the Arab era as that of the *hijra*"); and that the term "Muslim" was not commonly used in early Islam ("There is no good reason to suppose that the bearers of this primitive identity called themselves 'Muslims' [but] sources do... reveal an earlier designation of the community [which] appears in Greek as

'Magaritai' in a papyrus of 642, and in Syriac as 'Mahgre' or 'Mahgraye' from as early as the 640s").

Hagarism came under immediate attack, from Muslim and non-Muslim scholars alike, for its heavy reliance on hostile sources. ("This is a book," the authors wrote, "based on what from any Muslim perspective must appear an inordinate regard for the testimony of infidel sources.") Crone and Cook have since backed away from some of its most radical propositions—such as, for example, that the Prophet Muhammad lived two years longer than the Muslim tradition claims he did, and that the historicity of his migration to Medina is questionable. But Crone has continued to challenge both Muslim and Western orthodox views of Islamic history. In *Meccan Trade and the Rise of Islam* (1987) she made a detailed argument challenging the prevailing view among Western (and some Muslim) scholars that Islam arose in response to the Arabian spice trade.

Gerd-R. Puin's current thinking about the Koran's history partakes of this contemporary revisionism. "My idea is that the Koran is a kind of cocktail of texts that were not all understood even at the time of Muhammad," he says. "Many of them may even be a hundred years older than Islam itself. Even within the Islamic traditions there is a huge body of contradictory information, including a significant Christian substrate; one can derive a whole Islamic *anti-history* from them if one wants."

"The Koran is a scripture with a history like any other," one scholar says, "except that we tend to provoke howls of protest when we study it. But we are not trying to destroy anyone's faith."

Patricia Crone defends the goals of this sort of thinking. "The Koran is a scripture with a history like any other— except that we don't know this history and tend to provoke howls of protest

when we study it. Nobody would mind the howls if they came from Westerners, but Westerners feel deferential when the howls come from other people: who are you to tamper with *their* legacy? But we Islamicists are not trying to destroy anyone's faith."

Not everyone agrees with that assessment—especially since Western Koranic scholarship has traditionally taken place in the context of an openly declared hostility between Christianity and Islam. (Indeed, the broad movement in the West over the past two centuries to "explain" the East, often referred to as Orientalism, has in recent years come under fire for exhibiting similar religious and cultural biases). The Koran has seemed, for Christian and Jewish scholars particularly, to possess an aura of heresy; the nineteenth-century Orientalist William Muir, for example, contended that the Koran was one of "the most stubborn enemies of Civilisation, Liberty, and the Truth which the world has yet known." Early Soviet scholars, too, undertook an ideologically motivated study of Islam's origins, with almost missionary zeal: in the 1920s and in 1930 a Soviet publication titled *Ateist* ran a series of articles explaining the rise of Islam in Marxist-Leninist terms. In *Islam and Russia* (1956), Ann K. S. Lambton summarized much of this work, and wrote that several Soviet scholars had theorized that "the motive force of the nascent religion was supplied by the mercantile bourgeoisie of Mecca and Medina"; that a certain S. P. Tolstov had held that "Islam was a social-religious movement originating in the slave-owning, not feudal, form of Arab society"; and that N. A. Morozov had argued that "until the Crusades Islam was indistinguishable from Judaism and... only then did it receive its independent character, while Muhammad and the first Caliphs are mythical figures." Morozov appears to have been a particularly flamboyant theorist: Lambton wrote that he also argued, in his book *Christ* (1930), that "in the Middle Ages Islam was merely an off-shoot of Arianism evoked by a meteorological event in the Red Sea area near Mecca."

Not surprisingly, then, given the biases of much non-Islamic critical study of the Koran, Muslims are inclined to dismiss it outright. A particularly eloquent protest came in 1987, in the *Muslim World Book Review*, in a paper titled "Method Against Truth: Orientalism and Qur'anic Studies," by the Muslim critic S. Parvez Manzoor. Placing the origins of Western Koranic scholarship in "the polemical marshes of medieval Christianity" and describing its contemporary state as a "cul-de-sac of its own making," Manzoor orchestrated a complex and layered assault on the entire Western approach to Islam. He opened his essay in a rage.

The Orientalist enterprise of Qur'anic studies, whatever its other merits and services, was a project born of spite, bred in frustration and nourished by vengeance: the spite of the powerful for the powerless, the frustration of the "rational" towards the "superstitious" and the vengeance of the "orthodox" against the "non-conformist." At the greatest hour of his worldly-triumph, the Western man, coordinating the powers of the State, Church and Academia, launched his most determined assault on the citadel of Muslim faith. All the aberrant streaks of his arrogant personality—its reckless rationalism, its world-domineering phantasy and its sectarian fanaticism—joined in an unholy conspiracy to dislodge the Muslim Scripture from its firmly entrenched position as the epitome of historic authenticity and moral unassailability. The ultimate trophy that the Western man sought by his dare-devil venture was the Muslim mind itself. In order to rid the West forever of the "problem" of Islam, he reasoned, Muslim consciousness must be made to despair of the cognitive certainty of the Divine message revealed to the Prophet. Only a Muslim confounded of the historical authenticity or doctrinal autonomy of the Qur'anic revelation would abdicate his universal mission and hence pose no challenge to the global domination of the West. Such, at least, seems to have been the

tacit, if not the explicit, rationale of the Orientalist assault on the Qur'an.

Despite such resistance, Western researchers with a variety of academic and theological interests press on, applying modern techniques of textual and historical criticism to the study of the Koran. That a substantial body of this scholarship now exists is indicated by the recent decision of the European firm Brill Publishers—a long-established publisher of such major works as *The Encyclopaedia of Islam* and *The Dead Sea Scrolls Study Edition*—to commission the first-ever *Encyclopaedia of the Qur'an.* Jane McAuliffe, a professor of Islamic studies at the University of Toronto, and the general editor of the encyclopedia, hopes that it will function as a "rough analogue" to biblical encyclopedias and will be "a turn-of-the-millennium summative work for the state of Koranic scholarship." Articles for the first part of the encyclopedia are currently being edited and prepared for publication later this year.

The *Encyclopaedia of the Qur'an* will be a truly collaborative enterprise, carried out by Muslims and non-Muslims, and its articles will present multiple approaches to the interpretation of the Koran, some of which are likely to challenge traditional Islamic views—thus disturbing many in the Islamic world, where the time is decidedly less ripe for a revisionist study of the Koran. The plight of Nasr Abu Zaid, an unassuming Egyptian professor of Arabic who sits on the encyclopedia's advisory board, illustrates the difficulties facing Muslim scholars trying to reinterpret their tradition.

"A MACABRE FARCE"

THE Koran is a text, a *literary* text, and the only way to understand, explain, and analyze it is through a literary approach," Abu Zaid says. "This is an essential theological issue." For expressing views like this in print—in essence, for challenging the idea that the Koran must be read literally as the absolute and unchanging Word of God—Abu Zaid was

in 1995 officially branded an apostate, a ruling that in 1996 was upheld by Egypt's highest court. The court then proceeded, on the grounds of an Islamic law forbidding the marriage of an apostate to a Muslim, to order Abu Zaid to divorce his wife, Ibtihal Yunis (a ruling that the shocked and happily married Yunis described at the time as coming "like a blow to the head with a brick").

Abu Zaid steadfastly maintains that he is a pious Muslim, but contends that the Koran's manifest content—for example, the often archaic laws about the treatment of women for which Islam is infamous—is much less important than its complex, regenerative, and spiritually nourishing latent content. The orthodox Islamic view, Abu Zaid claims, is stultifying; it reduces a divine, eternal, and dynamic text to a fixed human interpretation with no more life and meaning than "a trinket… a talisman… or an ornament."

For a while Abu Zaid remained in Egypt and sought to refute the charges of apostasy, but in the face of death threats and relentless public harassment he fled with his wife from Cairo to Holland, calling the whole affair "a macabre farce." Sheikh Youssef al-Badri, the cleric whose preachings inspired much of the opposition to Abu Zaid, was exultant. "We are not terrorists; we have not used bullets or machine guns, but we have stopped an enemy of Islam from poking fun at our religion.… No one will even dare to think about harming Islam again."

Abu Zaid seems to have been justified in fearing for his life and fleeing: in 1992 the Egyptian journalist Farag Foda was assassinated by Islamists for his critical writings about Egypt's Muslim Brotherhood, and in 1994 the Nobel Prize-winning novelist Naguib Mahfouz was stabbed for writing, among other works, the allegorical *Children of Gabalawi* (1959)—a novel, structured like the Koran, that presents "heretical" conceptions of God and the Prophet Muhammad.

Deviating from the orthodox interpretation of the Koran, says the Algerian Mohammed Arkoun, a professor emeritus of Islamic thought at the University of Paris, is "a *very* sensitive business" with major implications. "Millions and millions of people refer to the Koran daily to explain their actions and to justify their aspirations," Arkoun says. "This scale of reference is much larger than it has ever been before."

MUHAMMAD IN THE CAVE

MECCA sits in a barren hollow between two ranges of steep hills in the west of present-day Saudi Arabia. To its immediate west lies the flat and sweltering Red Sea coast; to the east stretches the great Rub'al-Khali, or Empty Quarter—the largest continuous body of sand on the planet. The town's setting is uninviting: the earth is dry and dusty, and smolders under a relentless sun; the whole region is scoured by hot, throbbing desert winds. Although sometimes rain does not fall for years, when it does come it can be heavy, creating torrents of water that rush out of the hills and flood the basin in which the city lies. As a backdrop for divine revelation, the area is every bit as fitting as the mountains of Sinai or the wilderness of Judea.

The only real source of historical information about pre-Islamic Mecca and the circumstances of the Koran's revelation is the classical Islamic story about the religion's founding, a distillation of which follows.

In the centuries leading up to the arrival of Islam, Mecca was a local pagan sanctuary of considerable antiquity. Religious rituals revolved around the Ka'ba—a shrine, still central in Islam today, that Muslims believe was originally built by Ibrahim (known to Christians and Jews as Abraham) and his son Isma'il (Ishmael). As Mecca became increasingly prosperous in the sixth century A.D., pagan idols of varying sizes and shapes proliferated. The traditional story has it that by the early seventh century a pantheon of some 360 statues and icons surrounded the Ka'ba (inside which were found renderings of Jesus and the Virgin Mary, among other idols).

Such was the background against which the first installments of the Koran are said to have been revealed, in 610, to an affluent but disaffected merchant named Muhammad bin Abdullah. Muhammad had developed the habit of periodically withdrawing from Mecca's pagan squalor to a nearby mountain cave, where he would reflect in solitude. During one of these retreats he was visited by the Angel Gabriel—the very same angel who had announced the coming of Jesus to the Virgin Mary in Nazareth some 600 years earlier. Opening with the command "Recite!," Gabriel made it known to Muhammad that he was to serve as the Messenger of God. Subsequently, until his death, the supposedly illiterate Muhammad received through Gabriel divine revelations in Arabic that were known as *qur'an* ("recitation") and that announced, initially in a highly poetic and rhetorical style, a new and uncompromising brand of monotheism known as *Islam*, or "submission" (to God's will). Muhammad reported these revelations verbatim to sympathetic family members and friends, who either memorized them or wrote them down.

Powerful Meccans soon began to persecute Muhammad and his small band of devoted followers, whose new faith rejected the pagan core of Meccan cultural and economic life, and as a result in 622 the group migrated some 200 miles north, to the town of Yathrib, which subsequently became known as Medina (short for Medinat al-Nabi, or City of the Prophet). (This migration, known in Islam as the *hijra*, is considered to mark the birth of an independent Islamic community, and 622 is thus the first year of the Islamic calendar.) In Medina, Muhammad continued to receive divine revelations, of an increasingly pragmatic and prosaic nature, and by 630 he had developed enough support in the Medinan community to attack and conquer Mecca. He spent the last two years of his life proselytizing, consolidating political power, and continuing to receive revelations.

The Islamic tradition has it that when Muhammad died, in 632, the Koranic revelations had not been gathered into a single book; they were recorded only "on palm leaves and flat stones and in the hearts of men." (This is not surprising: the oral tradition was strong and well established, and the Arabic script, which was written without the vowel markings and consonantal dots used today, served mainly as an aid to memorization.) Nor was the establishment of such a text of primary concern: the Medinan Arabs—an unlikely coalition of ex-merchants, desert nomads, and agriculturalists united in a potent new faith and inspired by the life and sayings of Prophet Muhammad—were at the time pursuing a fantastically successful series of international conquests in the name of Islam. By the 640s the Arabs possessed most of Syria, Iraq, Persia, and Egypt, and thirty years later they were busy taking over parts of Europe, North Africa, and Central Asia.

In the early decades of the Arab conquests many members of Muhammad's coterie were killed, and with them died valuable knowledge of the Koranic revelations. Muslims at the edges of the empire began arguing over what was Koranic scripture and what was not. An army general returning from Azerbaijan expressed his fears about sectarian controversy to the Caliph 'Uthman (644–656)—the third Islamic ruler to succeed Muhammad—and is said to have entreated him to "overtake this people before they differ over the Koran the way the Jews and Christians differ over their Scripture." 'Uthman convened an editorial committee of sorts that carefully gathered the various pieces of scripture that had been memorized or written down by Muhammad's companions. The result was a standard written version of the Koran. 'Uthman ordered all incomplete and "imperfect" collections of the Koranic scripture destroyed, and the new version was quickly distributed to the major centers of the rapidly burgeoning empire.

During the next few centuries, while Islam solidified as a religious and political entity, a vast body of exegetical and historical literature evolved to explain the Koran and the rise of Islam, the most important elements of which are *hadith*, or the collected sayings and deeds of the Prophet Muhammad; *sunna*, or the body of Islamic social and legal custom; *sira*, or biographies of the Prophet: and *tafsir*, or Koranic commentary and explication. It is from these traditional sources—compiled in written form mostly from the mid eighth to the mid tenth century—that all accounts of the revelation of the

Koran and the early years of Islam are ultimately derived.

"FOR PEOPLE WHO UNDERSTAND"

ROUGHLY equivalent in length to the New Testament, the Koran is divided into 114 sections, known as *suras,* that vary dramatically in length and form. The book's organizing principle is neither chronological nor thematic—for the most part the *suras* are arranged from beginning to end in descending order of length. Despite the unusual structure, however, what generally surprises newcomers to the Koran is the degree to which it draws on the same beliefs and stories that appear in the Bible. God (*Allah* in Arabic) rules supreme: he is the all-powerful, all-knowing, and all-merciful Being who has created the world and its creatures; he sends messages and laws through prophets to help guide human existence; and, at a time in the future known only to him, he will bring about the end of the world and the Day of Judgement. Adam, the first man, is expelled from Paradise for eating from the forbidden tree. Noah builds an ark to save a select few from a flood brought on by the wrath of God. Abraham prepares himself to sacrifice his son at God's bidding. Moses leads the Israelites out of Egypt and receives a revelation on Mount Sinai. Jesus—born of the Virgin Mary and referred to as the Messiah—works miracles, has disciples, and rises to heaven.

The Koran takes great care to stress this common monotheistic heritage, but it works equally hard to distinguish Islam from Judaism and Christianity. For example, it mentions prophets—Hud, Salih, Shu'ayb, Luqman, and others—whose origins seem exclusively Arabian, and it reminds readers that it is "A Koran in Arabic,/ For people who understand." Despite its repeated assertions to the contrary, however, the Koran is often extremely difficult for contemporary readers—even highly educated speakers of Arabic—to understand. It sometimes makes dramatic shifts in style, voice, and subject matter from verse to verse, and it assumes a familiarity with language, sto-

ries, and events that seem to have been lost even to the earliest of Muslim exegetes (typical of a text that initially evolved in an oral tradition). Its apparent inconsistencies are easy to find: God may be referred to in the first and third person in the same sentence; divergent versions of the same story are repeated at different points in the text; divine rulings occasionally contradict one another. In this last case the Koran anticipates criticism and defends itself by asserting the right to abrogate its own message ("God doth blot out/Or confirm what He pleaseth").

Criticism did come. As Muslims increasingly came into contact with Christians during the eighth century, the wars of conquest were accompanied by theological polemics, in which Christians and others latched on to the confusing literary state of the Koran as proof of its human origins. Muslim scholars themselves were fastidiously cataloguing the problematic aspects of the Koran—unfamiliar vocabulary, seeming omissions of text, grammatical incongruities, deviant readings, and so on. A major theological debate in fact arose within Islam in the late eighth century, pitting those who believed in the Koran as the "uncreated" and eternal Word of God against those who believed in it as created in time, like anything that isn't God himself. Under the Caliph al-Ma'mum (813–833) this latter view briefly became orthodox doctrine. It was supported by several schools of thought, including an influential one known as Mu'tazilism, that developed a complex theology based partly on a metaphorical rather than simply literal understanding of the Koran.

By the end of the tenth century the influence of Mu'utazili school had waned, for complicated political reasons, and the official doctrine had become that of *i'jaz* or the "inimitability" of the Koran. (As a result, the Koran has traditionally not been translated by Muslims for non-Arabic-speaking Muslims. Instead it is read and recited in the original by Muslims worldwide, the majority of whom do not speak Arabic. The translations that do exist are considered to be nothing more than scriptural aids and paraphrases.) The adoption of the doctrine of inimitability was a major turning point in Is-

lamic history, and from the tenth century to this day the mainstream Muslim understanding of the Koran as the literal and uncreated Word of God has remained constant.

PSYCHOPATHIC VANDALISM?

GERD-R. Puin speaks with disdain about the traditional willingness, on the part of Muslim and Western scholars, to accept the conventional understanding of the Koran. "The Koran claims for itself that it is *'mubeen,'* or 'clear.'" he says. "But if you look at it, you will notice that every fifth sentence or so simply doesn't make sense. Many Muslims—and Orientalists—will tell you otherwise, of course, but the fact is that a fifth of the Koranic text is *just incomprehensible.* This is what has caused the traditional anxiety regarding translation. If the Koran is not comprehensible—if it can't even be understood in Arabic—then it's not translatable. People fear that. And since the Koran claims repeatedly to be clear but obviously is not—as even speakers of Arabic will tell you—there is a contradiction. Something else must be going on."

Trying to figure out that "something else" really began only in this century. "Until quite recently," Patricia Crone, the historian of early Islam, says, "everyone took it for granted that everything the Muslims claim to remember about the origin and meaning of the Koran is correct. If you drop that assumption, you have to start afresh." This is no mean feat, of course; the Koran has come down to us tightly swathed in a historical tradition that is extremely resistant to criticism and analysis. As Crone put it in *Slaves on Horses,*

> The Biblical redactors offer us sections of the Israelite tradition at different stages of crystallization, and their testimonies can accordingly be profitably compared and weighed against each other. But the Muslim tradition was the outcome, not of a slow crystallization, but of an explosion; the first compilers were not redactors, but col-

lectors of debris whose works are strikingly devoid of overall unity; and no particular illuminations ensue from their comparison.

Not surprisingly, given the explosive expansion of early Islam and the passage of time between the religion's birth and the first systematic documenting of his history, Muhammad's world and the worlds of the historians who subsequently wrote about him were dramatically different. During Islam's first century alone a provincial band of pagan desert tribesmen became the guardians of a vast international empire of institutional monotheism that teemed with unprecedented literary and scientific activity. Many contemporary historians argue that one cannot expect Islam's stories about its own origins—particularly given the oral tradition of the early centuries—to have survived this tremendous social transformation intact. Nor can one expect a Muslim historian writing in ninth- or tenth-century Iraq to have discarded his social and intellectual background (and theological convictions) in order accurately to describe a deeply unfamiliar seventh-century Arabian context. R. Stephen Humphreys, writing in *Islamic History: A Framework for Inquiry* (1988), concisely summed up the issue that historians confront in studying early Islam.

If our goal is to comprehend the way in which Muslims of the late 2nd/8th and 3rd/9th centuries [Islamic calendar/Christian calendar] understood the origins of their society, then we are very well off indeed. But if our aim is to find out "what really happened" in terms of reliably documented answers to modern questions about the earliest decades of Islamic society, then we are in trouble.

The person who more than anyone else has shaken up Koranic studies in the past few decades is John Wansbrough, formerly of the University of London's School of Oriental and African studies. Puin is "re-reading him now" as he prepares to analyze the Yemeni fragments. Patricia Crone says that she and Michael

Cook "did not say much about the Koran in *Hagarism* that was not based on Wansbrough." Other scholars are less admiring, referring to Wansbrough's work as "drastically wrongheaded," "ferociously opaque," and a "colossal self-deception." But like it or not, anybody engaged in the critical study of the Koran today must contend with Wansbrough's two main works—*Quranic Studies: Sources and Methods of Scriptural Interpretation (1977)* and *The Sectarian Milieu: Content and Composition of Islamic Salvation History* (1978).

Wansbrough applied an entire arsenal of what he called the "instruments and techniques" of biblical criticism—form criticism, source criticism, redaction criticism, and much more—to the Koranic text. He concluded that the Koran evolved only gradually in the seventh and eighth centuries, during a long period of oral transmission when Jewish and Christian sects were arguing volubly with one another to the north of Mecca and Medina, in which are now parts of Syria, Jordan, Israel and Iraq. The reason that no Islamic source material from the first century or so of Islam has survived, Wansbrough concluded, it that it never existed.

To Wansbrough, the Islamic tradition is an example of what is known to biblical scholars as a "salvation history": a theologically and evangelically motivated story of a religion's origins invented late in the day and projected back in time. In other words, as Wansbrough put it in *Quranic Studies, the canonization of the Koran—and the Islamic traditions that arose to explain it—involved the*

attribution of several, partially overlapping, collections of *logia* (exhibiting a distinctly Mosaic imprint) to the image of a Biblical prophet (modified by the material of the Muhammadan *evangelium* into an Arabian man of God) with a traditional message of salvation (modified by the influence of Rabbanic Judaism into the unmediated and finally immutable word of God).

Wansbrough's arcane theories have been contagious in certain scholarly cir-

cles, but many Muslims understandably have found them deeply offensive. S. Parvez Manzoor, for example, has described the Koranic studies of Wansbrough and others as "a naked discourse of power" and "an outburst of psychopathic vandalism" But not even Manzoor argues for a retreat from the critical enterprise of Koranic studies; instead he urges Muslims to defeat the Western revisionists on the "epistemological battlefield," admitting that "sooner or later [we Muslims] will have to approach the Koran from methodological assumptions and parameters that are radically at odds with the ones consecrated by our tradition."

REVISIONISM INSIDE THE ISLAMIC WORLD

INDEED, for more than a century there have been public figures in the Islamic world who have attempted the revisionist study of the Koran and Islamic history—the exiled Egyptian professor Nasr Abu Zaid is not unique. Perhaps Abu Zaid's most famous predecessor was the prominent Egyptian government minister, university professor, and writer Taha Hussein. A determined modernist, Hussein in the early 1920s devoted himself to the study of pre-Islamic Arabian poetry and ended up concluding that much of that body of work had been fabricated well after the establishment of Islam in order to lend outside support to Koranic mythology. A more recent example is the Iranian journalist and diplomat Ali Dashti, who in his *Twenty Three Years: A Study of the Prophetic Career of Mohammed* (1985) repeatedly took his fellow Muslims to task for not questioning the traditional accounts of Muhammad's life, much of which he called "myth-making and miracle-mongering."

Abu Zaid also cites the enormously influential Muhammad 'Abduh as a precursor. The nineteenth-century father of Egyptian modernism, 'Abduh saw the potential for a new Islamic theology in the theories of the ninth-century Mu'tazilis. The ideas of the Mu'tazilis gained popularity in some Muslim circles early in this century (leading the important Egyptian writer and intellectual Ahmad Amin to remark in 1936 that "the demise of Mu'tazilism was the greatest misfortune to have afflicted Muslims; they have committed a crime against themselves"). The late Pakistani scholar Fazlur Rahman carried the Mu'tazilite torch well into the present era: he spend the later years of his life, from the 1960s until his death in 1988, living and teaching in the United States, where he trained many students of Islam—both Muslims and non-Muslims— in the Mu'tazilite tradition.

Such work has not come without cost, however: Taha Hussein, like Nasr Abu Zaid, was declared an apostate in Egypt; Ali Dashti died mysteriously just after the 1979 Iranian revolution; and Fazlur Rahman was forced to leave Pakistan in the 1960s. Muslims interested in challenging orthodox doctrine must tread carefully. "I would like to get the Koran out of this prison," Abu Zaid has said of the prevailing Islamic hostility to reinterpreting the Koran for the modern age, "so that once more it becomes productive for the essence of our culture and the arts, which are being strangled in our society." Despite his many enemies in Egypt, Abu Zaid may well be making progress toward this goal: there are indications that his work is being widely, if quietly, read with interest in the Arab world. Abu Zaid says, for example, that his *The Concept of the Text* (1990)—the book largely responsible for his exile from Egypt—has gone through at least eight underground printings in Cairo and Beirut.

Another scholar with a wide readership who is committed to re-examining the Koran is Mohammed Arkoun, the Algerian professor at the University of Paris. Arkoun argued in *Lectures du Coran* (1982), for example, that "it is time [for Islam] to assume, along with all of the great cultural traditions, the modern risks of scientific knowledge," and suggested that "the problem of the divine authenticity of the Koran can serve to reactivate Islamic thought and engage it in the major debates of our age." Arkoun regrets the fact that most Muslims are unaware that a different conception of the Koran exists within their own historical tradition. What a re-examination of Islamic history offers Muslims, Arkoun and others argue, is an opportunity to challenge the Muslim orthodoxy from within, rather than having to rely on "hostile" outside sources. Arkoun, Abu Zaid, and others hope that this challenge might ultimately lead to nothing less than an Islamic renaissance.

THE gulf between such academic theories and the daily practice of Islam around the world is huge, of course—the majority of Muslims today are unlikely to question the orthodox understanding of the Koran and Islamic history. Yet Islam became one of the world's great religions in part because of its openness to social change and new ideas. (Centuries ago, when Europe was mired in its feudal Dark Ages, the sages of a flourishing Islamic civilization opened an era of great scientific and philosophical discovery. The ideas of the ancient Greeks and Romans might never have been introduced to Europe were it not for the Islamic historians and philosophers who rediscovered and revived them.) Islam's own history shows that the prevailing conception of the Koran is not the only one ever to have existed, and the recent history of biblical scholarship shows that not all critical-historical studies of a holy scripture are antagonistic. They can instead be carried out with the aim of spiritual and cultural regeneration. They can, as Mohammed Arkoun puts it, demystify the text while reaffirming "the relevance of its larger intuitions."

Increasingly diverse interpretations of the Koran and Islamic history will inevitably be proposed in the coming decades, as traditional cultural distinctions between East, West, North and South continue to dissolve, as the population of the Muslim world continues to grow, as early historical sources continue to be scrutinized, and as feminism meets the Koran. With the diversity of interpretations will surely come increased fractiousness, perhaps intensified by the fact that Islam now exists in such a great variety of social and intellectual settings—Bosnia, Iran, Malaysia, Nigeria, Saudi Arabia, South Africa, the United States, and so on. More than ever before, anybody wishing to understand global affairs will need to understand Islamic civilization, in all its permutations. Surely the best way to start is with the study of the Koran—which promises in the years ahead to be at least as contentious, fascinating, and important as the study of the Bible has been in this century.

Toby Lester is the executive editor of Atlantic Unbound, the *Atlantic Monthly* Web site.

From *The Atlantic Monthly*, January 1999, pp. 43-46, 48-51, 54-56. © 1999 by Toby Lester. Reprinted by permission of the author.

In the Beginning, There Were the HOLY BOOKS

The Bible and the Qur'an both reveal the word of God.
Both speak of prophets, redemption, heaven and hell.
So why the violence? Searching the sacred texts for answers.

By Kenneth L. Woodward

He was a pious family man, a trader from Mecca who regularly retreated into the hills above the city to fast and pray. In his 40th year, while he was praying in a cave on Mount Hira, the angel Gabriel spoke to him, saying, "Muhammad, you are the Messenger of God," and commanded him to "Recite!" Muhammad protested that he could not—after all, he was not gifted like the traditional tribal bards of Arabia. Then, according to this tradition, the angel squeezed him so violently that Muhammad thought he'd die. Again Gabriel ordered him to recite, and from his lips came the first verses of what eventually became the Qur'an, regarded as the eternal words of God himself by some 1.3 billion Muslims around the world.

Until that moment, 13 centuries ago, the Arabs were mostly polytheists, worshiping tribal deities. They had no sacred history linking them to one universal god, like other Middle Eastern peoples. They had no sacred text to live by, like the Bible; no sacred language, as Hebrew is to Jews and Sanskrit is to Hindus. Above all, they had no prophet sent to them by God, as Jews and Christians could boast.

Muhammad and the words that he recited until his death in 632 provided all this and more. Like the Bible, the Qur'an is a book of divine revelation. Between them, these two books define the will of God for more than half the world's population. Over centuries, the Bible fashioned the Hebrew tribes into a nation: Israel. But in just a hundred years, the Qur'an created an entire civilization that at its height stretched from northern Africa and southern Europe in the West to the borders of modern India and China in the East. Even today, in streets as distant from each other as those of Tashkent, Khartoum, Qom and Kuala Lumpur, one can hear from dawn to dusk the constant murmur and chant of the Qur'an in melodious Arabic. Indeed, if there were a gospel according to Muhammad, it would begin with these words: in the beginning was the Book.

But since the events of September 11, the Qur'an and the religion it inspired have been on trial. Is Islam an inherently intolerant faith? Does the Qur'an oblige Muslims to wage jihad—holy war—on those who do not share their beliefs? And who are these "infidels" that the Muslim Scriptures find so odious? After all, Jews and Christians are monotheists, too, and most of their own prophets—Abraham, Moses and Jesus especially—are revered by Muslims through their holy book. Listening to the rants of Osama bin Laden and other radical Islamists, Jews and Christians wonder who really speaks for Islam in these perilous times. What common ground—if any—joins these three "Peoples of the Book," as Muslims call their fellow monotheists? What seeds of reconciliation lie within the Qur'an and the Bible and the traditions that they represent? Does the battle of the books, which has endured for centuries between Muslims and believers in the West, ensure a perpetual clash of civilizations?

The Qur'an does contain sporadic calls to violence, sprinkled throughout the text. Islam implies "peace," as Muslims repeatedly insist. Yet the peace promised by Allah to individuals and societies is possible only to those who follow the "straight path" as outlined in the Qur'an. When Muslims run into opposition, especially of the armed variety, the Qur'an counsels bellicose response. "Fight them [nonbelievers] so that Allah may punish them at your hands, and put them to shame," one Qur'anic verse admonishes. Though few in number, these aggressive verses have fired Muslim zealots in every age.

To read the Qur'an is like entering a stream. At any point one may come upon a command of God, a burst of prayer, a theological pronouncement or a description of the final judgment.

The Bible, too, has its stories of violence in the name of the Lord. The God of the early Biblical books is fierce indeed in his support of the Israelite warriors, drowning enemies in the sea. But these stories do not have the force of divine commands. Nor are they considered God's own eternal words, as Muslims believe Qur'anic verses to be. Moreover, Israeli commandos do not cite the Hebrew prophet Joshua as they go into battle, but Muslim insurgents can readily invoke the example of their Prophet, Muhammad, who was a military commander himself. And while the Crusaders may have fought with the cross on their shields, they did not—could not—cite words from Jesus to justify their slaughters. Even so, compared with the few and much quoted verses that call for jihad against the infidels, the Qur'an places far more emphasis on acts of justice, mercy and compassion.

Indeed, the Qur'an is better appreciated as comprehensive guide for those who would know and do the will of God. Like the Bible, the Qur'an defines rules for prayer and religious rituals. It establishes norms governing marriage and divorce, relations between men and women and the way to raise righteous children. More important, both books trace a common lineage back to Abraham, who was neither Jew nor Christian, and beyond that to Adam himself. Theologically, both books profess faith in a single God (Allah means "The God") who creates and sustains the world. Both call humankind to repentance, obedience and purity of life. Both warn of God's punishment and final judgment of the world. Both imagine a hell and a paradise in the hereafter.

DIVINE AUTHORITY

AS SACRED TEXTS, however, the Bible and the Qur'an could not be more different. To read the Qur'an is like entering a stream. At almost any point one may come upon a command of God, a burst of prayer, a theological pronouncement, the story of an earlier prophet or a description of the final judgment. Because Muhammad's revelations were heard, recited and memorized by his converts, the Qur'an is full of repetitions. None of its 114 suras, or chapters, focuses on a single theme. Each sura takes its title from a single word—The Cow, for example, names the

THE ANNUNCIATION

In the Qur'an and the Bible the angel Gabriel is God's announcer. Through Gabriel, Muhammad hears the revelations that, for Muslims, is the Word of God made book. In the Bible, Gabriel tells the Virgin Mary she will give birth to Jesus who, for Christians, is the Word of God made flesh.

CREATION

Both the Qur'an and the Bible tell the story of Adam and Eve in the Garden of Eden. But for Muslims, as for Jews, their 'original sin' of disobedience is not passed on to humankind, so they don't require salvation through the sacrifice of Jesus on the cross—a central doctrine of Christianity.

THE ASCENSION

In one story extrapolated from a verse in the Qur'an, the Prophet Muhammad ascends to the throne of God, the model for the Sufis' flight of the soul to God. In the Bible, Jesus ascends to the Father after he is resurrected from the dead. For Muhammad, it was inconceivable that Allah would allow one of his prophets to be executed as a criminal.

HOLY PLACES

The Temple Mount is the holiest shrine for Jews. At first Muhammad directed his followers also to face Jerusalem when they prayed. But after the Jews of Medina refused him as their prophet, he directed Muslims to bow in the direction of the Kaaba in Mecca, now the holiest shrine in Islam.

PEACE AND WAR

Muhammad was not only a prophet but a military commander who led Muslim armies into battle. Jesus, on the other hand, refused even to defend himself against the Roman soldiers who arrested him in the Garden of Gethsemane after he was betrayed with a kiss by Judas, one of his own disciples. The difference helps explain the contrasting attitudes toward war and violence in the Qur'an and the New Testament.

longest—which appears only in that chapter. When Muhammad's recitations were finally written down (on palm leaves, shoulders of animals, shards of anything that would substitute for paper) and collected after his death, they were organized roughly from the longest to the shortest. Thus there is no chronological organization—this is God speaking, after all, and his words are timeless.

Nonetheless, scholars recognize that the shortest suras were received first, in Muhammad's Meccan period, and the longest in Medina, where he later became a political and military leader of the emerging community of Muslims. As a result, the longer texts take up matters of behavior and organization which are absent in the shorter, more "prophetic" suras that announce the need to submit. ("Muslim" means "submission" to God.) The Qur'an's fluid structure can be confusing, even to Muslims. "That's why one finds in Muslim bookstores such books as 'What the Qur'an says about women' or 'What the Qur'an says about a just society'," observes Jane McAuliffe of Georgetown University, editor of the new Encyclopaedia of the Qur'an.

Like the Bible, the Qur'an asserts its own divine authority. But whereas Jews and Christians regard the Biblical text as the words of divinely inspired human authors, Muslims regard the Qur'an, which means "The Recitation," as the eternal words of Allah himself. Thus, Muhammad is the conduit for God's words, not their composer. Moreover, since Muhammad heard God in Arabic, translations of the Qur'an are considered mere "interpretations" of the language of God's original revelation. "In this very important sense," says Roy Mottahedeh, professor of Middle Eastern history at Harvard, "the Qur'an is *not* the Bible of the Muslims." Rather, he says, it is like the oral Torah first revealed to Moses that was later written down. In gospel terminology, the Qur'an corresponds to Christ himself, as the *logos*, or eternal word of the Father. In short, if Christ is the word made flesh, the Qur'an is the word made book.

Compared with the few and much quoted verses that call for jihad against the 'infidels,' the Qur'an places far more emphasis on acts of justice, mercy and compassion.

The implications of this doctrine are vast—and help to explain the deepest divisions between Muslims and other monotheisms. For Muslims, God is one, indivisible and absolutely transcendent. Because of this, no edition of the Qur'an carries illustrations—even of the Prophet—lest they encourage idolatry *(shirk)*, the worst sin a Muslim can commit. Muslims in the former Persian Empire, however, developed a rich tradition of extra-Qur'anic art depicting episodes in the life of Muhammad, from which the illustrations for this story are taken. But for every Muslim, the presence of Allah can be experienced here and now through the very sounds and syllables of the Arabic Qur'an. Thus, only the original Arabic is used in prayer—even though the vast majority of Muslims do not understand the language. It doesn't matter: the Qur'an was revealed through the Prophet's ears, not his eyes. To hear those same words recited, to take them into yourself through prayer, says Father Patrick Gaffney, an anthropologist specializing in Islam at the University of Notre Dame, "is to experience the presence of God with the same kind of intimacy as Catholics feel when they receive Christ as consecrated bread and wine at mass."

'PEOPLE OF THE BOOK'

WHY THEN, DOES THE Qur'an acknowledge Jews and Christians as fellow "People of the Book," and as such, distinguish them from nonbelievers? Contrary to popular belief, "the Book" in question is not the Bible; it refers to a heavenly text, written by God, of which the Qur'an is the only perfect copy. According to the Qur'an, God mercifully revealed the contents of that book from time to time through the words of previous Biblical prophets and messengers—and also to other obscure figures not mentioned in the Bible. But in every case those who received his revelations—particularly the Jews and Christians—either consciously or inadvertently corrupted the original text, or seriously misinterpreted it. On this view, the Qur'an is not a new version of what is contained in the Bible, but what Jane McAuliffe calls a "rerevelation" that corrects the errors of the Hebrew and Christian Scriptures. Readers of the Bible will find in the Qur'an familiar figures such as Abraham, Moses, David, John the Baptist, Jesus and even the Virgin Mary, who appears much more often than she does in the New Testament, and is the only woman mentioned in the Qur'an by name. But their stories differ radically from those found in the Bible. In the Qur'an all the previous prophets are Muslims.

Abraham (Ibrahim), for example, is recognized as the first Muslim because he chose to surrender to Allah rather than accept the religion of his father, who is not mentioned in the Bible. Neither is the Qur'anic story of how Abraham built the Kaaba in Mecca, Islam's holiest shrine. Abraham's importance in the Qur'an is central: just as the Hebrews trace their lineage to Abraham through Isaac, his son by Sarah, the Qur'an traces Arab genealogy—and Muhammad's prophethood—back through Ishmael, a son Abraham had by Hagar.

The Qur'anic Moses (Musa) looks much like his Biblical counterpart. He confronts the pharaoh, works miracles and in the desert ascends the mountain to receive God's commandments. But in the Qur'an there is no mention of the Passover rituals, and among the commandments one of the most important for Jews—keeping the Sabbath—is absent. Obedience to parents is stressed repeatedly, but as in the Qur'anic story of Abraham, disobedience is required when parents are polytheists.

As a prophet rejected by his own people, the Qur'anic Jesus (Isa) looks a lot like Muhammad, who was at first rejected by the people of Mecca. He preaches the word of God, works miracles, is persecuted and—what is new, foretells his successor: Muhammad. But the Qur'an rejects the Christian claim that he is the son of God as blasphemous and dismisses the doctrine of the Trinity as polytheistic. The Crucifixion is mentioned in passing, but according to the Qur'an Jesus mysteriously does not die. Instead, Allah rescues him to heaven from where he will descend in the last days and, like other prophets, be a witness for his community of believers at the Final Judgment.

What Muhammad may have known about the Bible and its prophets and where he got his information is a purely scholarly debate. The Qur'an itself says that Muhammad met a Jewish clan in Medina. He even had his followers bow to Jerusalem when praying until the Jews rejected him as prophet. Some scholars claim that Muhammad had in-laws who were Christian, and they believe he learned his fasting and other ascetic practices from observing desert monks. But Muslims reject any scholarly efforts to link the contents of the Qur'an to the Prophet's human interactions. They cherish the tradition that Muhammad could not read or write as proof that the Qur'an is pure revelation. It is enough for them that Islam is the perfect religion and the Qur'an the perfect text.

That belief has not prevented Muslim tradition from transforming the Qur'an's many obscure passages into powerful myths. By far the most significant is the story developed from one short verse: "Glory be to Him who carried His servant at night from the Holy Mosque to the Further Mosque, the precincts of which we have blessed, that we might show him some of our signs" (sura 17:1). From this Muslims have elaborated the story of Muhammad's mystical nighttime journey from Mecca to Jerusalem, where he addresses an assembly of all previous prophets from Adam to Jesus. Yet another version of this story tells of his subsequent Ascension (mi'raj) from Jerusalem

to the throne of Allah, receiving honors along the way from the prophets whom he has superseded. For Sufi mystics, Muhammad's ascension is the paradigmatic story of the soul's flight to God. For many Muslim traditionalists, however, the journey was a physical one. Either way, its geopolitical significance cannot be ignored because the spot where the ascension began is Islam's third holiest shrine: the Dome of the Rock on Jerusalem's Temple Mount.

In Islam's current political conflicts with the West, the major problem is not the Muslims' sacred book but how it is interpreted. Muslims everywhere are plagued by a crippling crisis of authority. The Qur'an envisioned a single Muslim community (the *umma*), but as subsequent history shows, Muslims have never resolved the tension between religious authority and Islamic governments. When Islam was a great medieval civilization, jurists learned in the Qur'an decided how to apply God's words to changed historical circumstances. Their *fatwas* (opinions) settled disputes. But in today's Islamic states, authoritative religious voices do not command widespread respect. Like freewheeling fundamentalists of every religious stripe, any Muslim with an agenda now feels free to cite the Qur'an in his support. Osama bin Laden is only the most dangerous and obvious example.

Bin Laden's Twisted Mission

A bloody misinterpretation of the Qur'an's call to arms

BY CHRISTOPHER DICKEY

WHEN OSAMA BIN Laden proclaimed his "jihad against Crusaders and Jews" in 1998, he knew he was on shaky religious ground. This was his declaration of "holy war" to justify bombing U.S. embassies in Africa a few months later and, eventually, the attacks of September 11. It was his theological license "to kill the Americans and plunder their money wherever and whenever they are found." And it was based on a lie: that Islam itself was under attack by the United States, that "crimes and sins committed by the Americans are a clear declaration of war on God, his messenger and Muslims." The fact that Americans defended Muslims against the likes of Saddam Hussein and Slobodan Milosevic was ignored because, for bin Laden's bloody-minded purposes, it had to be.

Without that lie about American aggression, none of the many verses of the Qur'an that bin Laden cites would justify violence, much less the unholy slaughter of civilians. There are many interpretations of jihad—which means, literally, "effort." Often it describes the personal struggle merely to be a better, more pious Muslim. The empire builders of Islam waged military offensives in the name of jihad as late as the 17th century, and not a few turned their righteous doctrines on each other. But according to Gilles Kepel, author of the forthcoming book "Jihad: The Trail of Political Islam," the defensive holy war that bin Laden claims to fight is the most potent and most dangerous form of all. It is seen by many Muslims, if it is justified, as a personal obligation that supersedes all others, and may ultimately challenge all authority. "It's a two-edged sword,"

says Kepel. "Once you open the gate of defensive jihad, it's very difficult to close it again."

"To those against whom war is made, permission is given to fight," says the 22d chapter of the Qur'an—especially "those who have been expelled from their homes… for no cause except that they say, 'Our Lord is Allah'." Thus in Muslim theology defensive holy war was justified against European Crusaders and conquerors who attacked Muslims in the name of Christ and imposed the Inquisition, with all its horrors. Thus, in more recent times, Afghans could wage their war against the atheistic Soviets with plenty of religious backing. Few if any Muslim scholars will speak out against jihad by Palestinians fighting Israeli occupying troops. But bin Laden, a Saudi, was never persecuted for his faith. The goals he fought for initially were political and personal: to overthrow the Muslim rulers of his own country. And the jihad he declared against the United States, in the eyes of most religious scholars, was never a holy war, it was a blatant fraud.

DECIPHERING MEANINGS

BUT THE QUR'AN HAS ITS moderate interpreters as well. Since September 11, brave voices scattered across the Middle East have condemned the terrorist acts of killing civilians and judged suicide bombing contrary to the teaching of the Qur'an. Returning to the text itself, other scholars have found verses showing that Allah created diverse peoples and cultures for a purpose and therefore intended that the world remain pluralistic in religion as well. "The Qur'an," argues Muslim philosopher Jawat Said of the Al-Azhar Institute in Cairo, "gives support and encouragement to sustain the messengers of reform who face difficult obstacles."

America, too, has a core of immigrant and second-generation Muslim scholars who have experienced firsthand the benefits of democracy, free speech and the Bill of Rights. They think the Qur'an is open to interpretations that can embrace these ideals for Islamic states as well. Islam even has feminists like Azizah Y. al-Hibri of the University of Richmond Law School, who are laying the legal groundwork for women's rights through a careful reconsideration of the Qur'an and its classic commentators.

It is precisely here that the Bible and the Qur'an find their real kinship. As divine revelation, each book says much more than what a literal reading can possibly capture. To say that God is one, as both the Qur'an and the Bible insist, is also to say that God's wisdom is unfathomable. As the Prophet himself insisted, God reveals himself through signs whose meanings need to be deciphered. Here, it would seem, lie the promising seeds of religious reconciliation. Humility, not bravado, is the universal posture of anyone who dares to plumb the mind of God and seek to do his will.

The Dome of The Rock: Jerusalem's Epicenter

Written By Walid Khalidi

Islam is the third great monotheistic religion of the world. Its followers, about a billion people, constitute the majority of the population in some 50 countries. Like Judaism and Christianity, Islam has rich and deep associations with the city of Jerusalem.

Islam is an Arabic word which means "submission"; in its religious context it means submission to the will of God alone. The message of Islam was delivered by the Prophet Muhammad, who was born in Makkah, in present-day Saudi Arabia, in the year 570 and died in 632. Such was the power of the divine message he preached that, within 100 years of his death in Madinah, Islam had spread across North Africa, into Spain and across the borders of France in the West, and to the borders of India and China in the East. (See *Aramco World,* November/December 1991.)

Very early in this period—in 637—the forces of Islam won Jerusalem from the Byzantine Empire, whose capital was in Constantinople, signing a treaty by which the holy city was surrendered to 'Umar ibn al-Khattab, the second caliph, or successor, of Muhammad. For the following 1280 years, except for the period between 1109 and 1187, during the Crusades, Jerusalem remained in Muslim hands: In 1917, during World War I, the British took control of the city Muslims call al-Quds, "The Holy."

To understand Jerusalem's position in Islam, we need to look at how Islam sees itself in relation to Judaism and Christianity, to which of course Jerusalem is also sacred.

Islamic doctrine states that God has, since creation, revealed His teachings repeatedly to humankind through a succession of prophets and scriptures. The first of this line was the prophet Noah, according to many Muslim scholars; others believe Adam must be considered the first. But in this line of succession, Muhammad is the last, or "seal" of the prophets, and the teachings revealed to him are the culmination of all the previous messages. Muslims believe that the Qur'an, the literal word of God revealed to Muhammad, follows the Torah and the Gospels as God's final revelation. Thus the Qur'an accords great reverence to the Hebrew prophets, patriarchs and kings who received revelations from God and are associated with Jerusalem. Similarly, Jesus Christ is revered as one of God's most dedicated messengers, and Jerusalem, as the locus of much of his teaching, is further blessed by that association.

To Islam, then, Jerusalem is sacred for many of the reasons it is sacred to Judaism and Christianity, but in addition, it is sacred for specifically Muslim reasons. The most important of these is the Prophet Muhammad's miraculous nocturnal journey, or *isra',* to *Bayt al-Maqdis,* "the house of holiness," in Jerusalem and his ascent from there to heaven—the *mi'raj.* These events are mentioned in a number of verses of the Qur'an, most clearly in the first verse of Chapter 17, titled *Al-Isra'.* Accounts of the Prophet's life supply the details. Led by the angel Gabriel, Muhammad traveled in one night from Makkah to the site of *al-*

masjid al-aqsa, "the furthest mosque," on Mount Moriah, called the Temple Mount, in Jerusalem. The site derives its name from the temples and houses of worship built there over the millennia, including the temple of the prophet Solomon, the temple of Jupiter, the Herodian temple and the al-Aqsa Mosque.

There, Muhammad led Abraham, Moses, Jesus and other prophets in prayer. Then, from a rock on the Temple Mount, Muhammad was taken by Gabriel to heaven itself, to "within two bowlengths" of the very throne of God.

The spot from which the Prophet's ascent began was sanctified in the eyes of Muslims by the *mi'raj;* the Qur'an refers to the prayer site as *al-masjid al-aqsa.* From Muhammad's journey evolved a vast body of Muslim devotional literature, some authentic and some uncanonical, that places Jerusalem at the center of Muslim beliefs concerning life beyond the grave. This literature is in circulation in all the diverse languages spoken by the world's one billion Muslims, most of whom to this day celebrate the anniversary of the *mi'raj.*

Jerusalem is also uniquely linked to one of the "pillars" of the Muslim faith, the five daily prayers. The earliest Muslims, for a time, turned toward Jerusalem to pray. A later revelation transferred the *qibla,* the direction of prayer, to Makkah, but to this day Jerusalem is known as "the first of the two *qiblas.*" And according to Muhammad's teachings, it was during the *mi'raj* that Muslims were

THE NOBLE SANCTUARY

(Continued on next page)

THE NOBLE SANCTUARY

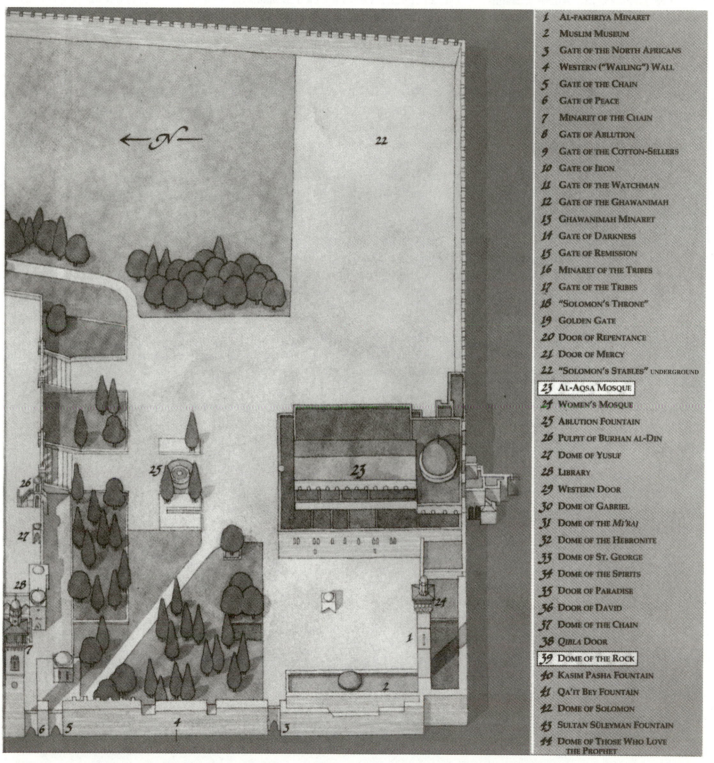

1. AL-FAKHRIYA MINARET
2. MUSLIM MUSEUM
3. GATE OF THE NORTH AFRICANS
4. WESTERN ("WAILING") WALL
5. GATE OF THE CHAIN
6. GATE OF PEACE
7. MINARET OF THE CHAIN
8. GATE OF ABLUTION
9. GATE OF THE COTTON-SELLERS
10. GATE OF IRON
11. GATE OF THE WATCHMAN
12. GATE OF THE GHAWANIMAH
13. GHAWANIMAH MINARET
14. GATE OF DARKNESS
15. GATE OF REMISSION
16. MINARET OF THE TRIBES
17. GATE OF THE TRIBES
18. "SOLOMON'S THRONE"
19. GOLDEN GATE
20. DOOR OF REPENTANCE
21. DOOR OF MERCY
22. "SOLOMON'S STABLES" UNDERGROUND
23. AL-AQSA MOSQUE
24. WOMEN'S MOSQUE
25. ABLUTION FOUNTAIN
26. PULPIT OF BURHAN AL-DIN
27. DOME OF YUSUF
28. LIBRARY
29. WESTERN DOOR
30. DOME OF GABRIEL
31. DOME OF THE *MI'RAJ*
32. DOME OF THE HEBRONITE
33. DOME OF ST. GEORGE
34. DOME OF THE SPIRITS
35. DOOR OF PARADISE
36. DOOR OF DAVID
37. DOME OF THE CHAIN
38. QIBLA DOOR
39. DOME OF THE ROCK
40. KASIM PASHA FOUNTAIN
41. QA'IT BEY FOUNTAIN
42. DOME OF SOLOMON
43. SULTAN SÜLEYMAN FOUNTAIN
44. DOME OF THOSE WHO LOVE THE PROPHET

The editors are grateful for the valuable help they received in compiling this map and checking it for accuracy. Thanks to architectural photographer Saïd Nuseibeh, whose book *The Dome of The Rock*, was published by Rizzoli (1996); to Jeff Spurr of the Aga Khan Program for Islamic Architecture and the Visual Collections of the Fine Arts Library at Harvard University; to Ahmad Nabal of the Aga Khan Visual Archives, Rotch Visual Collection, Massachusetts Institute of Technology; and to Dr. Walid Khalidi.

ordered by God to pray, and that the number of the daily prayers was fixed at five.

The center of Muslim power shifted, through the centuries, from one great capital to the next: from Madinah to Umayyad Damascus to Abbasid Baghdad to Mamluk Cairo and to Ottoman Constantinople. But after Jerusalem became part of the Muslim state in 637, whichever dynasty was in control of that city lavished it with care and attention in the form of public monuments: mosques, colleges for the study of the Qur'an and the traditions of the Prophet, hospitals, hospices, fountains, orphanages, caravansarais, baths, convents for mystics, pools and mausolea. This is why Jerusalem's Old City, within the 16th-century walls built by the Ottoman sultan Süleyman, strikes the modern-day visitor with its predominantly Muslim character.

Caliph 'Umar personally came to Jerusalem to accept the city's surrender from the Byzantines, and visited the site of *al-masjid al-aqsa,* known to some Muslims today as *al-Haram al-Maqdisi al-Sharif,* "the Noble Sanctuary of Jerusalem," or simply *al-Haram al-Sharif.* The site lay vacant and in ruins; 'Umar

ordered it cleaned, and, tradition says, took part in the work himself, carrying dirt in his own robe. When the site had been cleansed and sprinkled with scent, 'Umar and his followers prayed there, near the rough rock from which Muhammad had ascended to heaven.

Two generations later, about 691, the Umayyad caliph 'Abd al-Malik ibn Marwan's Syrian craftsmen built in the same location the earliest masterpiece of Islamic architecture, the Dome of the Rock *(Qubbat al Sakhra)*—the octagonal sanctuary, centered on the rock, whose golden dome still dominates the skyline of Old Jerusalem. 'Abd al-Malik's son al-Walid, who ruled from 705 to 715, built the second major monument, the al-Aqsa Mosque, also on the Temple Mount.

The octagonal plan of the Dome of the Rock may not have been accidental. Cyril Glassé, in his *Concise Encyclopedia of Islam,* points out that "the octagon is a step in the mathematical series going from square, symbolizing the fixity of earthly manifestation, to circle, the natural symbol for the perfection of heaven.... In traditional Islamic architecture this con-

figuration symbolizes the link between earth... and heaven...." Nor is it coincidence that the elegant calligraphy that encircles the structure inside and out—240 meters, or 785 feet, of it—includes all the Qur'anic verses about the prophet Jesus. "The calligraphic inscriptions," writes Glassé, "recall the relationship between Jerusalem and Jesus...; and the architecture, above all the octagonal form supporting a dome, is symbolic of the... ascent to heaven by the Prophet, and thus by man." Mount Moriah, with the Dome of the Rock at its center, is thus "the place where man, as man, is joined once more to God...."

History, tradition and symbolism intersect in this building, whose presence suffuses Jerusalem.

Dr. Walid Khalidi was educated in London and Oxford and has taught at Oxford University, the American University of Beirut and Harvard University. Since 1982, he has been a senior research fellow at Harvard's Center for Middle Eastern Studies. Members of his family have served Jerusalem as scholars, judges, diplomats and members of parliament since the late 12th century.

From *Aramco World,* September/October 1996, pp. 2-17. © 1996 Walid Khalidi and Tom McNeff. Reprinted by permission of Aramco World.

The Sacred Is Allah, the One True God

MOHAMMAD ZIA ULLAH

Many people in the Western world believe that Muslims worship a god named "Allah" who is distinct from the Christian God or the Jewish God. In fact, "Allah" simply means "God" in Arabic, and it is a central claim of Islam that there is only one god and wherever that one God is worshiped, the true God is worshiped. It does not matter what one calls this God; what is important is that one recognize that there is only one, and that this God is the all-powerful and all-merciful creator and lawgiver who rules over and guides the universe at all times. In the following viewpoint Mohammad Zia Ullah defends this Muslim view with quotations from the Quran and points out another central Muslim belief—that the existence of this God is obvious to all who look at the world, and that it is only the perversity of humans that causes us to deny this obvious fact. He also details the characteristics of God and the idea that we should worship God alone. To Muslims, the greatest sin is "shirk," to worship a created object instead of the true God who transcends all images. But if we turn to the true God, Ullah claims, we will find a powerful and loving Lord who protects us from adversity, forgives our sins, and guides the universe to its ultimate fulfillment.

QUESTIONS

1. How does Ullah refute what he calls the modern, materialistic denial of God?
2. Why should we worship only the one God, according to Ullah?
3. What characteristics of God does Ullah detail?

The basic values of modern civilization are purely materialistic. Its widespread evil influences permeate everywhere. As a result all religious truths are denied and religion is held in ridicule. The central point in religious faith is the being and person of God. But God is dismissed as an invention of the human mind. Man, it is said, invented gods and goddesses during the days of his infancy and ignorance. Thus, conception of God is an extension of the same infantile attitude of mind and amounts to no more than saying after Copernicus that the sun moves round the earth. But the truth is that belief in God is one of the natural dispositions of man. It is not a question requiring any subtlety of logical argumentation. Says God in the Holy Quran.

> And in the earth are Signs for those who have *certainty* of faith.
> And also in your own selves. Will you not then see? (51:21, 22)

There is evidence galore only if man would occasionally withdraw into solitude and contemplate with an unprejudiced mind. Did he come to birth of himself? Is he his own Creator? Who will say 'Yes' to such questions? So much will be obvious to anyone who consults his own conscience. No, his conscience will say. Then, if man is not his own creator, the Creator has to be someone else, outside of him. Could it be his parents? No, again. For, what is true of one man is true *ipso facto* of his parents. Man, in short, is himself proof of the existence of God....

All our little movements throughout our life are witness sure of the existence of the God of might and power, the God eternal. Just as the millstone of the water-mill is proof of the running stream of water. So is my life—and every movement of my life—proof of the existence and power of God. The watermill will not run without a running stream. Nor will life pulsate in me without the eternal and powerful Lord of Life.

Similarly the Quran bears witness to the sacred covenant between mankind and its creator:

> And when they Lord brings forth from Adam's children—out of their loins—their offspring and makes them witnesses against their own selves by saying: Am I not your Lord? they say, 'Yes, we do bear witness' (7: 173).

To a sane person, this covenant is undeniable evidence of the existence of the great Creator. Planted in man's nature is the vital seed of the Almighty's love and avowal of His existence. The seed needs life—giving sustenance to flourish and flower, and, unless denied this sustenance by a polluted environment, it remains a constant and continuous guide to the Lord, and the nature of man ever keeps proclaiming, irresistibly, at all times and all places, 'Yes, yes, we are witness to Thy creation'....

Alas the terrifying stresses of modern materialism have buried the sacred seed of the Almighty's love and avowal of His existence deep beneath a heavy weight of moral decay. But without these corrupting materialistic influences the existence of the Supreme Being remains the great, the ever-present and eternal truth. Compared to this truth nothing else could be more true, more real. Everything else but He would be as naught. Because everything would then be a manifestation, a sign, or a proof of Him. We know sunshine and we know shade. But could there be sunlight without the sun or shade without the tree?...

All religions have taught about Him. It is Him they have urged men to know and to love. It is He Who has been the centre of their teaching, their message. True, they have taught in the main two kinds of duties, duties we owe to God and duties we owe to fellow men. But these duties have one great end in view, and that is God.

Duties we owe to God are prescribed, so that we can get nearer and nearer to Him. Duties we owe to follow men have the same end in view. For, when we serve our fellow men we please our God and get closer to Him. In a sense, creatures of God are God's children. If we show love and affection to children—lift one to our lap and give a sweet to another—will it not please their parents? Will they not wish to show love and affection to you? So it is with God.

But for the moment we are not concerned so much with our duties to men. Therefore, we will deal rather with the duties we owe to God. And dealing with this subject every religion including Islam has laid special stress on two points.

Firstly, that in our faith we should associate no-one else with Him.

Secondly, we must love God more than anyone else.

It is a pity that with the passage of time Muslims also, like the followers of other religions, have mixed other things with the truth about God. Worship of tombs, of dead or hereditary saints goes on side by side with indifference to this our primary duty—to love God. Dividing our belief in one God with belief in other gods is prohibited because greater deviation from the true and straight path there could not be. This is disloyalty to God, *Shirk* in Islamic parlance. For one who has yet to find the object of true belief, the question of getting close to God does not arise. *Shirk* (associating other deities with the one God) is also self-degrading. Man has been created to subjugate, to use and to rule other things. Could he bow in obeisance to these things? It is unthinkable....

> ### IT IS GOD WHO CAUSETH
> The seed-grain
> And the date-stone
> The split and sprout.
> He causeth the living
> To issue from the dead,
> And He is the One
> To cause the dead
> To issue from the living.
> That is God: then how
> Are ye deluded
> Away from the truth?
>
> He it is that cleaveth
> The day-break (from the dark):
> He makes the night
> For rest and tranquillity,
> And the sun and moon
> For the reckoning (of time):
> Such is the judgment
> And ordering of (Him),
> The Exalted in Power,
> The Omniscient.
>
> **Quran, Surah 6.95–96**

Now let us ponder. The perfections worthy of God, perfections attributable to the divine being, are all to be found in Him. Only He possesses the most perfect attributes, only He is free from defects, weaknesses. He is one and the only one. He has no equal, no partner. He is all-powerful. He is beneficent; that is, He confers and endows without any deserts. He gives without our asking or deserving. He is merciful. That is, He rewards our deeds fully. He is the Lord of all worlds. That is, He is the nourisher, the developer, the guarantor of progress. He raises the imperfect to perfection. Ultimate rewards and punishment are in His hands. Everything in this world, this universe, owes its existence and excellence to Him. He is unique, He is not begotten, but He creates everything. He is selfsubsistent, but everything subsists because of Him. If He withdraws His sustaining hand, everything will come to naught. Death or decay or decline is not for Him. Everything without Him is subject to death and destruction. He is above want or need. But all things have wants and needs. He provides food and nourishment for everyone, everything, but Himself is above the need of food or drink. He is the supreme ruler. His rule is over everything, He Himself is free from all limitations, all constraints. He is all-hearing, all-seeing. Nothing is hidden from Him. Past, present or future are the same for Him. No-one can interfere in His plans, His wishes or wills. But not a leaf can move without His will. He is above the limitations of time and space. He is the originator, the source and spring of the entire universe.

He is all-wise, all-free in His actions and dealings, His power knows no limits, His knowledge no gaps. His mercy encompasses everything. His forgiveness has precedence over His wrath. His magnanimity knows no bounds, His mercy no limits. He forgives without cause, without atonement. His mercy is all-embracing, ultimate, basic. Yet He is master, mighty, and punishes when He should. He would not treat loyal and disloyal servants alike. If He did so, it would be a sign of weakness. He manifests Himself with a new glory every day, every moment. The most truly magnanimous is He. Others give in the hope of reward hereafter, or to be praised here in this world. And they only give out of what the Lord has given them. If the Lord had not given *them,* they would have had nothing to give. They give out of what the Lord has trusted them with. He provides for peace, protects us from all afflictions, guards us against mishaps. He is dominant over all, the One Who compensates us for our losses. He turns to us with mercy ever and ever. His greatness is unique. He shields us from the consequences of our mistakes, our sins. He resolves for us our difficulties. Honour and disgrace are in His hands, He is the One Who raises us in public esteem and pulls us down if He so wills. He is the true judge and real justice comes only from Him. His eye is on every small detail. His is the true appreciation. Glory and greatness belong only to him. He is the watcher of us all, the protector, the helper. He is the One Who listens to the prayers of men, the One Who accepts their prayers and their good deeds. He is most loving, most worthy. His attributes are ever with Him. He is the most manifest, the most hidden, the very first, the very last. He is the dispenser of forgiveness and He is the forgiver. Everything we have is His gift. He is most tolerant, most patient, even with those who are ungrateful or unmannerly. He is the One Who turns to men with mercy, and again and again. He is the possessor of all the good names. The Holy Prophet counted ninety-nine of them. But it would be wrong to think the ninety-nine names are the only names He has. This inadequate expression of His greatness and majesty is all that is possible for us earth-bound creatures of limited capacity and knowledge. His wonderful and glorious attributes surpass all description and understanding.

> Understanding and reasoning,
> and imagining besides,
> may do their utmost;
> but beyond, ever beyond,
> remains the core—the essence—of His Being.

Now you are the judge. A being, a person, of such attributes, who would say He is not entitled to our love and our worship? Shall we not give our full devotion, the devotion of our heart and soul to such a being? Is there another one deserving of our love in a like manner?

From *Enduring Issues in Religion*, 1995, pp. 114-120. © 1995 by Greenhaven Press, Inc.

The Islamic Counter-Reformation

PROFESSOR ABDULLAHI AHMED AN-NA'IM WAS A MEMBER OF THE FAC-
ULTY OF LAW AT THE UNIVERSITY OF KHARTOUM IN THE SUDAN AND A LEADING
MEMBER OF AN ISLAMIC REFORMIST GROUP CALLED THE REPUBLICAN BROTHERS
UNTIL HE WAS IMPRISONED WITHOUT CHARGE IN 1983–1984 BY THEN SUDANESE
PRESIDENT NUMIERY.

IN 1985, NUMIERY EXECUTED THE LEADER OF THE REPUBLICAN BROTHERS,
MAHMOUD MOHAMMED TAHA, FOR "APOSTASY." SUBSEQUENTLY, AN-NA'IM
TRANSLATED MOHAMMED TAHA'S *The Second Message of Islam* (SYRACUSE UNI-
VERSITY PRESS).

IN THE FOLLOWING, PROFESSOR AN-NA'IM, NOW ON THE LAW FACULTY AT
EMORY UNIVERSITY, ARGUES THAT THE EFFORT TO REFORM ISLAM IN ACCORD
WITH HUMAN RIGHTS AND CIVIL LIBERTIES MUST BE BASED ON THE EARLIEST MES-
SAGE OF ISLAM, THE "MECCA MESSAGE."

AUTHORS' NOTE: It would be totally inappropriate for me to consent to presenting this Universalist and inclusive vision of Islam introduced by a Sudanese Muslim reformer since the early 1950s, without registering my strongest protest against the military campaign of the United States of America that is killing innocent civilians in Afghanistan for the sins of their oppressors.

I remain fully committed to Taha's vision and continue to do my best to realize it. Nevertheless, and precisely because of that commitment, I also believe that the illegal, immoral and inhumane campaign by the US against the people of Afghanistan constitutes a fundamental betrayal of any possibility of the rule of law and respect for human rights in international relations, which are the underlying premise of Taha's ideas. In this context, I don't wish my representation of Taha's vision to be seen as saying that all will be well if only "moderate Muslims struggle for an Islamic reformation."

Taha proposed a paradigm shift in Islamic religious and legal thinking, including the total repudiation of the notion of *jihad* as aggressive war, on the premise that we all now live in a world that is governed according to the rule of law in international relations and protection of human rights and humanitarian legal principles. It is there-fore particularly discouraging that the US, as the world's sole superpower chooses to deliberately and persistently violate those civilized principles.

Nevertheless, I do hereby consent to the re-publication of this article, first published in spring 1987, because I refuse to allow American exceptionalism and unilateral-ism to defeat Taha's humane and civilized vision.

—Abdullahi An'Naim, November 1, 2001

CAIRO—The tragedy of Islam today is that the Muslim leadership has locked itself into being intimidated by its extremist elements. These Muslim leaders, whose moral bankruptcy and weakness are represented by the opulent lifestyles of the Saudi Sheikhs, live on the fringes of Islam as well as Western civilization. They lack the essence of either. In that sense, they are twice as corrupt and twice as Satanic as radical Muslims claim the West to be.

As a result, a few militant and highly motivated gang-sters—real criminals—are holding Muslim cultures and Muslim leadership hostage.

The primary motivation of radical Muslims is a reac-tion to Western neocolonialism and, more significantly, Western cultural domination. The revolt against Western cultural domination is legitimate, but how that revolt develops is the key question for Islam today.

> **The complete and immediate implementation of *Shari'a* (the historic code of Islam), which is what radical Muslims such as the Taliban demanded, is the least Islamic position for a Muslim to adopt today.**

The complete and immediate implementation of *Shari'a* (the historic code of Islam), which is what radical Muslims such as the Taliban demanded, is the least Islamic position for a Muslim to adopt today. To try to build a new Islamic identity in this way is tantamount to saying that Islam stands for repression and discrimination at home and aggressive war abroad.

In order to sustain and strengthen the Islamic faith, Muslims need to reassert in a modern context the fundamental truths of the Koran and the Prophet's original Mecca message which was based on broad principles of justice and equality. Only by removing the serious inconsistencies between their historical Islamic self-identity and the realities of the modern world can Muslims effectively challenge Western domination. If they fail, they will lose their Islamic identity and tradition altogether.

COUNTER-REFORMATION BEFORE REFORM

The benefits of Western secularism for the Muslim world, such as technology, human rights and civil international relations, are only superficially entrenched. In the Iranian revolution, these frail acquisitions of civilization were swept away wholesale because they were not indigenous or legitimized from within Islam itself.

> **The Islamic world never experienced the Enlightenment or had its own Reformation out of which the Islamic equivalent of Western concepts of democracy, human rights and civil liberties could have developed.**

The Islamic world never experienced the Enlightenment or had its own Reformation out of which the Islamic equivalent of Western concepts of democracy, human rights and civil liberties could have developed. The emergence of a bourgeoisie and heightened individual consciousness

which presaged these great European movements did not arise in the Muslim context until the present day.

Today, Islam is in a period of pre-Reformation. Paradoxically, the coming Islamic Reformation has its roots in the Muslim reaction to the muted influences of European modernity.

In the 19th century, Muslims thought they could reap the benefits of the European Enlightenment by emulating it—such as in Turkey and Egypt with the adoption of the European codes. Elitist Muslims saw that they could neutralize the rising expectations of the masses in this way. This has continued up to the present time.

Today, because advanced communications and transportation enable Muslims to travel, read and watch television, they readily see that their institutions and doctrines are extremely inadequate in terms of even superficially emulating the West. However, this surface modernization has raised the economic expectations and heightened the political frustration of Muslims because of the lack of freedoms at home.

At the same time it has made Muslims feel that they have lost touch with their own Islamic identity and tradition. Especially in the wake of decolonization, they understand that national self-determination must be of an Islamic nature. Caught in a kind of limbo between tradition and modernity, Muslims have found themselves where their leaders have taken them—superficially Islamic and superficially modern.

One attempt to resolve this dilemma has been the great Islamic "counter-reformation." This reaction against Western influence and the search for an historical Islamic identity is precisely why the Reformation will ultimately come about. The historical model promoted by Iran has remained an ideal which Muslims sentimentalize and glorify, believing that it can miraculously overcome all their problems. When it is seen to fail, a new Islamic identity that accommodates human rights and international law will come about. In this sense, our counter-Reformation is the prelude to the Islamic Reformation.

Meanwhile, the situation grows worse. There may be a great deal of killing and human suffering before things get better. Fundamentalism is growing. We have been visited with the experiences of Iran, Pakistan, the Sudan and Afghanistan. Egypt remains a target. It is extremely significant because it is the most vital and vigorous center of learning in the whole Muslim world. If Egypt should fall, many other Muslim countries would fall very quickly. Khomeini types or Sunni fundamentalists like the Muslim Brothers, who are also in Syria and Tunisia, are likely to succeed unless Muslims can develop progressive reforms that are Islamically genuine.

However, it is an optimistic and religiously determined path we are taking. We believe all this human suffering has been visited upon us to excite our religious imagination, to sharpen our intellect and our moral response. It has prepared us for the next step—realization that Islamic self-identity based on *Shari'a* is an historically dated identity that needs to be reformed.

SHARI'A AND HUMAN RIGHTS

Shari'a is the law of Islam developed by early jurists from basic sources: the Koran—which Muslims believe to be the final and literal word of God, and the living example of the Prophet Himself. *Shari'a* is very broad and comprehensive. It includes worship rituals—how to pray, cleanliness for worship, how to fast and rules for social etiquette—how to dress and how to wash. There is no inconsistency with these rituals and questions of human rights.

> **What is a problem with *Shari'a* is that part which has to do with penal law, rights and civil liberties and the treatment of minorities, non-Muslims and women.**

What is a problem with *Shari'a* is that part which has to do with penal law, rights and civil liberties and the treatment of minorities, non-Muslims and women. It is these aspects of the Islamic code that have tended to hit the Western headlines—the quick-justice amputations for theft or veils on women.

For political expediency, some Muslim governments emphasize the penal aspects as window dressing to publicize their commitment to *Shari'a* without genuinely being committed to other, more important rules about economic and social justice and legitimate political power. For example, if there were a genuine commitment to *Shari'a* in Saudi Arabia, the hereditary monarchy would be rejected as illegitimate because, according to *Shari'a*, the personal lifestyle and conduct of the ruler are alone the basis for his claim to rule.

> **The notion of aggressive *jihad* has become morally untenable as a means of conducting international relations; and the rise of the modern human rights movement has tumbled the moral foundations of segregation and discrimination against women and non-Muslims.**

Unfortunately, because they are afraid of creating the conditions for civil strife, many Islamic jurists have been co-opted by the regimes in power and have contributed to the distortion of Islam.

REFORM: THE CONTRIBUTION OF THE WEST

The first Islamic state was established in Arabia, around 622, in the city of Medina after the Prophet Mohammed's migration from Mecca. It is only in the last 100 years that the historical model of *Shari'a*, based on the circumstances of Medina, has lost its legitimacy and moral validity. The notion of aggressive *jihad* has become morally untenable as a means of conducting international relations; and the rise of the modern human rights movement has tumbled the moral foundations of segregation and discrimination against women and non-Muslims.

Human rights and the international rule of law were contributions to civilization from the West. Since the West has had a very significant role in developing the totality of the human experience, Muslims are entitled, even required, to take advantage of these positive achievements.

In each cycle of the growth of civilization, a new contribution is added to the total course of human experience. The ancient Romans incorporated what the Greeks had contributed. Roman civilization was, in turn, developed and promoted by Muslims. Then Muslims handed it back to Europe. The Islamic task now is to reconcile human progress with traditions; to reject the remnants of colonial domination and spiritual corruption, of whatever source, while accepting the standards of economic and political justice and the rights of individuals.

For example, as Muslims, we should accept female equality. That is a universal value. But the way we develop our indigenous response to this challenge is our business. Mahmoud Mohammed Taha, the leader of the Republican Brothers in the Sudan who was executed by President Numiery, was first imprisoned for challenging the colonial authorities who had arrested a woman for circumcising her daughter. Although Taha opposed the practice of circumcision as a means of subordinating women, he felt that such an unhealthy and oppressive practice should be countered by indigenous medical and moral education, not by the imposition of European norms by colonial authorities.

As Muslims, we should also accept the full human dignity of non-Muslims and their right to be equal citizens. The very ideas of the national state, constitutional government, limitations of power and equality regardless of sex or religion are part of the universal values to which Islamic law must adapt.

However, regarding penal law, I cannot find a way, in principle, to abolish what is perceived to be the harshest aspects of the law—amputations and floggings. But we can de-emphasize their importance as primary instruments of justice while we place the highest priority on social and economic justice.

> In considering the reform of Islam, it is useful to think in terms of the combined roles played by Thomas Aquinas and Martin Luther in the adaptation of Christian tradition to the development of the modern world.

Penal law should not be applied in the spirit of vengeance and intimidation. For example, in the Jewish tradition there is still a wide range of about 50 offenses punishable by death, but Jewish jurists have developed pre-requirements and procedural safeguards that effectively preclude application of penalties. Human judgment cannot abolish the offense because it is a matter of religious principle, but human judgment can decide whether the conditions for enforcement of the penalty have been satisfied.

SUPERFUNDAMENTALIST REFORM

In considering the reform of Islam, it is useful to think in terms of the combined roles played by Thomas Aquinas and Martin Luther in the adaptation of Christian tradition to the development of the modern world. This analogy illustrates both the commitment to tradition and fundamental religious notions, while at the same time seeking reformation and a challenge to orthodoxy.

In Mecca, for the 13 years before His migration to Medina, the Prophet received the first part of the Koran—the Mecca part. This Mecca period established the moral and ethical foundation of the Muslim community.

Because this peaceful and voluntary Mecca message of fundamental social and economic egalitarianism was violently rejected in Mecca and Arabia in general, the Mecca message was not suitable for that stage of human development. Thus, the Prophet's migration to Medina not only signified a tactical move to seek a more receptive environment, but also a shift in the content of the message itself.

The rest of the Koran—the Medina message—which later became codified in *Shari'a* as the model for an Islamic state by the majority of Muslims, was a step backward. For example, there are many verses in the Koran from the Mecca message which say there is no compulsion in matters of religion or belief and people should be left to decide for themselves whether they want to believe or not believe. In the Medina message, there are verses that say one should go out and fight infidels wherever one finds them and kill them. There are verses which say one should fight Christian and Jewish believers, making them submit to Muslim rule or be subjugated by force.

Now, according to Islamic belief, each message, including Judaism and Christianity, is valid only to the extent that it is relevant and applicable to changing people's lives. So, it was very necessary, logical and valid in that context for the Prophet to apply the Medina message. But the Medina message is not the fundamental, universal, eternal message of Islam. That founding message is from Mecca.

So, the reformation of Islam must be based on a return to the Mecca message. In order to reconcile the Mecca and Medina messages into a single system, Muslim jurists have said that some of the Medina verses have abrogated the corresponding earlier verses from Mecca. Although the abrogation did take place, and it was logical and valid jurisprudence at one time, it was a postponement, not a permanent abrogation. If we accept the process as a permanent abrogation, we will have lost the best part of our religion—the most humane and the most universal, egalitarian aspects.

> The Mecca verses should now be made the basis of the law and the Medina verses should be abrogated.

The Mecca verses should now be made the basis of the law and the Medina verses should be abrogated. This counter-abrogation will result in the total conciliation between Islamic law and the modern development of human rights and civil liberties. In this sense we reformers are superfundamentalists.

The key to our reformation will be a positive and receptive attitude toward the totality of the human experience. What we find to be consistent with our fundamental principles, we accept, whatever the source.

For example, the democratic component of Western experience, not the capitalistic component, is a positive aspect. The social component of the Marxist experience, not the atheist or totalitarian aspect, is a positive aspect. We would not accept the humanism of the Western Enlightenment unqualified. We accept that God is the Creator in the first place; Man the creator only in the second place—to the extent that he is a reflection of the original Creator. For this reason, the Islamic religious orientation would remain even in a neutral state that retains a functional separation between state and religion.

If universal values are not adapted from within indigenous traditions, reform only foments the very cultural reaction witnessed in the Islamic world today.

From *New Perspectives Quarterly*, Winter 2002, pp. 29-35. © 2002 by New Perspective Quarterly. Reprinted by permission.

UNIT 9
Religions in Dialogue and Confrontation

Unit Selections

Key Points to Consider

• Can someone practice both traditional Asian culture and Christianity simultaneously? Expain.

• Why do some religions appear to preach hate toward each other? Are there ways of interpreting scripture to avoid this? Explain.

• What are some of the problems that Muslims face living in a non-Muslim country?

• Suggest some approaches that Muslims and Christians can take to enhance understanding of each other?

 **Links: www.dushkin.com/online/**
These sites are annotated in the World Wide Web pages.

Center for Strategic and International Studies (CSIS)
http://www.csis.org/prevdip/cp_index.htm

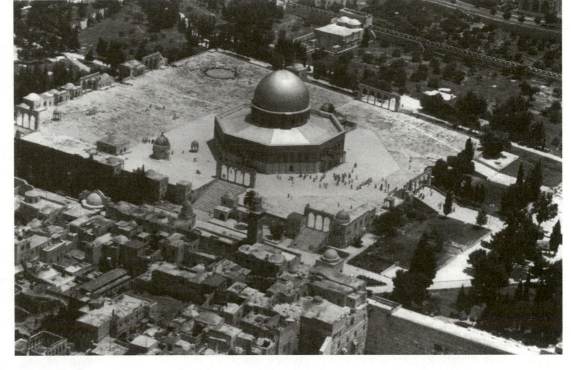

Religious traditions express, justify, and promote their views of the material and spirit worlds by means of constructed value systems. These systems, like social, political, and economic systems, classify the various elements of the world within which their focus lies hierarchically. In the case of religions, the focus can be narrow, dealing essentially with ritual activity and certain human interactions, or it can be broad, including nearly every aspect of human existence. Ethnic/indigenous religious tradition, as mentioned in unit 2, have values based primarily on the history, experiences, and beliefs of an ethnic or cultural group. Prophetic religious traditions, on the other hand, find their basis primarily, if not exclusively, in the experiences and teachings of a specific prophet, such as Jesus, the Buddha, or Muhammad, for example. In this unit, the discussion will primarily surround prophetic traditions, their value systems, and how they interact with others in dialogue and in confrontation.

The beliefs and values of ethnic traditions tend to be passed on orally through family and community interactions. As a result, they often remain unwritten. Prophetic traditions are usually contained in scripture. Furthermore, these are believed to contain a truth that transcends time and space, thereby taking the traditions beyond the confines of a particular group of people or a particular place. Such traditions also typically contain a missionary element within them, born out of the desire, and even need, to establish their version of truth throughout the world. As a consequence, the larger prophetic traditions, such as Christianity and Islam, can be found in vastly diverse geographic and cultural milieus around the world.

Whenever such traditions come into contact with each other, or even with secular value systems, the potential for tension and conflict is elevated, and the need for accommodation is necessary. If a prophetic tradition has within its philosophical framework, room for dialogue and adaptation, then the contact can be fruitful for both. In this way, both systems can learn from each other. However, when such accommodation is viewed instead as capitulation, then discord is the more likely outcome. One can see both occurring in the case of Christianity and Islam.

The history of the interactions between Christianity and Islam dates back to the seventh century and the founding of Islam.

Since that time, there have been countless battles between the two, and countless lives lost in the process. The Crusades of the thirteenth and fourteenth centuries are but one of the more egregious examples of this. It can be rightly said that religion can be the basis for war as much as the inspiration for peace. Conflict, however, has not been the only result of the interaction. Accommodation has also existed, and there are countless examples of harmonious relationships between members of both traditions as well.

As we enter the twenty-first century and the various value systems of the world come into closer contact, the need for dialogue as well as the potential for confrontation grow every day. The articles in this unit address some of the issues and opportunities that the contemporary world has precipitated. The first of these looks at the three Western religious traditions and attempts that are being made to get beyond the antagonism and find some common ground.

The vocation and goal of most missionaries is to convert outsiders to their way of thinking and believing. Because religious beliefs and cultural practices often go hand in hand, many missionaries attempt to have converts reject past practices as a part of adopting and following their new religion. This is especially the case with respect to Christian missionaries. In "The Case for 'Yellow Theology'," Dixon Yagi suggests that this process is not necessary and that traditional cultural beliefs and practices are not antithetical to the practice of Christianity.

The next two articles focus specifically on Christian-Muslim interactions, highlighting both the possibilities and the necessity of dialogue and accommodation.

Religion; It Sounds Like Hate, but Is It?

Most sacred texts contain passages shocking to modern sensibilities.
But experts say they need to be read in context.

by TERESA WATANABE

This month's flap over whether Korans containing anti-Jewish commentary should be pulled from public schools underscores a question of growing prominence in today's pluralistic times: How do you make sure ancient scriptures mesh with modern-day sensibilities?

The prevailing answer among scholars: You can't. No scripture is politically correct—nor, many scholars argue, should anyone expect it to be.

New religious movements emerge precisely because the prevailing faiths are deemed flawed in some major way, says Reuven Firestone, a professor of medieval Judaism and Islam at Hebrew Union College in Los Angeles. So if their scriptures rail against others as arrogant sinners, unbelievers, idol worshippers and the like—well, that's their job, Firestone says.

"Scripture is a divinely authoritative way to prove the old systems are no longer proper and that there is a need for a new religious expression," he says.

Religious scholars say there is a plenty of political incorrectness to go around in virtually all scriptures. The Hebrew Bible trashes the prevailing Canaanite religion—and even calls for the wholesale slaughter of those regarded as idol worshippers. In the New Testament Gospel of Matthew, Jesus condemns the Pharisees, a group of particularly observant Jews, as hypocrites and "sons of vipers" destined for the "judgment of hell."

The Koran urges believers to slaughter infidels "wherever you find them" and not to befriend Christians or Jews. The Buddha criticizes the Hindu priestly caste known as Brahmans, and Sikhism founder Guru Nanak rose up to declare deficiencies in both the prevailing Muslim and Hindu cultures of the time.

"There are things in every religion that contemporary followers of that faith are embarrassed by, and should be," says Elliot Dorff, a philosophy professor at the University of Judaism. "The question for believers is: How do you continue to have faith in your own tradition, and nonetheless shape it to accord with modern sensibilities?"

Many Muslims believe that question was never fully—or fairly—vetted before 300 Korans were pulled from the shelves of the Los Angeles Unified School District last week. The books, a 1934 translation and commentary by Abdullah Yusuf Ali, a British Muslim of Indian descent, were donated to the district in January by the Omar Al Khattab Foundation in Los Angeles. On Monday, district officials said a panel of Islamic experts and other educators will review potential substitute translations.

Ali's English translation of the Koran's original Arabic text is the most popular among Muslims because it was one of the first. But his commentary offended some school district personnel with such passages as: "The Jews in their arrogance claimed that all wisdom and all knowledge of Allah were enclosed in their hearts. Their claim was not only arrogance but blasphemy."

Scholars say it is crucial to understand such passages in their historical context. According to Mahmoud Abdel-Baset of the Islamic Center of Southern California, Ali's commentary was not smearing Jews per se, but only describing the attitude of the Jewish communities in the Arabian city of Medina at the time, who rejected Muhammad's message and claimed themselves as the sole recipients of divine revelation.

Ali's pique at those who refused to accept God's message was no different, scholars say, than Jesus' railings against the Pharisees or even the Hebrew prophets condemning their own spiritually wayward people as an "unwanted vessel," a "ravaged vine."

Singling out the Islamic sources for criticism was "unfair," says Muzammil Siddiqi, religious director of the Islamic Center of Orange County. "Why not pull out all of the religion books, and take out books of English literature as well—Shakespeare, because of Shylock," he says, referring to the unflattering Jewish character portrayed in "The Merchant of Venice."

Jewish texts have been misunderstood as well, says Rabbi Yitzchok Adlerstein, chairman of Jewish law and ethics at Loyola Law School in Los Angeles. He said Talmudic exhortations to kill "the best of non-Jews," refers only to wartime. Statements that most thieves in the world were descendants of Ishmael—the progenitor of Muslims—referred only to the way rabbis saw their neighbors at the time—not any "essential truths" about Muslims today, he says. And Jewish tradition offers at least eight interpretations of why the seemingly vengeful "eye for an eye" exhortation is not to be taken literally, Adlerstein says.

On the question of what to do about politically incorrect religious material, responses are mixed.

Some people, such as Firestone and UCLA Islamic law scholar Khaled Abou El Fadl, suggest taking care to choose material appropriate for today's climate of interfaith tolerance. Abou El Fadl, for one, favors a Koranic translation by Muhammad Asad, a convert to Islam, who sought to interpret the divine book in a universal manner.

For example, in examining the Koran's infamous passage to slaughter all unbelievers, Asad cautions readers to balance this command with more temperate ones—that there is no compulsion in religion, for instance. By contrast, a less flexible translation widely disseminated by Saudi Arabia, "The Noble Qur'an," emphasizes the need to fight non-Muslims until they accept the Islamic creed that there is no God but Allah and Muhammad is his messenger.

Abou El Fadl added that if objectionable commentaries are used, a note should be attached to them putting the work into historical context. Others, however, view that as a potentially endless task.

"If we start putting notes in everything that bothers us, we're going to be putting a lot of notes in a lot of books," says Marianne Meye Thompson, professor of New Testament at Fuller Theological Seminary in Pasadena.

University of Judaism professor Dorff says that religious communities have dealt with problematic material in a number of ways. The first is to repudiate it. In 1996, he says, the Evangelical Lutheran Church of America repudiated Martin Luther's anti-Semitic comments and has now formed a commission to create what he called a "more positive theology about Jews and Judaism."

Dorff says he himself wrote a ruling for the Conservative movement in 1985 that repudiated traditional Jewish law against drinking wine made by non-Jews, who were assumed to be idolaters. "We openly repudiated that law based on the fact that relations with non-Jews are different and we no longer consider Christians idolaters," he says.

For Orthodox Jews, however, throwing out tradition is not an option.

Instead, many seek to find acceptable understandings of seemingly offensive material. Every morning, for instance, Adlerstein recites a traditional blessing thanking God for not making him a non-Jew, slave or woman. Although other movements have eliminated that blessing, Adlerstein says he interprets it not as a criticism of others but as praise to God for giving him more responsibility. Under traditional law, he says, Jewish men were given more commandments than others to keep.

Another strategy for dealing with problem texts, Dorff says, is to limit the scope of the offensive material.

He says the Vatican has sought to alter perceptions of Jews as "Christ killers" by issuing statements that New Testament references to Jews at Jesus' crucifixion should not be taken to affix blame on Jews of today.

Limiting the scope of material can be tricky, however, if it is done inside the sacred scriptures themselves.

For example, Focus on the Family, a Colorado-based evangelical Christian organization, charges that a new revision of a Bible translation skews the sacred word in pursuit of political correctness. In John 19:12, which recounts a crowd of Jews urging Pilate not to release Jesus, the new revision narrows the scope of responsibility to "Jewish leaders"—an unacceptable liberty, in the eyes of Paul Hetrick, a spokesman.

"They are trying to isolate what happened in John 19:12 as the responsibility only of Jewish leaders, and they do not have the right or prerogative to introduce new words or editorialize like that," he says.

Dorff said a third approach to dealing with offensive texts is to create modern commentaries that point out their anachronistic nature.

For years, Catholic priests would read historical reproaches, or commentaries, during Lent that Dorff says scolded Jews for being involved in the crucifixion of Jesus. But as a result of a Jewish-Catholic dialogue in 1973, he says, the L.A. archdiocese instructed priests to drop these words or precede them with new commentaries urging Catholics to reflect instead on how they themselves may have failed in embracing Jesus' teachings.

For the long run, Firestone suggested that Muslim Americans commission a committee of scholars to write a new Koranic commentary suitable for modern times, just as Jews and Christians have done. "It has to reflect the values of a pluralistic society, and Islam does not contradict that," he says.

The Case for 'Yellow Theology'

A former Buddhist preaches a style of Christian evangelism
that is sensitive to Asian culture.

By K. CONNIE KANG
TIMES STAFF WRITER

For the first couple of years after he became a Christian, Dickson Yagi, born in a Buddhist family in Hawaii, could hardly contain his happiness at the thought of going to heaven.

Then, as his new religion took hold, he began to worry about his non-Christian relatives and friends. Were they headed for hell? Was there no hope even for devout Buddhists, such as his beloved grandfather, should they die without accepting Christ as their lord and savior?

Yagi went on to become a Southern Baptist minister, spending 27 years as a missionary in Japan, but he never forgot the way that question ate at him. It shaped the style he used in trying to bring Christianity to Japan, a style he calls "yellow theology": evangelism that is sensitive to the religious and psychosocial history of people of Asian ancestry.

The third-generation Okinawan American's personal experiences convinced him that the "good news" of Christianity can become alienating "bad news" to potential Asian converts.

"Many missionaries have ignored, condemned and ridiculed marvelous elements in Asian culture through ignorance and misunderstanding," said Yagi, 64, who retired from missionary work in 2000 because of prostate cancer, returned to the U.S. and eventually settled in Los Angeles, where he specializes in Buddhist-Christian relations.

Take ancestor worship. For centuries, Christian missionaries warned potential East Asian converts that they would no longer be able to engage in a practice Christians considered idolatry.

Telling tradition-minded Asians that they can no longer bow in front of the images of their ancestors at a memorial table,

laden with choice foods, was tantamount to condemning their way of life. It clashed with one of their most cherished precepts—filial piety.

Eventually, the Catholic Church dropped the prohibition. But Protestant churches have not, creating frictions within Asian families with Christian and non-Christian members.

Yagi, a graduate of seminaries in America and Japan, counsels Protestant missionaries to interpret ancestor worship less literally.

"Worship in the Western context brings images of a weak man standing before an omnipotent God," he writes in "Christ for Asia: Yellow Theology for the East" in the faculty journal of the Southern Baptist Theological Seminary.

"In ancestor worship in Japan, however, the opposite is true. Although the dead can haunt and harm the living, it is the dead who are so utterly dependent on the living for rituals that guarantee their well-being."

Thus, ancestor *respect*, not ancestor *worship*, would more accurately describe what takes place, Yagi said.

"Japanese speak to the dead in the funeral service, at the home Buddha altar and at the grave. They report family events. They talk as if the person were still alive," he said. "This is not prayers of adoration or prayers of supplication. They just say it feels good to get their feelings out."

Not Preaching a 'Terrible Message'

It is the task of yellow theology, he said, "to squeeze the Scriptures and see if any kind of minimum survival hope will ooze out to soothe the agony of Asian

Christians." In this case, the biblical command to honor one's parents should take precedence. Working in Japan, where Christians constitute less than 1% of the population, Yagi could not bring himself to preach that only one in 100 Japanese would go to heaven and the rest to hell. That sounded like a "terrible message."

So he delved into how to deal with the separation of a handful of Christians from their loved ones and made it his life's work.

The missionary's command to the boy that 'You must tear it down as Gideon did' touched Yagi deeply because of a concern in Asian and Asian American churches: In becoming a Christian, does a convert sever ties with his non-Christian loved ones?

He had been the first member of his Shingon Buddhist family to convert to Christianity. As a small boy, he heard a visiting American missionary from Japan speak at his church in Hilo, Hawaii. He was so impressed with the missionary's knowledge of Japanese culture and language that he felt as if he were hearing God himself.

But an issue the missionary raised during his exchanges with youngsters at Kinoole Baptist Church—whether their families kept a *butsudan* (Buddhist altar)

and his unequivocal stance that such symbols of idolatry must be destroyed—troubled young Yagi.

His grandfather kept a *butsudan* in the living room. He sat in front of it every morning and prayed.

The missionary's command to the boy that "You must tear it down as Gideon did," reciting the Old Testament story of prophet Gideon, touched him deeply. When he talks about it now, he explains it as part of a concern in Asian and Asian American churches: In becoming a Christian, does a convert sever ties with his non-Christian loved ones, who will be banished to hell?

"I'd rather go to hell and be with my family than go to heaven and spend the rest of eternity with white people I don't even know" is a familiar comment heard by Asian American pastors.

How, the young Yagi wondered, could he possibly tear down his grandfather's beloved altar and still remain his grandson? As far back as he could remember, his grandfather, Seiryu Yagi, who had immigrated to Hawaii in 1907 from Okinawa, Japan, to escape poverty, would sit cross-legged in front of the altar at the crack of dawn to pray, the fragrant scent of incense and the tinkle of prayer bells signaling the household that the patriarch of the clan was at intercessory prayers for four generations of Yagis in Okinawa, Hawaii, California, Brazil and Peru.

Images of Buddha as 'Evil and Demonic'

Like the missionary he encountered in his childhood, Yagi said, too many well-intentioned Christian workers from the West see the images of Buddha as "something evil and demonic." Yet even Christians growing up in Japan would understand the kindness and compassion each of the many Buddhas and bodhisattvas represent, Yagi said. Jizo is synonymous with compassion, as he leads dying children to heaven, and Kannon is the epitome of maternal love.

Yagi was in his 30s by the time his grandfather lay dying of cancer in a Hilo hospital. The family summoned Yagi, who was in Louisville, working on his doctorate at Southern Baptist Theological Seminary, to hurry home.

Calling him by his Japanese name, the grandfather asked: "Kazuo, will you pray for the family?" Of course, the grandson said.

The old man let out a sigh of relief, leaned back in his bed, and was at peace, Yagi recalled. For years, the elder Yagi had been deeply troubled by the fact that he could not count on any of his American-born sons to promise to take care of the *butsudan* after he died. But he remembered that he and his grandson had shared a "spirit of prayer."

The grandfather understood that the Buddhist prayers could not continue after his death, and that his grandson's prayers would be Christian. No matter. He was at peace, believing Buddha would understand. Yagi is certain he will revisit his grandfather in his eternal life.

Religions are about transforming peoples' hearts, Yagi said. "When I find kind people, to me, they are very precious to God," he said. "The labels, such as Christian, Buddhist, Hindu, [are] secondary because God sees the heart."

Cross meets crescent:
An interview with Kenneth Cragg

KENNETH CRAGG *has been a major figure in Christian-Muslim conversations. He has spent some 45 years in the Middle East as professor of philosophy, as a chaplain, and as assistant bishop in the Anglican Archdiocese of Jerusalem. He has also taught at the University of Sussex in England. His published works include hundreds of scholarly articles and more than 30 books, most recently* The Arab Christian *and* Palestine: The Prize and Price of Zion. *Now in his 80s, Bishop Cragg still lectures at Oxford University and in Europe and the U.S. We spoke to him recently at Chicago's North Park University.*

You've said that Christians and Muslims should be trying to work for religious ecumenism. What does ecumenism look like from a Muslim perspective?

It depends on which Muslim you ask, of course, as it would depend on which Christian you asked. The word *ecumenae* means the whole inhabited world. But we seem to have limited it to Christian togetherness, to Christian mutuality. Couldn't we have an *ecumenae* of religions?

The ecumenical movement has adopted the position that "whatever is Christian I will try to belong with, in some sense." Can we go on to say, "I will try to belong with anything that is religious" ? That, obviously, is vastly more difficult. But a good example of this happened at Temple University, where the *Journal of Ecumenical Studies* is produced. The journal started out dealing only with inter-Christian issues. Then the editors said, "Why not include Jews? They're part of the *ecumenae* of Abraham. Why not Muslims?" If you begin thinking that way, soon you ask, "Why not every religion—Jainism, Buddhism, Hinduism?"

The difficulty is that religion is such an omnibus term. Michael Ramsey, the former archbishop of Canterbury, once said, "Not everything religious is desirable." Would we want to align ourselves with the Hinduism that undergirds the caste system or the Hinduism of Gandhi, which repudiates the caste system? To which Islam can Christians relate—the Islam of Afghanistan's Taliban or the Islam of academics living in the West? But with due circumspection, I think it's possible to relate to those of other faiths. We must do so with patience and

modesty, with the honest recognition that the degree to which we can be together is partial, and that each faith has distinctive aspects which can't be reconciled. If we agree to agree, we must at the same time agree to disagree. Otherwise, we may be heading only for some kind of gooey sentimentalism.

In the U.S., there always seem to be far more Christians than Muslims involved in Islamic-Christian dialogue groups. Are Christians more open than Muslims to this kind of encounter?

Even those in the two faiths who are articulate and ready for dialogue do have a different kind of calendar. Christianity has had a longer confrontation with modernity than has Islam. Our experience or awareness of the issues now facing us is, consequently, different. Christians are more aware of the need to respond to pluralism.

If you feel your culture is being swamped by alien influences from the West, you may develop a mentality of resistance.

We have to be patient until Muslims feel they are more ready for dialogue. What I often find is that the Muslim participants in dialogue groups will make a kind of set statement reiterating how they see things. You get the impression that they haven't really taken in the things the Christians have said. But at least they have been willing to respond. Many of the same issues face people of all religions—ecology, the environment, population. In all these spheres we can, to an extent, cooperate. And religions need the criticism that those of other faiths can bring.

Aren't many Muslim countries trying to shut themselves off from the West and the West's religion?

There is a very deep-seated resentment of Western power, especially of American power. It's a love-hate relationship, because these countries need Western technology and expertise.

People come to the West for education, and some nations, such as Egypt and Jordan, are sustained by American aid. If you feel your culture is under threat, however, or is going to be swamped by what you regard as alien influences, or if you want to have some control over the degree to which another culture influences yours—then you may develop a mentality of resistance. We see an extreme form of this in Afghanistan. The more people see old securities threatened, the louder they tend to shout. So in that sense, fundamentalism is itself an index of the degree of inevitable change.

Is it possible for Muslim countries to develop a non-Western modernity, an Islamic modernity?

Yes. An example is the work of Ismail al-Faruqi, a Palestinian who taught at Temple University. Faruqi promoted the idea of what he called the "Islamization of all knowledge." Faruqi thought that Western science, especially the social sciences, had a harmful influence, particularly on the young. Sociology and psychology take up the subject of religious conviction and put a question mark around faith. They imply that there is no objective reality. According to the social sciences, if we hold religious beliefs it's because we've been conditioned to do so. To combat this mind-set, it's necessary to construct a system of knowledge consistent with Islamic premises—to make the social sciences consistent with Islamic doctrines. Faruqi developed these ideas in various books, most notably *The Cultural Atlas of Islam and An Islamic Formulation of the Social Sciences*.

What place does fundamentalism have within the full range of Islamic faith and practice?

This is difficult to discuss, because there is no equivalent for the word "fundamentalism" in Arabic. In one sense, Islam is inherently fundamentalist in that it understands the Qur'an to be a literal dictation to Muhammad of a book in heaven. His mental processes or personal preferences are not at all involved in the text of the Qur'an. It is simply the result of a mysterious process of inspiration or revelation that comes down upon him. The orthodox view (with which I don't agree) is that Muhammad was illiterate. That makes the text of the Qur'an all the more God's word, because it couldn't have come from Muhammad. The 13th-century mystic Jalal ed-Din Rumi gives a vivid image of Muhammad's role in transmitting the Qur'an: Muhammad is like a stone lion in a garden. Out of the lion's mouth comes a spout of water. Everyone knows that a cunning plumber has contrived a pipe to use as a conduit to conduct the water through the lion.

In Islam, the more something is of God, the less the human is needed. In contrast, the biblical view is that the more the divine is giving, the more the human is recruited. The biblical prophets are vivid personalities, not ciphers. Each has his own unique style and imagery.

But the Qur'an has been considered a literal scripture from the beginning. This is what accounts for the importance of calligraphy and recitation in Islam. One mustn't make a mistake in recitation, since one is repeating the very words of God. For most Christians, the New Testament is not that kind of writing. We see it as a book about what is antecedent to itself—the person and work of Christ, the Word made flesh, teaching and suffering among us.

Though the Qur'an does need interpretation, Muslims don't approach it with the kind of almost overconfidence that sometimes marks Christian exegesis of the Bible. A Muslim once said to me, "You play fast and loose with your scripture." That is how Muslims react to our sense that we need to discern what the text could mean—especially, for example, when we deal with the Gospel of John. We question whether we can accept the text as giving us the actual words of Jesus, as we think the parables do. Why do Jesus' words sound so different in the Fourth Gospel? What is John doing here? Those are legitimate questions for us, questions that are a part of the integrity of our faith. One Muslim has referred to "the liquidity of the Christian scriptures as you treat them." He says it's like the liquidity of capital—we make it do what we want it to do.

Another factor is that Muslims understand Islam as the final religion, and Jesus as the next-to-last in a long succession of prophets. The Qur'an is the book that perfects and, if need be, corrects all previous revelation, going right back to Abraham. That gives Muslims an enormous sense of finality, which tends to preclude a will to be really critical or even investigative about what they believe.

Is there a place for historical criticism in Islam, the kind of criticism Western scholars started applying to the biblical text in the 18th century?

Not that kind of textual criticism. But Muslims do have a principle of exegesis: the horizontal plain of Muhammad's revelation, which he received over 23 years, from 609, when he was 40, until his death in 632. To understand the text, you need to know what Muslims call the "occasions of revelation," that is, when and in what circumstances a verse or chapter came to Muhammad. The context is the clue to the content.

There's a second very interesting interpretive question that some Muslims will recognize and take up, but others tend to ignore because it's too daunting—they see it as a slippery slope. The question has to do with the finality of the text. Why does this final revelation come to Arabia in the seventh century of the Christian era? How do we take a revelation there and then into the 20th-century global culture?

We now have all sorts of issues that technology off-loads onto ethics. How do we behave about birth control? How do we respond to the idea of international human rights now that we have the United Nations and the concept of common human values? Can we still hold that what happens in our country is our own affair, and that no others have a right to intrude? Does world opinion have the right to concern itself with how women are treated in Saudi Arabia? The 20th century is very different from the seventh. You can claim that the revelation is final, but it becomes a museum piece unless it continues to apply to your time.

How might Muslims—and Christians—deal with these intellectual problems now confronting Islam?

There are ambiguities in the Qur'an, and passages that can be interpreted in different ways. One can, for example, base the argument for the equality of the sexes on certain Qur'anic passages. And there are articulate and courageous Muslim women—like Fatima Mernissi in Morocco—who are making this point. It's important for us not to say, "Look here, the West has Jeffersonian values about the rights of women, values we'd like to see you adopt," but to argue instead from the Qur'an itself, citing verses like the one stating that God has ordained love and tenderness between the male and female in marriage, or that no man has two hearts in one bosom. I take that to mean that polygamy is impossible because no man can love two wives equally.

Even the verse that has been interpreted for centuries as giving men permission to marry up to four women says a man can do so only if he treats them all equally. But what does equality mean in this context? If it means dividing the budget equally between the wives or spending an equal number of nights with each, then it's feasible to marry more than one. But if it means having an equal affection of the heart for each, the proviso is unattainable and the permission lapses. By this exegesis, the verse does not legitimate plural marriage; it requires monogamy. This is the kind of exegesis by which women can have the text on their side. And it's not dishonest to do this.

The best way to deal with religious persecution is to promote liberty of conscience for people of all faiths.

On the interfaith question, the Qur'an contains passages that say God himself ordained human diversity in order that people might compete together to be the best. God has sanctified diverse cultures by giving each a pattern of worship, a ritual to follow. Another verse says that there is no people to whom a prophet has not been sent. Does that make Socrates a prophet to the Greeks? Is the Buddha a prophet? Of course, there are other verses that seem to restrict pluralism. If a text is ambiguous, you might as well interpret it in the ways that seem the best and most just. That's how reformers work.

What do you make of the current U.S. focus on curbing the persecution of Christians in other countries, particularly Islamic countries?

We must, of course, try to make sure that religious persecution isn't covered up, and we must try to get the facts straight, avoiding exaggeration. I think that the best way to approach this problem is to promote liberty of conscience for people of all faiths, not just for Christian minorities. Liberty of soul and the freedom to change one's religious affiliation are human rights that should be asserted on behalf of all.

We must be concerned with how Muslim, as well as Christian, minorities are treated in Islamic countries. We must be concerned about the Muslim scholars who are persecuted in their own countries or are forced into exile. We don't want our concern about religious persecution to come across as a Western power's concern about Christians only. We want to dispel the old suspicion that the Christians in the East provide a way for Western interests to gain a toehold in Eastern societies. Christians in places like Egypt and Palestine want to cast their lot with the others of their own societies; they don't want to be thought of as dubious citizens. We don't want to compromise their situations still more by making them seem a kind of enemy in the camp.

What about the Muslim minorities in the West?

A big dilemma for Muslims today is that many have lost the shelter of the Islamic state. About a quarter of the world's Muslims live as minorities in places where they must practice Islam as "just a religion," to use a Western phrase. For them, Islam is a system of worship and ethics and a community, but not a source of social and political power.

There is a precedent for this in Islam in the first 13 years of Muhammad's mission. There are passages in the Qur'an where God says that Muhammad has no responsibility except to preach the message. It wasn't until after the Hijrah—Muhammad's flight from Mecca to what became Medina—in 622 that Islam became a political force.

Now many Muslims find themselves in that pre-Hijrah situation in which the faith began. If we believe in the hand of God behind historical developments, then today's Muslim diaspora—Turks in Germany, Algerians in France, Pakistanis in Britain, Indonesians in Holland, people from many Islamic countries in Canada and the U.S.—seems a call for Muslims to coexist with those of other religions. Many Muslims are being called to live in varying circumstances, as fellow citizens, voting, getting elected, taking part in local and national government—but all in the context of remaining a minority, with the psychological uncertainty that all minorities experience.

What problems does Islam without statehood pose for Muslims, and what effect might it have on Islam?

I think that this is, paradoxically, a realm of hope for the world and for Islam. Muslims in this condition are forced to interrogate the very core of their faith. How can Islam be true, full and authentic when it lacks one element that historically has been understood as a sine qua non of the faith? Two new journals in Britain are devoted to thinking through this problem: the *Journal of the Institute of Muslim Minority Affairs* and the *Journal of Qur'anic Studies*. The brochure for the latter states that it is open to the free exercise of scholarship in the interpretation of the Qur'an and invites non-Muslims to share in the debate.

The rise of Muslim minority populations makes urgent the question of international law: What is the appropriate treatment for religious minorities? To its credit, Islam has a long tradition of conditional toleration for Jewish and Christian minorities, to whom it gives *dhimmi* status—the freedom to practice their religion, and to educate their progeny in it, on condition that they submit politically to the Islamic state. In some places this took the form of a kind of contract: a minority had to submit or forfeit its right to remain in the country. Such an approach is not viable in the modern world, where we have the concept of equal citizenship. The status of minorities must not include political subservience.

The position of Muslim minorities raises the whole question of the nature of religious authority. Can Islam move toward accepting the secular state—secular in the sense that the state treats equally citizens of any and every tradition, consonant with public order and the common good? There is, of course, always prejudice against minorities on the part of majorities; there are all kinds of ways to put minorities in an inferior position. But the ideal of the secular state—that all may be what they are, that believers in all faiths are common subjects of the state—can be argued on the basis of Islam itself, if one goes back to pre-Hijrah times and to the concept of the *dhimmi*. This makes religion a private affair in terms of how the government views religious practice. But it does not imply that belief is nothing more than a private option. It doesn't require the kind of secularity that means nobody has any belief at all. We need urgently to make this distinction. As Islam recognizes its vocation to be just a religion in situations where it is a minority faith, the quality of Islamic faith in its cohesion and understanding of compassion can contribute to the common good of other faiths as well.

International law requires us to get away from the notion that national boundaries are frontiers across which ideas may not cross. The concept of international human rights from which no country is exempt is consonant with the idea that Shari'a, the large body of legal tradition that informs the Muslim community about how God requires it to live, is in some sense the rule of God.

How might Christians counter the view that Islam is a great threat to Western civilization?

This image of a confrontation between Islam and the West is much more prevalent in the U.S. than it is in Europe, and the American media seem to promote it. But we can give the lie to this reading of history. There is an understanding, both Christian and Muslim, that we should keep in mind: With what measure you mete, it shall be meted out to you. In other words, the way you treat another party is likely to contribute to the response that party makes to you. If you are ready to assume a capacity that is positive and reciprocal, there's a better chance that you will find it.

A verse from the Sermon on the Mount is very appropriate to this context—"Judge not and you shall not be judged." Like many of the sayings of Jesus, this could be misread. It doesn't mean that you should never have an opinion. The point is that your judgment is an index to your character. The way we judge has a way of judging us. Our judgments must be based on a perceptive honesty and a wide compassion. When two cultures accuse each other of satanism, the only one who gains is Satan himself.

The openhearted observer of Islam in the West can discern the shape of hope in the increasing willingness of people of the two faiths to come together for dialogue and consultation on the mutual problems they face; in the reevaluation of Islam forced upon Muslims by their minority status in many places; and in the development of the concept of international law and universal human rights. We must do our best to contribute to the fullfillment of that hope.

ISLAM & CHRISTIANITY FACE TO FACE

An old conflict & prospects for a new ending

John L. Esposito

The recent Taliban capture of Kabul and control of much of Afghanistan, Hamas's continued threats to disrupt the Palestinian-Israeli peace process, bombing attacks targeting American military in Saudi Arabia, attacks by Muslim extremists against Christians in Egypt and the Sudan, the brutal murder of Trappist monks in Algeria, communal riots from Nigeria to Indonesia between Muslims and Christians—these are the events associated with Islam that capture headlines and cause grave concern.

At the same time, Islamic political and social activism have become powerful institutionalized forces in mainstream society. Islamic candidates have held cabinet-level positions and been elected parliamentarians, mayors, and city officials in countries as diverse as Tunisia, Algeria, Egypt, Sudan, Lebanon, Turkey, Pakistan, Yemen, Kuwait, Malaysia, and even Israel. Secular Turkey has its first Islamist prime minister, Malaysia's deputy prime minister was the founder of a major Malaysian Islamic movement, and Bosnia has a president often identified as an Islamist.

Islam has also proved a potent social force in civil society. Islamically inspired institutions—schools, hospitals, clinics, legal aid societies, social services, banks, publishing houses—have proliferated. Islamists have won elections in professional associations from faculty and student groups to organizations for physicians, lawyers, and engineers.

While there is much that could be written about the positive interaction and exchanges between Islam and Christianity, the realities of contemporary politics and the media have produced a different set of issues. Some speak of a clash of civilizations and a new Crusade, others warn of the dangers of demonizing this major world religion, and there is the tendency of some in the post-cold war period to identify Islam as the new global threat.

Ironically, all too often we seek understanding and answers as though we are inquiring about a "foreign" or alien faith. In fact, Islam is well on the way to becoming the second largest religion in the United States and Europe in the twenty-first century. Thus, we are not just talking about strangers who are Muslims but, in a very real sense, our neighbors as well.

History of Conflict and Misunderstanding

Despite many common theological roots and beliefs, Muslim-Christian relations have often been overshadowed by conflict as the armies and missionaries of Islam and of Christendom have been locked in a struggle for power and for souls: from the fall of the Byzantine (eastern Roman) Empire before Muslim armies in the seventh century to the Crusades during the eleventh and twelfth centuries; the expulsion of the "Moors" from Spain and the Inquisition; the Ottoman threat to overrun Europe; European (Christian) colonial expansion and domination from the eighteenth to the early twentieth centuries; the political and cultural challenge of the superpowers in a period of "neocolonialism" during the latter half of the twentieth century; the creation of the state of Israel by Western "Christian" countries and consequent Palestinian exile; the competition of Christian and Muslim missionaries today, from Africa to Southeast Asia; and the contemporary reassertion of Islam in politics around the world.

Ironically, the very theological similarities of Christianity and Islam had put the two on an early collision course. Both religions had a universal message and mission. Both possessed a supercessionist theology; that is, each community believed that its covenant with God was the fulfillment of God's earlier revelation to a previous community that had gone astray. While Christians had little problem with their supercessionist views toward Judaism, a similar claim by Muslims to have the final revelation was unacceptable and, more than that, a threat to the uniqueness and divinely mandated role of Christianity to be the only means to salvation.

Christendom experienced the early conquests and expansion of Islam as a theological, political, and civilizational challenge to its religious and political hegemony. Muslim rule, and with it the message of Islam, quickly spread from the Byzantine and Persian Empires to Syria, Iraq, and Egypt, and swept across North Africa and into Europe where Muslims ruled Spain and the Mediterranean from Sicily to Anatolia.

Non-Muslims in the Islamic State

For non-Muslim populations in Byzantium and Persia, who were subjugated to foreign rulers, Islamic rule meant an exchange of rulers rather than a loss of independence. Many in Byzantium willingly exchanged Greco-Roman rule for new Arab masters—fellow Semites—with whom they had closer linguistic and cultural affinities. Christians and Jews were regarded as "People of the Book" (those who had possessed a scripture/revelation from God). In exchange for allegiance to the state and payment of a poll (head) tax, these "protected" (*dhim-mi*) peoples could practice their faith and be governed by their religious leaders and law in matters of faith and private life (family laws).

Thus, Islam proved more tolerant than imperial Christianity, providing greater religious freedom for Jews and indigenous Christians; most local Christian churches had been persecuted as schismatics and heretics by a "foreign" Christian orthodoxy. As Francis E. Peters, writing about the early Muslim empires, has observed:

> The conquests destroyed little: what they did suppress were imperial rivalries and sectarian bloodletting among the newly subjected population. The Muslims tolerated Christianity but they disestablished it; henceforth Christian life and liturgy, its endowments, politics, and theology, would be a private not a public affair. By an exquisite irony, Islam reduced the status of Christians to that which the Christians had earlier thrust upon the Jews, with one difference. The

reduction in Christian status was merely judicial; it was unaccompanied by either systematic persecution or blood lust, and generally, though not everywhere and at all times, unmarred by vexatious behavior.

The rapid spread and development of imperial Islam produced a rich Islamic civilization, which reflected religious and cultural synthesis and exchange. With significant assistance from Christian and Jewish subjects, Muslims collected the great books of science, medicine, and philosophy from the West and the East and translated them into Arabic from Greek, Latin, Persian, Coptic, Syriac, and Sanskrit. The age of translation was followed by a period of great creativity as a new generation of educated Muslim thinkers and scientists made their own contributions to learning: in philosophy, medicine, chemistry, astronomy, algebra, optics, art, and architecture. The cultural traffic pattern was again reversed when Europeans, emerging from the Dark Ages, turned to Muslim centers of learning to regain their lost heritage and to learn from Muslim advances in philosophy, mathematics, medicine, and science.

From the Crusades to European Colonialism

Few events have had a more shattering and long-lasting effect on Muslim-Christian relations than the Crusades. For many in the West, the specific facts regarding the Crusades are but a dim memory. Few remember that it was the pope who called for the Crusades, and that on balance the Crusaders lost. For Muslims, the memory of the Crusades lives on as the clearest example of militant Christianity, an early harbinger of the aggression and imperialism of the Christian West. If many in the West have regarded Islam as a religion of the sword, Muslims through the ages speak of the Christian West's crusader mentality and hegemonic ambitions.

For Muslim-Christian relations, it is less a case of what actually happened in the Crusades than how they are remembered. Each community looks back with memories of its commitment to defend its faith and with heroic stories of valor and chivalry against "the infidel." Both Muslims and Christians saw the other as militant, somewhat barbaric, and fanatic in religious zeal, determined to conquer, convert, or eradicate the other, and thus an enemy of God.

A second far-reaching and influential event affecting the relationship of Islam to the West is the experience of European colonialism. Its impact and continued legacy remain alive in Middle East politics and throughout the Muslim world today. No one who has traveled in and studied the Muslim world can be oblivious to the tendency of many Muslims to associate their past and current problems in large part with the legacy of European colonialism.

European colonialism abruptly reversed a pattern of self-rule that had existed from the time of the Prophet. The vast majority of the Muslim community had possessed a sense of history in which Islam had, over the centuries, remained triumphant, and Muslims lived under Muslim rule. As the balance of power and leadership shifted to Europe, much of the Muslim world found itself either directly ruled or dominated by the Christian West, threatened by "crown and cross." On the other hand, many Europeans believed that modernity was not only the result of conditions producing the Enlightenment and the Industrial Revolution, but also due to the inherent superiority of Christianity as a religion and culture. The British spoke of the "white man's burden" and the French of their "mission to civilize" as they colonized much of Africa, the Middle East, and South and Southeast Asia.

The external threat to Muslim identity and autonomy from European Christendom raised profound religious as well as political questions for many in the Muslim world: What had gone wrong? Why had Muslim fortunes been so thoroughly reversed? Was it Muslims who had failed Islam, or Islam that had failed Muslims? How were Muslims to respond?

Western Neocolonialism and the Islamic Resurgence

The creation of Israel and the politics of the cold war were regarded as signs of a new colonialism in the post–World War II period, a hegemonic chess game between the United States and the Soviet Union that threatened the identity and integrity of the Muslim world.

Israel was considered a European/American colony in the midst of the Arab nation. For Arab leaders, Palestine provided a cause that they could exploit to buttress their power domestically and internationally. The struggle against Israel symbolized the battle against imperialism, provided a common cause and sense of unity, and distracted from the failures of many regimes. Both the secular and the religiously oriented—Arab nationalists and Islamic activists—found common ground in their focus on liberating Palestine, the great *jihad* ("struggle," holy war) against Western imperialism.

The Iranian revolution of 1978–79 focused attention on "Islamic fundamentalism" and with it the spread of political Islam in other parts of the Muslim world. However, this contemporary revival had its origins and roots in the late 1960s and early 1970s in such disparate areas as Egypt and Libya as well as Pakistan and Malaysia. The ongoing failures of many of these countries' economies, the growing disparities between rich and poor, corruption, and the general impact and disruption of modernity spawned disillusionment and a sense of failure within modern Muslim states. In addition, American ignorance of and hostility toward Islam and the Middle East, often seen by Muslims as a "Christian Crusader" mentality in-

fluenced by Orientalism and Zionism, were blamed for misguided U.S. political-military policies: support for an "un-Islamic," authoritarian Shah of Iran, massive military and economic funding of Israel, and the backing of an "unrepresentative" Christian-controlled government in Lebanon. These crises reinforced a prevailing sense of impotence and inferiority among many Muslims, the product of centuries of European colonial dominance that left a legacy of admiration (of the West's power, science, and technology) as well as deep resentment (of its dominance, penetration, and exploitation).

For Islamic political activists, Islam is a total or comprehensive way of life as revealed in the Qur'an, God's Word, mirrored in the example of the Prophet Muhammad and the first Muslim community-state, and embodied in the Shariah, Islamic law. Thus, for Islamists the renewal and revitalization of governments and societies require the restoration or reimplementation of Islamic law, which is the blueprint for an Islamically guided and socially just state and society. While Islamists reject the Westernization and secularization of society, modernization through science and technology is accepted. However, the pace, direction, and extent of change should, they believe, be subordinated to Islamic belief and values, so that the penetration and excessive dependence on Western values can be avoided.

In the 1990s, Islamic revivalism has developed from small radical groups or organizations on the periphery of society to a significant part of mainstream Muslim society. This "quiet revolution" has produced a new class of modern, educated, but Islamically oriented elites and organizations that exist alongside their secular counterparts. They have become part and parcel of mainstream religion and society, found among the middle and lower classes, educated and uneducated, professionals and workers, young and old, men, women, and children. A new generation of Islamically oriented leaders may be found in Egypt, the Sudan, Tunisia, Turkey, Jordan, Iran, Malaysia, Indonesia, Yemen, Kuwait, Saudi Arabia, and Pakistan.

Islam & the West: Challenge or Threat?

According to some, Islam and the West are on a political, demographic, and religio-cultural collision course. Past images of a Christian West turning back threatening Muslim armies are conjured up and linked to current political as well as demographic realities. Immigrants and immigration have become an explosive political issue in Europe and America.

If the 1980s were dominated by fear of "other Irans" or of underground terrorist groups, the emergence of Islam's "quiet revolution" has increased fears of political Islam. Its global force is now seen not only in the Islamic Republics of Iran, Sudan, and Afghanistan, but also in the emergence of Islamists as effective political and social actors in Turkey, Egypt, Jordan, Lebanon, Kuwait, Yemen, Pakistan, Bangladesh, Malaysia, and Indonesia.

Governments in the Middle East, both Arab states and Israel, play on such fears, warning of the dangers of "fundamentalism," domestically and internationally. Often their appeals conveniently obscure their own domestic political, economic, and social problems and causes for opposition and instability. The "fundamentalist" threat, described monolithically and equated solely with radicalism and terrorism, becomes a convenient pretext for crushing political opposition, nonviolent as well as violent, and backing away from previous commitments to democratization or greater political participation. For example, Tunisia's Zeine Abedin Ben Ali used such an excuse to "decapitate" his Islamic opposition (the Renaissance party which had emerged as the leading opposition in elections), as well as to silence secular opposition and thus win the elections of 1993 with 99.91 percent of the vote. With the end of the cold war and the threat of communism, a similar mission with a new threat, "Islamic fundamentalism," has become a primary excuse for Israel and Egypt to attract foreign aid or excuse human rights records of abuses. Fear of fundamentalists coming to power has often influenced European and American attitudes toward Turkey, Bosnia, Chechniya, Central Asia and, more broadly, the promotion of democratization in the Muslim world.

At the same time the record of Islamic experiments in Iran, Sudan, Pakistan, and, most recently, Afghanistan has reinforced fears of the export of terrorism. Reports of the forced veiling and seclusion of women, militant attacks against Christians in Egypt and Sudan, and discrimination against the Bahai in Iran and the Ahmadiyya in Pakistan exacerbate concerns about the rights of women and minorities. While many modern Muslim states granted equality of citizenship to all regardless of religious faith, the contemporary resurgence has resurrected pressures to reimplement classical Islamic laws which inform traditional attitudes and values that have remained operative in the minds and outlooks of many traditionally minded Muslims. Legal change implemented or imposed from the top down by a minority elite has not in many cases significantly changed popular culture and values.

In recent years, there are those who speak of a clash of civilizations, a clash between Islam and "our" modern secular (or Judaeo-Christian) democratic values and culture. Those who contrast Islamic civilization or culture with "our" modern Western culture conveniently slip into an "us and them" mentality that obscures the diversity of both sides, and implies a "static, retrogressive them" and a "dynamic, progressive us." Several things should be kept in mind. The history of religions demonstrates that all three Abrahamic faiths (as indeed all religions) change; the issue is not change but degrees of change. All three traditions have within them divergent orientations: orthodox, conservative, reformist, fundamentalist, "secularist," etc. Judaism and Christianity, responding to pressing modern political, social, economic or cultural challenges/realities, experienced their reformations, but with diverse responses that continue to be reflected in their differing communities. For example, think of the vast diversity that exists between Orthodox and Reform Jews, Southern Baptist and Unitarian Christians on issues ranging from evolution to abortion.

Islam is experiencing, sometimes in similar and sometimes in dissimilar ways, the tensions and conflicts that accompany the interactions between tradition and change. The West, and Judaism and Christianity, experienced centuries-long struggles as a result of the political revolutions that accompanied the emergence of modern states and societies to the Reformation (which included warfare as well as theological disputation). Islam and Muslim communities have been severely limited by a lack of freedom and autonomy, first because of European colonialism and more recently, in many countries, by authoritarian governments. As with the Western experience, this political, social, and religio-cultural reformation or revolution is at times one of radical change whose experiments and progress can in the short term degenerate into violent revolution and radicalism, provoked by both political and religious authoritarianism and demagoguery.

Most Muslims are not Islamic political activists. In fact, such activists constitute only a minority, albeit a significant minority. Moreover, we must distinguish between a violent minority, bent upon the overthrow of governments, and a majority that, given the opportunity, will work within the system to bring about change. Even more difficult, of course, is distinguishing between legitimate and illegitimate uses of violence. When are revolutions just? When is violence or warfare defensive rather than offensive? When is it just or unjust?

Islam in the West

The remarkable growth of Islam in Europe and America, where it is now the second- or third-largest religion, has raised fears about whether Muslims can be loyal citizens and even whether they will bring "fundamentalist" violence to the West. The World Trade Center bombing as well as bombings in Paris and France help to feed such fears. France has insisted on integration, not multiculturalism. Muslims have experienced levels of discrimination in society and the media in Europe and America that would simply not be tolerated by Christians and Jews.

Islam, like Christianity and Judaism, is a religion that provides a framework of faith and meaning that has transformed lives and societies. At the same time, again like Judaism and Christianity, it has been used or abused to justify violence and oppression. We can speak equally about militant Judaism and Christianity as we can about militant Islam. Part of our problem of interpretation is that when a Jewish extremist murdered Muslims at

France & Algeria

Judging from the forensic evidence, investigators have indicated that a December 3, 1996 subway bombing in Paris was likely perpetrated by the same Algerian terrorists responsible for similar attacks the year before. In 1995, the violence swirled around the *ex post facto* election of Algerian President Liamine Zeroual. Zeroual had been made president in 1994 by fiat of the military, which had seized power in 1992 to pre-empt the election of an Islamic government that was, ironically, antipathetic to democracy. This time, the violence came on the heels of a new constitution that banned Islamic parties and granted the president discretionary power. The Armed Islamic Group, militants in Algeria's raging civil war, has repeatedly demanded that France cut its political and economic ties with Zeroual's régime.

Despite these pretexts, however, it is clear that the indiscriminate killings served no positive political goals. The subway bombings, as well as the May 1996 executions of seven French monks who lived in the mountains of Algeria, did little more than play into the hands of belligerents in a purported "clash of civilizations."

Terrorists like the Armed Islamic Group cast a pall upon Islam and give ammunition to French xenophobes like Jean-Marie Le Pen and his National Front faithful. But do things really come down to Islam versus "the West," or to humanity against barbarity, here *and* there? The rhetoric of opposing cultures disguises a primitive lust for power and disparages civilization and culture. In what the French newspaper *Le Monde* has called "the Algerian night," this manipulation cries out.

The reaction to the monks' murders makes for an instructive example. While the French Islamic community expressed its outrage that such crimes would be committed in the name of Islam, Le Pen shamelessly exploited "this tragic incident." First he took a swipe at the French government for having imperiled the monks, then he turned on the monks themselves for having cared for injured fighters on both sides in the French-Algerian colonial war. "A different conception from ours of civic loyalism," he noted—as if the monks had thereby made themselves anathema (*Le Monde*, May 26–27, 1996).

Like today's Chinese and Iraqi Tyrants, Le Pen & Co. and the Algerian terrorists have all stigmatized "globalization." But indifferent to contradiction, they preach the same hate and practice the same stupid acts of violence the whole world over. As the philosopher Paul Feyerabend reflected toward the end of his life, there is no such thing as a "culturally authentic" murder. Against his own earlier relativism, he argued that culture is not an envelope, but the mode of our openness to life and its mysteries.

A friend has told me that now, on the Paris subway, there is only silence and suspicion. Will the barbarians win? In the aftermath of the latest bombing, Henri Tincq, *Le Monde*'s religion correspondent, quoted the hopeful words of the rector of a suburban Paris mosque: "It is in distress and misfortune that we recognize one another as brothers" (December 6, 1996).

BERNARD G. PRUSAK

Bernard G. Prusak *is Commonweal's 1996–1997 editorial intern.*

---

prayer in the Hebron mosque or assassinated Prime Minister Itzhak Rabin, or when Christian extremists, calling themselves the army of God, blew up an abortion clinic, we reflexively distinguished between the mainstream faith of Jews and Christians and the twisted use of religion by fanatics. Making an equivalent distinction with regard to Islam does not regularly occur. Similarly, while some do not object to the mixing of religion and politics in Israel, Eastern Europe, or Latin America (liberation theology), they will do so in a blanket way when it comes to Islam.

As Jews faced the challenges of preserving a sense of identity, community, and faith within an American society dominated by Christian culture and values, Muslims today as a religious minority face a similar challenge within a Judaeo-Christian or secular America. Real understanding can begin when we, the majority, come to realize that, despite our differences, there is a common Judaeo-Christian-Islamic heritage shared by all the children of Abraham, and that Islam is not a "foreign" or Middle Eastern religion any more than Judaism and Christianity. The Muslim presence in America spans centuries, not decades, and with a population of at least from 4 to 6 million, Muslims are indeed "us." The failures of our educational system to make us aware of these facts and our media's presentation of present Islam and Muslims only through "headline events" have distorted or obscured these realities.

Conclusion

This is an exceptionally dynamic and fluid period in Muslim history. Diverse voices in the Muslim world are grappling with issues from scriptural criticism and exegesis, modernism, democracy, and pluralism to women's rights and family values. The voices for substantive change are a minority and themselves divided, much as was the case, for example, in Roman Catholicism in the late nineteenth and the first half of the twentieth century regarding modernism, pluralism, biblical criticism, and dissent. The days of excommunication, silencing, or banishment, the index of forbidden books, the easy consignment of "others" to hell, the struggle between the religious establishment and the laity may be in large part gone, but are not all that far behind us. For Muslims, who struggle with similar problems in many societies where political participation and freedom of expression have been restricted, and authoritarianism, patriarchy, and violence all too common, the battle can be especially contentious.

The fundamental question or issue for contemporary Muslims, one which affects Muslim-Christian relations as well, is the direction of Islamic revival or reform. Will it simply be a process of restoration of classical law, or will it be one of reformation: a reformulation of Islamic law that distinguishes between the immutable and the mutable, between that which is divine and that which is the product of human interpretation? For believers everywhere, this is an all-too-familiar question.

Contemporary Islam challenges us all to know and understand the richness and diversity of the Muslim experience. Followers of Christianity and Judaism are specifically challenged to recall or to become aware of the faith of Islam, to acknowledge their Muslim brothers and sisters as children of Abraham. Muslim governments are challenged to be more responsive to popular demands for political liberalization and greater popular participation, to tolerate rather than repress opposition movements (including Islamic organizations and parties), and to build viable, democratic institutions. At the same time, new Islamic governments and movements are challenged to demonstrate by word and action that they acknowledge the rights of others, that pluralism and human rights are not valued only when Muslims seek access to power but also when they are in power. Self-criticism and the denunciation of religious extremism, intolerance, and authoritarianism are the only means by which Islamist claims can be credible.

Western powers are challenged to stand by the democratic values they embody and to recognize authentic populist movements and the right of the people to determine the nature of their governments and leadership, whether they choose a secular or a more Islamically oriented path.

And finally, as Christians and Jews, or their secular counterparts, view the changing specter of Islam, they need to remember their own histories. Moreover, they must seek to understand before they judge, not to excuse, but to be sure that their judgments, which have implications both internationally and domestically, are fair and informed.

John L. Esposito *is professor of religion and international affairs and director of the Center for Muslim-Christian Understanding at Georgetown University. Editor-in-chief of* The Oxford Encyclopedia of the Modern Islamic World, *Esposito's other publications include* The Islamic Threat: Myth or Reality? *and* Islam: The Straight Path *(all Oxford University Press).*

From *Commonweal,* January 31, 1997, pp. 11-16. © 1997 by Commonweal Foundation. For subscriptions, call toll-free: 1-888-495-6755 www.commonwealmagazine.org. Reprinted by permission.

UNIT 10

Religion Facing the Modern World

Unit Selections

49. **Religion Makes a Comeback (Belief to Follow)**, Jack Miles
50. **Oh, Gods!** Toby Lester
51. **Doper or Devotee?** Kim Leighton
52. **Fundamentalism**, R. Scott Appleby and Martin E. Marty

Key Points to Consider

- What are some of the factors that have led to the growth of "institutionalized anti-institutionalism" in contemporary American religion?

- Why are there so many different religions in the world today?

- Can science and religion coexist? Defend your answer.

- Should drug use be legal if it has a ritual role in an accepted religious tradition? Why or why not?

- What is fundamentalism? What role does it play in contemporary American religion?

 **Links: www.dushkin.com/online/**
These sites are annotated in the World Wide Web pages.

American Religion Resources
http://www.academicinfo.net/amrelig.html

New Religious Movements Resources
http://www.gtu.edu/library/LibraryNRMLinks.html

In contemporary American society, a conscious involvement in and commitment to the practice of religion is on the decrease. Moreover, urban peoples worldwide are moving in a similar direction. This has been an ongoing trend since the latter half of the twentieth century. While most Americans continue to profess a belief in the Divine, relatively few find a need to purposely integrate more than a modicum of sectarian religious involvement and values into their daily lives. Consequently, there has been a gradual movement in America away from active participation in organized religion.

A major stimulus for this move away from religion seems to be the increasing dependence on science over belief and faith. As humans become more dependent on technology, there tends to be a diminished dependence on the spirit world. For an ever-increasing number, science is their religion. It is the foundation upon which their beliefs and understandings of the world are built. They perceive it to be based on fact rather than faith, and therefore it is seen as far more dependable. It is the domain of truth. Another reason for this shift is the growing sense of indi-

viduality, in which independence becomes the goal. Dependence on a divinity or a religion is seen, then, as a weakness.

But, religious belief has not yet died. In many ways, it is actually making a comeback. However, for the most part it is not a return to traditional religion. Instead, Americans are finding innovative ways to express their faith and to find meaning in religious belief and affiliation. Every day, new forms of religious expression emerge, new movements to meet the changing demands of the contemporary world.

The first two articles in this unit look at some of the new forms that Americans are finding to involve themselves in religion. While some find comfort in traditional avenues, others seek out innovative paths for participation in religion.

The final two articles deal with the issue of religious belief, commitment, and practice. The first of these looks at the case of the Jamaican Ras Tafari religious tradition and the confrontation between religious freedom and current drug laws. The final article attempts to present an accurate picture of contemporary religious fundamentalism, its inspirations and its goals.

Faith Is an Option

Religion Makes a
Comeback

(Belief to Follow)

**America has outgrown its 'take it or leave it' attitude toward religion.
Now, even people without faith are looking for God.**

By JACK MILES

Is America in the grip of a religious revival? Hundreds of thousands of Christian Promise Keepers rally in Washington, and hundreds of thousands of black men gather, at a Muslim's call, to make "atonement." Religion comes to life on television in series like "Seventh Heaven," "Touched by an Angel" and "Nothing Sacred." Religious books, once ghettoized by the publishing trade, are promoted heavily by the biggest chains, reviewed in major newspapers and monitored closely by Publishers Weekly. The Pope, of all people, writes a runaway best seller. Time and Newsweek seem virtually obsessed with religion: everything from the Infant Jesus to the Baby Dalai Lama.

Or is religion continuing the slow fade perennially lamented by religious leaders? Jews worry about the high rate of intermarriage. Catholics worry that too few young people seem willing to serve as nuns or priests. Mainstream Protestants worry that parish rolls are shrinking, with national budgets shrinking apace. And then there is unbelief, the ever popular default option. On a head count of purest honesty, would not these unbelievers constitute the biggest "church" in America?

One key to making sense of these contradictory indicators is the unique functioning of individualism in American religious culture. As long ago as 1840, Alexis de Tocqueville wrote of the pervasiveness in American life of "a calm and considered feeling which disposes each citizen to isolate himself from the mass of his fellows and withdraw into the circle of family and friends; with this little society formed to his taste, he gladly leaves the greater society to look after itself."

What this "calm and considered feeling" produces in the realm of religion is an institutionalized anti-institutionalism. Americans are particularly at ease with forms of religious expression that require little in the way of organizational commitment and impose little in the way of group identity. Religious books, television shows and one-time events like marches and revivals all meet those criteria. Less in the individualist American grain is church or synagogue or mosque membership, which does indeed impose a group identity and which, even more important, demands regular attendance, steady financial support and religious education of the young. In general, classic organized religion functions more as a corrective to American individualism than as an expression of it; for that very reason, it is both prized and resisted.

Collective religious identity is further weakened and individual religious autonomy further strengthened by the separation of religion and nationality in American culture—the fact that an American may be of any religion or none and still be fully an American. In Bosnia, if you are a Catholic, you are a Croat, and vice versa, to the point that if you change your religion from Catholicism to Orthodoxy or Islam, you will feel as if you have also changed your nationality to Serb or "Turk." In this country, by sharpest contrast, your American identity remains unchanged when you change your religion, a fact that makes such a change considerably easier to undertake, even repeatedly.

But if American religious individualism smoothes the path to conversion, it also smoothes the path to apostasy. Until recently, this may be what happened most often. Even though conversion in the U.S. was easy by European standards, it was easier still to drop out of religion totally. The complications facing a back-slid Protestant, a lapsed Catholic or a nonobservant Jew were simple compared with those facing a Southern Baptist converting to Catholicism or a Catholic converting to Judaism or a Jew converting to any form of Christianity. By condemning the turncoat so much more harshly than the deserter, organized religion may have actually fostered desertion.

By the same token, if Americans now take conversion more casually, the result may be an aggregate *increase* in religious participation. Two years ago I attended the wedding of a Catholic and a Jew, blessed jointly by a priest and a rabbi. Forty years ago, the marriage itself could doubtless have taken place one way or another, but not the doubly sanctified wedding. Instead, quite probably, the young wedding partners would have become dropouts from their respective traditions. In one way, the joint wedding ceremony represents the confounding of two proud and ancient traditions by the youthful spirit of American religious individualism. In another, it represents a victory for both over the tendency of American religious individualism to make each man and woman a happy sect of one.

THAT TENDENCY IS SCARCELY TO BE COUNTED OUT. UNBELIEF remains omnipresent in American life, the position one takes by taking no position. Is there any reason to believe that fewer Americans are defaulting to this position and that, as a result, religion in the United States is experiencing a net gain at the expense of irreligion?

A recurring experience that I had as the author of "God: A Biography" suggests to me that there has been such a gain. In that book, I wrote about God as—and only as—the literary protagonist of the Old Testament, but my very abstention from theology seemed to embolden people to tell me what they thought about God. Over time, what struck me most about these conversations was a note of defiance, the defiant rejection of the widespread assumption that doubt and religion are incompatible. "Take it (belief) or leave it (religion)"—this was the dilemma I heard brusquely rejected in favor of a third alternative: *If I may doubt the practice of medicine from the operating table, if I may doubt the political system from the voting booth, if I may doubt the institution of marriage from the conjugal bed, why may I not doubt religion from the pew?*

Why this mood of challenge or dare? Because this was a novel attitude for the people expressing it. Some were newcomers to the expression of doubt, but others were newcomers to the pew. They were excited and a bit combative, as people tend to be when they are doing something they have been told

they may not do. But *why* were they doing it? Why not just vacate the pew (or never enter it) if you have doubts about God?

In answering that question, it matters greatly where one imagines the doubting to originate. Is religion in question? Are the doubts mainly doubts about God? Or is society in question and religion one of the proposed answers, notwithstanding the difficulty of belief?

It may well be true that organized religion has functioned as a corrective to American individualism. But religion has not been the only corrective available. Innumerable secular forms of association have also tried to deliver the psychological and moral counterbalance that American individualism requires. There are Americans for whom knowledge or politics or career or therapy provides sanctuary, collective purpose and a measure of personal transcendence. There are even those for whom, as we say, bodybuilding is a religion. The question that must now be asked is whether the society that has relied so heavily on such alternatives to religion is succeeding or failing. Have its own citizens lost confidence in it? Are they suffering a secular loss of faith?

One who believes they are is the Mexican poet-philosopher Octavio Paz. In his recent memoirs, "In Light of India," Paz maintains that capitalist democracy has turned us all into "hermits," replacing "fraternity with a perpetual struggle among individuals." An admirer of Tocqueville, Paz finds the Frenchman's worst fears about the corrosive effect of individualism "utterly fulfilled in our time" and in a rather violent reaction, manages a degree of sympathy for India's religiously grounded caste system. (Paz was once Mexico's ambassador to India.) That system is full of disgraceful abuses, Paz admits, and yet, he insists, it at least brings an entire population into a stable and understood relationship.

Paz does not endorse a systematic rejection of capitalist democracy. He simply looks at what it has become and recoils. Though he cannot be said to proclaim his faith in religion, he confesses a loss of faith in the viability of Western society *without* religion. If Americans of some indeterminate number are finding themselves where Paz finds himself, we should not wonder that a religious revival may be under way. These would be Americans who, like Paz, have looked at what their society has become and recoiled, who are weary of being hermits, who want to place some collective check on their relentless competitiveness. Like Paz, these Americans have not so much recovered their faith in religion as lost their faith in the alternatives.

Several months ago, I came across a recent anthology of essays titled "Outside the Law: Narratives on Justice in America." One scathingly brilliant contribution, "The Myth of Justice," announces that "religion isn't the opiate of the people, the conception of justice is." Mere atheism, the essay explains, is for beginners. Real unbelief requires flushing out and crushing delusions like "As you reap, so will you sow" and "Whatever goes around comes around." "In your dreams, sucker," the writer sneers, and the empirical evidence for his view is undeniably enormous. Still, what his lacerating bitterness most bespeaks is the personal cost to him of his own conclusion. I read his statement with sadness, for I knew him, and I knew that shortly after writing it, he committed suicide.

Neither Octavio Paz's social despair nor this kind of personal despair leads infallibly to religion, much less to suicide, yet the alternatives can seem almost that stark. It thereby follows that, though many people who turn up in church or synagogue are not truly believers, they are not hypocrites either. What appeals to them in the first instance may be the social and esthetic refuge provided by religion, but they arrive with open minds regarding belief. This openness is the defiance I noticed in my book-tour conversations. It is the defiance of the doubter in the pew.

Organized religion typically provides for the seasons of life: for birth, childhood and coming-of-age; for marriage and other forms of life companionship; for old age and death, bereavement and remembrance; and even for a harmonious division of the calendar year into seasons of mourning and joy, repentance and triumph. Though some will always find this rigmarole repellent, more find it calming and attractive. To make their attraction intellectually acceptable, they do not require that an irrefragable case for belief be established. They require only that the case for unbelief be somewhat neutralized.

This may be little to ask, but that little is indispensable. Accordingly, even if few people have the patience or the intellectual preparation for theology, those few are disproportionately important. If the social viability of religion for the many depends significantly on the intellectual viability of religion for the few, then the question becomes: Can a post-modern path be opened for the few to a form of religion they can honestly practice?

IF THE ANSWER IS YES, I SUSPECT THAT THE FIRST STEP ON THAT path will be religious reflection on secular uncertainty—a reversal of the familiar phenomenon of secular reflection on religious uncertainty. The question "Does God really exist?" takes on a different coloring when and if the reality of other things now confidently thought to exist also comes into question. Take mathematics, for example, the paradigm of clear answers to clear questions. Reuben Hersh, in a new book titled "What Is Mathematics, Really?" writes that "mathematics is like money, war or religion—not physical, not mental, but social." There is no mathematical reality "out there," he maintains, and his mathematical agnosticism would seem rather clearly to have implications for the reality behind any theory that depends on mathematics.

Most mathematicians do not share Hersh's agnosticism, but none can deny that, despite it, he is a practicing mathematician. This state of affairs—a theory standoff between agnostics and believers that leaves practice surprisingly untouched—can be documented in many other disciplines. Why may it not be so in theology as well? Some who come to worship believing in the old way might find this stance strange, just as some mathematicians find Hersh's stance strange, but would they bar the door?

Religion has always been, among other things, a response to the intellectual inadequacy of the human species: neither individually nor collectively can we know all that we need to know, much less all that we might wonder about. Recalling that fact and taking full note of the current state of secular dubiety at the highest intellectual levels, a man or woman who decides to practice a religion may do so not to acknowledge the mystery *of* religion but to acknowledge, first, the mystery *in response to which* religion has come into being and, second, the felt necessity—somewhat mysterious in itself—to live a moral life even when the grounds of morality cannot be known.

Like a jury summons that can be put off no longer, the long-postponed questions are being taken up. At the deepest level, nothing else can explain the recent resurgence of interest in religion.

In short, to ask "Does God really exist, yes or no?" may not be the right question. It might be better to ask, "Is the word 'existence' really just another word, yes or no?" When the latter question is in the air (and it increasingly is), an intellectual decision pro or con religious affiliation need not wait on a final verdict about whether God (or anything else) "really exists."

"TWO THINGS FILL THE MIND WITH EVER-INCREASING ADMIRA-tion and awe, the oftener and the more steadily we reflect on them," Immanuel Kant wrote 200 years ago, "the starry heaven above and the moral law within." Judeo-Christian morality has linked these two sources of wonder through God, the creator and guarantor of the physical as well as the moral order:

Thy steadfast love, O Lord, extends to the heavens,
thy faithfulness to the clouds.
Thy righteousness is like the mountains of God,
thy judgments are like the great deep. (Psalm 36: 5-6)

Even when silence is maintained about God, the fact that existence can be predicated of cosmos and conscience alike creates a link between the two. If, however, we begin to entertain doubts about existence as such, then all links become dubious, not just the link between the heavens above and the moral law within. Once the philosophical glue is gone, everything comes unstuck. Our various intellectual enterprises, call them what we will, may go forward unchecked, but they will go forward under an enormous question mark.

The armed-and-dangerous ignorance of religious fanaticism deserves to be quarantined. Let's be clear about that. I dread it as much as any atheist does. All the same, the trouble in which secular ideology finds itself—and it does find itself in some kind of trouble—does not seem to me to be generated wholly from without. During the cold war, Americans dared not consider the erosion of our interlocking secular beliefs any more than we dared consider the nuclear contamination of our landscape. Now, like a jury summons that can be put off no longer, the long-postponed questions are being taken up. At the deepest level, nothing else can explain the recent resurgence of interest in religion. Alas, there is a vast difference between taking the questions up and answering them.

DESPAIR, ACCORDING TO A STUDY PUBLISHED IN THE AMERICAN Heart Association's journal, is as bad for the human heart as a pack-a-day smoking habit. "Steps should be taken," writes one

Belief by the
Numbers

Who's reading which Good Book, who's praying for what and why, who's going to heaven (hint: almost all of us, or so we think).

Compiled by RUSSELL SHORTO

Just How Religious Are We?

Americans plainly have a gut feeling that they are in the midst of a secular era: in a recent survey, 60 percent of the respondents said that religion is a waning force in American life. But how accurate is that perception? Fifty years ago, 95 percent of the population said they believed in God—compared with 96 percent now. The same percentage of Americans pray today (90 percent) as did in 1947; the same percentage also still attends church once a week (41 percent), while 63 percent of the population regularly gives thanks before meals, compared with 43 percent in 1947.

It is true that American church *membership* peaked 50 years ago. But … America is still a far more observant place than it was in its earlier years.

The more than 40 percent of the population that attends weekly services places the U.S. among the most actively religious countries. Nigeria (89 percent), Ireland (84 percent) and the Philippines (68 percent) are more observant, but Canada (38 percent), Spain (25 percent), France (21 percent) and Australia (16 percent), among many others, are less so.

The Evangelical Boom

About 87 percent of Americans consider themselves Christians. And most of them attend church, at least sometimes. But the churches they go to are hardly the same old churches. Of the approximately 1,600 religions and denominations in the U.S. today, about 800 were founded since 1965.

Mainline Protestant churches have lost ground to evangelical churches; Catholicism, which has grown by nearly 400 percent in Africa since 1967, represents a slightly smaller proportion of the American population today (22 percent) than it did 30 years ago. Here's a look at how some established denominations have floundered while churches that favor evangelism have flourished.

Increase or decrease, over the past 30 years, as a proportion of the U.S. population, in percentages:

Episcopal..................-44
Methodist..................-38
Roman Catholic..............-3
Southern Baptist............+8
Mormon.....................+96
Jehovah's Witnesses.......+119
Assemblies of God.........+211
Church of God in Christ...+863

The evangelical boom has been fueled in large part by the rise of the megachurch (a church with more than 2,000 attendees as a given service). In 1970 there were 10 megachurches in America; now there are 400. How big do they get? Consider the Saddleback Valley Community Church in Lake Forest, Calif. In 1980, 8 people attended its first gathering; it now pulls 13,000 to the four services it holds over a weekend.

Not Just Christian

America's non-Christian landscape has also undergone considerable change. There are now approximately 800,000 Hindus in the country, compared with about 70,000 in 1977. The growth of Islam has been especially pronounced. There are now about as many Muslims in the U.S. (at least 3.5 million) as there are Presbyterians. The largest group of Muslims (30 percent) is from South Asia; about 25 percent are African-American; only 20 percent are Arabs (and, contrary to popular belief, only about 33 percent of Arab-Americans are Muslim).

Buddhism appears to be the fastest-growing Eastern religion, with an estimated 750,000 adherents now living in the U.S. Tibetan Buddhism is the highest-profile subgroup (thanks, in part, to celebrity converts like Richard Gere and Steven Seagal) and includes some 100,000 American converts.

The American Jewish population, meanwhile, is virtually the same size today as it was in 1960, about 5.5 million, but as a percentage of the population, Jews have slipped from 3 percent to just over 2 percent. The leading cause of the decline is intermarriage; some scholars estimate that 50 percent of the Jews who married this year married outside their religion (compared with 10 percent who did so before 1960).

The Good Book and Other
Media Properties

Americans love their Bibles: 93 percent of the homes contain at least one, and 33 percent of American adults say they read the Bible at least once a week. But as surveys have revealed, their devotion may overshadow their retention. Below, the percentage of respondents who:

Can't name the authors of the four Gospels: 54.
Don't know what a Gospel is: 63.
Can't name five of the Ten Commandments: 58.
Think Joan of Arc was Noah's wife: 10.

One of the country's largest religious publishing houses, Thomas Nelson of Nashville, reports selling about 8 million Bibles in the U.S. each year. The King James Version is easily the most popular translation. ("John seeth Jesus coming unto him, and saith, 'Behold the Lamb of God.'") The International Bible Society's "Free on the Inside" Bible, tailored for prison inmates, has sold 525,000 copies since 1994. Zondervan publishes 400 Bible editions and formats, including one aimed at the 400 million American adults who read at or below the fourth-grade level. ("John said, 'Look! The Lamb of God!'") In its first year, it has sold more than 300,000 copies.

(continued)

Sales of what Bill Anderson, president of the Christian Booksellers Association, calls "Christ-honoring product"—from books to bumper stickers to CD's—grew from $1 billion on 1980 to $4 billion in 1996. Brok and Bodie Thoene, a husband and wife who write Christian historical fiction, have 6 million books in print. The hottest knickknack is anything bearing the legend "WWJD?" (for "What Would Jesus Do?"): coffee mugs, key rings, bracelets, etc. This year, Bob Siemon Designs of Santa Ana, Calif., has sold more than 2.5 million WWJD pieces.

Television, too, has found God to its liking. In 1974, there were 9 religious TV stations in the country; by last year, there were 257. In 1974, only 1 percent of all television programming was religious, compared with 16 percent in 1996.

God does less well in cyberspace. One survey found that only 40 percent of on-line users consider themselves Christians, while just 65 percent believe in a supreme being. And 11 percent call themselves atheists (compared with 3 percent in the American population—though surveys on atheism, depending on how the questions are phrased, produce widely varying results).

Heaven? Absolutely. Hell? Well....

About 90 percent of Americans say they believe in heaven. But even some nonbelievers feel pretty good about their futures: 94 percent of all respondents say they have a fair-to-excellent chance of going to heaven. Meanwhile, 65 percent of Americans believe in the Devil (compared with the more than 75 percent who believe that angels exist and affect human affairs). And 75 percent believe in hell, though only 6 percent think they'll wind up there.

Selective Belief

In one study, 87 percent of American adults said they "believe in the resurrection of Christ." But another found that 39 percent feel Jesus did not return bodily from death; even 35 percent of born-again Christians agree.

Catholics remain among the most devoted worshipers, albeit selectively so. About 85 percent consider themselves "religious," and 75 percent say the belief in Mary as the mother of God is "very important." Meanwhile, 82 percent of Catholics say that using birth control is "entirely up to the individual," and 64 percent agree that "one can be a good Catholic without going to Mass."

American Jews, too, remain unbound by traditional guidelines. According to a recent poll of Conservative Jews, 62 percent believe that they are "obligated to obey" traditional Jewish law, but 62 percent believe that they can be "religious" without being "particularly observant." Meanwhile, 67 percent do not support the law that a child must be born of a Jewish mother to be considered Jewish.

Godlessness 101

In a recent survey of college freshmen, 15 percent indicated no religious preference—the highest figure ever and two and a half times as much as the nation as a whole.

The Christian Right: Not a Monolith

A recent poll of conservative evangelical Christians revealed a more complex set of beliefs than is commonly presented. Though 38 percent support conservative political organizations, 49 percent believe religious leaders shouldn't tell people how to vote. While 82 percent believe Christian sand Jews share the same value system, and 79 percent might vote for a Jew for President, 58 percent believe Jews need to be converted to Christianity. And 79 percent think that homosexuals are too influential in American society.

God is in the Decimal Points

Conventional wisdom holds that religioun is the balm of the oppressed. Conventional wisdom may be wrong. Americans who earn more than $75,000 are more likely to have gone to a religious service in the previous week than those earning less than $15,000 (44 percent compared with 28 percent). One possible reason: The people in the high-income group were more likely to have done something in the previous week that they later regretted doing (24 percent to 17 percent).

About 60 percent of those in the low-income group see God in Cecil B. De Mille terms: creator of the universe, bringer of rewards and punishments. Only 34 percent in the high-income group agree, with an equal percentage just as likely to think of God as a "force" that maintains the balance of nature.

The Power of Prayer

Nearly everyone in America prays at least once in a while. And among those who do, 98 percent pray for their family's health and happiness. Below, a list in percentages, of some of the other things they pray for:

World peace: 83.
Personal salvation: 78.
The return of Jesus Christ: 55.
Good Grades: 42.
The end of an addiction: 30.
Victory in sports: 23.
Material possessions: 18.
Bad tidings for someone else: 5.

Russell Shorto is a journalist and the author of "Gospel Truth."

doctor in the study, "to try to change" the cardiac patients' situation "so they gain hope or become more optimistic."

Steps should be taken by whom? In our day, religion often begins in despair—in personal despair that hardens the arteries, in cultural despair that darkens the heart, in intellectual despair that humbles the mind—and moves from there to hope, not through argument but through affiliation. (I hesitate to use the word love.) Just how anyone makes the decision to affiliate—to go it, but not alone, to be (gag) a joiner—is diffi-cult to describe and impossible to recover, but it happens, this decision, and many such decisions can accrue to a movement. A movement toward hope? Perhaps. A refusal, at least, to despair.

Jack Miles is the author of "God: A Biography," which won a Pulitzer Prize. He is the Mellon Visiting Professor Humanities at the California Institute of Technology.

OH, GODS!

Religion didn't begin to wither away during the twentieth century, as some academic experts had prophesied. Far from it. And the new century will probably see religion explode—in both intensity and variety. New religions are springing up everywhere. Old ones are mutating with Darwinian restlessness. And the big "problem religion" of the twenty-first century may not be the one you think.

BY TOBY LESTER

In 1851 the French historian and philosopher Ernest Renan announced to the world that Islam was "the last religious creation of humanity." He was more than a bit premature. At about the time he was writing, the Bahai faith, Christian Science, Mormonism, the Seventh-Day Adventists, and a major Japanese religious movement known as Tenrikyo were all just coming to life. Falun Gong and Pentecostalism—both of which now have millions and millions of members—had yet to emerge. Whoops.

Contemporary theories of social and political behavior tend to be almost willfully blind to the constantly evolving role of religion as a force in global affairs. The assumption is that advances in the rational understanding of the world will inevitably diminish the influence of that last, vexing sphere of irrationality in human culture: religion. Inconveniently, however, the world is today as awash in religious novelty, flux, and dynamism as it has ever been—and religious change is, if anything, likely to intensify in the coming decades. The spectacular emergence of militant Islamist movements during the twentieth century is surely only a first indication of how quickly, and with what profound implications, change can occur.

It's tempting to conceive of the religious world—particularly when there is so much talk of clashing civilizations—as being made up primarily of a few well-delineated and static religious blocs: Christians, Jews, Muslims, Buddhists, Hindus, and so on. But that's dangerously simplistic. It assumes a stability in the religious landscape that is completely at odds with reality. New religions are born all the time. Old ones transform themselves dramatically. Schism, evolution, death, and rebirth are the norm. And this doesn't apply only to religious groups that one often hears referred to as cults. Today hundreds of widely divergent forms of

Christianity are practiced around the world. Islam is usually talked about in monolithic terms (or, at most, in terms of the Shia-Sunni divide), but one almost never hears about the 50 million or so members of the Naqshabandiya order of Sufi Islam, which is strong in Central Asia and India, or about the more than 20 million members of various schismatic Muslim groups around the world. Think, too, about the strange rise and fall of the Taliban. Buddhism, far from being an all-encompassing glow radiating benignly out of the East, is a vast family of religions made up of more than 200 distinct bodies, many of which don't see eye-to-eye at all. Major strands of Hinduism were profoundly reshaped in the nineteenth century, revealing strong Western and Christian influences.

The fact is that religion mutates with Darwinian restlessness. Take a long enough view, and all talk of "established" or "traditional" faith becomes oxymoronic: there's no reason to think that the religious movements of today are any less subject to change than were the religious movements of hundreds or even thousands of years ago. History bears this out. Early Christianity was deemed pathetic by the religious establishment: Pliny the Younger wrote to the Roman Emperor Trajan that he could get nothing out of Christian captives but "depraved, excessive superstition." Islam, initially the faith of a band of little-known desert Arabs, astonished the whole world with its rapid spread. Protestantism started out as a note of protest nailed to a door. In 1871 Ralph Waldo Emerson dismissed Mormonism as nothing more than an "after-clap of Puritanism." Up until the 1940s Pentecostalists were often dismissed as "holy rollers," but today the *World Christian Encyclopedia* suggests that by 2050 there may be more than a billion people affiliated with the movement. In the period after World War II so many new religious movements came into being in Japan that local scholars of religion were forced to distinguish between *shin-shukyo* ("new religions") and *shin-shin-shukyo* ("new new religions"); one Western writer referred to the time as "the rush hour of the gods." The implication is clear: what is now dismissed as a fundamentalist sect, a fanatical cult, or a mushy New Age fad could become the next big thing.

Anybody who doubts the degree to which the religious world is evolving should have a look at the second edition of the *World Christian Encyclopedia*, published last year by Oxford University Press in two oversized volumes of more than 800 pages each. The encyclopedia's title is misleading: the work is not devoted exclusively to Christianity. It is, in fact, the only serious reference work in existence that attempts both to survey and to analyze the present religious makeup of the entire world. It tracks the birth of new movements, records recent growth patterns, and offers scenarios for future growth. It divides major religions into different denominations and classifies each by country of origin and global reach. It records the dates that movements were founded and the names of their founders. It's the place to turn if you want to know how many Bahais there were in 2000 in the Bahamas (1,241), how many Jews in Yemen (1,087), how many Zoroastrians in Iran (1,903,182), how many Mormons in South Africa (10,200), or how many Buddhists in the United States (2,449,570).

The prime mover and longtime editor of the encyclopedia is a soft-spoken Anglican Charismatic named David B. Barrett. A former missionary in Africa, Barrett began working on the encyclopedia in the 1960s. His idea, which explains the work's title, was to create a reliable and richly informative tool for Christian evangelists around the world. Barrett is now affiliated with the Global Evangelization Movement, in Richmond, Virginia, and with Pat Robertson's Regent University, in Virginia Beach, where he is a research professor of "missiometrics"—the science of missions.

I recently asked Barrett what he has learned about religious change in his decades of working on the encyclopedia. "The main thing we've discovered," he said, "is that there is *enormous* religious change going on across the world, all the time. It's massive, it's complex, and it's continual. We have identified nine thousand and nine hundred distinct and separate religions in the world, increasing by two or three new religions every day. What this means is that new religious movements are not just a curiosity, which is what people in the older denominations usually think they are. They are a very serious subject."

THE SECULARIZATION MYTH

Long the subject of ridicule and persecution, derided as cults, alternative religions are finally being taken seriously. The study of new religious movements—NRMs for short—has become a growth industry. NRM scholars come from a variety of backgrounds, but many are sociologists and reli-

gious historians. All are sympathetic to the idea that new religious movements should be respected, protected, and studied carefully. They tend to avoid the words "cult" and "sect," because of the polemical connotations; as a result NRM scholars are often caricatured in anti-cult circles as "cult apologists." They examine such matters as how new movements arise; what internal dynamics are at work as the movements evolve; how they spread and grow; how societies react to them; and how and why they move toward the mainstream.

The NRM field is only a few decades old, but already it has made its mark. NRM scholars were pivotal in the defanging of the anti-cult movement in the United States, which exercised considerable influence in the 1970s and 1980s and often engaged in the illegal—but frequently tolerated—practice of kidnapping and "deprogramming" members of new religious movements. In the aftermath of Waco, of the Heaven's Gate and Solar Temple suicides, and of the subway poisonings in Tokyo by Aum Shinrikyo, NRM scholars are now regularly consulted by the FBI, Scotland Yard, and other law-enforcement agencies hoping to avoid future tragedies. They are currently battling the major anti-cult legislation-directed explicitly at the "repression of cultic movements which undermine human rights and fundamental freedoms"—that was passed last year in France. (The legislation was implicitly rooted in a blacklist compiled in 1996 by a French parliamentary commission. The blacklist targets 173 movements, including the Center for Gnostic Studies, the Hare Krishnas, some evangelical Protestant groups, practitioners of Transcendental Meditation, Rosicrucians, Scientologists, Wiccans, and the Jehovah's Witnesses.)

NRM scholars have even influenced the Vatican. In 1991, as part of what was then the largest gathering of Catholic cardinals in the history of the Church, an Extraordinary Consistory was held to discuss just two matters: the "threats to life" (that is, contraception, euthanasia, and abortion) and the challenges posed to the Church by "neo-religious, quasi-religious and pseudo-religious groups." NRM scholars were involved as advisers, and the result was a surprisingly liberal report, written by Cardinal Arinze, that referred to "New Religious Movements" rather than to "cults" or "sects" and even suggested that these movements have something to teach the Church. "The dynamism of their missionary drive," the report said of the NRMs, "the evangelistic responsibility assigned to the new 'converts,' their use of the mass media and their setting of the objectives to be attained, should make us ask ourselves questions as to how to make more dynamic the missionary activity of the Church."

That dynamism also speaks to one of the significant facts of our time: the failure of religion to wither away on schedule. This is a state of affairs that the sociologist Rodney Stark addresses in the book *Acts of Faith* (2000). "For nearly three centuries," he writes, "social scientists and assorted Western intellectuals have been promising the end of religion. Each generation has been confident that within another few decades, or possibly a bit longer, humans will 'outgrow' belief in the supernatural. This proposition soon came to be known as the secularization thesis." Stark goes on to cite a series of failed prophecies about the impending demise of religion, concluding with a statement made by the American sociologist Peter Berger, who in 1968 told *The New York Times* that by "the 21st century, religious believers are likely to be found only in small sects, huddled together to resist a worldwide secular culture."

Secularization of a sort certainly has occurred in the modern world—but religion seems to keep adapting to new social ecosystems, in a process one might refer to as "supernatural selection." It shows no sign of extinction, and "theodiversity" is, if anything, on the rise. How can this be? Three decades ago the British sociologist Colin Campbell suggested an answer. A way to explore the apparently paradoxical relationship between secularization and religion, Campbell felt, might be to examine closely what happens on the religious fringe, where new movements are born. "Ironically enough," he wrote, "it could be that the very processes of secularization which have been responsible for the 'cutting back' of the established form of religion have actually allowed 'hardier varieties' to flourish."

A THEODIVERSITY SAMPLER

The variety of flourishing new religious movements around the world is astonishing and largely unrecognized in the West. The groups that generally grab all the attention—Moonies, Scientologists, Hare Krishnas, Wiccans—amount to a tiny and not particularly significant proportion of what's out there. Here are just a few representatively diverse examples of new movements from around the world:

THE AHMADIS. A messianic Muslim sect based in Pakistan, with perhaps eight million members in seventy countries, the Ahmadi movement was founded by Mirza Ghulam Ahmad, a Punjabi Muslim who began receiving divine revelations in 1876. "In order to win the pleasure of Allah," he wrote, "I hereby inform you all of the important fact that Almighty God has, at the beginning of this 14th century [in the Islamic calendar], appointed me from Himself for the revival and support of the true faith of Islam." Ahmad claimed to have been brought to earth as "the Imam of the age today who must, under Divine Command, be obeyed by all Muslims." Members of the movement are considered heretics by most Muslims and are persecuted accordingly. They are barred entry to Mecca. In the Ahmadi version of religious history Jesus escaped from the cross and made his way to India, where he died at the age of 120.

THE BRAHMA KUMARIS WORLD SPIRITUAL UNIVERSITY. A prosperous ascetic meditation movement based in India, with some 500,000 members (mostly women) worldwide, the group was founded by Dada Lekh Raj, a Hindu diamond merchant who in the 1930s experienced a series of powerful visions revealing "the mysterious entity of God and explaining the process of world transformation." Its establishment was originally rooted in a desire to give self-determination and self-esteem to Indian women. Members wear white, abstain from meat and sex, and are committed to social-welfare projects. They believe in an eternal, karmic scheme of time that involves recurring 1,250-year cycles through a Golden Age (perfection), a Silver Age (incipient degeneration), a Copper Age (decadence ascendant), and an Iron Age (rampant violence, greed, and lust—our present state). The group is recognized as a nongovernmental organization by the United Nations, with which it often works.

CAO DAI. A syncretistic religion based in Vietnam, with more than three million members in fifty countries, Cao Dai combines the teachings of Confucianism, Taoism, and Buddhism, and also builds on elements of Judaism, Christianity, Islam, and Geniism. The movement was formally established in 1926, six years after a government functionary named Ngo Ming Chieu received a revelation from Duc Cao Dai, the Supreme Being, during a table-moving séance. The movement's institutional structure is based on that of the Catholic Church: its headquarters are called the Holy See, and its members are led by a pope, six cardinals, thirty-six archbishops, seventy-two bishops, and 3,000 priests. Cao Dai is elaborately ritualized and symbolic—a blend of incense, candles, multi-tiered altars, yin and yang, karmic cycles, seances for communication with the spirit world, and prayers to a pantheon of divine beings, including the Buddha, Confucius, Lao Tzu, Quan Am, Ly Thai Bach, Quan Thanh De Quan, and Jesus Christ. Its "Three Saints" are Sun Yat-sen; a sixteenth-century Vietnamese poet named Trang Trinh; and Victor Hugo. The movement gained more adherents in its first year of existence than Catholic missionaries had attracted during the Church's previous 300 years in Vietnam.

THE RAËLIANS. A growing new international UFO-oriented movement based in Canada, with perhaps 55,000 members worldwide, primarily in Quebec, French-speaking Europe, and Japan, the group was founded in 1973 by Ra'l, a French race-car journalist formerly known as Claude Vorilhon. Ra'l claims that in December of 1973, in the dish of a French volcano called Puy-de-Lassolas, he was taken onto a flying saucer, where he met a four-foot humanoid extraterrestrial with olive-colored skin, almond- shaped eyes, and long dark hair. The extraterrestrial's first words, in fluent French, were "You regret not having brought your camera?" On six successive days Raël had conversations with the extraterrestrial, from whom he learned that the human race was the creation (by means of DNA manipulation) of beings known as the Elohim—a word that was mistranslated in the Bible as "God" and actually means "those who came from the sky." Past prophets such as Moses, the Buddha, Jesus, and Muhammad had been given their revelations and training by the Elohim, who would now like to get to know their creations on equal terms, and demystify "the old concept of God." To that end the Ra'lians have raised the money to build "the first embassy to welcome people from space." (Originally Ra'l was told that the embassy should be near Jerusalem, but Israel has been less than co-operative, and a recent revelation has led Ra'l to investigate Hawaii as a possibility.) Ra'l has also recently attracted international attention by creating Clonaid, a company devoted to the goal of cloning a human being.

SOKA GAKKAI INTERNATIONAL. A wealthy form of this-worldly Buddhism, based in Japan and rooted in the teachings of the thirteenth-century Buddhist monk Nichiren, Soka Gakkai has some 18 million members in 115 countries. It was founded in 1930 by Makiguchi Tsunesaburo and Toda Josei and then re-established after World War II, at which point it began to grow dramatically. "*Soka gakkai*" means "value-creating society," and the movement's members believe that true Buddhists should work not to escape earthly experience but, rather, to embrace and transform it into enlightened wisdom. Early members were criticized for their goal of worldwide conversion and their aggressive approach to evangelism, a strategy referred to as *shakubuku,* or "break through and overcome." In recent years the intensity has diminished. The movement is strongly but unofficially linked to New Komeito ("Clean Government Party"), currently the third most powerful group in the Japanese parliament. It is also registered as an NGO with the United Nations, and recently opened a major new liberal-arts university in southern California.

THE TORONTO BLESSING. An unorthodox new evangelistic Christian Charismatic movement, based in Canada, the movement emerged in 1994 within the Toronto Airport branch of the Vineyard Church (itself a remarkably successful NRM founded in 1974), after a service delivered by a Florida-based preacher named Rodney Howard Browne. To date about 300,000 people have visited the movement's main church. Services often induce "a move of the Holy Spirit" that can trigger uncontrollable laughter, apparent drunkenness, barking like a dog, and roaring like a lion. The group finds support for its practices in passages from the Bible's Book of Acts, among them "All of them were filled with the Holy Spirit and began to speak in other tongues as the Spirit enabled them" and "Some, however, made fun of them and said, 'They have had too much wine.'" The Vineyard Church no longer recognizes the Toronto Blessing as an affiliate, but the two groups, like many other new Christian movements, put a markedly similar emphasis on spontaneity, informality, evangelism, and a lack of traditional organizational hierarchy.

UMBANDA. A major syncretistic movement of spirit worship and spirit healing based in Brazil, with perhaps 20 million members in twenty-two countries, Umbanda emerged as an identifiable movement in the 1920s. It fuses traditional African religion (notably Yoruban) with native South American beliefs, elements of Catholicism, and the spiritist

ideas of the French philosopher Allan Kardec. In 1857 Kardec published, in *The Spirits' Book,* transcripts of philosophical and scientific conversations he claimed to have had (using mediums from around the world) with members of the spirit world. The movement grew phenomenally in the twentieth century and is sometimes considered the "national religion of Brazil," uniting the country's many races and faiths.

RELIGIOUS AMOEBAS

Last April, hoping to learn more about such groups and the people who study them, I attended an academic conference devoted to new religious movements and religious pluralism. The event, held at the London School of Economics, was put together and hosted by an influential British organization called the Information Network Focus on Religious Movements (INFORM), in cooperation with an Italian group known as the Center for Studies on New Religions (CESNUR). The conference sessions were dominated by a clubby international crew of NRM scholars who travel around the world presenting papers to one another. The American, English, formerly Soviet, and Japanese contingents seemed particularly strong. People regularly referred to articles that they had published or read in the new journal *Nova Religio,* a major outlet for NRM scholarship. Much of the buzz in the corridors had to do with the French anti-cult legislation, which was soon to be voted on. Everywhere I turned I seemed to bump into avuncular bearded American sociologists. "I'm so damn sick of the cult-anti-cult debate, I could just puke!" one of them told me heatedly over dinner, gesticulating with his fork. I hadn't brought the subject up.

What made the London conference distinctive was its nonacademic participants. At the opening reception I drank orange juice and munched on potato skins with a tall Swedish woman who had introduced herself to me as a member of the International Society for Krishna Consciousness—a Hare Krishna. I was joined at lunch one day by a nondescript elderly gentleman in a coat and tie who turned out to be a wry Latvian neo-pagan. Among the others I came across were European Bahais, British Moonies, a Jewish convert to the Family (a sort of "Jesus Freak" offshoot formerly known as the Children of God), members of a small messianic community known as the Twelve Tribes, and several representatives from the Church of Scientology, including the director of its European human-rights office. (Scientology is trying hard to gain formal status as a religion in Europe and the former Soviet Union, but many countries—notably France, Germany, and Russia—consider it a cult to be eradicated.)

That sounds like an exotic cast of characters, but actually it wasn't. The NRM members I encountered at the London conference were no more or less eccentric, interesting, or threatening than any of the people I rode with every morning on the London Underground. I found this oddly oppressive; I thought I'd be getting strangeness and mystery, but instead I got an essential human blandness. The people I met were just people.

This was a point made explicitly by the conference's organizer, Eileen Barker, an eminent British sociologist based at the London School of Economics. Barker is a genial and apparently tireless scholar who is often credited with having popularized the academic use of the term "new religious movement." She made a name for herself in 1984, with her influential book-length study *The Making of a Moonie: Choice or Brainwashing?* (the answer was choice), and she now devotes most of her spare time to INFORM, which she founded. The group is dedicated to making available—to concerned relatives, government officials, law-enforcement agencies, the media, representatives of mainstream religions, researchers, and many others—balanced, accurate, and up-to-date information on NRMs from around the world. Speaking at one of the conference sessions, Barker emphatically reminded her audience of "just how very ordinary the people in the cult scene are." When I asked her later about this remark, she elaborated.

"New religious movements aren't always as exotic as they are made out to be," she said. "Or, indeed, as they *themselves* would make themselves out to be. They're interesting in that they're offering something that, they claim, quite often correctly, isn't on sale in the general mainstream religions. So almost by definition there's a sort of curiosity value about them. They're comparatively easy to study—I knew pretty well all of the Moonies in Britain by the time I completed my study of them. They're interesting because you can see a whole lot of social processes going on: conversion, leaving, bureaucratization, leadership squabbles, ways in which authority is used, ways in which people can change, the difference that people *born* into a religion can make."

I asked a lot of the scholars at the conference why they thought it was important to study new religious movements. Perhaps the most succinct answer came from Susan Palmer, a Canadian who in recent years has become an expert on the Ra'lians (and whose ancestors were Mormon polygamists who fled U.S. persecution in the nineteenth century). "If you're interested in studying religion," she told me, "NRMs are a great place to start. Their history is really short, they don't have that many members, their leader is usually still alive, and you can see the evolution of their rituals and their doctrines. It's a bit like dissecting amoebas instead of zebras."

The ultimate dream for any ambitious student of NRMs, of course, is to discover and monitor the very early stirrings of a new movement and then to track it as it evolves and spreads around the globe. Everybody acknowledges how unlikely this is. But the idea that it *could* happen is irresistible. One scholar I met in London who admitted to harboring such hopes was Jean-François Mayer, a tall, bearded, boyishly enthusiastic lecturer in religious studies at the University of Fribourg, in Switzerland. For the past twenty years Mayer has been following a small French movement known as the Revelation of Arès. Founded in 1974 by a former Catholic deacon named Michel Potay, and based near Bordeaux, the movement describes itself as the corrective culmination of Christianity, Judaism, and Islam. "It is an NRM," Mayer told me, "that has all of the constitutive elements of a new religion of the book: new scriptures incorporating previously revealed scriptures, new rituals, and a new place of pilgrimage. When I study such a group, I see such obvious similarities with the birth of Christianity and the birth of Islam that for me it's fascinating and exciting. Sometimes I let myself think that I might be witnessing something similar at its initial stage." Even if the movement doesn't take off—which, Mayer readily admits, is likely—it is a perfect example of what many NRM scholars like to study.

What have the NRM scholars learned? The literature is copious and varied, but several ideas recur again and again. In an environment of religious freedom NRMs emerge constantly and are the primary agents of religious change. They tend to respond quickly and directly to the evolving spiritual demands of the times. It is often said that they are "midwives of new sensibilities." They exist at a high level of tension with society, but they nevertheless represent social and spiritual reconfigurations that are already under way—or, to put it differently, they almost never emerge out of thin air. Their views can rapidly shift from being considered deviant to being considered orthodox. The people who join NRMs tend to be young, well educated, and relatively affluent. They also tend to have been born into an established religious order but to profess a lack of religious belief prior to joining. They are drawn to new religious movements primarily for social reasons rather than theological ones—usually because of the participation of friends or family members. And (*pace* the anti-cultists) most of them soon leave of their own free will.

This last phenomenon is profoundly symptomatic. Because the fact is that almost all new religious movements fail.

THE RELIGIOUS MARKETPLACE

The sociologist Rodney Stark is one of the few people who have been willing to develop specific ideas about what makes new religious movements succeed. This is inherently speculative territory (as with stocks, past performance is no guarantee of future returns), but it also has the potential to be one of the most interesting areas of NRM scholarship, in that such ideas can be applied to all religious movements.

Stark, a professor of sociology and comparative religion at the University of Washington, is blunt, amiable, and a classically American maverick. He does scholarship with an often irreverent swagger. Knowing that he had written specifically on how and why religious movements succeed, I called him and asked him to summarize his thoughts on the subject. "The main thing you've got to recognize," he told me, "is that success is really about relationships and *not* about faith. What happens is that people form relationships and only then come to embrace a religion. It doesn't happen the other way around. That's really critical, and it's something that you can only learn by going out and watching people convert to new movements. We would never, ever, have figured that out in the library. You can never find that sort of thing out after the fact—because after the fact people do think it's about faith. And they're not lying, by the way. They're just projecting backwards.

"Something else: give people things to do. The folks in the Vineyard are geniuses at that. It's quite an adventure to go off somewhere and set up a new church for them. The Mormons are great at giving people things to do too. You know, they not only tithe money but they also tithe time. They do an enormous amount of social services for one another, all of which builds community bonds. It also gives you this incredible sense of security—I'm going to be okay when I'm in a position of need; there are going to be people to look out for me. That makes a difference. And if you want to build commitment, send your kids out on missions when they're nineteen! Go out and you save the world for two years! Even if you don't get a single convert, it's worth it in terms of the bonds you develop.

"You've also got to have a serious conception of God and the supernatural to succeed. Just having some 'essence of goodness,' like the Tao, isn't going to do it. It just isn't. It doesn't even do it in Asian countries, you know. They hang a whole collection of supernatural beings around these essences. So to succeed you do best by starting with a very active God who's virtuous and makes demands, because people have a tendency to value religions on the basis of cost."

This last idea is at the heart of much of Stark's work. It is a component of the major sociological model for which Stark is perhaps best known: the rational-choice theory of religion, which proposes that in an environment of religious freedom people choose to develop and maintain their religious beliefs in accordance with the laws of a "religious economy." This model of religious history and change, Stark feels, is what should replace the traditional model—which, he has written, is based on the erroneous and fundamentally secular idea of "progress through theological refinement." It's a controversial model (some find the science of economics only dimly enlightening even when applied to financial markets), but it has become a major force in recent theorizing about religion. Many of the presentations at the London conference used it as a starting point.

The essence of the idea is this: People act rationally in choosing their religion. If they are believers, they make a constant cost-benefit analysis, consciously or unconsciously, about what form of religion to practice. Religious beliefs and practices make up the product that is on sale in the market, and current and potential followers are the consumers. In a free-market religious economy there is a healthy abundance of choice (religious pluralism), which leads naturally to vigorous competition and efficient supply (new and old religious movements). The more competition there is, the higher the level of consumption. This would explain the often remarked paradox that the United States is one of the most religious countries in the world but also one of the strongest enforcers of a separation between Church and State.

The conventional wisdom is that religion is the realm of the irrational (in a good or a bad sense, depending on one's point of view), and as such, it can't be studied in the way that other aspects of human behavior are studied. But Stark argues that all of social science is based on the idea that human behavior is essentially explainable, and it therefore makes no sense to exclude a major and apparently constant behavior like religion-building from what should be studied scientifically. The sources of religious experience may well be mysterious, irrational, and highly personal, but religion itself is not. It is a social rather than a psychological phenomenon, and, absent conditions of active repression, it unfolds according to observable rules of group behavior.

I asked Stark if he could give me an example of what's happening in the contemporary American religious marketplace. "Sure," he said. "I happen to have grown up in Jamestown, North Dakota. When I left, if you had asked me what the religious situation was going to be like a couple of generations later, I would have told you that it would have stayed pretty much the same: the Catholics would be the largest single group, but overall there would be more Protestants than Catholics, with the Methodists and the Presbyterians being the two largest. But that's not what happened at all. Today the Assemblies of God and the Nazarenes are the two biggest religious bodies in Jamestown. These are new religious movements. There were no Mormons in Jamestown when I was a kid, by the way, and now there's a ward hall. There were two families of Jehovah's Witnesses, and now there's a Kingdom Hall. Evangelical Protestants of all kinds have grown a lot. What's happened is that people have changed brands. They've changed suppliers. Writ small, this is what has happened to the country as a whole. There are new religious movements everywhere—and what this tells me is that in a religious free market institutions often go to pot but religion doesn't. Look at the Methodists! They were nothing in 1776, they were everything in 1876, and they were receding in 1976."

Stark has applied his ideas to the study of the history of Christianity. He suggests, in *The Rise of Christianity* (1996), that early Christianity was a rational choice for converts because its emphasis on helping the needy "prompted and sustained attractive, liberating, and effective social relations and organizations." People initially became Christians for a number of rational, nontheological reasons, he argues, and not, he told me, because "two thousand people on a Tuesday afternoon went and heard Saint Paul." People converted because Christianity *worked*. The Christian community put an emphasis on caring for its members, for example; that emphasis allowed it to survive onslaughts of disease better than other communities. People also converted, he writes, because, contrary to the standard version of events, Christianity's initial membership was not drawn predominantly from among the poor. Stark argues that in

Roman society Christianity's early members, like members of most other new religious movements, were relatively affluent and highly placed, and thus weren't treated as a social problem to be repressed. In this view, although Christians were subjected to their share of anti-cult persecution, they were largely ignored by the Romans as a political threat and therefore were able quietly to build their membership. Early growth, Stark writes, involved the conversion of many more members of the Jewish community than has traditionally been acknowledged; Christianity offered disaffected Jews a sort of higher-tension new religion that nevertheless maintained continuity with some established Jewish orthodoxies. Why else—rationally speaking—would the Christians have held on to the Old Testament, a sacred text that in so many ways is at theological odds with the New Testament?

Stark has no shortage of critics. Bryan Wilson, a venerable scholar of NRMs based at Oxford, told me that the rational-choice theory of religious economics is "really rather ludicrous" and said that "most European sociologists of religion would quarrel with it." Steve Bruce, a sociologist based at the University of Aberdeen, in Scotland, has complained about the creeping prevalence of the theory, which he attributes (clearly with Stark in mind) to "the malign influence of a small clique of U.S. sociologists."

It does seem dangerously easy to approach any subject—love? music?—with a grand rational-choice framework in mind and then suddenly to see everything in terms of a marketplace of "products" subject to the laws of supply and demand. What does such an approach really say about specific situations? And what constitutes "choice" or "supply" anyway? How does being born into a religion, which is what happens to most people, affect the idea of a "free market"? These are questions that will be debated for years. In the meantime, one can safely say that, misguided or not, rational-choice theory is a serious attempt to grapple with the reality of continual and unpredictable religious change.

FUTURE SHOCK

What new religious movements will come to light in the twenty-first century? Who knows? Will that raving, disheveled lunatic you ignored on a street corner last week turn out to be an authentic prophet of the next world faith? All sorts of developments are possible. Catholicism might evolve into a distinctly Charismatic movement rooted primarily in China and headed by an African pope. India's *Dalits*, formerly known as Untouchables, might convert en masse to Christianity or Buddhism. Africa might become the home of the Anglican Church and of Freemasonry. Much of the Islamic world might veer off in Sufi directions. A neo-Zoroastrian prophet might appear and spark a worldwide revival. Membership of the Mormon Church might become predominantly Latin American or Asian. Scientology might become the informal state religion of California. The Episcopalians might dwindle into something not unlike the Amish or the Hutterites—a tiny religious body whose

members have voluntarily cut themselves off from the misguided world around them and have chosen to live in self-sustaining hamlets where they quaintly persist in wearing their distinctive costumes (ties with ducks on them, boat shoes) and in marrying only within the community. The next major religion might involve the worship of an inscrutable numinous entity that emerges on the Internet and swathes the globe in electronic revelation. None of these possibilities is as unlikely as it may sound.

One of the most remarkable changes already taking place because of new religious movements is the under-reported shift in the center of gravity in the Christian world. There has been a dramatic move from North to South. Christianity is most vital now in Africa, Asia, and Latin America, where independent churches, Pentecostalism, and even major Catholic Charismatic movements are expanding rapidly. The story of Christianity in twentieth-century Africa is particularly noteworthy. There were fewer than 10 million Christians in Africa in 1900; by 2000 there were more than 360 million. And something very interesting is happening: ancient Christian practices such as exorcism, spirit healing, and speaking in tongues—all of which are documented in the Book of Acts—are back in force. In classic NRM fashion, some of these Christianity-based movements involve new prophet figures, new sacred texts, new pilgrimage sites, and new forms of worship.

"New movements are not only a part of Christianity but an enormous part of it," I was told by David Barrett, the editor of the *World Christian Encyclopedia*, when I asked him about Christian NRMs. "According to our estimates, the specifically new independent churches in Christianity number about three hundred and ninety-four million, which is getting on for twenty percent of the Christian world. So it starts to look faintly ridiculous, you see, when the 'respectable' Christians start talking patronizingly about these new, 'strange' Christians appearing everywhere. In a very short time the people in those movements will be talking the same way about us."

One of the stock Northern explanations for these new movements has been that they are transitional phases of religious "development" and represent thinly veiled manifestations of still potent primitive superstitions. That's a line of thinking that Philip Jenkins—a professor of history and religious studies at Penn State, and the author of the forthcoming *The Next Christendom: The Coming of Global Christianity*—dismissed to me as nothing more than a "racist, they've-just-come-down-from-the-trees" kind of argument. Recent NRM scholarship suggests a less condescending view: in a lot of places, for a lot of reasons, the new Christianity works. Just as, in Rodney Stark's opinion, early Christianity spread throughout the vestiges of the Roman Empire because it "prompted and sustained attractive, liberating, and effective social relations and organizations," these early forms of new Christianity are spreading in much of the post-colonial world in large part because they provide community and foster relationships that help people deal with challenging new social and political realities.

Rosalind I. J. Hackett, who teaches religious studies at the University of Tennessee at Knoxville, is a specialist in African religious movements. "African NRMs have been successful," she told me, "because they help people *survive*, in all of the ways that people need to survive—social, spiritual, economic, finding a mate. People forget how critical that is. In Western academic circles it's very fashionable these days to talk about the value of ethnic identity and all that. But that's a luxury for people trying to feed families. To survive today in Africa people have to be *incredibly* mobile in search of work. One of the very important things that many of these NRMs do is create broad trans-ethnic and trans-national communities, so that when somebody moves from city to city or country to country there's a sort of surrogate family structure in place."

Some of the most successful African Christian NRMs of the twentieth century, such as the Zion Christian Church, based in South Africa, and the Celestial Church of Christ, in Nigeria, are very self-consciously and deliberately African in their forms of worship, but a new wave of African NRMs, Hackett says, now downplays traditional African features and instead promotes modern lifestyles and global evangelism. The International Central Gospel Church, in Ghana, and the Winner's Chapel, in Nigeria, are examples of these churches; their educated, savvy, and charismatic leaders, Mensa Otabil and David Oyedepo, respectively, spend a good deal of time on the international preaching circuit. The emphasis on global evangelism has helped to spur the development of what Hackett has called the "South-South" religious connection. No longer does Christian missionary activity flow primarily from the developed countries of the North to the developing countries of the South. Brazilian Pentecostal movements are evangelizing heavily in Africa. New African movements are setting up shop in Asia. Korean evangelists now outnumber American ones around the world. And so on.

The course of missionary activity is also beginning to flow from South to North. Many new African movements have for some time been establishing themselves in Europe and North America. Some of this can be attributed to immigration, but there's more to the process than that. "Many people just aren't aware of how active African Christian missionaries are in North America," Hackett says. "The Africans hear about secularization and empty churches and they feel sorry for us. So they come and evangelize. The late Archbishop Idahosa [a renowned Nigerian evangelist and the founder of the Church of God Mission, International] once put it to me this way: 'Africa doesn't need God, it needs money. America doesn't need money, it needs God.' That's an oversimplification, but it gets at something important."

David Barrett, too, underscores the significance of the African missionary presence in the United States. "America is honeycombed with African independent churches," he told me. "Immigrants from Nigeria, Kenya, South Africa, and Congo have brought their indigenous churches with them. These are independent denominations that are very vibrant in America. They're tremendous churches, and they're winning all kinds of white members, because it's a very attractive form of Christianity, full of music and movement and color."

Asian and Latin American missionaries of new Christian movements are also moving north. A rapidly growing and controversial Brazilian Pentecostal movement called the Universal Church of the Kingdom of God—founded in 1977 and often referred to by its Portuguese acronym, IURD—has established an aggressive and successful evangelistic presence in both Europe and North America. A revivalist, anti-institutional movement founded in China in the 1920s and referred to as the Local Church has made considerable inroads in the United States. El Shaddai, a lay Catholic Charismatic movement established in the Philippines in 1984 to compete with Pentecostalism, has now set up shop in twenty-five countries. Another Christian group, the Light of the World Church, a Pentecostal movement based in Mexico, has spread widely in the United States in recent years.

The present rate of growth of the new Christian movements and their geographical range suggest that they will become a major social and political force in the coming century. The potential for misunderstanding and stereotyping is enormous—as it was in the twentieth century with a new religious movement that most people initially ignored. It was called fundamentalist Islam.

"We need to take the new Christianity very seriously," Philip Jenkins told me. "It is *not* just Christianity plus drums. If we're not careful, fifty years from now we may find a largely secular North defining itself against a largely Christian South. This will have its implications."

Such as? I asked.

Jenkins paused, and then made a prediction. "I think," he said, "that the big 'problem cult' of the twenty-first century will be Christianity."

From *The Atlantic Monthly,* February 2002, pp. 37–45. © 2002 by The Atlantic Monthly. Reprinted by permission of Toby Lester, senior editor of The Atlantic Monthly.

DOPER
OR DEVOTEE?

Cameron Best Admitted He Smoked Marijuana; So Why, Under RFRA, Is He Getting a New Trial?

BY KIM LEIGHTON

Things don't augur well for Rastafarian Cameron Best at his trial on 55-count drug possession and trafficking charges in Billings, Montana.

First, he refused to stand when Chief U.S. District Judge Jack Shanstrom entered and left the courtroom, because a basic Rastafarian tenet holds that all men are equal, and to pay homage to one is to violate the faith.

"I have no fear of the court," said the five-foot-four-inch black Montana native. "I have no fear of the law, because I believe that one day the Lord will prevail."

Next, Best kept his hair in signature Rastafarian dreadlocks during the trial. "There have been many situations where so-called Rastafarians faced with marijuana charges have cut their locks and caved in," said Best. "I didn't do that."

Finally, Best never attempted to conceal or deny his marijuana use at any time during the proceedings. In fact, Best rolled two "joints" (marijuana cigarettes) while on the witness stand, in order to settle a dispute over the amount of marijuana a single joint contains. Moreover, he spent an entire day on the stand detailing his marijuana-related activities for the jury.

Thus, it wasn't surprising that the 12 white women on the jury found Best guilty, which resulted in a 35-year term in a federal prison.

Yet what elevates the case is the unprecedented action of three federal appellate judges in San Francisco who reversed Best's marijuana possession conviction, citing violations of the 1993 Religious Freedom Restoration Act (RFRA). Specifically, the Ninth Circuit Court of Appeals noted that Best's use of marijuana as a Rastafarian sacra-

ment was largely and wrongly proscribed by the lower court as an element in his defense. The 1996 appeals court decision is the first time that a drug conviction has been overturned on the basis of RFRA.

"Under RFRA," the Ninth Circuit Court ruled, "the government had the obligation, first, to show that the application of the marijuana laws to the defendants was in furtherance of a compelling governmental interest, and second, to show that the application of these laws to these defendants was the least restrictive means of furthering these interests."

RFRA was enacted in response to a 1990 U.S. Supreme Court ruling that allowed a peyote prosecution despite a claim that use of the drug was central to Native American religion. It requires the government to prove a compelling justification for any prosecution that substantially burdens the defendant's exercise of religion, and then prove that its action "is the least restrictive means of furthering that compelling governmental interest."

Despite that ruling, Best remains in federal prison, because the reversal of his conviction on possession did not turn back the jury's guilty verdict for trafficking. The appellate decision merely opens the possibility of a new trial for Best (and codefendants convicted along with him) on the marijuana possession charges, one that would allow the defendants to present a religious-use defense.

"The court may conduct a preliminary hearing," said the Ninth Circuit, "in which the defendants will have the obligation of showing that they are in fact Rastafarians and that the use of marijuana is part of the religious practice of Rastafarians."

SMOKING OUT RASTAFARIANISM

Because of the pervasive and profound misunderstanding of Rastafarianism in the twentieth century, it is often easier to define the Jamaica-based theology by dispelling the myths and misconceptions that shroud it, according to its closest adherents.

"Lots of people feel that we have no theology, that we're the mystics of the Caribbean," laments Imani Nyah, who founded and chairs the Association of Rastafarian Theologians, in Chicago.

The blame for that erroneous perception, she concedes, arises from Rastafarianism's lack of the strong organizational structures that characterize most Judaeo-Christian religions in the United States.

Fueling the misperceptions are what Nyah calls "wolves in sheep's clothing." Typically, she says, they are highly visible individuals—fixtures now in most major metropolitan areas—who wear their hair in dreadlocks and abuse marijuana, using Rastafarian theology as a pretext. As well, she adds, the recent spate of Hollywood movies depicting Rastafarians as thugs and drug dealers has further embedded the stereotype in the American psyche.

However misperceived, the estimated 1 million Rastafarians worldwide do have a core theology. "We are African-centered Christians who proclaim that Ethiopia is Judah, and that Jesus Christ was manifested in the person of His Imperial Majesty Haile Selassie [Ethiopia's late emperor, who changed his name from Ras Tefari at his coronation]," explains Nyah, adding that Rastafari beliefs are grounded in the Bible. She points to Revelation 5:2–5 and 19:16, Psalm 68:31, and Daniel 7:9, among many other verses, as core Rastafarian scripture.

Additionally, Rastafari believe that the late Bob Marley, who popularized reggae music worldwide, including in the U.S., in the 1970s with his band "The Wailers," was a musical prophet.

"To Rastafari," says Nyah, "he was like John the Baptist. He sowed the seeds of Rastafarianism with his music."

Why Rastafarians' unique appearance? "We follow in the way of the Nazarites, which is why many Rastafari wear dreadlocks," says Nyah. She compares Rastafari dreadlocks to "the collar worn by a priest or the crown worn by rabbis."

A theology born in the slums of Kingston, Jamaica, in the 1920s, Rastafarianism includes marijuana as a sacrament. "Smoking marijuana is not a requirement," says Nyah, "but it is a sacrament in the sacred circles of the Rastafari. Marijuana use in Rastafarian worship is what incense is to the Roman Catholic Mass."

An outgrowth of Ethiopian Christianity, Rastafarianism and its followers were persecuted without mercy in Jamaica for decades. But in the mid-1960s Rastafarians began penetrating Jamaica's middle and upper classes. Now Jamaica is nearly synonymous with Rastafarianism. Its influence is pervasive at all socioeconomic and political levels of the island nation. From Jamaica, Rastafarians have spread throughout the world, and because of their grassroots, inclusive theology, are seen by many as a force for integration in countries with multicultural populations.

An afterlife? Nyah describes heaven as a reincarnation of sorts where the spirit becomes part of the natural world, a belief, she said, that shares parallels with Native American pantheism. And hell?

"It's anywhere on earth where humanity lives in oppression."

—K.L.

For the moment, though, it's a Pyrrhic victory in terms of Best's freedom, according to Best's lawyer, Don Fiedler.

"The United States Supreme Court could have some interest in this case by the year 2000," Fiedler speculated. "In the meantime, we'd like to prevail on RFRA issues to the point where we get a new trial—a fair trial."

From court records and press accounts, both the pretrial proceedings and the eight-week trial in Billings, Montana, were contentious. Defense motions to recuse the judge for his rulings in similar cases were denied. Allegations of Best being the target of selective prosecution, which is illegal, were similarly rejected, along with defense claims that the jury selection was not done fairly or legally. The trial itself was punctuated by mistrial motions (all denied) arising from alleged discrepancies between prosecution evidence and the corroborative testimony of investigators and other witnesses.

Fiedler conceded that Best's strict adherence to his religious principles throughout the trial did not bode well for his client.

"I've never had a client more courageous," said Fiedler. "Cameron knew that he was rolling the dice, but he felt that his religious beliefs were more important to him than the laws of man. If he had wanted to, he could have cut his exposure down and gotten what everybody else got—eight or nine years."

Fiedler bristled at the hypothesis that Best used Rastafarianism as a pretext for his personal marijuana use and its distribution to others.

"Cameron's distributing marijuana is similar to Christian Scientists handling out pamphlets about their religious beliefs. To understand the Rastafarian way, you need to use the sacraments, and enlightenment follows. It's consistent with their religious principles."

The defense attorney also rebutted the suggestion that Best's successful use of RFRA could provide a legal loophole for unscrupulous marijuana defendants.

"That's ludicrous, and it's opposed to the spirit under which RFRA was passed," Fiedler said. "There's a reason the First Amendment mentions religious freedom. It's a paramount right in our country. And there's no doubt in my mind about Cameron Best's sincerity."

Of the 25 people indicted with Best, many were called by Assistant U.S. Attorney Jim Seykora to testify against him. But under cross-examination, many who turned state's evidence described the diminutive Best as principled and benevolent, a man steeped in Rastafarian beliefs who eschewed alcohol, tobacco, and all other drugs, in keeping with his faith. Rastafarians do not consider marijuana a drug.

The government contended that for at least a decade leading up to the trial Best and his alleged coconspirators imported thousands of pounds of marijuana into Billings for resale—essentially a drug cartel with Best as its leader. During the trial Best vehemently denied those allegations as overblown, contending that he was simply part of a loose association of Rastafarians and other friends who pooled their money to get a better price on marijuana.

Best's jury, all of whom came from farms and ranches well away from Billings, Montana's largest city, didn't see it Best's way. It is, of course, likely that the jury judged fairly, based on the evidence and testimony; it's equally likely that Cameron Best is the victim in a clash of irreconcilable cultures. Or, as the Ninth circuit Court of Appeals has framed the question: Is Best a doper or a devotee?

The middle child of a family of seven, Cameron Best was raised in South Side, a working-class Billings neighborhood that was long the home of Burlington-Northern Railroad workers, a company that has since relocated. Billings (population 90,000) is the eastern gateway to Montana, a sprawling former cow town bounded by the Yellowstone River and the breaks, bluffs, and rimrock the river has carved out of the high plains over the centuries. By Montana standards Billings is culturally diverse, with some 2,500 blacks, Hispanics, and Native Americans among its populations.

In a state where people take pride in tracing their heritage back to Montana's territorial days, Eugene Best, Cameron Best's father, is no exception. "My grandfather was a Buffalo soldier from Kentucky who was stationed out here during the Civil War. He was a gambler, and won a small business in Billings in a poker game. We stayed."

Edna Best, his wife of 41 years and Cameron's mother, is an affable and articulate woman who clearly feels betrayed by a system that imprisons her sons Cameron and 31-year-old Jason. Jason, she said, was found guilty of marijuana charges when authorities "found his fingerprint on a bag of pot related to Cameron's case."

Despite his Roman Catholic upbringing, Cameron Best was leaning toward Rastafarianism when he was 19. "The first inkling I had of it was when he became a vegetarian," his mother said. "He was always so resolute in everything; he was very strict about his vegetarian diet."

It was shortly after his conversion to Rastafarian theology that Cameron Best left home for his own place—a mobile home on the outskirts of Billings, across the street from his childhood friend Calvin Treiber, who would later be a central codefendant at Cameron's trial.

Although neither Cameron Best, Treiber, nor the other 24 people who would be indicted a decade later on drug charges had a police record, within two years of leaving home Best was the subject of a police investigation (called Operation Reggae North) that would eventually include city and county law enforcement, the FBI, and the IRS, and would result in his arrest for attempting to "corner the market on the Billings marijuana trade."

It was well into that investigation that Best, concerned about Billings' burgeoning problems arising from the widespread use of crack cocaine, offered to help police stem the flow of the drug by identifying the city's major dealers, according to trial testimony. His offer was refused. Since mid-1995 the abuse of crack and the crime, misery, and death that accompany it have become rooted in Billings, according to regular reports in the Billings *Gazette*.

Instead, Best wound up in prison, where, according to his parents, he has opted to remain in maximum security, away from the much larger hierarchy and greater dangers of the prison's general population. A food service worker in prison, according to his mother, Best is able to stick to his Rastafarian diet, which prohibits pork and most red meat. And despite maximum security, his religious beliefs have not gone unchallenged.

"He had an experience with Islamic leaders in prison and he found it interesting," Edna Best said. "But since he has five interracial children, Cameron said he could not support the idea of black supremacy, which is a central theme of the Nation of Islam but not the Rastafarians."

Proffering a recent letter from Cameron, Edna Best said that far from blunting his zeal for the Rastafarian faith, prison seems to have heightened her son's resolve as a Rastafarian disciple.

Of the Court of Appeals decision, she says it offers a ray of hope. "They're heading in the right direction. They have an understanding.

If and when Cameron Best gets his second day in court, Rastafarian theology will certainly weigh in as part of his defense. But it's questionable that he'll win, even with the court obliged to follow the principles set forth by RFRA. It's not likely that the prosecution would have trouble convincing a judge that, considering the pervasive drug problem, the state does indeed have a compelling interest in prohibiting marijuana use, even for religious reasons. In another case *(Leary v. United States)*, the Fifth Circuit Court said, "It would be difficult to imagine the harm which would result if the criminal statutes against marijuana were nullified as to those who claim the right to possess and traffic in this drug for religious purposes. For all practical purposes the anti-marijuana laws would be meaningless, and enforcement impossible." And, as Ninth Circuit Court Judge John Noonan wrote in Best's case: "We do not exclude the possibility that the government may show that the least restrictive means of preventing the sale and distribution of marijuana is the universal enforcement of marijuana laws."

Whatever the outcome, federal prisoner Cameron Best feels he did the right thing, knowing that at least he has pioneered a bridge across the yawning chasm that separates two vastly different cultures and theologies. And despite his situation he doesn't feel bitter against those who have put him away.

"I don't hate the U.S.," he said. "This is one of the best places in the world to live. I'd like to see the U.S. government learn more about the Rastafarians and our beliefs, instead of simply putting us in jail."

Kim Leighton is a freelance writer in Livingston, Montana.

From *Liberty*, November/December 1996, pp. 6-9. © 1996 by Liberty. Reprinted with permission of the author, Kim Leighton, who is a Montana-based freelance writer and book author.

FUNDAMENTALISM

For all the current focus on fiery Islamic extremists, religious fundamentalists are not confined to any particular faith or country, nor to the poor and uneducated. Instead, they are likely to spring up anywhere people perceive the need to fight a godless, secular culture—even if they have to depart from the orthodoxy of their traditions to do it. In fact, what fundamentalists everywhere have in common is the ability to craft their messages to fit the times.

By R. Scott Appleby and Martin E. Marty

"All Fundamentalism Is Religious"

Yes. It's true that many sorts of groups share basic characteristics of religious fundamentalists: They draw lines in the sand, demand unconditional obedience from the rank and file, expend enormous energies maintaining boundaries between the pure and impure, build impenetrable dogmatic fortresses around "the truth," and see their version of it as absolute, infallible, or inerrant. Indeed, some may be tempted to seek manifestations of "secular fundamentalism" in Marxism or Soviet-era state socialism, in the many virulent strains of nationalism in evidence today, or in the unqualified extremism of ideologically driven revolutionary or terrorist movements, from Peru's Shining Path to Germany's Baader-Meinhof gang. In a similar vein, one might speak of "scientific fundamentalism" to connote the assumption, held by many modern scientists, that empirically based knowledge is the only reliable way of knowing reality.

But we hesitate to call such secular groups "fundamentalist." They may call upon followers to make the ultimate sacrifice, but unlike the monotheistic religions, especially Christianity and Islam, they do not reassure their followers that God or an eternal reward awaits them. The absence of a truly "ultimate" concern affects how such secular groups think about and carry out their missions,

and the belief in heaven or paradise serves as a very different kind of framework for and legitimation of self-martyrdom in the monotheistic religions.

"Fundamentalism Is Limited to Monotheism"

No. Let us put aside for the moment the observation that Hinduism and Buddhism are not religions in the Western sense of the word and that Hindus and Buddhists do not believe in a personal God. Like another major South Asian religion, Sikhism, which has produced its fair share of candidates for the fundamentalist family, these great traditions of belief and practice orient devotees to a reality (or nonreality) that transcends or renders illusory the mundane world. And they have produced powerful modern, antisecular, antimodernist, absolutist, boundary-setting, exclusionary, and often violent movements that bear startling resemblances to fundamentalism within the Jewish, Christian, and Islamic worlds.

Indeed, the Hindutva movement in India has consciously borrowed elements from the theistic Western traditions, including a supernatural patron, the Lord Rama, with his own sacred birthplace, in order to give Hinduism the kind of prickly spine that allows Western theistic fundamentalists to get their backs up when threatened. Sikh radicals exhibit a sense of apocalyptic expectation more natural in non-Asian cultures. And Buddhist "warriors" in Sri Lanka have transformed segments of the *sangha*, or monastic order, into an implacable force for religious and cultural nationalism. These "synthetic" Asian variants of fundamentalism select and canonize sacred epics, poems, and other open-ended genres into the stuff of fundamental, inerrant scripture.

"Fundamentalists Are Literalists"

Not so. Fundamentalists lay claim to preaching and practicing "the unvarnished word of God" as revealed in the Hebrew Bible, the New Testament, or the Koran. This claim undergirds the fundamentalists' larger assertion that their authority comes directly from God and thus their program for reform and transformation is, in principle, beyond criticism. Such claims are patently false. Religious traditions are vast, complex bodies of wisdom built up over generations. Their foundational sources (sacred scriptures, codified oral teachings, and commentaries) express and interpret the experiences of the sacred that led to the formation of their religious communities. Religious traditions are not less than these sources; they are always more. Interpretation is nine tenths of the law—even religious law—and the sources of religious law are often multivalent and contradictory. One verse of the Koran condemns killing while another commands the slaying of infidels. How to choose? The art is called hermeneutics—developing a theory that guides the interpretation.

Fundamentalists claim not to interpret, but they are the narrowest and most ideologically guided interpreters. West Bank settlers of Gush Emunim in Israel, the most prominent fundamentalist movement in Judaism, depend not only on one esoteric way of reading the Torah but on the mystical utterances of two 20th-century rabbis, Rabbi Zvi Yehuda Kook the Elder and his son. The rabbis selected one of the 613 mitzvahs, or Torah duties—to settle "the whole land of Israel"—and elevated it above all others. Similarly, one of American Protestant fundamentalism's main themes, "premillennial dispensationalism," a form of apocalypse that proclaims that the world is deteriorating morally and that Christ will soon return in vengeance, is not "traditional." It was developed in England in the middle of the 19th century.

Fundamentalists are eager to adapt to the exigencies of the moment if it suits the movement's needs. In Lebanon, the militant Hezbollah benefited in the 1980s from Muslim clerics' promotion of the injunction to "be fruitful and multiply": From 1956 to 1975 the Shiite minority population tripled, so that in 20 years the Shiite representation in the population jumped from 19 to 30 percent. In postrevolutionary Iran, by contrast, officials argued that modification of birth control teaching did not violate traditional norms. Ministry of Health officials publicized how unchecked population growth hurt families and lauded the virtues of the small family and its quality of life. Officials then promoted birth control measures, a serious step given what had been interpreted as Islamic injunctions against such measures.

To gain support beyond small cadres of followers, fundamentalist leaders must persuade ordinary believers to suspend existing teachings that condemn violence and promote peacemaking. Believers who are theologically informed and spiritually well formed tend not to be susceptible to such arguments. Unfortunately, ordinary believers are not always sufficiently grounded in the teachings and practices of their traditions to counter fundamentalists' selective reading of sacred texts. Thus religious extremists tend to prey upon the young and untutored.

"Fundamentalism Attracts the Poorest"

A common misperception. Without question, fundamentalist groups often recruit among and appeal to people on the short end of economic development. Often the followers are poor, jobless people, lacking worldly prospects. But they are not the poorest of the poor, who do not have the luxury of becoming disciples—much less leaders of fundamentalist movements—and are more preoccupied with "the fundamentals" of basic survival. More commonly, recruits come from the educated unemployed or underemployed, or from gainfully employed teachers, engineers, medical technicians, and other professionals in the applied sciences, areas of specialization in which modernizing societies are playing catch-up.

In Algeria, "the young men who hold up the walls" swelled the ranks of Islamist cadres in the 1980s and 1990s. The Algerian state had educated a generation of young men but had not developed an economy that could employ novice engineers and technocrats. Un- or underemployed, these young men, entering their sexual prime but frustrated because they could not support brides, hung out on street corners in Algiers and other urban centers, awaiting social salvation. They were thus particularly receptive to the slogan, "Islam is the solution."

Across the Middle East, such desperate but capable men signed on to destroy the corrupt, repressive, ineffective, and nominally Muslim leadership of the Arab world. The daring joined the ranks of the transnational mujahedin—the Islamist "freedom fighters" dispatched to Afghanistan in the 1980s to thwart the godless Soviet invaders. The graduates of that campaign made their way into the ranks of al Qaeda, Islamic Jihad, and other terrorist networks.

The second category, gainfully employed but spiritually unfulfilled, swells the ranks of Jewish, Christian, and Islamic fundamentalist groups. As conservative Christian denominations in the United States split and fundamentalists left them during the 1920s and 1930s, many rural, culturally sheltered, traditionally religious people joined the newly formed independent churches, and fundamen-

What's in a Name?

While the word "fundamentalism" is here to stay, not everyone is at ease with it, and maybe no one ever should be. Clustering movements, for comparative purposes, that share broad "family resemblances" may lead untutored onlookers to wrongly conclude that all believers are fundamentalists, that all fundamentalists are terrorists, and therefor that every form of orthodox religion should be banished from public expression. Phrases like "the rage of Islam" don't help.

For a time, some newspapers chose to avoid the term and referred to fundamentalist movements only as "extremist," "militant," or "fanatic." Readers had a hard time making out just what people were "extremist" about. Militias are militant but not often fundamentalist. Football fans can be fanatic.

Yet many who shunned the word fundamentalist did so with good reason, and what they say gives pause to those who would use it casually. The main argument has been that the term belonged only in the United States, where Protestant fundamentalist Curtis Lee Laws coined the term and where famous nonfundamentalist minister, Harry Emerson Fosdick, once defined a fundamentalist as "a mad evangelical."

Substitutes have not been satisfying. Call something a "neoreformist radical revolutionary Islamism" and you may well point to some features of one movement. But how then may it be compared to others?

Some who attack the use of the word fundamentalism will use "capitalist" or "liberal" without batting an eye, even though both terms were born somewhere in some specific circumstance. Careful scholars and publics will take care to see exactly how various fundamentalist groups invest their movements with meaning and what particular meanings give life to their movements. They will pick their language with care. but to deny use of the term "fundamentalist" because it did not exist in other languages a century ago is not distinctive. It di not exist in English either. A new phenoenon was on the scene and it needed a name.

–R.S.A., M.E.M.

boasting Ph.D.'s. Today, Christian fundamentalists live in Dallas suburbs as well as in the Tennessee hill country. They drive BMWs in Nashville and own malls and Bible-based radio stations and cable channels.

The Jewish movements attracted affluent American Jews who made aliyah and upon their return to Israel turned super-Orthodox. The Islamic cadres hail from a variety of backgrounds, including extremely wealthy families, and have advanced degrees from Western universities. Mohammed Atta, the Hamburg-based student who learned to pilot jetliners in preparation for American Airlines Flight 11 (which crashed into the World Trade Center), is typical of the 21st-century fundamentalist—the illiterate or semiliterate peasant is not.

The fact that fundamentalist movements middle management and rank and file frequently have educational and professional backgrounds in applied sciences, technical, and bureaucratic fields helps explain why fundamentalists tend to read scriptures like engineers read blueprints—as a prosaic set of instructions and specifications. In fundamentalist hands, the complex, multivocal, ambiguous treasury of mysteries is reduced to a storehouse of raw materials to be ransacked as needed for building a political program. Few poets or cosmologists find their way into fundamentalist cadres.

"Fundamentalism Leads to Violence"

Not necessarily. Social context and the local or regional political culture have much to say about the directions that fundamentalism takes. Within the abode of Islam, nation-states are either weak or failing, on the one hand, or dictatorial and repressive, on the other. Both contexts encourage violent variants of fundamentalism bent on replacing the state (as the Taliban did in Afghanistan) or overthrowing it (as the Shiites did in Iran and as radical Islamic groups have hoped to do in Egypt, Algeria, Saudi Arabia, and elsewhere).

American Christian fundamentalists would argue they are and always have been law-abiding citizens. "Why do you compare us to extremist Arabs and gun-toting Jewish settlers?" a fundamentalist friend once demanded. "We do not stockpile arms in the basement of Moody Bible School in Chicago!" Although they may sometimes be associated with abortion-clinic bombers and white supremacist or antigovernment militias—neither of which qualify as fundamentalists because of their tenuous connections to organized Christianity—American Christian fundamentalists do not resort to violence. But that may have more to do with the character of their society—open, pluralist, governed by the rule of law, and tolerant of moderate expressions of fundamentalism—than with their principled rejection of violence.

Many hard-bitten policymakers assume there is no such thing as a moderate fundamentalist—especially in the Islamic cases. Such a view allowed the U.S. govern-

talists got typed and dismissed as redneck, dirt-poor, backwoods people who had nothing to gain on earth and everything to gain by hope of heaven. But identifying Christian fundamentalists with hillbillies and rednecks is a half-truth, at best. Protestant fundamentalist leaders have included Princeton professors and "creationists" ment, the putative champion of democracy and free elections, to turn a blind eye to the 1991 invalidation and subsequent cancellation of democratic elections in Algeria, when the Islamic Salvation Front won at the ballot box and appeared poised to assume control of the parliament. The Islamic form of democracy, according to the conventional wisdom in the State Department, means "one man, one vote—one time."

There is insufficient evidence to support such a conclusion. Indeed, the majority of fundamentalist Muslims, including Islamists who serve in the parliaments of Jordan, Indonesia, and Malaysia, have consistently refused to identify their movements with the terrorist fringe.

Deadly violence does occur, however, when brands of fundamentalism clash, as in the case of religiously motivated Jewish settlers and Islamic militants fighting for the same territory on the West Bank and Gaza. In Africa, a bitter contest for souls between Christianity and Islam has led to the torture, murder, and, reportedly, the crucifixion of Christians by Islamic extremists. In Pakistan, blasphemy laws putatively based in Islamic law are used to justify the persecution of Christians and other religious minorities.

"Fundamentalists Oppose Change"

Hardly. Fundamentalists are dedicated to changing a world they see as godless, but their remedy is not to preserve or recreate the past. Amish they are not. In an odd way, they are "progressives," not conservatives; most people simply do not agree that the world they envision could be called "progress." They have inhabited the modern material and technical world while attempting to cast off its pernicious, dehumanizing, materialistic philosophy.

How does this profile of the thoroughly modern, change-oriented fundamentalist square with the image of the angry rebel? Fundamentalists are, indeed, reactive: Their independent churches, mosques, and yeshivas and their cadres, networks, and movements originated in heated, defiant opposition to some trend—be it the invasion of Bible criticism and evolutionists into Protestant seminaries and churches, the narrowly secular vision borne out in Israeli policies, or the corruption of "establishment" imams in Cairo and across the Sunni world.

But notice how they reacted. Not by yearning for the return of the golden age of medieval Islam, but by transforming the Prophet into an icon of global jihad who delivers modern nation-states to Islam. Not by hiding out in the ultra-Orthodox enclave of Mea Sharim in Jerusalem, but by forming political parties and playing power politics in the Knesset. Not merely by invoking 16th-century Protestant reformers such as Martin Luther and John Calvin, who defended the su-

preme authority of the Bible, but by inventing the concept of strict inerrancy.

Likewise, Sayyid Qutb, the major ideologue of the Muslim Brotherhood before his 1966 execution in Egypt, claimed, that reputed Muslim societies had descended into a state of *jahiliyya* (pre-Islamic barbarism and ignorance). Under Qutb's teaching, everyone had to pass litmus tests designed to separate the true believer from the infidel, in order to wage jihad against the latter. He thereby displaced the concept of jihad as a believer's internal struggle against his profane passions with jihad as an external war against the unbeliever.

The examples abound: Fundamentalists do not oppose change; they specialize in it.

"Cults of Personality Drive Fundamentalism"

No. It would be comforting to think so. Unfortunately for those who would like to see their influence diminished, fundamentalist movements are not cults. Fundamentalist leaders may be charismatic, as is Sheik Muhammad Hussein Fadlallah, Hezbollah's spiritual guide, or they may not be, but they are always authoritarian. In other words, such leaders' appeal for potential recruits is their continuity with the ancient religious tradition, which they claim to uphold and defend. Thus, fundamentalist leaders, even the firebrands, must be perceived as acting and interpreting within the bounds of the tradition. And although Osama bin Laden pushes the envelope in this regard, he still argues his case on traditional grounds.

Scholars thus avoid lumping fundamentalists with cult leaders such as Branch Davidian leader David Koresh, Jim Jones in Guyana, or Aum Shinrikyo's Shoko Asahara because the cultic leaders have decisively broken with tradition, in rhetoric as well as behavior. They claim the ancient prophecies are being fulfilled in their persons; apocalypse is now, and because they say so. Cult leaders have a problem, then, that most fundamentalist movements avoid. When cult leaders die, sometimes at their own beckoning, and the End does not arrive, most of their movements flare out as well. Fundamentalists, by contrast, aspire to be fixed stars in the firmament.

Accordingly, Fadlallah may deliver a radical ruling and support it with a fiery homily, but he always genuflects in the direction of Islamic law. And when he departs the scene, the Shiite community will raise up another leader authoritarian, yes, and charismatic, perhaps. But fundamentalism doesn't require it. Certainly many of the early leaders of U.S. Protestant fundamentalism—Curtis Lee Laws and J. Gresham Machen—lacked charisma.

Most congregations have relied on their local pastors to decree what "the Bible says." Islam, too, is a village religion. It is true that electronic communications make it

[Want to Know More?]

From 1988 to 1993, the **Fundamentalism Project**, directed by Martin E. Marty and R. Scott Appleby, convened 10 conferences involving more than 100 scholars with expertise in fundamentalist movements around the world. The project produced five volumes of case studies and analytical essays edited by Marty and Appleby and published by the University of Chicago Press between 1991 and 1995. Marty and Appleby also produced a distillation of the Christian, Jewish, and Islamic cases in *The Glory and the Power: The Fundamentalist Challenge to the Modern World* (Boston: Beacon Press, 1992). *Spokesmen for the Despised. Fundamentalist Leaders of the Middle East* (Chicago: University of Chicago Press, 1997), edited by Appleby, profiles many prominent fundamentalists. In *The Ambivalence of the Sacred: Religion, Violence, and Reconciliation* (Lanham: Rowman & Littlefield Publishers, 2000), Appleby places the findings of the Fundamentalism Project within the wider context of religious violence and peacemaking.

One important, single-volume study of comparative fundamentalism is Bruce Lawrence pioneering *Defenders of God: The Fundamentalist Revolt Against the Modern Age* (San Francisco: Harper & Row, 1989). In addition, there are many first-rate works on individual movements, including George Marsden's *Fundamentalism and American Culture: The Shaping of 20th-Century Evangelicalism* (New York: Oxford University Press, 1982). William Martin looks at **"The Christian Right and American Foreign Policy"** (FOREIGN POLICY, Spring 1999). Two scholarly but still accessible works on Sunni and Shiite movements are Emmanuel Sivan's *Radical Islam: Medieval Theology and Modern Politics* (New Haven: Yale University Press, 1990) and Said Arjomand's *The Turban for the Crown: The Islamic Revolution in Iran* (New York: Oxford University Press, 1988). A detailed account of Hindu movements' politics and organization is in Christophe Jaffrelot's *The Hindu Nationalist Movement in India* (New York: Columbia University Press, 1998).

The **Religious Movements Home Page** of the University of Virginia has a fundamentalism section that discusses problems in analyzing fundamentalism and provides links to the sites of prominent U.S. fundamentalist groups.

easier for leaders to reach many congregations. But technology is not the primary impetus for such movements. Fundamentalism appears almost as if by spontaneous combustion, or as if spread by capillary action, under the guidance of leaders who mumble, stumble, and falter but who are tagged as authorized agents of God because they properly interpret "the word."

R. Scott Appleby is professor of history and the John M. Regan Jr. director of the Joan B. Kroc Institute for International Peace Studies at the University of Notre Dame. He is the author of The Ambivalence of the Sacred: Religion, Violence, and Reconciliation *(Lanham: Rowman & Littlefield, 2000). Martin E. Marty is Fairfax M. Cone distinguished service professor emeritus of the history of modern Christianity at the University of Chicago Divinity School. His most recent book is* The One and the Many: America's Struggle for the Common Good *(Cambridge: Harvard University Press, 1997).*

Index

Index

H

hadith, 158

Hagarism: The Making of the Islamic World (Cook), 156, 160

hallucinations, 60

Han dynasty, Confucius and, 78, 81, 82

hand gestures, Hula and, 29

Harappa, 34

Heaven and Earth, creation of, 96

Heavenly Masters School, 91

Hebrew literature, Jerusalem and, 118

hermeneutics, 43, 215

Herodotus, 35

Herzl, Theodor, 114

Himiko, Fujita: and her Dragon Palace Family, 102–105; initiation of, 102–103

himsa, 49, 52

Hindus, 34, 40, 41; ethic of, nonviolence and, 49–52

Hinduism, 3, 35, 49, 53, 202; image-making religious tradition and, 42

Historical Records (Ch'ien), 81

Holocaust Remembrance Day, 126–127

holy places, 163

"holy-mouth-men," 5

Homily on Simeon the Stylite (Jacob of Serug), 92–93

"House of Wisdom," 36–37

Huang Zhengyuan, 83, 84

Huangdi sijing, 90

hula dancing, in Hawaii, 28–31

Humphreys, R. Stephen, 160

Huzruiwuhti, Woman of the Hard Substances, story of, 18–19

I

"I Become Part of It" program, 22–25

"idols," 46

Image and Pilgrimage in Christian Culture (Turner), 40

images, of the Hindu religious tradition, 43

immaculate conception, 151

immortality, 88, 89, 90–91

In Light of India (Paz), 197

independent churches, 145–147

India, 34–38, 40, 41, 42–43; Christianity in, 131

Indian Buddhist, 65–66

Indian Running (Nabokov), 23

individualism, in American religious culture, 196, 197

inferior Brahman, 53

Information Network Focus on Religious Movements (INFORM), 205

International Association for the History of Religions, 3

international law, Muslims and, 186–187

Islam, 117, 121, 167, 185, 202; and Christianity, conflict between, 188–193

Islamic counter-reformation, 174–177

Islamic fundamentalism, 190, 191

Islamic history, controversial theories about, 154–161; revisionist study of, 160–161

Islamic History: A Framework for Inquiry (Humphreys), 160

Islamic revivalism, 190

islands and gods, production of, 96–97

Israel, 114–116, 190

Izanami-no-mikoto, 96–98

Izumo, myths of, 96–98

J

Jagannath Deities, 41

Jain asceticism, 91

Jaina-Barsu, 39

Jainism, 61

Japan, 70, 182; Buddhism in, 68; history of the development of Pure Land Buddhism in, 69; matsuri in, 106

Japanese religions, in the new millennium, 99–101

Jerusalem Studies in Arabic and Islam, 155–156

Jerusalem: Dome of the Rock in, 167–170; politics of holiness in, 117–121

Jewish texts, 180–181

jihad, 174, 176, 190

Jihad: The Trail of Political Islam (Keppel), 165

jina, 39

Jodo Buddhism, 70

Jodoshinshu, 68–73

Journal of Higher Criticism, The (Luling), 155

Judaism, 117, 118, 121, 170, 191; sacred space of, 112–113

K

Kaelber, Walter O., 88

kaimyo, 100

Kalevala, as national epic of Finland, 20–21

Kamakau, S. M., 29

kami, 104, 105, 106, 108

Kant, Immanuel, 198

karma, 50, 51, 58, 94; theory of, 68

Karpatri, Swami, 40

Kashta-Sanghi-Swetambara, 39

Kautilya, 60–61

Knock, Ireland, Marian pilgrimage at, 148

Knox, Ronald, 2

Koran, 162–166, 167, 169–170, 171, 172–173, 177, 180, 181, 185, 186, 190; Buddhism in, 68; controversial theories about the history of, 154–161; revisionist study of, 160–161

Korea, history of the development of Pure Land Buddhism in, 69

Kramrisch, Stella, 42

Krsna, 40

Kumulipo, 29, 31

Kuyo ritual, 74

L

language: Native Americans and, 23–24; oral communication and, 28; photographs and, 45; religion and, 12

Laozi, 88–89, 90, 91

Latin America, Christianity in, 131

latipso ceremonies, 5

Latter Han Dynasty, 90–91

Laws, Curtis Lee, 216

Layne, Daniel, 143–144

Leadership Network, 146

Leary v. United States, 213

linearity, 23

linga-worship, 39

"listener," 5–6

literalists, fundamentalists as, 215

literary text, the Koran as, 157

Lonnrot, Elias, 20

Lourdes, Marian pilgrimage at, 148

Luling, Gunter, 155

Lunheng, 90

Lwa, 26

M

Madonna, 148

Mahavira, teacher of the Jain religion in India, 58

Mahayana principle, of dependent origination, 69, 71

mai nei loko, 28

Malinowski, Bronislaw, 7, 11

Manichaean ascetics, 91

Manzoor, S. Parvez, 157

Marrow of Zen, 63–64

Marshall, John, 34

Maspero, Henri, 91

mathematics, religion and, 198

matsuri, in Japan, 106–109

maya, concept of, 36

Mecca, as a pagan sanctuary, 158

Meccan Trade and the Rise of Islam (Crone), 156

Medina, 158

Merit Field, 66

Mernissi, Fatima, 186

Milarepa, 65, 66

Mill, John Stuart, 137

Misogi, 97–98

mitama-matsuri, 103

mizuko, 74–75

Mizuko Kuyo, religious phenomenon of, 99–100

modern civilization, basic values of, 171

modern study, of religion, 2, 3

Mohenjo-Daro, 34

monks, Buddhist, 59–60, 65; role as a physician, 62; in training, 60

monotheism, fundamentalism and, 214–215

morality books, 83–87

Moses, 164

mouth-rite, as a daily body ritual, 5

Muhammad, 120, 155, 156, 157, 158–159, 160, 162, 163, 164–165, 167

Muiyinwuh, god of All Life Germs, story of, 18–19

Muslim traditions, 120

Muslims, interview with Kenneth Cragg about Christians and, 184–187

Mu'tazilism, 159, 161

"myokonin," 72, 73

mysticism, 2

N

Nabokov, Peter, 23

Nachman, Rabbi, sayings of, 122–123

Nacirema, body ritual among, 4–6

Native Americans, sacred dimensions of, 22

Nembutsu, 69–70, 71

neo-Confucian ideas, on morality books, 83

Nevo, Yehuda D., 156

new religious movements (NRM), 205, 206; scholars, 203

New Society, Altneuland as, 114–116

Nirvana, 69

noninjury, inner source of, 51

non-literate societies, 23

non-Muslims, in the Islamic state, 189

nonviolence, Hindu ethic of, 49–52

O

Ochre Robe, The (Bharati), 40

Ojoyoshu (Genshin), 70

On Liberty (Mill), 137

Test Your Knowledge Form

We encourage you to photocopy and use this page as a tool to assess how the articles in *Annual Editions* expand on the information in your textbook. By reflecting on the articles you will gain enhanced text information. You can also access this useful form on a product's book support Web site at *http://www.dushkin.com/online/*.

NAME: DATE:

_____

TITLE AND NUMBER OF ARTICLE:

_____

BRIEFLY STATE THE MAIN IDEA OF THIS ARTICLE:

_____

LIST THREE IMPORTANT FACTS THAT THE AUTHOR USES TO SUPPORT THE MAIN IDEA:

_____

WHAT INFORMATION OR IDEAS DISCUSSED IN THIS ARTICLE ARE ALSO DISCUSSED IN YOUR TEXTBOOK OR OTHER READINGS THAT YOU HAVE DONE? LIST THE TEXTBOOK CHAPTERS AND PAGE NUMBERS:

_____

LIST ANY EXAMPLES OF BIAS OR FAULTY REASONING THAT YOU FOUND IN THE ARTICLE:

_____

LIST ANY NEW TERMS/CONCEPTS THAT WERE DISCUSSED IN THE ARTICLE, AND WRITE A SHORT DEFINITION:

We Want Your Advice

ANNUAL EDITIONS revisions depend on two major opinion sources: one is our Advisory Board, listed in the front of this volume, which works with us in scanning the thousands of articles published in the public press each year; the other is you—the person actually using the book. Please help us and the users of the next edition by completing the prepaid article rating form on this page and returning it to us. Thank you for your help!

ANNUAL EDITIONS: World Religions 03/04

ARTICLE RATING FORM

Here is an opportunity for you to have direct input into the next revision of this volume.
We would like you to rate each of the articles listed below, using the following scale:

1. **Excellent: should definitely be retained**
2. **Above average: should probably be retained**
3. **Below average: should probably be deleted**
4. **Poor: should definitely be deleted**

Your ratings will play a vital part in the next revision.
Please mail this prepaid form to us as soon as possible.
Thanks for your help!

RATING	ARTICLE	RATING	ARTICLE
	1. The "Comparative" Study of Religion		35. Pluralism and the Catholic University
	2. Body Ritual Among the Nacirema		36. Raising Christian Children in a Pagan Culture
	3. Baseball Magic		37. Child's Death Raises Questions About Faith
	4. Each Religion Expresses an Important Part of the Truth		38. Resuscitating Passion
	5. Sun Mother Wakes the World: Australian Aborigine		39. Handmaid or Feminist?
	6. First Tale		40. What Is the Koran?
	7. Kalevala: An Epic Poem That Gave Birth to a Nation		41. In the Beginning, There Were the Holy Books
	8. Becoming Part of It		42. The Dome of the Rock: Jerusalem's Epicenter
	9. Veve: The Sacred Symbol of Vodoun		43. The Sacred Is Allah, the One True God
	10. The Hula in Hawaiian Life and Thought		44. The Islamic Counter-Reformation
	11. Ancient Jewel		45. Religion; It Sounds Like Hate, but Is It?
	12. The Jain Deities		46. The Case for 'Yellow Theology'
	13. Seeing the Sacred		47. Cross Meets Crescent: An Interview With Kenneth Cragg
	14. The Hindu Ethic of Nonviolence		48. Islam & Christianity Face to Face: An Old Conflict: Prospects for a New Ending
	15. The Sacred Is the One True Reality of Brahman		49. Religion Makes a Comeback (Belief to Follow)
	16. The Beginnings of Buddhism		50. Oh, Gods!
	17. The Marrow of Zen		51. Doper or Devotee?
	18. An Essential Commitment		52. Fundamentalism
	19. "Shinran and Jodoshinshu"		
	20. Buddhism and Abortion: "The Way to Memorialize One's Mizuko"		
	21. Confucius		
	22. Stories from an Illustrated Explanation of the *Tract of the Most Exalted on Action and Response*		
	23. Asceticism in Early Taoist Religion: Introduction		
	24. Izanagi-No-Mikoto and Izanami-No-Mikoto		
	25. Japanese Religions in the New Millennium		
	26. The Goddess Emerges From her Cave: Fujita Himiko and her Dragon Palace Family		
	27. Matsuri		
	28. The Sacred Space of Judaism		
	29. Dreaming of Altneuland		
	30. The Politics of Holiness in Jerusalem		
	31. Sayings of Rabbi Nachman		
	32. He Who Was Caught in His Own Trap		
	33. Holocaust Remembrance Day Brings Memories of Evil, Courage		
	34. The Changing Face of the Church		

(Continued on next page)

BUSINESS REPLY MAIL
FIRST-CLASS MAIL PERMIT NO. 84 GUILFORD CT

POSTAGE WILL BE PAID BY ADDRESSEE

McGraw-Hill/Dushkin
530 Old Whitfield Street
Guilford, Ct 06437-9989

Ill....ll.....l....l...l.ll...lll.l.l..l.l.l..l.l.l..l.ll

ABOUT YOU

Name   Date

Are you a teacher? ❑   A student? ❑
Your school's name

Department

Address   City   State   Zip

School telephone #

YOUR COMMENTS ARE IMPORTANT TO US!

Please fill in the following information:
For which course did you use this book?

Did you use a text with this ANNUAL EDITION?   ❑ yes ❑ no
What was the title of the text?

What are your general reactions to the *Annual Editions* concept?

Have you read any pertinent articles recently that you think should be included in the next edition? Explain.

Are there any articles that you feel should be replaced in the next edition? Why?

Are there any World Wide Web sites that you feel should be included in the next edition? Please annotate.

May we contact you for editorial input?   ❑ yes ❑ no
May we quote your comments? ❑ yes ❑ no